I0834158

DAG. BY [illegible] SMITH. ENG. BY J. SARTAIN, PHILA.

CHARLES PETTIT McILVAINE, D.D.,

BISHOP OF THE PROTESTANT EPISCOPAL CHURCH IN THE STATE OF OHIO

THE EVIDENCES OF CHRISTIANITY;

IN THEIR

EXTERNAL, OR HISTORICAL, DIVISION:

EXHIBITED IN A

COURSE OF LECTURES,

BY

CHARLES PETTIT M'ILVAINE, D. D.,

BISHOP OF THE PROTESTANT EPISCOPAL CHURCH IN THE STATE OF OHIO.

Sint castæ deliciæ meæ scripturæ tuæ; nec fallar in eis, nec fallam ex eis.—AUGUSTINE.

TWENTY-SEVENTH THOUSAND.

REVISED AND IMPROVED BY THE AUTHOR, WITH THE ADDITION OF A PREFACE,

BY OLINTHUS GREGORY, D.D., LL.D.

Philadelphia:

SMITH, ENGLISH & CO.,

40 NORTH SIXTH ST.

1861.

COLLINS, PRINTER.

PREFACE TO THE ENGLISH EDITION.

BY OLINTHUS GREGORY, D.D., LL.D.

The English friends of the author of these Lectures on the Evidences of Christianity are unanimous in deciding that they will constitute a valuable addition to our sacred literature. On a subject which has been repeatedly treated, and often by men of distinguished talent and learning, *much* that is essentially new is not to be expected. Yet the specific purpose for which a work of this kind is undertaken may cause the main arguments to be placed in such a position, while some of the subordinate topics may be exhibited in so strong a light, as to give to the whole an air of light and freshness well fitted to convey high gratification in union with rich instruction. Several, indeed, of the trains of reasoning pursued by the author seem to be entirely original; at the same time that they are conducted with considerable skill, and by their accumulative property, lead to an ultimate issue that *must* make a deep and salutary impression on the mind of any candid investigator of this ever momentous subject. It may, farther, be added, that the Christian feeling, benevolence, and warmth with which the author conducts his inquiry, in its several stages, honourably distinguish this work from many of its predecessors; while they show that, instead of regarding Christian truth as supplying matter for a pleasing speculation, he considers it as that which alone can make men truly holy, happy, honourable, and useful, and transform the world from an Aceldama to the Paradise of God.

May 1st, 1833.

PREFACE.

THE history of the following lectures may be given in few words. In the autumn of eighteen hundred and thirty-one, when the University of the City of New York had not yet organized its classes, nor appointed its instructers, it was represented to the Council, that a course of lectures on the Evidences of Christianity was exceedingly needed, and would probably be well attended by young men of intelligence and education. On the strength of such representation, the author of this volume was requested, by the Chancellor of the University, to undertake the work desired; not, he is well aware, on account of any special qualifications for a task which many others in the city would have executed much more satisfactorily; but because, having lectured on the Evidences of Christianity, while connected with the Military Academy at West Point, he was supposed to be in a great measure prepared at this time for a similar effort. It was under a considerable misunderstanding of the extent to which the proposed engagement would be expected to go, that the author expressed a hesitating willingness to assume its responsibility. The next thing was the honour of an appointment, by the Council of the University, to the office of "Lecturer on the Evidences of Christianity." Alarmed at the prospect of so much additional work, but desirous of serving a rising and most hopeful institution, as well as of advocating the gospel of the Lord Jesus Christ; he consented to the appointment, with the expectation of finding, in the manuscripts of the former course, enough preparation already made to prevent any considerable increase to his accumulated engagements. What was his disappointment, on inspecting those compositions, to find himself so little satisfied with their plan and whole execution, that instead of attempting to mend their infirmities and supply their deficiencies, it seemed much better to lay them all aside in their wonted retirement, and begin anew both in study and writing! Thus, in the midst of exhausting duties, as a parish minister,* and in a state of health by no means well established, he was unexpectedly committed to an amount of labour which, had it been all foreseen, he would not have dared to undertake. Mean while, a class of many hundreds, from among the most intelligent in the community, and composed, to a considerable

* The author was at that time Rector of St. Ann's Church, Brooklyn, N. Y.

extent, of members of the "New York Young Men's Society for Intellectual and Moral Improvement," had been formed, and was waiting the commencement of the course. A more interesting, important, or attentive assemblage of mind and character, no one need wish to address. The burden of preparation was delightfully compensated by the pleasure of speaking to such an audience. The lecturer could not but feel an engrossing impression of the privilege, as well as responsibility of such an opportunity of usefulness. He would thankfully acknowledge the kindness of divine Providence, in his having been permitted and persuaded to embrace it, and for a measure of health, in the prosecution of its duties, far beyond what he had reason to expect. His debt of gratitude is inexpressibly increased by the cheering information, that much spiritual benefit was derived from the lectures by some whose minds, at the outset of the course, were far from the belief of the blessed gospel, as a revelation from God.

The idea of publication did not originate with the author. He began the work with no such view. Had it not been for the favourable opinion of the Council of the University, as to the probable usefulness of the step, and the urgent advice of distinguished individuals of that body; he would have shrunk from contributing another volume to a department of divinity, already so well supplied by authors of the highest grade of learning and intellect. After the recent lectures of Daniel Wilson, D. D., the present excellent bishop of Calcutta, not to speak of many other and earlier works in the same field, it will not seem surprising to the present author if some should think it quite presumptuous, at least unnecessary, for a writer of such inferior qualifications, in every sense, to offer an additional publication. But all have not read, nor may all be expected to read the books which have already been issued. Nothing can be more conclusive; and yet, to multitudes of readers, they must remain as if they were not. A work of inferior claims may find readers, and do much good, in consequence of local circumstances drawing attention to its pages, where all others would be overlooked. Vessels of moderate draught may go up the tributary streams of public thought, and may deal advantageously with the minds of men, where others of heavier tonnage could never reach. Should such be an advantage of this unpretending publication, its apparent presumption may be pardoned, and its author will, by no means, have laboured in vain. That many faults will be found in it, he cannot but anticipate. That any have arisen from haste, carelessness, or want of pains, he will not dishonour his sense of duty, however he might excuse his understanding, by the plea. He can only say that he has tried to do well, and to do good. If, in the opinion of any qualified critic, he has succeeded, he desires to regard it as a matter of thankfulness to God, not of praise to himself. If he has failed, let the infirmities of the lecturer, not the merits of the subject, receive the blame.

That many books have been consulted in the preparation of this volume, and that the author is greatly indebted to the more learned labours of numerous predecessors, he need not acknowledge. It seems unnecessary to mention more particularly than is done in the margin, the various works from which assistance or authority has been derived. Wherever quotations occur they are marked, and almost always credited to their respective authors. The elaborate work of Lardner on the Credibility of the Gospel History, and the books of Josephus, being more frequently cited than any other; it may be well to mention that the edition of Josephus, referred to in the marginal notes, is that of Whiston's translation, in one volume octavo, London, 1828; and the quotations from Lardner are out of the quarto edition of his works, in five volumes, London, 1815.

And now, without further preface, let this humble attempt to promote the saving truth of Jesus Christ be committed to Him whose blessing alone can honour it. Should it receive but little favour from man, and yet be made, in the Lord's hand, the instrument of leading some misguided soul from the darkness and barrenness of infidelity to the precious light and hope of the gospel, its name will then be written in heaven, and its unworthy author will have a rich reward.

C. P. M.

PREFACE TO THE SIXTH EDITION.

So many, and such remarkable instances of a divine blessing having been graciously vouchsafed in the reading of this book, have come to the author's knowledge, that he cannot but regard it as a duty to see that it be no longer allowed to remain out of print, as it has been for some time past. It would make a very interesting little book were it in the power of the author to recollect and relate the particulars of the many cases of persons who have ascribed their conversion from infidelity, and their affectionate embracing of the gospel, under the blessing of God, to the use of this little, unpretending work. In many instances, the accounts were given to the author by the persons themselves, earnestly seeking an interview for the purpose; in others, by their friends made happy by their conversion; or by those who had advised the reading of the book, and wished its writer to be partaker, with them, in the joy of knowing that it had been made a signal blessing. Some are now in the ministry of the gospel, who, when they began the perusal, were in the darkness of infidelity. A copy of the first edition was sent by the author, as a present, to the library of a literary institution. Some time after, he received a request for another copy, with the reason that the first had got worn out before it ever reached its destination. The explanation was, that an officer of the institution had lent it to a person living in a neighbouring village, who was well known among the inhabitants as an infidel, and who had succeeded in poisoning the minds of many in the vicinity against the gospel. God blessed the book to the breaking up of that man's whole boasted system of opinion. He became a Christian, and then sent the volume, as a missionary, among those whom he had poisoned. When its rounds were done (which were greatly blessed), it was worn out, and a new one was requested for the library.

The author is sensitively aware of the delicacy of his speaking of these things, lest he should seem to regard them with feelings of self-complacency, and to mention them with a view to his own praise. God forbid! How can he take praise to himself for that which is, and must be so exclusively, the work of the mighty power and unsearchable grace of God, as the conversion of a sinner from a hardened infidel to being an humble, obedient follower of Christ? He has three motives in speaking of these things. One is, that he may thankfully acknowledge the goodness and condescension of God in having made use of an instrument so humble and unworthy, for the accomplishment of such a wonderful and infinitely precious end as the turning of immortal souls "from darkness to light, and from the power of Satan unto God." Certainly, when these lectures were composed, and when the author concluded to print them, he little suspected ever to be greeted with such accounts of their usefulness as have come to his ears.

Another motive is, that persons may be encouraged to put this, or similar books, into the hands of those who unhappily have taken up with sentiments opposed to the gospel of Christ. There is a mass and a solemnity of strength in the evidences of Christianity, when properly presented; there is visible upon them so distinctly the handwriting of God, that they cannot fail to be exceedingly impressive to any mind that is once induced to consider them. The author is persuaded that professing Christians are too little informed on this subject for their own benefit and usefulness, and that the importance of the general circulation of well-digested, serious, earnest, spiritually-minded works thereon is not rightly appreciated by the Christian community.

A third motive is, to point out one reason which may account for the fact that, in the circulation of this book and others of the same class, in a certain respect which will presently be mentioned, there have occurred so many more instances, not merely of the removal of skeptical doubts, but also of the actual work of God's grace in turning sinners to himself, than have usually been known in connection with books on the Evidences of Christianity. No explanation can be found in any greater skill, or weight of argument; in any new evidences, or any new logical method of arraying what had often been exhibited before. It seems to be in this, that the argument is not presented merely *as an argument*, abstractedly from the great and infinitely momentous interests which depend upon the conclusion to which the reader shall come, but is kept in close connection with the question, *What must I do to be saved?* and thus its whole force becomes a matter of serious and solemn impression, as well as of intellectual conviction. This is seen in the admirable lectures on the Evidences, by Bishop Wilson, and also in the forcible volume on the same subject, by one whom the present writer cannot speak of without an expression of veneration and love for one of the most eminent Christians and philosophers of his age—his deceased friend, the late Olinthus Gregory, LL.D. Those books *exhibit* gospel truth, as well as prove that he gospel is true. The earnestness of the Christian preacher accompanies the argument of the scholastic reasoner. The question stands before the reader as one of conscience as well as of judgment. It seems invested with all that is serious in the worth of his soul and in the consideration of eternity. God blesses such books of Evidences more than others, as He blesses those sermons more than others which, though they may be inferior in argument, in talent, in eloquence, have more of the seriousness and earnestness of the gospel. Perhaps the writer may be allowed to insert here, in confirmation of these views, the opinion of one whose judgment he is glad of an opportunity of honouring. The present noble president of the British and Foreign Bible Society, Lord Bexley, addressed to the writer, in 1833, a very kind letter concerning this volume, in which he said, "In one important respect, it seems to excel other works of a similar kind, namely, that while the chain of argument is deduced with great clearness and force, no opportunity is lost of giving it a practical application, and of impressing holiness on the heart, as well as conviction on the understanding. The want of this renders many books dry and repulsive, which are much to be admired for sagacity and extent of information."

In the year 1833, this work was reprinted in England, under the advice and superintendence of the late Dr. Olinthus Gregory, of the Royal Military Academy; and to that edition it is probably owing that a communication has been received from the committee of the venerable society of the Church of England "for the Promotion of Christian Knowledge,' requesting the author's approbation to its being adopted by that society and printed as one of its works for distribution.

C. P. M'ILVAINE.

Gambier (Ohio), Jan., 1844.

CONTENTS.

LECTURE I.

LECTURE II.

LECTURE III.

LECTURE IV.

LECTURE V.

MIRACLES, p. 126.

LECTURE VI.

MIRACLES, p. 155.

LECTURE VII.

PROPHECY, p. 184.

LECTURE VIII.

LECTURE IX.

LECTURE X.

LECTURE XI.

LECTURE XII.

LECTURE XIII.

EVIDENCES OF CHRISTIANITY.

LECTURE I.

INTRODUCTORY OBSERVATIONS.

I APPEAR before those who have come this evening to favour me with their attention, as sustaining, under appointment from the University of the city of New York, the office of Lecturer on the Evidences of Christianity. It is but justice to my own feelings, to assure you that I had not thought of entering on so much responsibility until earnestly requested to do so by respected individuals belonging to the Council of that institution. I am not without much apprehension of having ventured far beyond my qualifications in acceding to their desires. When I think of the many in this city of much superior furniture of mind and spirit, to whom the office might have been intrusted, and of my own daily and engrossing occupations in the duties of the ministry, leaving so little time or strength for any other occupation, however important, it is a matter almost of alarm that I find myself committed to a series of lectures for which the very best intellect, the soundest judgment, and the most deliberate study, are so much needed. But having undertaken the work, I trust the Lord has ordered the step in wisdom, and, if I seek his guidance, will enable me to go forward in a strength above my own; so that I may be the instrument, under his hand, of contributing something to promote the improvement and everlasting happiness of those to whom I may have the pleasure of speaking.

The present lecture will be exclusively of an introductory kind. I pause at the threshold, in remembrance of the word and promise of God: "*In all thy ways acknowledge Him, and He shall direct thy steps.*" I would devoutly acknowledge God as the omniscient witness in this undertaking; the only source of wisdom, strength, and blessing, "from whom all holy desires, all good counsels, and all just works do proceed." May his Holy Spirit, through the mediation of his Son, our Lord Jesus Christ, who is "the way, the truth, and the life," "God, blessed for ever," condescend to guide our way and help our infirmities, that all may see and embrace the TRUTH.

The subject to which we are to direct our attention, has engaged the powers of wise, learned, and good men, in almost all ages since the promulgation of christianity. Minds of every class, and in all departments of intellectual occupation, have directly or indirectly, by design or unwittingly, contributed materials for its elucidation. Thus it has come to pass that the difficulty of an appropriate exhibition of the evidences of christianity is rather on the side of selection and arrangement and the just proportioning of arguments, than of their sufficient multiplication. To give the various branches of the subject their just measure of relief and prominence; to determine what should be displayed strongly and completely, and what should be sketched with a lighter pencil, and placed in the background of the picture; to adjust the numerous parts in such symmetry as will present the whole with the most undivided and overcoming effect, is a difficulty of no little magnitude, where attention to space and time is of so much consequence as in the present undertaking. The nicest discrimination, the most logical taste, and a talent for extensive combination, may here find room for the exercise of all their powers. The danger is that one will lose himself amidst the wide spread and accumulated treasures of illustration and evidence; that he will fail so entirely in their classification as to see and exhibit them confusedly and unjustly, and for want of a good discipline among his own thoughts will lead out his forces in feeble detail, instead of forming them into compact masses, and meeting the enemy on every side with a self-sustained combination of strength.

Before we proceed to the main question on which our subsequent lectures are to be employed, it will be well to call your attention to,

I. *The high importance of the investigation on which we are about to enter.* You are to unite with me in examining the grounds on which the religion of the gospel claims to be received, to the exclusion of every other religion in the world, as containing the only way of duty and the only foundation of a sinner's hope of salvation; so that you may be enabled to answer satisfactorily to your own consciences and to all who may ask a reason of your belief, this great question: *Is the religion of Jesus Christ as exhibited in the New Testament, a revelation from God, and consequently possessed of a sovereign right to universal faith and obedience?*

There are considerations intrinsically belonging to this question, which place it in an aspect of unrivalled importance.

We must have the religion of Christ or none. A very little reflection will make it apparent, that the question as to the truth of christianity is not one of preference between two rival systems of doctrine, having conflicting claims and nearly balanced arguments and benefits; it is not whether the gospel is more true and salutary than some other mode of religion, which though inferior would still secure many of the most essential and substantial benefits for which religion is desirable. But it is no other than the plain and solemn question, shall we believe in the faith of Christ, or in none? Shall we receive and be comforted by the light which the gospel has thrown over all our present interests and future prospects; or shall our condition in this life—our relation to the future—what we are to be, and what we are to receive hereafter and for ever, be left in appalling, impenetrable darkness? Such is the real question when we inquire whether christianity is a revelation from God. Do any ask the reason? Because if such be the divine origin and authority of the religion of Christ, there can be no other religion. It claims not only to stand—but to stand alone. It demands not only that we believe it—but that, in doing so, we consider ourselves as denying the truth of every other system of faith. Like the one living and true God, whose seal and character it bears, it is *jealous*, and will not share its honour with another; but requires us to believe that, as there is but one Lord, so there is but one faith—*the truth as it is in Jesus.* On the other hand, if christianity be not of divine origin, it is no religion; its essential doctrines must be false; its whole structure baseless. Suppose then, for a moment, that such were the case, what could we substitute for the gospel? We must either plunge into the abyss of atheism, or find something in the regions of paganism that would answer; or be content with the religion of Mohammed; or else find what our nature wants in that which is unjustly distinguished as *the Religion of Nature*, in other words, we must *become Deists.* But is there a creed among the countless absurdities of pagan belief and worship which any of us could be persuaded to adopt? Could we be convinced of the prophetic character of the Arabian impostor, and receive as of divine authority the professed revelations and unrighteous features of the Koran, after having rejected such a book as the New Testament, and such evidences as those of Jesus? Where else could we flee? To atheism? But that is the gulf in which all religions are lost.—Darkness is on the face of the deep. Nothing remains that does not acknowledge the divine revelation of christianity, but the self-styled religion of nature—*deism.* And what shall be said of this? I am unable to give an account of it more definite than that it is the denial of christianity, on the one hand, and of atheism, on the other, and is to be found somewhere between these two infinitely distant extremes; but is never stationary, changing place with the times; accommodating its character to the disposition of every disciple, and permitting any one to assume the name of Deist who will only believe these two articles of faith—*that there is a God, and that christianity is untrue.* Such is the religion which, according to Paine, "teaches us without the possibility of being mistaken all that is necessary or proper to be known." And yet notwithstanding this boasted fulness and infallibility of instruction, there is no agreement among Deists as to what their natural religion consists in, or as to the truth of what some of them consider its most fundamental doctrines. Their chief writers are altogether at variance as to whether there is any distinction between right and wrong, other than in the law of the land, or the customs of society; whether there is a Providence; whether God is to be worshipped in prayer and praise, or the practice of virtue is not the only worship required, whether the practice of virtue forbids or encourages deceit, suicide, revenge, adultery, and all uncleanness; whether the soul is mortal or immortal; whether God has any concern with human conduct. Now without spending a moment upon the question as to what evidence or what adaptation to the wants of men and of sinners, deism could pretend to, after the rejection of evidence and excellence such as those of the gospel; let me ask whether deism can with any propriety be called religion? Does that deserve the name of a system of religious faith which has no settled doctrine upon the most essential points of belief and practice? which may acknowledge as many contradictory forms, at the same moment, as it has disciples, and never could remain long enough in one position or under one countenance for the most skilful pencil to take its portrait? But aside from all this, it is too notorious to be argued, that whatever pretensions may have been advanced by Deists to something like a theory of religious belief, it is at best a mere theory; utterly powerless in practice, except to liberate its disciples from all conscientious restraint upon their passions, and promote in the public mind the wildest licentiousness as to all moral obligation. Substitute deism for christianity, and none acquainted with the nature or history of man can help acknowledging that as to all the beneficial influence of religion upon heart and life, in promoting either the moral purity of individuals, or the happiness of society, we shall have no religion at all. When have Deists ever maintained a habit of private, family, or public worship? Attempts have been made among them to keep up some mode of congregational service, but total failure, in every instance, has proved how forced was the effort, and how little it would have been thought of, had it not been for the surrounding influence of christianity. The first attempt was by a man in England, who styled himself the Priest of Nature. He relapsed from being a dissenting preacher in England, of an orthodox creed, to socinianism, thence to deism; after which he set up in London a house of worship, formed a liturgy, was patronised by some persons of influence, preached and collected some disciples. But most of his people became Atheists; and after an experiment of four years, the congregation was reduced to nothing, funds failed, and the effort was abandoned. The most formidable enterprise in this way took place in France during the revolution. Having found by some experience that to acknowledge no God was to have no law; and to be without religious institutions was to want civilization and peace; certain persons distinguished for learning, and calling themselves *Theophilanthropists*, set up a society for the worship of God on the principles of deism. The desolated churches of Paris were given for their object. A directory of deistical worship was published, containing prayers and hymns. Lectures were substituted for sermons. The ceremonies were simple, tasteful, and classical. Music added its charms. The form of worship was sent into all parts of the country, and great exertions were made by the powers of the state to get up this religion in every town. Circumstances were exceedingly propitious to the enterprise. Christianity had been banished. Her witnesses were in sackcloth. She had none to oppose themselves to the scheme of her enemies. The country was sick of the horrors of atheism. Some religion was demanded by public feeling. This contrivance had nothing in it offensive to the sinner, while it seemed to be skilfully adapted to the people and the times. Moreover, it was patronised by government, and conformed to by the learned. The ceremonies were well performed—the musical accompaniments excellent. But all would not do. No sooner had novelty ceased, than the assemblies were thinned. The trifling expenses of music and apparatus could not be raised out of the liberality of the people. The society was split up with dissensions, some refusing the manual of worship; others complaining against the lecturers as aiming at too much power; others demanding that the creed of the society should be more liberal and allow a greater latitude of belief. None at last could be got to lecture. To keep up the popular interest, and to escape the charge of bigotry, religious festivals were appointed, in which a union of service was attempted to be formed between Jews, Protestants, Catholics, Deists, and Atheists. There were festivals in honour of Socrates, of Rousseau, and of Washington. At one of these a banner inscribed with the name *Morality* was carried by a man notorious as a professor of atheism. But all would not do. The great principle of religion was wanting. There was no devotional spirit. The body was dead, and therefore soon tumbled to dust. A short time after, a counsellor of France, in a public address, declared the result of the experiment in these words: "For want of a religious education for the last ten years, our children are without any ideas of a

Divinity, without any notion of what is just and unjust; hence arise barbarous manners, hence a people become ferocious. Alas! what have we gained by deviating from the path pointed out by our ancestors? What have we gained by substituting vain and abstract doctrines for the creed which actuated the minds of Turenne, Fenelon, and Pascal?"* I cannot omit, in connexion with these striking confessions, the description given by one of the most famous infidels in those times, of all that class of philosophers whose views and schemes we have been noticing. Thus writes Rousseau: "I have consulted our philosophers, I have perused their books, I have examined their several opinions, I have found them all proud, positive, and dogmatizing even in their pretended scepticism, knowing every thing, proving nothing, and ridiculing one another; and this is the only point in which they concur, and in which they are right. If you count their number, each one is reduced to himself; they never unite but to dispute. I conceived that the insufficiency of the human understanding was the first cause of this prodigious diversity of sentiment, and that pride was the second. If our philosophers were able to discover truth, which of them would interest himself about it? Where is the philosopher who for his own glory would not willingly deceive the whole human race? Where is he who in the secret of his heart proposes any other object than his own distinction? The great thing for him is to think differently from other people. Under pretence of being themselves the only people enlightened, they imperiously subject us to their magisterial decisions, and would fain palm upon us, for the true causes of things, the unintelligible systems they have erected in their own heads. Whilst they overturn, destroy, and trample under foot, all that mankind reveres; snatch from the afflicted the only

* For more particulars, see Alexander's Evidences—Dwight's Sermons I. 191.

comfort left them in their misery; from the rich and great the only curb that can restrain their passions; tear from the heart all remorse of vice, all hopes of virtue; and still boast themselves the benefactors of mankind. 'Truth,' they say, 'is never hurtful to man.' I believe that as well as they; and the same, in my opinion, is a proof that what they teach is not the truth."* Such are the singular expressions of a noted infidel, into whose mind the truth sometimes forced an entrance, in spite of all his levity of mind and profligacy of life. They are the confessions of one of the chief actors in the farce of natural religion, and by leading us behind the scenes, display in a most impressive light, that if deism be the only substitute of christianity, we must have no religion or that of Jesus. So that, in examining the evidences of christianity, we should solemnly feel that the question before us is of no less magnitude than whether life and immortality have been brought to light by the gospel, or they are still involved in deep and confounding darkness; whether religion is revealed in the Bible, or every thing on earth under the name of religion is false and impotent. Now, when it is considered what desolation would sweep at once over all the interests of society, were the restraint of religion withdrawn from the flood-gates of human corruption; what immense benefits have ensued, and must ensue, even by the confession of some of its most violent opposers, from the diffusion of the gospel; what happy effects upon the character and present happiness of its genuine disciples it has always produced; reforming their lives, purifying their hearts, elevating their affections, healing the wounds of the guilty, taking away the sting of death, and lighting even the sepulchre with a hope full of glory; when it is considered what high claims the gospel asserts to an unlimited sovereignty over all

* Gandolphy's Defence of the Ancient Faith: quoted in Gregory's Letters, i., p. p. 6 and 7.

our affections and faculties, requiring our entire submission, promising to every devout believer eternal life, and to all that refuse its claims everlasting wo: it must at once be evident that the subject before us is no matter of mere intellectual interest, but one in which every expectant of eternity has an immeasurable stake. No mind has any right to indifference here. Without the most wonderful folly no mind *can* be indifferent here. Whether the claims of the gospel are the claims of God is a question to which in point of importance no other can pretend a comparison, except this one—*Believing in those claims, am I surrendered to their governance?*

But I speak to a great many who have no difficulty on this head, being fully satisfied that the gospel of Christ is a divine revelation. What concern have they with the investigation before us? "Much every way." The question for them to ask, is, *on what grounds are we satisfied? Are we believers in christianity because we were born of believing parents, and have always lived in a Christian country; or because we have considered the excellence and weighed the proofs of this religion, and are intelligently persuaded that it deserves our reliance?* I am well aware that there are many truly devoted followers of Christ who have never made the evidences of christianity their study, and in argument with an infidel, would be easily confounded by superior skill and information; but whose belief nevertheless is, in the highest degree, that of rational conviction, since they possess *in themselves* the best of all evidence that the gospel of Christ is "the power and wisdom of God," having experienced its transforming, purifying, elevating, and enlightening efficacy upon their own hearts and characters. Did such believers abound, christianity would be much less in need of other evidence. Were all that call themselves Christians thus experimentally convinced of the preciousness of the gospel, I would still urge upon them the duty and advantage of studying as far as possible the various arguments which illustrate the divinity of its origin. I would urge it on considerations of *personal pleasure and spiritual improvement.* There is a rich feast of knowledge and of devout contemplation to be found in this study. The serious believer, who has not pursued it, has yet to learn with what wonderful and impressive light the God of the gospel has manifested its truth. Its evidences are not only convincing, but delightfully plain; astonishingly accumulated, and of immense variety, as well as strength. He who will take the pains not only to pursue the single line of argument which may seem enough to satisfy his own mind; but devoutly to follow up, in succession, all those great avenues which lead to the gospel as the central fountain of truth, will be presented, at every step, with such evident marks of the finger of God; he will hear from every quarter such reiterated assurances of: "*this is the way*; *walk thou in it*;" he will find himself so enclosed on every hand by insurmountable evidences shutting him up unto the faith of Christ, that new views will open upon him of the real cause and guilt and danger of all unbelief; new emotions of gratitude and admiration will arise in his heart for a revelation so divinely attested; his zeal will receive a new impulse to follow and promote such heavenly light.

But I would urge this study on all serious believers, who have the means of pursuing it, *as a matter of duty.* It is not enough that *they* are well satisfied. They have a cause to defend and promote, as well as a faith to love and enjoy. It is enjoined on them, by the authority of their Divine Master, that they be ready to give to every man that asketh them, *a reason* of the hope that is in them. They must be able to answer intelligently the question: *Why do you believe in christianity?* For this purpose, it is not enough to be able to speak of a sense of the truth, arising from an inward experience of its power and blessedness. This is excellent evidence for one's own mind; but it cannot be felt or under stood by an unbeliever. The Christian advocate must have a knowledge of the arguments by which infidelity may be confounded; as well as an experience of the benefits for which the gospel should be loved. To obtain this in proportion to his abilities, he is bound by the all-important consideration that the religion of Jesus cannot be content while one soul remains in the rejection of her light and life. She seeks not only to be maintained, but to bring all mankind to her blessings. The *benevolence* of a Christian should stimulate him to be well armed for the controversy with unbelievers. Benevolence, while it should constrain the infidel most carefully to conceal his opinions lest others be so unhappy as to feel their ague and catch their blight, should invigorate the believer with the liveliest zeal to bring over his fellow-creatures to the adoption of a faith so glorious in its hopes and so ennobling in its influence. Even on the supposition that christianity were false, unspeakably better should we think it, to be deluded by consolations which, though groundless, would be still so precious; than enlightened by an infidelity which shrouds its disciples in such darkness, and drowns them in such confusion.

But if such are the weighty considerations which should induce an experienced Christian to study the evidences of christianity, while he carries in his own breast the strongest of all assurances of its having the witness of the Spirit of God, how much more should this subject receive the attention of that numerous portion of the population of a Christian land who, while they are called Christians, have never experienced in their hearts the blessedness of the gospel. These are eminently dependent on this study for all rational and steadfast belief. Being destitute of the anchor obtained by an inward sense of the divine excellence of the truth as it is in Jesus, they must spread their sails to the influence of external evidence, or be liable to be tossed about with every wind of doctrine, and wrecked against the cliffs of infidelity

It is a matter of great importance that the attention of this class should be much more extensively obtained to the proofs of the religion in which they profess to believe. Multitudes of men, well informed on other subjects, are believers, for hardly any other reason than because their parents were so, and the fashion of society is on this side. The same considerations that make them Christians in this land, would have made them enemies of christianity in others: Pagans in India, Mohammedans in Turkey. They can give a better reason for every other opinion they profess, than for their acknowledgment of the gospel of Christ. The efforts of infidels, combining ingenious sophistry with high pretensions to learning, and coming into alliance with strong dispositions of human nature, have an open field, and must be expected to do a fearful work among minds thus undisciplined and unarmed. It is only in the lowest possible sense of the word that they can receive the name of believers. Instead of adding strength to the cause of christianity, by their numbers, they rather embarrass it by their ignorance of its weapons, and bring it into disrepute by the ease with which they are entrapped in the snares of the enemy. They have no conception what a truth that is which they so carelessly acknowledge; *how impressively it is true;* with what awful authority it is invested; what a wonder is involved in professing to believe and refusing to obey it. Do I speak to any who are thus situated? I would earnestly exhort them, for their own satisfaction and steadfastness as believers in revelation, for the purpose of realizing how solemnly the living God has called them to submit as well as assent, to the gospel of Christ, and for the honour of a religion which so abounds in the best of reasons, to make a serious study of the evidences of christianity.

To any whose minds are not settled with regard to this momentous question; or who consider themselves as having arrived at a definite opinion against the divine authority of the gospel, need I say a word to show why *they*, of all others, should give the subject in view their most serious and diligent attention? Suppose they should become fixed in the rejection of christianity, and to the influence of their example on the side of infidelity, should add the effort of argument, tending to weaken the faith of others, and to increase the number of enemies to Christ; and finally, should be convinced on the verge of the grave (as many of this mind have been most painfully convinced,) or in eternity, should have it discovered to them that what they have been setting at nought was no less than God's own revelation, the gospel of him who cometh to judge the quick and dead; and that what they had embraced, and led others to embrace, in its stead, was only a miserable offspring of human pride and folly, a spirit of delusion and eternal destruction; what then would seem the importance of a serious application of mind and heart to this study; the madness of treating it with indifference, or pursuing it without the strictest impartiality? That such a discovery is at least as likely as the contrary, even infidels, in their continual declarations that all beyond the grave is unknown, have given impressive confessions. That it is at least exceedingly probable, independently of positive evidence, the unbeliever cannot but fear when he surveys the history of the world, and sees what minds and what hearts, what men of learning and of holiness have been ready to suffer any earthly loss or pain, rather than be unassociated with the eternal blessedness of the discipleship of Christ.

I have now exhibited something of the incomparable importance of the question before us, as considered *by itself.* There is an additional importance in its present investigation, arising out of *the peculiar character of the present times.*

We rejoice with others in the belief that this age, in comparison with all before it, merits distinction *as an age of free-*

dom. We rejoice that it is an age of freedom, as well in the investigation of all truth as in the assertion of all political rights. But what is called the spirit of freedom is not every where identical with the cause of truth and right. In one region, it is the calm, deliberate determination to be governed only by just and equal laws; in another, it is the furious, desolating despiser of all laws, but those of one's own passion and selfishness. This is seen, as well in the discussion of religious truth, as in the vindication of assumed principles of civil liberty. There are certain just and necessary laws to govern us in reasoning, as much as in acting; to regulate the investigation of moral and religious, as well as physical and political subjects. True liberty of mind consists in the right of being governed by these laws, and no other; and at the same time asserts their absolute necessity. But there is a spirit abroad which, under the name of freedom of opinion, would set at defiance all the fundamental laws of reasoning and denounce, as the offspring of intellectual despotism, whatever principles of moral evidence are at variance with itself. This is licentiousness; not freedom. It is the enemy of *law*, not of *oppression:* the very menial of mental degradation, instead of what it boasts itself, the prompter of manly, elevated, independent intellect. This spirit of evil is greatly on the increase, because the name and boast of freedom are circulating far more rapidly in this world, than the knowledge of its character or the possession of its blessings; because it is so much easier for the mass of society to burst at once the whole body of law by which mind is restrained, than to separate between the precious and the vile; and chiefly because with the many, there is too little reflection and too little moral principle, when religion is in question, to appreciate the important difference between the oppression of opinion in matters of reason, and the just government of reason in matters of opinion. Nothing, in truth, has so promoted the freedom of thought, of opinion, and of action, as christianity. If any thing, under her name, has been guilty of the opposite, it has been, so far forth, the corruption of her character and the denial of her principles. Pure christianity has ever proclaimed liberty to the captive, as well in mental as in physical slavery. The ages of the purest freedom have been those of her greatest advancement. She courts investigation when it is free; but rejects it when licentious. She is the patroness of law, and will be judged only by law. Bring her trial to the judgment seat of that inductive philosophy which one of her own children first illustrated, and which, on other subjects, the world has learned to use so well and prize so highly: let her be judged by the evidence of fact, and she is satisfied. But this reasonable privilege it is more than ever the spirit of self constituted philosophers, in their loud declamation against the slavery of opinion, and their licentious rebellion against all the laws of reasoning, to refuse. Hence the greater importance that our present subject, in all its departments, from the most fundamental principles of evidence, to the highest point of inductive argument, should be thoroughly studied by all whose interest it is to know, and whose duty it is to vindicate, the truth.

But there is one more consideration, in connexion with the present age, illustrating the peculiar importance of the study you are now commencing. The evidences of christianity, while specially assailed, in these times, with a licentiousness and effrontery which the dignity of no truth can countenance, and the chastity of religious truth should never meet, are favoured, at the same time, with advantages for convincing illustration such as no preceding age ever furnished. Time, while it has impaired the strength of none of our ancient arguments, has greatly increased the weight of some, and has added, and is daily adding, new auxiliaries to a body of proof which its enemies have never ventured to attack in front. Every new year, in the age and trials of our holy faith, is an additional evidence that, like the pyramids of Memphis, it was made to endure. It wears well. Christianity has been journeying, for the last eighteen hundred years, through unceasing trials. While as yet an infant in a land of almost Egyptian darkness, a Jewish Pharaoh attempted to strangle her in the cradle. She grew up in contempt and poverty, and began her course, like Israel of old, through a Red Sea of relentless persecution. Bitter waters awaited her subsequent progress. Amalek with all the principalities and powers of earth, during more than three centuries, opposed her march. Fiery serpents in the wilderness of sin have ever been stinging at her feet. The world has opened no fountain, nor vouchsafed any bread to sustain her. What alliances the nations have ever made with her cause have only given them the greater power to encumber and divide her strength. Her drink has been drawn from the rock; her bread has been gathered in the desert. Nothing that malice, or learning, or power, or perseverance, could do to arrest her goings, has been wanting. Even treachery in her own household has often endeavoured to betray her into the hands of the enemy. No age has encountered her advance with such a dangerous variety of force; or with a more boastful confidence of success, than the present. And yet in none, since that of the primitive Christians, has her triumph been so glorious, or her conquest so extensive. At a time of life when, considering her fiery trials, one ignorant of her nature would expect to see her wrinkled with age and crippled with manifold infirmities, it may be said of her, with perfect truth, that though for more than eighteen hundred years she has been journeying through conflicts and trials innumerable, *her eye is not dim, nor her natural force abated.* She remains unchanged by time, the same precisely as when first proclaimed in the streets of Jerusalem. The shield of faith, the breastplate of righteousness, the helmet of salvation, the sword of the spirit are neither broken nor decayed, but as ready as in the beginning, to go forth "conquering and to conquer." This long and hard experiment proves that she is made for eternity. It is the privilege of our age to appreciate the evidence of this with more satisfaction than any preceding it. But how different, this sublime immutability of christianity, so much like the eternity of God, from the childish fickleness of infidelity. What is the history of infidelity, but a history of changes? Where is the resemblance between the writings of its modern and those of its ancient disciples? What Celsus and Porphyry attempted to maintain against primitive christianity, none at present would think of advocating; while the positions and reasonings of recent infidels would have been subjects of ridicule among their earliest brethren. "The doctrines which Herbert and Tindal declared to be so evident that God could not make them more evident, were wholly given up as untenable by Hume; and the scepticism of Hume sustained no higher character in the mind of D'Alembert. Mere infidelity gave up natural religion, and atheism mere infidelity. Atheism is the system at present in vogue. What will succeed it, cannot be foreseen. One consolation, however, attends the subject, and that is: no other system can be so groundless, so despicable, or so completely ruinous to the morals and happiness of mankind."*

But there is another aspect in which the study of the evidences of christianity is presented as especially interesting, in connexion with the present age. *This is an age peculiarly distinguished for scientific research and discovery.* Never did science travel so widely, explore so deeply, analyze so minutely, compare so critically the present with the past, principles with facts; histories of ancient times, with monuments of ancient things; truths of revealed religion, with results of experimental philosophy. And what is the con-

* Dwight on Infidel Philosophy.

sequence? Has the Pentateuch suffered by him who found the key, and applied it to the hieroglyphical memorials on the marbles and porphyries of Egypt? Did the geological researches of the lamented Cuvier enfeeble his belief in the Mosaic history?*

I venture to say there never was an age in which it could be asserted, with so much practical witness, that science and every extension of human knowledge are strengthening and multiplying the evidences of christianity. Add to this, the ever accumulating force of the argument from prophecy, a source of evidence in which we exceed by far the primitive times of the gospel, and which must be increasing as long as one prediction of the Bible remains to be fulfilled. Then consider what new exhibitions the present age of signal enterprise, in all things, has furnished, and is daily presenting of the power attendant upon the gospel to overcome every obstacle, and make the moral desert a garden, and savages meek and lowly of heart. Look at the missionary stations of the Pacific and of Hindoostan, and among our own frontier tribes. There it will be seen that christianity has still her apostles, her martyrs, her conquests. The idol cast to the ground; the idol temple purged of its pollutions, and consecrated to Jehovah; the multitude, once naked devotees of demons, now clothed and in their right mind, and sitting at the feet of Jesus; these are some of our additional testimonies to the gospel, that her arm is not shortened that it cannot save. But they are not all. Every new traveller into regions hitherto but little known, as he developes the condition of nations destitute of the gospel, increases our evidence of the utter helplessness of human reason, and the total prostration

* It is an interesting fact, well worthy of being recorded, that Cuvier, whose death has been recently announced, was to have presided at the next annual meeting of the Bible Society of Paris; and had proposed, as the topic of his address, *the agreement between the Mosaic history and the modern discoveries in geology.*

of human nature, without the light which we enjoy, and consequently, our evidence of the universal need of a revelation like ours, as well as of the benefits which have followed in the train of christianity wherever she has been received. And last, but not least, our experience of the tender mercies of infidelity is more impressive than that of preceding ages. Its nature, spirit, personal and public consequences have now had time to speak out, and make a full display of their benefits to all classes of mankind. Our times have seen enough; any of us have heard enough to form some adequate idea of what society would be favoured with, in personal consolations; in domestic peace and purity; in public security and order, should the principles of infidelity be generally adopted as the basis of individual, family, and national government.

I have now endeavoured to illustrate the importance of a diligent attention to the great subject we have undertaken to treat, by considerations arising out of its own intrinsic nature, and from its special aspect as associated with the distinctive character of the present age. I will occupy but a little while longer in speaking of,

II. *The importance of strict attention to the spirit in which we should examine the evidences of christianity.*

"Blessed (said the Saviour) is he whosoever shall not be offended in me." There is a great deal in the religion of Jesus at which the natural dispositions of man are offended. He is proud—the gospel demands humility; revengeful—the gospel demands forgiveness. Man is prone to set his affections on things on the earth; the gospel requires him to set them on those which are above. He is wedded to self-indulgence, glories in being his own master, idolizes himself, encourages self-dependence, boasts his own goodness, lives without God in the world. All this the gospel peremptorily condemns; requires him to repent of it, to deny himself, renounce all right over himself, give up his will to that of

God, live for the Lord Jesus, and lean upon and glory in him alone as all his strength, hope, and righteousness. Hence it is evident that the natural heart and the precepts of christianity are directly at variance. "The mystery of an incarnate and crucified Saviour must necessarily confound the reason and shock the prejudices, of a mind which will admit nothing that it cannot perfectly reduce to the principles of philosophy. The whole tenor of the life of Christ, the objects he pursued, and the profound humiliation he exhibited, must convict of madness and folly the favourite pursuits of mankind. The virtues usually practised in society, and the models of excellence most admired there, are so remote from that holiness which is enjoined in the New Testament, that it is impossible for a taste which is formed on the one to perceive the charms of the other. The happiness which it proposes in a union with God, and a participation of the image of Christ, is so far from being congenial to the inclinations of worldly men, that it can scarcely be mentioned without exciting their ridicule and scorn. General speculations on the Deity have much to amuse the mind, and to gratify that appetite for the wonderful, which thoughtful and speculative men are delighted to indulge. Religion viewed in this light appears more in the form of an exercise to the understanding, than a law to the heart. Here the soul expatiates at large, without feeling itself controlled or alarmed. But when evangelical truths are presented, they bring God so near, if we may be allowed the expression, and speak with so commanding a voice to the conscience, that they leave no alternative, but that of submissive acquiescence or proud revolt."*

Hence the question as to the truth of christianity is peculiar. You can investigate the truth of a narrative in com-

---

* Robert Hall

mon history, or of a phenomenon in physical science, or of a principle of political economy, with the coolness of a mere intellectual exercise. One sets out in such pursuits with no feelings already enlisted. Had this been the case, with regard to the divine origin of christianity, "a tenth part of the testimony which has actually been given, would have been enough to satisfy us; the testimony, both in weight and quantity, would have been looked upon as quite unexampled in the whole compass of ancient literature."* But here the question is one of feeling, as well as evidence; enlisting the heart, as well as the head. Powerful dispositions crowd around the investigation. Hence one is in danger, unless his natural inclinations be subdued, of looking at the argument through a medium which, while it diminishes the importance of the evidence, will magnify the objections. This explains sufficiently how it has happened that there have been men of learning and talents and much practical wisdom, in many departments, who have become and continued unbelievers. Their dispositions were stronger than their talents, and moulded the latter to their own service, instead of yielding to their guidance. The examination was conducted rather by the test of inclination, than of evidence. Now it is no part of the profession of christianity to furnish eyes to those who will not see. Evidence that will force its way irresistibly through prejudice and unwillingness, compelling submission, she does not promise. Enough to satisfy, abundantly, every candid, serious, diligent, humble inquirer, she does profess to give. If she ever exhibit more, it is beyond her stipulation, and more than any have reason to demand.

The pride of human reason is often deeply offended at the claims of christianity. The gospel demands to be received as a revelation of truth, communicated by autho-

---

* Chalmers.

rity, so that a wise man shall have no room to ascribe his knowledge of God and of His will, to his own powers of discovery; but has to sit, just where the ignorant and lowly must sit, at the feet of Jesus. This pleases not the speculative and ambitious turn of the human intellect. Men like to find out truth by reasonings of their own, instead of the authoritative declarations of another, even though that other be infallible wisdom. They love to theorize and conjecture, and try the ingenuity of their own faculties, so as to praise themselves for whatever is ascertained. Hence, in matters of science, there was a long and hard struggle before they could be brought down from the proud flights of speculation, and consent to the self-denial of the inductive method, submitting to be instructed only by the revelations of experiment, and in the unpretending school of fact. To adopt the same method in matters of religious investigation, many are not yet willing. To give up all speculation—*philosophy*, "falsely so called"—and consent to *receive*, instead of being ambitious to *discover*, religious truth; to receive it at a source where the humblest and the loftiest mind must drink together, out of the same cup; to receive it on the simple testimony of a well attested revelation, which lies as open to the peasant as the philosopher: this the wise men of the world are slow of heart to consent to. Their pride of reason is offended. Did an account come to them from the other continent of certain novel and interesting phenomena recently observed in the heavens; they would see at once how unphilosophical it would be to commence theorizing upon the question of their truth, and then reject them because inconsistent with certain previous speculations of their own. They would institute but the one inquiry: Is there reason to depend upon the accuracy of the observations, and the honesty of the reports of those from whom these statements proceed? Satisfied on this head, they would at once receive the phenomena, and every truth resulting therefrom, on the great principle of modern science, that *whatever is thus collected by induction must be received, notwithstanding any conjectural hypothesis to the contrary, until contradicted or limited by other phenomena equally authenticated.* Now we only ask them, not to disown the philosophy of Newton in examining the evidence of the religion of Christ; to try the celestial wonders, the "*mecanique celeste*," as given by Christ and his apostles, not by theory or speculation, but precisely as they would try any other, in the open field of fact and induction. We do not ask them to believe, unless upon the credit of facts. But we do ask that whatever is thus proved, they will receive, notwithstanding any conjectural hypothesis to the contrary. The whole argument for christianity, so far from being in any degree theoretical or speculative, is eminently one of experimental evidence and inductive simplicity. We take the position that our Lord Jesus Christ professed to make a revelation from God. It is conceded that if he attested his communications by miracles, he sealed that profession as true. We say he did thus attest them. But miracles are facts—*phenomena*—to be proved by the testimony of eye-witnesses, like any phenomena in physics. To such testimony we appeal. We ask the unbeliever to refute it; and if he cannot, to receive the revelation, and bow to its declarations as the attested word of God. But here, unfortunately, we set the rule of sound philosophy against the dispositions of an unhumbled heart. The latter has the victory, often; and the wise man goes to work to oppose our facts, with his theories; our testimony, with his speculations, till he flatters himself, because he has covered up his eyes in his own mazes, that he has refuted the evidences of christianity. Hence, therefore, another cause that learned men are not all believers in christianity. They are not all humble enough, in a question with which heart and life are so much connected, to abide by the results to which the principles of philosophical investigation would naturally lead them. But hence, also, a most important reason that whoever of you may have doubts as to the gospel of Christ, should, in the pursuit on which we have entered, be cautious, candid, ready to learn, and determined to embrace the truth wherever it should be found.

One consideration more. It is true of christianity, as of many other excellent subjects, that *objections are more easily invented than answered.* Objections in such matters are usually light affairs, floating on the surface of men's thoughts. Answers, to be solid, must be heavier and lie deeper, requiring like the pearl, both labour and skill to bring them up and fashion them for use. But christianity is peculiarly exposed to objections; from the simple fact that as it meets every body and compels every body to say *yea* or *nay* to its requirements, every body must needs have something to say, however unreasonable, in its favour or against it. Few indeed would venture to give an opinion, without some study, on a question in science or polite literature; but the most ignorant and unthinking will undertake an opinion upon the merits of the gospel, and raise an objection in a breath which would require much patience and some learning to refute. Hundreds hear the objection; thousands relish, retain, and are poisoned by it; while, perhaps, not one of them has the disposition to hear, or patience enough to understand, the reply. Evil hearts can do what only good and well instructed minds can undo. "Pertness and ignorance may ask a question, in three lines, which it will cost learning and ingenuity thirty pages to answer. When this is done, the same question will be triumphantly asked again the next year, as if nothing had ever been written on the subject. And as people, in general, for one reason or another, like short objections better than long answers; in this mode of disputation (if it can be styled such) the odds must ever be against us; and we must be content with those for our friends who have honesty and erudition, candour and patience, to study both sides of the question."*

These observations explain the lamentable fact, that, in a large portion of society, there is so much more acquaintance with the cant and slang of infidelity, than with the reasonings in support of christianity; that our young men are often so familiar with the boasting and floating calumnies which the troubled sea of infidelity is ever casting up, with its mire and dirt, in the face of the gospel; while, with the innumerable efforts by which christian science has scattered all such poisonous exhalations to the winds, many have not the most trifling acquaintance.

All these considerations are at least sufficient to impress us with the eminent importance of the most serious attention to the spirit and manner in which one proceeds in the study of the evidences of christianity.

Let me urgently recommend *docility*, in this pursuit. By this, I mean nothing resembling *credulity;* but an open-hearted and humble-minded readiness to weigh evidence with simplicity of purpose in the most even scales of truth; and then to submit to, and follow the truth, wherever it may lead, with singleness of heart, in the fear of God.

Let me also recommend *a deep seriousness of purpose*, in this pursuit. I mean that calm and settled earnestness of mind, which a just sense of the unspeakable importance of the subject, and of the responsibility under which all, even the most indifferent, must treat it, will necessarily inspire.

Lastly, *prayer* is by all means to be employed in this pursuit. It is written most wisely: "If any man lack wisdom, let him ask of God." But do I forget that I am speaking from the chair of a lecture room, instead of the pulpit of a church? Prayer! How do I know but that I am addressing many who are already on the side of infidelity? Would I

---

* Horne's Letters on Infidelity.

say to them, study the evidences of christianity *with prayer*? Is it not equivalent to begging the question? Is it not asking them to do what, as professors of infidelity, they object to? In one sense, I verily believe it is begging the question. A spirit of serious, earnest prayer, for the knowledge of truth, is utterly inconsistent with the spirit of infidelity. Who does not feel the singularity involved in the idea of seeing a thorough infidel engaged in secret, earnest prayer, to be preserved from all bias in search of truth, and to be led in the way in which God would have him to go? And yet, if he be not an Atheist, he can have nothing to say against the propriety of such a step. But is it true that infidelity and the spirit of prayer are practically so inconsistent? Is it true that we have already accomplished at least half our work of conviction, when we have persuaded an unbeliever to make religious truth a subject of serious supplication at the throne of grace? What does this say for the gospel?

Any, who are very anxious to continue in unbelief, had better not pray. They might find out more than would be convenient, by such an effort. Infidelity cannot tolerate so much seriousness. But if any feel that they lack wisdom, in this great concern of eternity, and desire to know the way of light and life: "*let them ask of God, who giveth to all men liberally and upbraideth not; and it shall be given them.*"

LECTURE II.

AUTHENTICITY OF THE NEW TESTAMENT.

Our last lecture was only introductory to the importan subject to which I have undertaken to lead your attention. In the present, we enter directly upon one of its principal branches.

The study of the evidences of christianity may be either brief or extended, according to the object with which it is pursued. If it be merely the possession of some one distinct and conclusive train of reasoning, perfect in itself, the investigation may soon be ended. The student may take any single miracle or fulfilled prophecy; he may choose his premises from the narrative of the resurrection of Christ, or the conversion of St. Paul, or the propagation of christianity, and, confining his argument to the point selected, may deduce a finished proof of the divine authority of the gospel. But if he desire not only rational satisfaction for his own mind, but a full view of all those great highways of evidence which, from every quarter, concentrate upon christianity; if he would behold, not only that it is capable of conclusive proof, but how variously and wonderfully its Divine Author has encompassed it with proofs of every kind, drawn from innumerable sources, and prepared, at all points, for every objection, he may lay himself out for a work of extensive research, as well as of rich gratification and improvement.

The evidences of christianity are classed under two general denominations: *external or historical*, and *internal evidence.* Under the latter, are included whatever proofs of divine original may be drawn from the doctrines of the gospel; its incomparable system of morality; the adaptation of the religion of Christ to the condition and wants of mankind;

the holy and elevated character of its Founder; together with all those incidental, but striking and various marks of uprightness, accuracy, and benevolence, which appear in the spirit and manner of the New Testament writers, or which are seen by a comparison of their several books one with another. Such are the principal heads of *internal evidence.* Under the name of *external* or *historical evidence,* we find whatever exhibits the need of a revelation, as apparent in the state of human opinion and practice among the most enlightened nations at the commencement of the gospel; the argument establishing the authenticity of the scriptures, and the credibility of the history contained therein; the proofs arising from miracles; from fulfilled prophecy; from the propagation of christianity, and from the social and personal benefits which have always accompanied its promotion, according to the degree in which its native character and influence have had room to appear. Such are the principal heads of *external evidence.*

The present course of lectures, for want of time to carry it further, will be confined to the department last described; which is chosen in preference to the other, not because it is more important or conclusive, but as more capable of having justice done it, in a series of discussions such as that to which the circumstances of these lectures restrict us.

Should we embrace in our view of this grand division of evidence whatever belongs to it, your attention would first be called to *the indispensable necessity of a divine revelation,* as the history of the ancient world displays it, and as it is still exhibited in the dark places of the earth. This, however, we have not room to include in our course. Though extremely impressive, and worthy of investigation, it is not an essential argument. The straight forward method of philosophical inquiry directs its attention to the testimony simply that an event did occur, and will not suspend assent till the *need* of such an event shall have been fully explained

If convincing evidence be adduced to the matter of fact that a *revelation has been given;* we may be reasonably content, while our limits forbid the proof that *it was needed.* Whoever should desire to read on this head will find it well discussed in the first volume of ***Wilson's Lectures on the Evidences***, &c., or in the admirable letters on the same subject, by ***Olinthus Gregory, L. L. D., Professor of Mathematics in the Royal Military Academy at Woolwich***, one of the most scientific and pious laymen of the age; or, more at large, in the learned volume of ***Leland, on the Advantages and Necessity of a Divine Revelation.***

Let us begin with the *authenticity of the New Testament.* We possess a venerable volume, under this title, consisting of twenty-seven independent books or writings, reputed to have been composed by eight different authors. It professes to contain, and is continually appealed to as containing, not only an accurate account of the history and doctrine of Jesus Christ, but an account written in the first age of christianity, by its earliest disciples and advocates, who were contemporaneous with its author, and were, most of them, eyewitnesses of the events related. Now, before we can be reasonably warranted in placing implicit reliance in the New Testament, as *the book* of the facts and doctrines of the gospel, two important questions must be determined. First: *is there satisfactory evidence that the several writings, of which it is composed, were written by the men to whom they are ascribed?* This involves the AUTHENTICITY OF THE NEW TESTAMENT. Secondly: *is the New Testament deserving of implicit reliance as to matters of historical detail, so that we may receive any narrative, as unquestionably true, because contained therein?* This refers to the CREDIBILITY OF THE NEW TESTAMENT.

Thus you perceive, that whether a volume be authentic, and whether credible, are two widely separate questions, neither, necessarily implying the other, however the evidence of one may bear upon the proof of the other. Writings may be *authentic*, composed by the men whose names they bear, and yet not credible. They may be *credible*, because correct in their statements, and yet not authentic. The question of authenticity refers to the author; that of credibility to the narrative. "The Pilgrim's Progress" is authentic, because it was actually composed by John Bunyan, to whom it is ascribed; but as a narrative, it is not credible, being an allegory throughout. The book entitled "Travels of Anacharsis the Younger," is credible, so far as it professes to exhibit a view of the antiquities, manners, customs, religious ceremonies, &c., of ancient Greece; but it is not authentic, having been written in the eighteenth century by Barthelemy, and fictitiously ascribed to the Scythian philosopher. "Marshall's Life of Washington" is both authentic and credible, being a true history, and worthily honoured with the name of that eminent and excellent man, from whose pen it professes to have come. That the New Testament is also authentic and credible, we undertake to show. We exclude the more ancient portion of the sacred volume, not because of any deficiency in its evidence, but for the sake of unity and clearness in our inquiries; and because, when the argument for the New Testament is set forth in a conclusive form, the authenticity and credibility of the other is rendered, as will hereafter appear, a necessary inference. The two questions will be the subjects of different lectures. To that of *authenticity* our attention will, this evening, be confined. Let us begin with the following:

How does it appear that the several writings composing the volume of the New Testament were written by the men to whom they are ascribed—the original disciples of Christ—and are consequently authentic?

We pursue precisely the same method in determining the authorship of the New Testament, as in ascertaining that of any other book of a passed age. For example; we possess a celebrated poem entitled Paradise Lost. It bears the name of Milton. How do we know that Milton composed it? The answer is easy. Our fathers received it, as his production, from their fathers; and they, from theirs. By such steps, we ascend to the very year in which the book was first published, and find it invariably ascribed to Milton. Moreover, the history of the age in which he lived, speaks of it as unquestionably and notoriously his work. Writers of every succeeding age refer to, and quote it as well known to be his. The language of the poem bears the characteristic marks of Milton's times. Its spirit, genius, and style, display the distinctive features of Milton's mind and character. And, finally, though Milton had many enemies, and lived in a time of great divisions, and this poem redounded greatly to his praise, and many must have been disposed, had they been able, to discover some false pretensions in his claim to its authorship; no other person in that age was ever mentioned as disputing his title, but all united in acknowledging him as the writer of Paradise Lost. On this evidence, although the poem professes to have been written as far back as the year 1674, we are so perfectly certain of its authenticity, that the man who should dispute it would be justly suspected of idiocy or derangement. And had Milton lived in the 7th, instead of the 17th century, a similar body of evidence would have been equally satisfactory. If, instead of the 7th century, he had lived in the first of the Christian era, similar evidence, reaching up to his time, would still prove, beyond a question, that he wrote Paradise Lost. Thus it is evident that time has no effect to impair the force of such proof. Whether a book be ascribed to the Christian era or to five centuries before or after; the evidence, being the same, is equally satisfactory. It as well convinces us that the history ascribed to Herodotus, in the 5th century, before Christ, was written by that historian, as that the *Æneid* was written by Virgil, a little before the birth of

Christ; or the "*Faerie Queene*" by Spenser, in the 1590th year after that event. We are no less satisfied of the authenticity of the orations of Demosthenes, than of Newton's Principia;—though between the dates of their publication, there is an interval of more than two thousand years. So little does the age of a book affect the evidence required to establish its authenticity.

Now in ascertaining the authorship of the New Testament, we are furnished with evidence precisely similar to that which settles the question so conclusively as to either of the works above mentioned.* An unbroken chain of testimony ascends from the present generation to the preceding, and thence to the next beyond, and thence onward again, till it reaches the very age of the apostles, exhibiting an uninterrupted series of acknowledgments of the New Testament, as having been written indeed by those primitive disciples to whom its several parts are ascribed. Besides this, historians and other writers of the age ascribed to this volume, as well Heathen and Jewish, as Christian, not only recognise its existence in their day, but speak of it as notoriously the production of its reputed authors. The language is characteristic of their age, nation and circumstances. The style and spirit exhibit the well-known peculiarities of their respective minds and dispositions. And again, although the New Testament at the time of its first appearance, either in parts or collectively, was surrounded with numerous, learned, and ingenious, as well as most bitter enemies, both among Heathens and Jews; and although there arose at an early period, many animated controversies between the real believers in gospel truth, on one side, and sundry heretical

* "We know," says St. Augustine, "the writings of the Apostles, as we know the works of Plato, Aristotle, Cicero, Varro, and others; and as we know the writings of divers ecclesiastical authors; for as much as they have the testimony of contemporaries, and of those who have lived in succeeding ages."

pretenders to the christian faith, whose cause would often have been materially served by a well sustained denial of the authenticity of certain of the books of the New Testament; none in the primitive ages, whether heretics or open enemies, ever denied that this volume contained the genuine writings of the original apostles and disciples of Christ. On the contrary, all received, argued, and acted upon it as unquestionably authentic. Thus we have the same evidence that the books of the New Testament were written by those whose names they bear, as that Paradise Lost was written by the man whose name it bears. The force of this evidence is in no wise diminished by the consideration that the apostles lived in the first, and Milton in the seventeenth century.

Thus have you received a general outline of the argument. We proceed to a more particular view.

I. *The books of the New Testament are quoted or alluded to by a series of writers who may be followed up in unbroken succession from the present age to that of the apostles.* In proof of this, it is unnecessary for the satisfaction of any person of ordinary information to trace the line of testimony from the present time, or from any point of departure lower down than the fourth century. Whoever has the least acquaintance with the history of the civilized world, as far upward as the fourth century, must know that the acknowledgment of the New Testament, as composed of authentic writings, is interwoven with all the literature, science, and political, as well as religious institutions, of every subsequent age. We begin, therefore, the chain of testimony at the fourth century.

It is a very impressive evidence of the high estimate in which the New Testament was universally held at this period, that beside innumerable quotations in various writings, no less than eleven distinct, formal catalogues of its several books, were composed at various times, during the fourth century, by different hands; and two of them by large and solemn councils of the heads of the christian church. All of these are still extant; and all agree, in every particular important to the present argument, with the list of the New Testament writings as at present received. In the year 397, a national or provincial council assembled at Carthage, consisting of forty-four bishops—Augustine, bishop of Hippo, was a member. The 47th canon of that council is thus written: "It is ordained that nothing beside the canonical scriptures be read in the church under the name of divine scriptures; and the canonical scriptures are these," &c. In the enumeration, we find precisely our New Testament books, and no more.*

About the same time Augustine wrote a book entitled "*Of the Christian Doctrine*," in which is furnished a catalogue of what he considered the authentic writings of the evangelists and apostles, agreeing entirely with ours. "*In these books* (saith he) *they who fear God, seek his will.*"†

A short time before this, Rufinus, a presbyter of Aquileia, published an "*Explication of the Apostles' Creed*," in which he includes a catalogue of the scriptures. It commences thus: "It will not be improper to enumerate here, the books of the New and Old Testament, which we find, by the monuments of the fathers, to have been delivered to the churches, as inspired by the Holy Spirit." This list differs in nothing from ours.‡

Jerome, a contemporaneous writer, universally allowed to have been the most learned of the Latin fathers, in a letter concerning the study of the scriptures, enumerates the books of the New Testament in precise correspondence with our volume. With regard to the Epistle to the Hebrews, he states that by some it was not considered as the work of Paul; though it is evident, from other places of his writings, that he was satisfied of its authenticity, and numbered it among the canonical scriptures.§

* Lardner's Credibility of the Gosp. Hist. ii. 574.

† Lardner, ii. 578. ‡ Ib. ii. 573. § Ib. ii. 548.

In the year 380, wrote Philastrius, bishop of Brescia. In a book "*Concerning Heresies*," he gives a catalogue agreeing entirely with ours, except that it omits the Epistle to the Hebrews, and the Book of Revelation. But it does not follow that these were not considered canonical. The object of his catalogue is to enumerate the books appointed to be read in the churches. The Epistle to the Hebrews, he says, was read in the churches "sometimes." "Some pretend (he writes) that additions have been made to it by some heterodox persons, and that for that reason it ought not to be read in the churches, though it is read by some." Philastrius himself received it, and frequently quoted it as the work of St. Paul, and reckoned it a heresy to reject it. He received also the book of Revelation, mentioning its rejection by some *among the heresies of the age.* "There are some (he writes) who dare to say that the Revelation is not a writing of John the apostle and evangelist."*

About the year 370, flourished Gregory Nazianzen, bishop of Constantinople, who in a work "*On the True and Genuine Scriptures*," enumerates all the present books of the New Testament, except that of Revelation. This however he has quoted in his other works.†

At the same time, wrote Epiphanius, bishop of Constantia, in Cyprus; "a man of five languages." He wrote against heresies, and gave a list of the New Testament books which agrees exactly with ours.‡

About the year 350, another catalogue was published by the Council of Laodicea, differing in nothing from ours but in the omission of Revelation. The decrees of this council were, in a short time, received into the canons of the universal church; so that as early as about the middle of the 4th century, we find a universal agreement, in all parts of the world in which christianity existed, as to the constituent

---

* Lardner, ii. 522. † Ib 470, 71. ‡ Ib. 416.

parts of the New Testament, with the single exception of the book of Revelation. That this was also generally received, and why any doubted its authenticity, will appear in our subsequent progress.*

Athanasius and Cyril, the latter bishop of Jerusalem, a little earlier in the century, have furnished catalogues—that of the former agreeing entirely with ours—that of the latter in every thing but the omission of the Revelation of St. John.

The last catalogue to be mentioned in the 4th century, is that of Eusebius, bishop of Cæsarea, who flourished about the year 315. "A man (says Jerome) most studious in the divine scriptures, and very diligent in making a large collection of ecclesiastical writers." In his Ecclesiastical History, he mentions, as belonging to the canon of scripture, all our present books. While he speaks of the Epistle of James, the second of Peter, the third of John, and the book of Revelation, as questioned by some, he states that they were generally received, and declares his own conviction that they ought not to be doubted.†

The above testimonies, though capable of great multiplication, are amply sufficient to exhibit the universal confidence of Christians, of the fourth century, in the authenticity of the New Testament. Let us proceed to the *third*. In this, among other important names, we find that of the celebrated Origen, who flourished about the year 230, having been born A. D. 184. Jerome speaks of him, as the greatest doctor of the churches, since the apostles—that he had the scriptures by heart, and laboured day and night in studying and explaining them.‡ Great numbers of all descriptions of men attended his lectures. Heathen philosophers dedicated their writings to him, and submitted them to his revisal. He

---

* Lardner, ii. 414. Alexanderon the Canon, p. 150.
† Ib. ii. 368 &c. ‡ Ib i. 527.

wrote a three-fold exposition of the books of scripture, on which he bestowed all his learning. He lived within a hundred years of the death of St. John, and was therefore so near the time of the publication of the books of the New Testament, that he could hardly avoid obtaining the most accurate knowledge of their origin and authors. His enumeration of these writings contains no other books than those of our sacred volume, and includes all that we receive, except the Epistles of James and Jude, which could not have been omitted by design, as in other places he expressly acknowledges them as part of the sacred canon.

Beside Origen, we have in the third century, Victorinus, a bishop in Germany; Cyprian, bishop of Carthage; Gregory, of Neo-Cæsarea, and Dionysius, of Alexandria, in whose writings are found most copious quotations from almost every book of the New Testament.

We proceed to the *second* century. Here we meet with Tertullian, a native of Carthage, born about the year 150, within fifty years of the last of the apostles, and renowned in his day as a learned, vigorous, and voluminous writer in defence of christianity. His works abound in quotations of the most direct kind, and with long extracts from all the books of the New Testament, except four of the minor Epistles, which, as he nowhere professes to give a formal catalogue, he may easily be supposed to have passed unquoted, without entertaining any opinion unfavourable to their authenticity. Tertullian's quotations occupy nearly thirty folio pages. "There are more and larger quotations of the small volume of the New Testament in *this one christian author*, than of all the works of Cicero—in the writers of *all characters for several ages*."*

The same is true with regard to Irenæus and Clement, of Alexandria, both writers of the second century. In what

* Lardner, i. 435.

spirit these early Christians regarded the authority of the New Testament books, may be judged from the manner of their quotations. Irenæus writes: "*As the blessed Paul* says, in the Epistle to the Ephesians, v. 30: 'For we are members of his body, of his flesh, and of his bones.'" And so Clement, "*The blessed Paul*, in the first Epistle to the Corinthians: 'Brethren, be not children in understanding,'" &c.

It deserves to be specially noted that, in this early age, the book of Revelation is expressly ascribed to St. John. The testimony of Irenæus to this effect is so full and strong, that it may justly be considered as putting its authenticity entirely beyond reasonable dispute.*

There is abundant evidence that, in the second century, the books of the New Testament were open to all, and well known in the world. In Tertullian's Apology, addressed to the Roman presidents, he challenges an inspection of the scriptures. "Look into the words of God, our scriptures, which we ourselves do not conceal, and many accidents bring into the way of those who are not of our religion." In this appeal, he calls the attention of the heathen rulers to the Epistles and Gospels, as constituting, "the words of God, our scriptures."†

There is good reason to believe that, in the time of Tertullian, the very autographs, or original letters of the apostles, were in the possession of those churches to which they had been specially directed. "If (says this ancient writer) you be willing to exercise your curiosity profitably in the business of your salvation, visit the apostolical churches, in which the very chairs of the apostles still preside; in which *their very authentic letters* are recited, sounding forth the voice, and representing the countenance, of each one of them. Is Achaia near you? You have Corinth. If you

---

* Lardner, i. 372

† Ib. i. 434.

are not far from Macedonia, you have Philippi, you have Thessalonica," &c.* If Tertullian did not mean that the original manuscripts, but only authentic *copies* of the Epistles to the Corinthians, Philippians, &c., were to be seen by application to those churches, why send inquirers thither? Could an *authentic copy* of the Epistle to the Philippians be seen nowhere but at Philippi; or of that to the Corinthians, nowhere but at Corinth?†

The quotations from the New Testament, in the writings of the second century, are so numerous that were the sacred volume lost, a large part of it might be collected from them alone. Passing by the testimonies of Melito, bishop of Sardis, who wrote a commentary on the book of Revelation, and of Hegesippus, converted from Judaism, and of Tatian, who composed a harmony of the gospels, all born about the time of the death of St. John, we come to Justin Martyr, born about ten years prior to that event. Before his conversion from heathenism, he studied philosophy in the schools of the Stoics, Peripatetics, Pythagoreans, and Platonics. After becoming a Christian, he occupied a high stand in learned writing and holy living. His remaining works contain numerous quotations from, as well as allusions to, the four Gospels, which he uniformly represents as containing "the genuine and authentic accounts of Jesus Christ and of his doctrine." The same is true in relation to the Acts of the Apostles, and the greater part of the Epistles. The book of Revelation is expressly said by Justin to have been written by "John, one of the apostles of Christ." Having lived before the death of that apostle, he had the best opportunity of knowing.

We finish the second century with Papias, bishop of Hierapolis in Asia, whom Irenæus speaks of as a hearer of John, and a disciple of Polycarp, a pupil of John the apostle.‡

Lardner, i 424. † Alexander on the Canon, p. 143. ‡ Lardner, i. 336.

How he obtained his information, will appear from the only fragment of his writings remaining. It is found in Eusebius. "If at any time, I met with one who had conversed with the elders, I inquired after the sayings of the elders (presbyters): what Andrew or what Peter said; or what Philip, Thomas, or James, had said; what John or Matthew, or what any other of the disciples of the Lord, were wont to say."* Thus we have a witness who lived near enough to the beginning, to inquire of those who had conversed with the apostles, if not to listen to St. John himself. Too little remains of his writings to furnish many testimonies, especially as he had it not in view to confirm the authenticity of any part of scripture; but still he gives a very valuable testimony to the Gospels of Matthew and Mark, and the first Epistles of Peter and John. He alludes to the Acts and the book of Revelation.

Thus we have ascended to the *apostolic age.* But we may reach still higher. We have in our possession the well authenticated writings of five individuals and fathers in the primitive church, who, because they were contemporary with the apostles, are called *apostolical fathers.* Three of them, Barnabas, Clement, and Hermas, are mentioned by name in the New Testament;† the fourth, Polycarp, was an immediate disciple of St. John; the fifth, Ignatius, enjoyed the privilege of frequent intercourse with the apostles. There is scarcely a book of the New Testament, which one or another of these writers has not either quoted or alluded to. Though what is extant of their works is very little, it contains more than two hundred and twenty quotations, or allusions to the writings of our sacred volume, in which they are uniformly treated with the reverence belonging to inspired books, calling them "*the Sacred Scriptures;*" "*the*

---

* Lardner, i. 337.

† Acts xiii. 2, 3; 46, 47. 1. Cor. ix. 4—7. Phil. iv. 3. Rom. xvi. 14

Oracles of the Lord." Their testimony is not universal, inasmuch as it is incidental. They had no design of enumerating for posterity, or their contemporaries, the books of scripture. There was no controversy on that subject in their age. It would have seemed a needless waste of words, had they attempted to decide a question which no one asked. It is very natural, therefore, considering the brevity of their remaining works, and the incidental character of their quotations, that some of the shorter writings of the New Testament should not be alluded to; while the fact that, by one or another, almost every book is quoted or alluded to, and that the whole number of quotations or allusions is upwards of two hundred and twenty, accompanied with every mark of reverence and submission, is a most impressive proof that the authenticity and inspired authority of the New Testament books were then notorious and unquestioned among Christians.

Thus we have ascended the line of testimony into the presence of the apostles. Our evidence has been collected from only a few out of the many witnesses that might have been cited. It has been derived from writers of different times, and of countries widely separated—from philosophers, rhetoricians, and divines, all men of acuteness and learning in their days, all concurring in their testimony that the books of the New Testament were equally known in distant regions, and received as authentic by men and churches that had no intercourse with one another. The argument is now, therefore, reduced to this. The apostles and disciples of Christ are known to have left some writings. That those writings have been lost, none can give a reason for believing. It is not pretended that any other volume than that of the New Testament contains them. The books contained in this volume, were considered to be the writings of the apostles, by the whole christian church, as far back as those who were their contemporaries and companions, being continually quoted and alluded to as such. It was impossible that such witnesses should be deceived. Contemporaries and companions must have known whether they quoted the genuine works of the apostles, or only forgeries pretending to their names. Our evidence, therefore, is complete. What I have presented, exceeds, above measure, the evidence for the authenticity of any other ancient book. Should the fiftieth part of it be demanded for any Roman or Grecian production, its character must be condemned as unworthy of confidence.

Before relinquishing this department of evidence, there are certain very important particulars which, though embraced in what has been already advanced, require a more special notice.

1st. It is worthy of distinct remark, that when the books of the New Testament are quoted or alluded to by those whose testimony has been adduced, *they are treated with supreme regard, as possessing an authority belonging to no other books, and as conclusive in questions of religion.* For example; Irenæus, born about A. D. 97, calls them "*divine oracles*;" "*scriptures of the Lord.*" He says that the Gospel was "committed to writing, by the will of God, that it might be, for time to come, the foundation and pillar of our faith."* "He fled to the Gospels, which he believed no less than if Christ had been speaking to him; and to the writings of the apostles, whom he esteemed as the presbytery of the whole christian church." Origen, born about A. D. 184, says, "Christians believe Jesus to be the Son of God, in a sense not to be explained and made known to men, by any but by that scripture alone *which is inspired by the Holy Ghost; that is, the evangelic and apostolic* scripture, as also that of the law and the prophets."† Cyprian, bishop of Carthage, born about the end of the second cen-

* Lardner, i. 372.

† Ib. i. 545.

tury, earnestly exhorts "all in general, but especially christian ministers, in all doubtful matters, to have recourse to the Gospels and the Epistles of the apostles, as to the fountain where may be found the true original doctrine of Christ." "The precepts of the Gospel (he says) are to be considered as the lessons of God to us; as the foundations of our hope, and the supports of our faith."*

2d. *The books of the New Testament were united at a very early period in a distinct volume.* Not to mention, in evidence of this, that in all the earliest writers, the Gospels and Epistles are spoken of as constituting a notorious collection of sacred authorities, divided into those two parts; we have Tertullian, born only fifty years after the death of St. John, calling the collection of the Gospels the "*evangelical instrument;*" the whole volume, the "*New Testament;*" and the two parts, the "*Gospels and apostles.*"

3d. *The books of the New Testament were, at a very early period, publicly read and expounded in the congregations of Christians.* Chrysostom, born about A. D. 347, testifies that "the Gospels, when written, were not hid in a corner, or buried in obscurity, but made known to all the world, before enemies as well as others, even as they are now." Irenæus, about two hundred years earlier, says that, in his time, "all the scriptures, both prophecies and Gospels, are open and clear, and *may be heard of all.*"† Still earlier, we find Justin Martyr giving the emperor an account of the christian worship, in which it is written: "The memoirs of the apostles or the writings of the prophets are read, according as the time allows; and when the reader has ended, the president makes a discourse, exhorting to the imitation of so excellent things."‡ The custom here mentioned, is evidently spoken of as notorious and universal. This was about the year 140. But a practice thus general and familiar could

* Lardner, ii. 27, and 592, 3. † Ib. i. 372. ‡ Ib. i. 345.

hardly have grown up in less than forty years before the writing of this last witness. Thus we reach the life of St. John, and may, therefore, consider it as satisfactorily proved that, at a period as early as the last years of St. John, the scriptures of the New Testament were publicly read and expounded in the churches of Christians. Such is the natural inference, from many passages in the works of Augustine, of the fourth century. For example, "The canonical books of scripture being read every where, the miracles therein recorded, are well known to all people." "The Epistles of Peter and Paul are daily recited to the people." And to what people? And to how many people? Listen to the Psalm: "*Their sound hath gone out into all the earth.*" Again: "The genuineness and integrity of the same scriptures may be relied on, which have been spread all over the world, and *which from the time of their publication were in the highest esteem, and have been carefully kept in the churches.**

4th. *During the primitive ages of christianity, commentaries were written upon the books of the New Testament; harmonies of them were formed, copies diligently compared, and translations made into different languages.* In proof of these assertions, it is needless, after the citations already made, to call up testimony. It may be found abundantly in Paley's Evidences;† where it is well said, that "no greater proof can be given of the esteem in which these ancient books were holden by the ancient Christians, or of the sense then entertained of their value and importance, than the industry bestowed upon them. Moreover, it shows that they were *then* considered as ancient books. Men do not write comments upon publications of their own times: therefore the testimonies cited under this head, afford an evidence which carries up the evangelic writings much be-

* Lardner, ii. 593, 4. † P. 1. c. ix. c vi.

yond the age of the testimonies themselves, and to that of their reputed authors." There is but a single example of a christian writer during the three first centuries, composing comments upon any other books than those in the New Testament. Clement, of Alexandria, is mentioned by Eusebius as having written short notes upon an apocryphal book, called the Revelation of Peter; but that he did not consider it as having authority, may be inferred from the fact mentioned by Eusebius, that in his other works it was nowhere quoted.*

5th. From the view we have taken of primitive testimony, it appears that *the agreement of the ancient church as to what were the authentic books of the New Testament, is complete.* Out of twelve catalogues, the earliest of which was furnished by Origen, living within a hundred years of St. John; all of which were drawn up, either by solemn councils, or distinguished heads of the church residing in various and widely remote parts of the world; out of twelve, seven, including the earliest, agree exactly with our New Testament list; three others differ only in the omission of the book of Revelation, for which they had a special reason not implicating its authenticity; and in the two which remain, the books omitted and spoken of as doubtful, in the estimation of some, were acknowledged and quoted as authentic by the framers of the catalogues. The fathers, in all their writings and of all ages and countries, appeal to the same scriptures as infallible authority. The consent of the ancient church was therefore universal. So far as the argument for the divine revelation of the Gospel is connected with the authenticity of any of the books it was without exception. The books omitted in some writers and catalogues, have no essential reference to the great question whether the Gospel of Christ is of divine revelation.

---

* Lardner, i. 410.

6th. *The agreement among the various sects of heretics in the earliest centuries, is as entire as that of the orthodox fathers.* The authenticity of the books of the New Testament was acknowledged even by those to whose sectarian interest their authority was extremely detrimental. Instead of venturing to dispute their having been written by their reputed authors, they sought refuge in arbitrary interpretations of such passages as opposed their favourite views. Some among the Gnostics, for example, unable to escape the apostolic character of the sacred books, maintained the necessity of giving an allegorical turn to their declarations. And when, in the course of time, heretics did undertake to question the authenticity of some portions of the New Testament, their accusation was not based upon any historical or testimonial objections, but confined to some trifling and pretended internal causes of exception, which only their own convenience could discover. Some of these later heretics, being opposed to the doctrine of the influences of the Holy Spirit, denied the gospel of St. John, because it contains the promise of that divine Teacher and Comforter. But with regard to those of an earlier date, Irenæus of the second century, writes, "So great is the certainty in regard to our Gospels, that even the heretics themselves bear testimony in their favour; and all acknowledging them, each endeavours to establish from them his own opinions."* Origen, on account as well of his candour and acquaintance with the heresies of his times as of the early age in which he lived, should be considered a competent witness on this head. He states that the heretics endeavoured to impose upon people by alleging texts of scripture for their particular tenets, though they quoted them in a very unfair and mutilated manner; and that they appealed to them because they were the only writings whose authority was univer-

* Storr & Flatt's Bib. Theol. i. 67.

sally allowed.* Testimony more impressive than this, to the apostolic authorship of the New Testament books, cannot be demanded.

7th. *The several heads of evidence which have now been made out in proof of the authenticity of the New Testament, cannot be pretended to with regard to any of those writings which are called Apocryphal Scriptures.* To some who are aware that in the early ages of christianity there existed a variety of apocryphal gospels and other compositions, pretending to have been written by the apostles, it may be difficult to imagine by what rule the true works of the inspired writers were separated, without embarrassment and with sufficient confidence, from all mere pretenders to that high original. But it greatly enhances one's sense of the prodigious weight of evidence in support of the true scriptures, to learn how broad and unquestionable was the distinction.

Among the apocryphal writings, there are two classes. One is that of *histories* which assumed the names of the apostles, but were literally forgeries and therefore *spurious*, as well as apocryphal. The other consists of certain writings of a christain character, and either entirely or in part historical, which are not *spurious*, but called apocryphal because their age and authors are unknown, or their authority is of no weight.

Of the first class, it may be asserted, without any hazard, that none are quoted within three hundred years after the birth of Christ, by any writer now extant or known; or if any are quoted, it is invariably with marks of censure and rejection.† The only possible exception is the *gospel according to the Hebrews*, "which (says Lardner) was probably either St. Matthew's gospel in his original Hebrew, with some additions; or, as I rather think, a Hebrew translation of St.

* Lardner, iv. 521, 2.

† 6 Paley's Evidences.

Matthew's Greek original, with the additions above mentioned." But this is quoted nowhere, without marks of discredit except *in one place* in the works of Clement of Alexandria.

Of the second class, none but a book called the *Preaching of Peter*, and another entitled the *Revelation of Peter*, are quoted, without positive condemnation, by any writer of the three first centuries. These are spoken of only by the same Clement of Alexandria. Compare with these facts, the immense mass and variety of concurrent testimonies to the books of the New Testament in the writers of the three first centuries; testimonies from all countries and all classes—orthodox or heretics; remember for example that you may find in the extant works of Tertullian, or of Irenæus, or of Clement of Alexandria, more and larger quotations of the small volume of the New Testament, than you can find in writers of all characters, for several ages, of the works of Cicero, though voluminous and always so universally popular; and it will be evident that the apocryphal writings could have presented no difficulties in ascertaining the authentic books of the apostles. None of them were read as having apostolic authority in the churches of Christians; nor admitted into their sacred volume; nor included in their catalogues; nor noticed as authentic by the adversaries of christianity; nor appealed to by all parties calling them selves Christians, as authority in their controversies; nor treated with sufficient respect to be made the subjects of commentaries, collections or translations, unless the brief notes on the Revelation of Peter, by Clement of Alexandria, should merit exception. So wide was the contrast between the true and the false; so easily were the true scriptures dis tinguished from all unauthorized pretenders to that honourable name.

But this is capable of being exhibited still more impressively. We have stated several important evidences of *authenticity*, all of which are found in the New Testament.

and none in any of the apocryphal writings. We will now exhibit certain evidences of *spuriousness*, all of which are found in the apocryphal writings, and none in those of the New Testament. The reasons which render the authenticity of a work suspicious, are thus enumerated in the learned *Introduction to the New Testament* by *Michaelis:* 1. When doubts have been entertained, from its first appearance, whether it was the work of its reputed author. 2. When his immediate friends who were able to judge, have denied it to be his. 3. When a long series of years has elapsed after his death, in which the book was unknown, and in which it must have been mentioned or quoted, had it been in existence. 4. When the style is different from that of his other writings; or in case no others remain, different from what might be reasonably expected. 5. When events are recorded which happened later than the time of the pretended author. 6. When opinions are advanced contradictory to those which he is known to have maintained in other writings.* Now it may be affirmed, without fear of contradiction, that the apocryphal books exhibit all these evidences of spuriousness; none of them being exempt from nearly the whole list, and few of them deficient in any particular. While, with equal confidence, it is asserted that the books of the New Testament exhibit none of them. In no book of that holy volume, are opinions professed that are contradictory to any which the reputed author is known elsewhere to have maintained; nor are facts recorded which happened later than the age in which he lived; nor is the style different from that of his other writings, or from what might reasonably have been expected from his pen. No book of the New Testament was unknown during a long series of years subsequent to the death of the individual to whom it is ascribed; none can be shown to have been denied by the

* Michaelis' Int., i. p. 25.

near friends of the reputed author as his production; no doubts can be proved to have been entertained of the au thenticity of any part of the New Testament at the time of its first publication.

That apocryphal writings existed in the first centuries, is a fact which so far from embarrassing the evidence for the authenticity of the New Testament books, and the truth of the gospel history, very materially confirms it. Had it not been notorious that the apostles did write Gospels and Epistles, it is not likely that so many would have attempted to pass off spurious Gospels, &c., in their names. Had it not been that the fame of Christ and his apostles was very great in all lands, from the beginning, it is not probable that all these apocryphal authors would have thought of writing about them, or in their names; much less that they would have expected a market for their works. Had it not been notorious and universally allowed that Christ and his apostles wrought miracles, and did many wonderful works, it is not probable that all these writers would have taken it for granted, and sought to build up their particular opinions upon the assumption. "They all suppose the dignity of our Lord's person, and a power of working miracles, together with a high degree of authority, as having been conveyed by him to his apostles."*

That apocryphal books should have been published in the name of the apostles, is precisely what was to be expected from the wide circulation, great popularity, and eminent reverence, which their authentic writings had obtained. Current notes soon awaken a disposition to counterfeit them. Popular medicines soon bring into the market apocryphal inventions wearing their names. The effort to pass off the latter is the best proof of the estimation of the former.

The New Testament writers have been treated, in this

* Lardner, iii. 131

respect, precisely like others. So writes Augustine: "No writings ever had a better testimony afforded them than those of the apostles and evangelists; nor does it weaken the credit and authority of books received by the church from the beginning, that some other writings have been without ground, and falsely, ascribed to the apostles; for the like has happened, for instance, to Hippocrates; but yet his genuine works have been distinguished from others, which have been published under his name."* Such, also, has been the case with many others. Several spurious orations were published under the names of Lysias and Demosthenes. Works were ascribed to Plautus, and Virgil, and Horace, which had no title to their names. But it was no difficult matter for the Greek and Roman critics to separate the genuine from the apocryphal works of those authors. Thus it was also with the early Christians. *They proved all things, and held fast that only which was good.* "We receive Peter and the other apostles, as Christ (said Serapion, bishop of Antioch); but as skilful men, we reject those writings which are falsely ascribed to them."

Here we might safely leave the question of authenticity; for, if the evidence adduced does not prove the New Testament books to have proceeded from the apostles, no book of a passed age has any pretension to authenticity; that Milton wrote Paradise Lost must be considered unworthy of credit; that the orations bearing the name of Cicero, were composed or delivered by that orator, must be condemned as one of the apocryphal inventions of some age of monks and darkness "I find more sure marks of authenticity in the New Testament (said Sir Isaac Newton), than in any profane history whatever."

But inasmuch as your minds cannot be furnished with too much information on this fundamental subject, I

* Lardner, iii. 134.

will reserve some important views for a subsequent lecture.

There is a lesson for the believer, in what has been exhibited, of great practical interest. It is manifest, from the testimonies adduced, that the scriptures of the New Testament were treated, among the primitive Christians, not only as true and possessed of inspired authority, in reference to all questions of doctrine and obedience; but as very precious, "more to be desired than gold." They loved them as an inestimable treasure; they kept them, consulted them, and exalted them in their hearts, and houses, and assemblies, as a companion for every trial; a guide in every difficulty; a gift of God, for the preservation and honour of which they were ready to shed their blood. They felt them to be "profitable for doctrine, reproof, correction, and instruction in righteousness." How does all this rebuke the lukewarmness with which the scriptures are regarded by too many professing Christians of the present day. In primitive times, believers would read them, though they paid for the privilege with their lives. In these days, multitudes who call themselves believers, can hardly be persuaded to search the scriptures, though every facility is afforded, and the Bible is in honour. What a tremendous account must he give to God, who neglects His word! Let us imitate not only the affectionate devotion with which the primitive Christians read the Bible, but also the diligent zeal with which they surmounted innumerable obstacles, in circulating copies of its books through the world. We possess facilities for such an object which they had not. The press is placed in our hands for this very purpose. It is our gift of tongues. Let us realize the responsibility we are under, for the improvement of so rich a talent; and speed its work, and multiply its branches of application, till the sound of the Gospel has gone out into all the earth, and the words of Jesus to the ends of the world; and there is nothing hid from the light thereof.

LECTURE III.

AUTHENTICITY AND INTEGRITY OF THE NEW TESTAMENT.

Our attention was exclusively occupied, during the last lecture, in tracing up the line of testimony by which the church of Christ, in these days, is certified that her sacred books, composing the volume of the New Testament, are those very books which were written by the apostles of the Lord Jesus. A series of attestations was followed up, by which we were conducted into the very age and presence of the apostles, and enabled to inquire of those who, having been their contemporaries, and in habits of intercourse with them, must necessarily have known what books they wrote. A mass of evidence was obtained, by which the authenticity of the New Testament was placed on the most immoveable basis. But, inasmuch as we are now laying the foundation of our subsequent and more direct arguments for the truth of christianity as a divine revelation, it is of the greatest importance that, in respect to this preliminary subject, every mind be well assured, and that nothing of importance to the impressiveness, as well as sufficiency, of the evidence, be omitted. In the present lecture, therefore, we pursue still farther the question to which the last was devoted.

From the whole tenor of the previous lecture, it is evident that the *canon of the New Testament;* in other words, the collection of those books which were considered as the inspired and authoritative writings of the apostles and evangelists, to the exclusion of all others, *was not made without great care, and the most deliberate, intelligent investigation* Such is the witnessing of an eminent writer of the fourth century. "Our canonical books (says Augustine), which are of the highest authority among us, *have been settled with great care:* they ought to be few, lest their value should be diminished; and yet they are so many, and written by so many persons, that their agreement, throughout, is wonderful."* The method pursued by the early Christians in determining what books had a just claim to the character of canonical scriptures, was precisely that by which we have been investigating the same subject. It was not enough, for the reception of a writing, that it came to them under the name of an apostle, and was considered by some as justly entitled to that honour. Its descent was carefully traced. How was it regarded by the preceding generation, and by the generation before that? Was it known by those who lived nearest the time and the person associated with its claims? Had it been received by the churches; referred to and quoted, as possessing canonical authority, by christian writers since the period of its general publication? Had it been handed down by the general and concurrent tradition of the church, written and unwritten, as the work of the writer whose name it bears? Such was the mode which, we know from the remaining works of Irenæus, Tertullian, Eusebius, Cyril, and Augustine, &c., was employed in their days, and in all times of the primitive church. "The books of the canonical scriptures (says Augustine), established in the times of the apostles, and confirmed by the testimony of the succession of bishops and churches, in all following times, are placed in a peculiar degree of authority, to which the judgment and understanding of all pious men are subject."

The numerous catalogues which have descended to us from the early centuries, are sufficient evidence of the care with which the canon of the New Testament was settled. In primitive times, when, from a variety of causes, spurious

* Lardner, ii. 596.

books abounded, and the distant and scattered churches, incapable of much intercourse with those near the centre of christian light, were most liable to be deceived, these catalogues were of the greatest importance. How numerous they must have been, may be, in somewise, conceived from the fact that, although a very small portion only of the works of the first four centuries are extant, there are among them no less than thirteen independent catalogues, all of them composed by authors scattered over only about one hundred and eighty, out of the first four hundred years after the birth of Christ.

The same care is seen in the pains that were taken to obtain the most exact information as to the authenticity of the books bearing apostolic names; as well as from the decisive censure and aversion with which an attempt to pass a spurious work upon the church, was visited. Pious and learned heads of the churches used to journey to Palestine, and reside there for a considerable length of time, for the express object of obtaining whatever valuable knowledge might be found there, as to the New Testament writings. And of the treatment bestowed upon attempted forgeries, we have an example in the case of a certain presbyter of Asia, soon after the death of St. John, who published a book, which is still extant, under the title of the *Acts of Paul and Thecla.* The attempt at imposition was charged upon the author, and confessed. Whereupon he was degraded from his office, and the whole matter was notified to the churches, that they might feel the need of the strictest care thereafter.*

The gradual steps by which the books of the New Testament were multiplied to their present number, afforded the best opportunity for a careful and accurate determination of their authenticity. Had they all appeared at once, claiming, in their collective form, to be received by the churches as in-

---

* Lardner, i. 435.

spired scripture; the attention of Christians being thus divided among twenty-seven independent writings which professed to have been written by eight different authors, the diligence of their investigation would have been also divided; its accuracy would have been endangered, and the opportunity of imposition greatly increased. But such was not the case. The books of the New Testament were published singly. They came before the churches, one by one, with considerable intervals between them, thus giving time for the claims of each to be deliberately and singly examined. The Epistle to the Romans appeared at the bar of the church in the city of Rome, and had its authority as a writing of St. Paul determined, without embarrassment from any question as to the authenticity of the Epistle to the Ephesians. The Ephesians received the Epistle directed to them, and could sit in judgment upon its claims, without any necessity of deciding, at that time, upon the authenticity of the Epistle to the Romans, or Corinthians, or Philippians. Thus were there several years between the beginning and completion of the canon of the New Testament. For a little while, a portion of the church might possess an additional book, which a distant region, on account of the difficulty of multiplying and transmitting copies, would not have received. It may have been a period of some years before a church in the distant parts of Asia received and was enabled satisfactorily to authenticate the Epistle to the Romans. Meanwhile the canon of scripture might be composed of more books at Rome than at the church supposed.

How long this state of things continued; or when precisely the canon was closed, is a question rather of curiosity than of importance; the authenticity and canonical character of any particular book being independent of its determination. We know that the principal parts of the New Testament were collected before the death of St. John, or at least not long subsequent to that event. But what individual, or what assemblage of persons, collected them; *where*, and precisely *when*, the work was done, we may indulge in plausible conjecture, but cannot certainly ascertain. But what connexion have such matters with the question of apostolic origin? If the Epistle to the Romans, or the gospel of Matthew was written by the disciple whose name it bears, it surely matters little when it became the companion of other authentic books in the formation of a separate volume; or who arranged its place in that volume; or when an assemblage of christian fathers inserted its name in a catalogue, and published it to the churches as a canonical writing. It was canonical as soon as it was composed. It was a part of the New Testament from the moment of its birth. Had the books of scripture never been collected into a volume, but kept in separation, as they were first published, to the present time, although their preservation would have been more difficult, their authority would have been the same, and the canon of the New Testament complete. Had no father of the church, nor any ecclesiastical council ever issued a declaration of opinion as to what writings should be included in the list of canonical scriptures, we should have wanted indeed much valuable testimony now possessed from such sources; but the essential claim of each inspired book to a place in the canon would have remained unaltered. To substantiate the title of any portion of the New Testament to so honourable a place, we need only the proof that it was written by the apostle or evangelist to whom it is ascribed. For this we require the testimony of primitive antiquity. So far as the opinion of ancient councils or authors is deserving of attention, as a matter of testimony, it is of value in the settlement of the canon; and in this view, such opinion is unquestionably of the highest importance; and what we have already exhibited of this kind, deserves the greatest consideration. But the point to be especially noted is, that the proof of *authenticity* in the subject before us, is the proof of *canonical autho-*

rity, that the canon began when the first Gospel or Epistle was published; that it increased with every additional publication by inspired men, and was complete and closed, the moment the last writing of the New Testament was issued to the churches; though at the same time but few of them may have been acquainted with it; no ecclesiastical assembly may have sanctioned it, and no union had been made with other inspired books, so as to present them to the churches as a collection of canonical writings, under the general name of the New Testament.

As to the arrangement of these books in a single volume, it must have been a work of time, according to the relative situation and intercourse of any particular region of christianity. "Those churches which were situated nearest to the place where any particular books were published, would, of course, obtain copies much earlier than churches in remote parts of the world. For a considerable period the collection of these books in each church must have been necessarily incomplete, for it would take some time to send to the church or people with whom the autographs were deposited, and to write off fair copies. This necessary process will also account for the fact, that some of the smaller books were not received by the churches so early, nor universally, as the larger. The solicitude of the churches to possess, immediately, the more extensive books of the New Testament, would doubtless induce them to make a great exertion to acquire copies; but, probably, the smaller would not be so much spoken of, nor would there be so strong a desire to obtain them without delay. Considering how difficult it is now, with all our improvements in the typographical art, to multiply copies of the scriptures with sufficient rapidity, it is truly wonderful how so many churches as were founded during the first century. to say nothing of individuals, could all be supplied with copies of the New Testament, when there was no speedier method of producing them than by writing every letter with the pen. Even as early as the time when Peter wrote his second Epistle, the writings of Paul were in the hands of the churches, and were classed with the other scriptures.* And the citation from these books by the earliest christian writers, living in different countries, demonstrates that, from the time of their publication, they were sought after with avidity, and were widely dispersed." "How intense the interest which the first Christians felt in the writings of the apostles can scarcely be conceived by us, who have been familiar with these books from our earliest years. How solicitous would they be, for example, who had never seen Paul, but had heard of his wonderful conversion and extraordinary labours and gifts, to read his writings? And probably they who had enjoyed the high privilege of hearing this apostle preach would not be less desirous of reading his Epistles! As we know from the nature of the case, as well as from testimony, that many uncertain accounts of Christ's discourses and miracles had obtained circulation, how greatly would the primitive Christians rejoice, to obtain an authentic history from the pen of an apostle, or from one who wrote precisely what was dictated by an apostle? We need no longer wonder, therefore, that every church should wish to possess a collection of the writings of the apostles; and knowing them to be the productions of inspired men, they would want no further sanction of their authority. All that was requisite, was to be certain that the book was indeed written by the apostle whose name it bore."† Hence the care of St. Paul, as he commonly wrote by an amanuensis, to have the salutation in his own hand, or to annex his signature: as, for example, in the second Epistle to the Thessalonians: "*The salutation of Paul with mine own hand, which is the token in every Epistle: so I write.*" Hence, also, the care so often manifest in the Epistles, to designate

---

* 2 Peter, iii. 14, 15. † Alexander on the Canon, p. 138, &c.

those by name to whom the office of carrying them, whither they were addressed, was intrusted.

From the authorities quoted in the previous lecture, it must be full in your recollection that while the agreement of the ancient churches may be considered to have been complete, so far as is important to the argument for the divine origin of Christianity; still there was a difference of opinion as to the authenticity and canonical authority of the Epistle to the Hebrews; of the Epistle of James; the second of Peter; the second and third of John; the Epistle of Jude; and the book of Revelation. This diversity was not, by any means, so great or important as some suppose. Had it not been for the great care and candour of those early Christians, from whom we learn the fact, it would have seemed of too limited an extent, and too inconsiderable in its origin, to merit any more than a very transient notice in their writings. But we have no reason to regret the publicity they have given it. They have thus put into our hands a very strong proof of the discriminating care and jealous vigilance with which the primitive churches investigated the title of any book to admission into the canon of the New Testament. That some were doubted, though afterwards universally acknowledged, exhibits in a very strong light the certain authenticity of all those of which there was never a question.

The canonical authority of the six Epistles above named, as well as of the Apocalypse, has no material connexion with the argument of the ensuing lectures. The evidence of the divine origin and revelation of christianity is entirely independent of the question of their authenticity. Should we acknowledge them to be spurious, no point of christian doctrine or duty would be removed; no gospel truth would be shaken; no evidence of divine revelation would be diminished. To vindicate their authenticity cannot, therefore, be required of a lecturer on the evidences of christianity. It is the appropriate office of the biblical critic, and belongs to discussions on the canon of scripture, and to the prolegomena of a commentary, instead of the course we are now pursuing. But lest the mere statement of the fact that doubts were once entertained as to the authenticity of these writings, should leave on some minds an impression unfavourable to their character, as inspired scriptures, it will be well to bestow a moment's attention to the amount of importance to which those doubts are justly entitled.

With regard to the Epistle to the Hebrews, no question was entertained as to its being the work of St. Paul, among the churches of the earlier centuries, except those of the Latin Christians. The fact that the Arians were the first in the Greek churches who are said to have denied that it was written by St. Paul, is an important testimony in its favour. The objections of the Latins did not pretend to any ecclesiastical tradition, or any authority of earlier churches, in opposition to its Pauline origin; but were based entirely on its internal character, and especially on the handle which the fourth and fifth verses of the sixth chapter seemed to afford the sect of the Montanists, in vindication of their prominent doctrine, that those guilty of grievous transgressions should be irrevocably cut off from the church. Hence it was that Jerome and Augustine, though of the Latins, could not adopt the opinions held by many of their contemporaries, being convinced of their incorrectness, by the testimony of the ancient churches to the authenticity of the Epistle.

It should be remarked, that all those who questioned the canonical authority of this Epistle, treated it with high respect as a christian and very ancient writing of the apostolic age, if not by an apostle's hand. They ascribed it either to Barnabas or Clement. But for this they had no testimony to appeal to. On the contrary, the testimony of the earliest christian writers is very decidedly for St. Paul. The fathers of the Greek church unanimously ascribed it to him. Jerome, of the fourth century, testifies that it was received as a production of that apostle, not only by the eastern churches, but *by all the Greek ecclesiastical writers.* "I receive it (said he) as genuine—guided by the authority of the ancient writers." Eusebius, the historian of the church of the fourth century, quotes it as the work of St. Paul, and says it had, not without reason, been reckoned among the other writings of the apostle. Theodoret positively asserts that Eusebius received this Epistle as St. Paul's, and that he manifested that almost all the *ancients* were of the same opinion. Augustine said "he followed the opinion of the churches of the east, who received it among the canonical scriptures." Origen, born A. D. 184, expresses his opinion that "it was not without cause that the *ancients* (i. e. the immediate successors of the apostles) regarded this as an Epistle of Paul." The internal evidence is decidedly in favour of its having been written by that apostle. The salutation from the Jewish Christians who had been driven out of Italy (Heb. xiii. 24.), and the mention of Timothy as his fellow traveller (xiii. 23.), are very applicable to Paul. Not only does the general scope of this Epistle tend to the same point on which so much stress is laid in his other writings, that we are justified only by faith in Christ, and that the works and institutions of the law are of no avail to our salvation; but there are also various propositions found in it which are conspicuous in his other works. The same characteristic warmth and energy of expression appear in this as in all writings ascribed in the New Testament to the pen of St. Paul. Hebraisms abound in it as in his other Epistles. It contains particular expressions, phrases, and collocations of words, which are either peculiar to him, or are most frequent in his compositions.* But as this is not the place to do justice to a question of so much importance, and yet not material to the argument

---

* Smucker's translation of Storr and Flatt's Bib. Theology.

of these lectures, I must refer you, for further knowledge and satisfaction, to the learned and complete work of professor Stuart, of Andover, on the Epistle to the Hebrews, or to an excellent article in the "Biblical Notes and Dissertations," recently from the pen of Joseph John Gurney, of the society of Friends, in England.

The Epistle of James, being addressed to Jewish believers, was for some time, to a considerable extent, unknown to the Gentile Christians. While this was the case, its authenticity was questioned, or rather was not certified among the Gentiles. As soon as this ceased to be the case, its authenticity was undoubted. It is of great importance to the character of this Epistle, that in the Syriac version, made at the end of the first or the beginning of the second century, while the second Epistle of Peter, the second and third of John, and the Apocalypse, are omitted, the Epistle of James, written particularly to the people for whom the version was made, is included and placed on an equality with all those books about which there was never a question in the church. In proportion as it became known among the Gentile Christians, it passed through a severe and accurate scrutiny, till, in a short time, it was universally received, and has ever since been universally honoured, as an authentic and inspired portion of the oracles of God.

With regard to the remaining Epistles, concerning the authenticity of which doubts were for a while entertained, it will suffice to remark in this place, that the fact of their not having been immediately recognised throughout the church as the works of the apostles, only shows that the persons who were in doubt had not yet received sufficient information to make up their judgment; and that the primitive Christians, so far from being so greedy after additions to the sacred canon as to be easily deceived by a plausible pretension to apostolic origin, were extremely deliberate and cautious in examining every candidate for admission into the catalogue of scripture. Such being the case, the subsequent reception of these Epistles, as soon as full time was given them to be universally circulated and known, is perfect proof that they were capable of enduring the most trying investigation of their inspired origin, and were honoured with a unanimous verdict as the veritable writings of those to whom they were ascribed, and as part and parcel of the word of God. The reader may find abundant satisfaction, with regard to them, in Dr. Alexander's excellent work on the canon of scripture.

It has been stated, that at one period doubts were entertained in the churches as to the authenticity of the book of Revelation. Those doubts imply no deficiency of testimony. Until the fourth century, the character of this book was undoubted, and its authority was universally acknowledged; only one writer questioning whether John the evangelist was its author, and even he admitting that it was written by inspiration of God. About the commencement of the fourth century, the Millenarian controversy having arisen and distracted the churches, and the mysterious character of the book having been extensively employed in the support of new and extravagant doctrines, its character declined; and without any reference to testimony in the case, its authenticity was by some, though by no means universally or for a long time, brought into question. Thus Eusebius, of that century, after having given a catalogue of the books universally acknowledged, writes: "After these, if it be thought fit, may be placed the Revelation of John, concerning which we shall observe the different opinions at a proper time." And in another place: "There are, concerning this book, different opinions." "This is the first doubt expressed by any respectable writer, concerning the canonical authority of this book; and Eusebius did not reject it, but would have placed it next after those which were received with universal consent. And we find, at this very time, the most learned and judicious of the fathers received the Revelation without scruple, and annexed it to their catalogues of the books of the New Testament."* It is of no small importance that a book so full of evidence against the heresies of the celebrated Dr. Priestley, should have received from his pen the following testimony: "This book of Revelation, I have no doubt, was written by the apostle John. Sir Isaac Newton, with great truth, says, *he does not find any other book of the New Testament so strongly attested, or commented upon so early as this.* Indeed I think it impossible for any intelligent and candid person to peruse it without being struck, in the most forcible manner, with the peculiar dignity and sublimity of its composition, superior to that of any other writing whatever; so as to be convinced that, considering the age in which it appeared, none but a person divinely inspired could have written it."† It is true, and at first may seem surprising, that while a majority of the ancient catalogues contain this book, there are many in which it is omitted; though it is known that the authors of some of these acknowledged its authenticity. The omissions are satisfactorily explained by the consideration that the object of these catalogues was the guidance of the people in reading the scriptures; and since the mysteriousness of this book and the use made of it, on the side of the Millenarian errors, when the catalogues were chiefly composed, seemed to render it inexpedient that it should be as generally read as the other scriptures, its name was excluded from several lists of books for universal use, without any intention of pronouncing upon its canonical character.

Having now exhibited satisfactory evidence of the authenticity of all the books of the New Testament, be it remarked that, while every part of the sacred volume is of inspired authority, and therefore of such importance as that no man can take away from it or add unto it without heinous offence

* Alexander on the Canon. † Priestley's Notes on Scripture.

against God; still the argument for the divine mission of Jesus and for the divine origin of christianity depends chiefly upon *the historical portions*, and would exhibit no deficiency were no attention paid to the authenticity of the others. In what remains to be said, by way of addition to the various and unequalled evidence already adduced, we shall have a view particularly to the Gospels and Acts of the Apostles.

The testimony of the adversaries of christianity.

It may be said, with some appearance of a plausible objection to the testimony hitherto produced, that it is all derived, either from the devoted friends of the gospel, or else from those who professed to be its disciples. Is there no testimony from enemies? The books of the New Testament were widely circulated; christian advocates, in their controversies with the Heathen, freely appealed to them; Heathens, in their works of attack and defence, must have spoken of them. In what light did they regard them? Did they ascribe them to their reputed authors, or question their authenticity? Now we do not grant that the testimony already produced is justly liable to the least disparagement on account of its having been derived exclusively from the friends of Christ. That certain ancients *believed* the facts contained in Cæsar's Commentaries has never been supposed to diminish the value of their testimony to the authenticity of that work. We will take occasion, by and by, to show that the very fact that an early witness to the New Testament history was not an enemy, but a friend, of the gospel, and had become a friend from having been once an enemy, is just the ingredient in his testimony that gives it peculiar conclusiveness. Still, however, we are under no temptation to undervalue the importance of an appeal to the opinions of adversaries. Let us inquire of enemies as well as friends—and first of *Julian*.

Julian, the emperor, united intelligence, learning, and power, with a persecuting zeal, in a resolute effort to root out christianity In the year 361, he composed a work against its claims. We may be well assured that if any thing could have been said against the authenticity of its books, he would have used it. His work is not extant; but from long extracts, found in the answer by Cyril, a few years after, as well as from the statements of his opinions and arguments by this writer, it is unquestionable that Julian bore witness to the authenticity of the four Gospels and of the Acts of the Apostles. He concedes, and argues from, their early date; quotes them by name as the genuine works of their reputed authors; proceeds upon the supposition, as a thing undeniable, that they were the only historical books which Christians received as canonical—the only authentic narratives of Christ and his apostles, and of the doctrine they delivered. He has also quoted, or plainly referred to, the Epistles to the Romans, Corinthians, and Galatians, and nowhere insinuates that the authenticity of any portion of the New Testament could reasonably be questioned.* Let us ascend a little higher.

Hierocles, president of Bithynia, and a learned man, of about the year 303, united, with a cruel persecution of Christians, the publication of a book against christianity, in which, instead of issuing even the least suspicion that the New Testament was not written by those to whom its several parts were ascribed, he confines his effort to the hunt of internal flaws and contradictions. Besides this tacit acknowledgment, his work, or the extracts of it that remain, refer to, at least, six out of the eight writers of the books of the New Testament.† Let us ascend still higher.

Porphyry, universally allowed to have been the most severe and formidable adversary, in all primitive antiquity, wrote, about the year 270, a work against christianity. It is evident that he was well acquainted with the New Testament.

---

* Lardner, iv. 341. † Ib. iv. 259.

In the little that has been preserved of his writings, there are plain references to the Gospels of Matthew, Mark, and John, the Acts of the Apostles, and the Epistle to the Galatians.* Speaking of Christians, he calls Matthew *their* evangelist. "He possessed every advantage which natural abilities or political situation could afford, to discover whether the New Testament was a genuine work of the apostles and evangelists, or whether it was imposed upon the world after the decease of its pretended authors. But no trace of this suspicion is any where to be found; nor did it ever occur to Porphyry to suppose that it was spurious."† How well this ingenious writer understood the value of an argument against the authenticity of a book of scripture, and how greedily he would have enlisted it in his war against christianity, could he have found such a weapon, is evident from his well known effort to escape the prophetic inspiration of the book of Daniel, by denying that it was written in the times of that prophet. We may ascend still higher.

Celsus, esteemed a man of learning among the ancients, and a wonderful philosopher among modern infidels, wrote a laboured argument against the Christians. He flourished in the year 176, or about *seventy-six years after the death of St. John.* None can accuse him of a want of zeal to ruin christianity. None can complain against his testimony, as deficient in antiquity. An industrious, ingenious, learned, adversary of that age, must have known whatever was suspicious in the authorship of the New Testament writings His book entitled "*The True Word*," is unhappily lost, but in the answer, composed by Origen, the extracts from it are so large, that it is difficult to find of any ancient book, not extant, more extensive remains. The author quotes, from the Gospels, such a variety of particulars, even in these fragments, that the enumeration would prove almost

* Lardner, iv. 234. † Marsh's Michaelis, i. 43.

an abridgement of the Gospel narrative.* Origen has noticed in them about eighty quotations from the books of the New Testament, or references to them. Among these there is abundant evidence that Celsus was acquainted with the Gospels of Matthew, Luke and John. Several of Paul's Epistles are alluded to. His whole argument proceeds upon the concession that the christian scriptures were the works of the authors to whom they were ascribed. Such a thing as a suspicion, to the contrary, is not breathed; and yet no man ever wrote against christianity with greater virulence. Hence it appears, "by the testimony of one of the most malicious adversaries the christian religion ever had, and who was also a man of considerable parts and learning, that the writings of the evangelists were extant in his time, which was the next century to that in which the apostles lived; and that those accounts were written by Christ's own disciples, and, consequently, in the very age in which the facts there related, were done, and when, therefore, it would have been the easiest thing in the world to have convicted them of falsehood, if they had not been true."† "Who can forbear (says the devout Doddridge) adoring the depth of divine wisdom, in laying up such a firm foundation of our faith in the gospel history, in the writings of one who was so inveterate an enemy to it, and so indefatigable in his attempts to overthrow it."‡ Who, I will add, can help the acknowledgment that in Celsus, Porphyry, Hierocles, and Julian, all of them learned controversionalists, as well as devoted opponents and persecutors of Christians, extending their testimony, from the seventieth year after the last of the apostles, to the year of our Lord 361—every reasonable demand for the testimony of enemies is fully met, and a gra-

* Doddridge, in Lardner, iv. 145 and 7.

† Answer to "Christianity as old as the Creation," by Leland, vol. ii. c. v. p. 150—154.

‡ Doddridge, in Lardner, iv. 147

cious Providence has perfected the external evidence for the authenticity of the New Testament?

We proceed to confirm the abounding proof, already adduced, by a brief reference *to the language and style of the New Testament.*

I. *The language and style are in perfect accordance with the local and other circumstances of the reputed writers.* They were Jews by birth; Jews by education; Jews by numerous and strong attachments; Jews in all their associations of thought and feeling. Jews were, in great part, the persons to whom they wrote. Jewish prejudices, objections, and peculiarities, were, to a great extent, the obstacles in their way. The religious and political institutions of the Jewish nation, though perfectly exterminated in a few years after they wrote, were in full establishment till after the death of all of them except St. John. Hence it is reasonably expected that Jewish peculiarities should be found frequently and broadly stamped upon any writings truly professing to have proceeded from their pens. Such, notoriously, is the case with the writings of the New Testament. None but Jews could have composed them. None but Jews who lived before the destruction of their temple, and city, and polity, and nation, could have cast them in their present mould; or marked them with all those indescribable and inimitable touches of a Jewish hand, which their style and language every where exhibit. The use of words and phrases which are known to have been peculiar to Judea in the times of the apostles; the continual, familiar, and natural allusions to the ceremonies and temple service of the Jews, as then existing, and which soon passed away; the universal prevalence of a mode of thinking and of expression, which none but a Jew, brought up under the Old Testament, always accustomed to think of religion through the types and shadows of the law, and reared amidst the usages, prejudices, associations, and errors of the Jewish people, as subsisting in the times of the apostles, could have introduced without awkwardness and obvious forgery; all bear decided witness, not only that the writers of the New Testament were Jews originally, in every sense; but that they must have formed their habits of thinking, feeling and writing, *before the destruction of the Jewish state;* in other words, *before the fortieth year after the death of Christ.* From that time, so entirely was every vestige of the religion and polity of the Jews destroyed, that, except among those whose minds had been moulded under pre-existing circumstances, the writing of a book in the language and style, and abounding in the peculiarities of the New Testament, would have been, at least, next to impossible.

This conclusion will appear the more inevitable, when you consider the characteristic features by which the Greek of the New Testament is distinguished. In the times of the apostles, Greek was almost a universal language. It was spread over all Palestine. The Jewish coast, on the Mediterranean, was occupied by cities, either wholly, or half Greek. On the eastern border of the land, from the Arnon upwards, towards the north, the cities were Greek; and, towards the south, in possession of the Greeks. Several cities of Judea and Galilee were either entirely, or, at least, half peopled by Greeks. "Being thus favoured on all sides, this language was spread, by means of traffic and intercourse, through all classes, so that the people (though with many exceptions), considered generally, understood it, although they adhered more to their own language."* But the Greek, thus spoken in Palestine, was not like that of Attica, nor of the cities of Asia Minor; but having become degenerated, in consequence of its associations with people whose native tongue was Hebrew, by means of Chaldee and

* Hug on the Greek languages in Palestine.—*Bib. Repository, No. III.* Andover

Syriac intermixtures, into Western Aramean, it contained a large share of the idioms and other peculiarities belonging to this heterogeneous neighbour. Such was the language in which the apostles must have written. Now, if *the books of the New Testament be their writings*, they must contain the characteristic features of that Palestine Greek. Such is most manifestly the case. These books are in Greek, but not pure and classic, such as a native and educated Grecian would have written; but in *Hebraic* Greek; in a language mixed up with the words and idioms of that peculiar dialect of the Hebrew which constituted the vernacular tongue of the inhabitants of Judea and Galilee in the age of the apostles. Had it been otherwise; were the language of the New Testament pure and classic; then the writers must have been either native and educated Grecians, or else Jews, of much more Attic cultivation than the apostles of Christ. In either case a suspicion would attach to the authenticity of our sacred books. Neither case being true, the evidence of authenticity is materially confirmed.

But we go further. The Greek of the New Testament could not have been written by men who had learned their language after the age of the apostles. This mingling of Grecian and Aramean, as it is preserved in the New Testament, ceased to be the familiar tongue of Christians in Palestine before the death of St. John. When Jerusalem, with the whole civil and religious polity of the Jews, was, in the seventieth year of the christian era, entirely destroyed, and the descendants of Abraham were rooted out of the land, and foreigners came in from all quarters to take their places; the language of the country underwent such a change that, except with the scattered few who had survived the desolation of their country, the Greek of the New Testament was no more a living language. When St. John died, there was probably not a man alive who could speak or write precisely that tongue. In the second century, an attempt to compose a book in the name of the apostles, and in imitation of their Greek, would have been detected as easily as if a full bred Frenchman, never out of France, should attempt to compose a volume in a dialect of English, and endeavour to pass it off as the work of a plain, sensible, but unpolished Yorkshireman. Hence, while doubts were entertained for a while, in some parts of the church, as to the authenticity of some portions of the New Testament, it was never doubted whether they were written by men who had lived when the Greek of Palestine, as it had been in the apostolic age, was yet alive.

II. *The language and style of the New Testament are in perfect harmony with the known characters of the reputed writers.* The apostles and evangelists were men of plain, sound understanding, but without any polish of education, and not likely to adorn their writings with much rhetorical dress. Paul, the only exception to this character, was well read in Jewish, and, we have reason to believe, in Grecian literature. From other sources, besides the New Testament, we are informed of certain peculiarities of natural character, as having distinguished some of those to whom the books of the New Testament are ascribed. John, for example, is always represented in ecclesiastical history as having been remarkable for meekness, and gentleness, and a manner and spirit full of mild affection. Paul, we always read of as characterized by prompt, energetic zeal and animated boldness. If the books bearing their names were written by those apostles, we must expect to find in them the distinctive stamp of their respective characters. So it is. In the historical books, *none of which the educated Paul composed,* there is no ornament of style; but merely the simplicity, and directness, of plain, sensible men, honestly relating what they familiarly knew, and disregarding style in their intentness upon truth. In the Epistles of Paul, however, the case is entirely different. There we behold the style of a writer brought up in the schools, though obviously in the schools of Judea. Accustomed to writing and to argument, he reasons precisely as we should expect of Saul of Tarsus, after having been educated at the feet of Gamaliel, and arrested by divine power and grace on the road to Damascus and made to "count all things but loss for the excellency of the knowledge of Christ." Every where in the epistles, bearing his name, are written the strong characters of the peculiar zeal and boldness, as well as education, that belonged to Paul; while throughout the writings ascribed to John, there breathes the sweet spirit of gentleness and tender affection, so characteristic of "that disciple whom Jesus loved." Similar statements might be made with regard to other writers of the New Testament, in proportion as their peculiarities of temperament are known and conspicuous.

From all that has now been said, it may easily be made to appear, that if the historical books of the New Testament, *the Gospels and Acts of the Apostles*, on which our subsequent argument will chiefly depend, be not authentic; in plainer terms, if they be forgeries, ***nothing less than a miracle can account for their early and universal currency.*** Remember that John lived to the end of the *first century.* It cannot be supposed that books, falsely pretending to have been written by those very evangelists, with whom he had been so intimately associated, and one of them professing to have been written by himself, could have gained a reputable currency in the churches while he lived. He certainly knew what he and the other evangelists had published; and no motive can be assigned that could have induced him to suffer a forgery to pass unexposed. We conclude, therefore, that if these books be not authentic, they must have been palmed on the churches after the death of John; that is, after the beginning of the *second* century. Suppose we descend to the *third.* Can it be imagined that the deception was introduced after this century commenced? Impossible; since by this time, the books in question were read, every Lord's Day, in all the churches; quoted by writers of all countries; universally received as the oracles of God. If a deception was introduced at all, it was brought in somewhere between the death of John and the third century—somewhere in the course of the *second.* Now, to obtain a clearer view of the difficulties which such an attempt must have had to overcome, let it be supposed that during the present year, a volume containing a digest of laws, under the title of "*Laws of the city of New York*," should appear among us, pretending to be a code of municipal regulations, composed, about seventy years ago, by a few of the most distinguished inhabitants of that period; and to have been received by the citizens, and appealed to in their municipal courts ever since, as the book of the laws of this city; claiming, moreover, to be acknowledged and obeyed by the present generation as the very code inherited from their fathers. What would be its chance? A moral impossibility would prevent its success. Nothing but lunacy would undertake such a scheme. It would be enough for lawyers and judges and people to say: "It was never heard of before. It has never been known in our courts." But this is only a feeble illustration of the case before us. If the books in question were forged in the name of the evangelists, you must suppose, that at some period, within a hundred years of St. John, while many were living who had either known him personally or conversed with those who did enjoy that privilege, a volume appeared among the churches, differing widely from those books which, as works of the evangelists, they had received and read from the beginning, and yet demanding to be considered as nothing more nor less than those very works. You must suppose the abettors of the imposition to have said to the various nations of Christians: "These are the genuine Gospels in which you were educated; which your fathers died for; which your persecutors endeavoured to destroy, and your martyrs laboured to save; which have been daily read in your families, expounded in your churches, quoted in your writings, and appealed to in all your controversies with heretics and enemies." And yet it must be supposed that Christians, notwithstanding their notorious love for the writings of the evangelists, and their great care in preserving them, were so easily and universally imposed on, as never to perceive that these fraudulent works, instead of having been expounded and read and quoted and appealed to in all their churches, had never been heard of before. You have to suppose, moreover, that while christianity was surrounded on all sides and opposed at every step by keen-sighted and determined enemies—Jews, on the one hand, with all their cunning—Greeks and Romans on the other, with all their skill and power, ever watching, accusing, and persecuting—none of them ever pretended to the discovery that these books, so fraudulently introduced, were not those which the apostles wrote and Christians had always read; but all believed them to be the identical writings to which the churches had invariably referred as the law and the testimony.

You must go still further, and suppose that notwithstanding the wide publicity which the genuine works of the apostles had obtained among the primitive churches, so immediately did these spurious productions expel them from the notice and recollection of all people, that no interval is known during which the question between the two conflicting volumes was so much as even debated. Instantly, (you must suppose), that the spurious were treated every where with the reverence belonging to inspired books; that though divers sects of heresies were starting up in various parts, all recognised their authority; that the churches of Rome, Corinth, Ephesus, Colosse, Philippi, Galatia, and Thessalonica, all believed that these several epistles, falsely pretending to have come to them from St. Paul, were those very ones, the autographs of which were then in their possession, and copies of which they had been continually reading in public from the time the originals were received from the apostle. Lastly, it must be supposed, that so perfect was the forgery, that although every weapon and artifice that wit, and learning, and power, could contrive, has been employed, during eighteen hundred years, for the single purpose of undermining the foundations of christianity, no labourer in the cause has yet succeeded in picking a flaw in the authenticity of its books. He that can digest all this for the purpose of maintaining that our sacred writings are not authentic, can swallow the most abject absurdity. He supposes an endless succession of miracles wrought upon innumerable minds for the promotion of imposture. He believes the laws of nature to have been continually violated, under the government of a holy God, to countenance unrighteousness. In sustaining this belief, he must adopt a principle with regard to miracles, the boldness and novelty of which, even Hume would have been jealous of. *He* was so modest as only to maintain that *no testimony can prove a miracle.* Here, however, the sceptic must maintain that the most absurd miracle can be proved, not only without any testimony, but *against all testimony.*

Enough has now been said to enable you to judge whether the learning or the honesty of the miserable Paine is most to be admired, when he says: "Those who are not much acquainted with ecclesiastical history, may suppose that the book called the New Testament has existed ever since the time of Jesus Christ; but the fact is historically otherwise. *There was no such book as the New Testament till more than three hundred years after the time that Christ is said to have lived.*" Whether we ought to save this poor sceptic from the charge of a gross and deliberate falsehood, by imputing to him disgraceful ignorance, I leave you to decide.

And now, having maintained our cause, permit me to say, that in argument with unbelievers, we cannot, in justice, be required to present any of the evidence to which you have been listening. The whole burden of proof lies with the objector. Should the authenticity of Paradise Lost be called in question, no believer in its Miltonian origin would feel himself called upon to prove it. We should wait in calmness, till the sceptic had sustained his objection. The book has lived long enough with a fair reputation to be considered authentic, till proved to be spurious. So would common justice warrant us in saying with regard to the New Testament. Eighteen centuries of high and holy reputation are enough to sustain its authenticity, till sceptics, besides *pronouncing*, shall *prove* it a forgery. Let the objector be kind enough to state the proof of its spuriousness; let him show the deficiencies in its evidence; let him establish objections to its legitimacy, which all the enemies that surrounded its birth were unable to venture; then will it be time for friends to stand on the defensive, and prove its apostolic parentage. But this we know not that any opposer of christianity ever pretended to have done. *How* these books were forced upon the world; *when* Christians were so asleep as not to perceive that they were not the books which they had always been reading, and consulting, and expounding, and loving, and suffering for; *when* the enemies of Christians were so miraculously blinded and the den of lions in which the church for so many centuries existed, was so miraculously hushed and overruled, that such an imposture could gain admission, and dwell in universal quietness, without so much as one paw to pounce on the prey, or one vigil ant foe to discover its existence—*what* is *the evidence* that such an event ever took place; I never heard of a human being undertaking to show. You might as well pretend to prove that the Declaration of Independence, circulated in numberless copies through the country, is not authentic; that our revolutionary fathers published no such document, or else that ours is not the declaration which they published

The adversaries of christianity are wary. It would require learning, and time, and talents, to make even a plausible show of strength, in conflict with the testimony to the authenticity of the New Testament; but it takes no time, requires no talent, or knowledge, for such persons to *insinuate* that its books are forgeries—to put out a *wise suspicion* that they were not written by the original disciples. No argument can refute a sneer, nor any human skill prevent its mischief. They know that many a mind will catch the plague of infidelity by the touch of their insinuation, without ever finding, or caring to seek, the antidote. Any body can soil the repute of an individual, however pure and chaste, by uttering a suspicion, which his enemies will believe, and his friends never hear of. A puff of idle wind can take up a million of the seeds of the thistle, and do a work of mischief which the husbandman must labour long and hard to undo; the floating particles being too trifling to be seen, and too light to be stopped. Such are the seeds of infidelity—so easily sown—so difficult to be gathered up, and yet so pernicious in their fruits. It is the work of God, much more than of man, that they do not spread more rapidly and widely. The hand of Divine Providence interposes to arrest it, where the regular array of human reasoning would have no room to use its strength.

Here we should leave the subject, were it not that one question of importance remains to be answered. How do we know that the New Testament has preserved its *integrity?* While it appears so conclusively that our present books are verily those which the evangelists and apostles wrote, and the primitive churches loved and read; how does it appear that they have undergone no material alteration since those times? On this head, the answer is complete.

We may reason from *the perfect impossibility of any material alteration.* The scriptures, as soon as written, were published. Christians eagerly sought for them; copies were multiplied; carried into distant countries; esteemed a sacred treasure, for which disciples were willing to die. They were daily read in families, and expounded in churches; writers quoted them; enemies attacked them; heretics endeavoured to elude their decisions; and the orthodox were vigilant, lest the former, in their efforts to escape the interpretation, should change the text. In a short time, copies were scattered over the whole inhabited portion of the earth. Versions were made into different languages. Harmonies, and collations, and commentaries, and catalogues, were carefully made and published. Thus universal notoriety, among friends and enemies, was given to every book. How, in such circumstances, could material alterations be made without exposure? If made in one copy, they must have been made universally; or else some unaltered copies would have descended to us, or would have been taken notice of and quoted in ecclesiastical history, and the writings of ancient times. If made universally, the work must have been done either by *friends*, or by *heretics*, or by *open enemies*. Is it supposable that *open enemies*, unnoticed by Christians, could have altered *all* or a hundreth part of the copies, when they were so continually read, and so affectionately protected? Could the sects of *heretics* have done such a work, when they were ever watching one another as jealously, as all their doings were continually watched by the churches? Could *true Christians* have accomplished such a task, even if any motive could have led them to desire it, while heretics on one hand, and innumerable enemies on the other, were always awake and watchful, with the scriptures in their hands, to lay hold of the least pretext against the defenders of the faith? It was at least as unlikely that material alterations in the New Testament should pass unnoticed and become universal, in the early centuries and in all succeeding ones, as that an important change in a copy of the constitution of the United States should creep into all the copies scattered over the country, and be handed down as part of the original document, unnoticed by the various parties and jealousies by which that instrument is so closely watched, and so constantly referred to. Such was the precise assertion of a writer of the fourth century, on this very subject. "The integrity (says Augustine) of the books of any one bishop, however eminent, cannot be so completely kept as that of the canonical scripture, translated into so many languages, and kept by the people of every age; and yet some there have been, who have forged writings with the names of apostles. In vain, indeed, because that scripture has been so esteemed, so celebrated, so known."* Reasoning with a heretic, he says: "If any one should charge you with having interpolated some texts alleged by you, would you not immediately answer that it is impossible for you to do such a thing in books read by all Christians? And that if any such attempt had been made by you, it would have been presently discerned and defeated by comparing the ancient copies? Well, then, for the same reason that the scriptures cannot be corrupted by you, neither could they be corrupted by any other people."†

The *agreement among the existing manuscripts* of the New Testament, proves that this holy volume has not been corrupted. Of no ancient classic are the extant manuscripts so numerous, as those of the New Testament. Griesbach, in making his edition, collated more than three hundred and fifty. These were written in different ages and countries. Some of them are as old as the fourth or fifth century. Some contain all, others only particular books or parts of books of the New Testament. Several contain detached portions or lessons, as appointed to be read on certain occasions in the churches. In none of them have we any thing differing in essential points from the text at present received. It is true, and it sounds to uninformed ears quite alarming

---

* Lardner, ii. 594. † Ib. ii. 228.

that in the manuscripts collated for Griesbach's edition of the New Testament, as many as *one hundred and fifty thousand various readings* are said to have been found. But all alarm will seem gratuitous when it is known that not one in a thousand of these various readings makes any perceptible, or at most any important variation of meaning; that they consist almost entirely in manifest mistakes of transcribers, such as the omission or transposition of letters, errors in pointing, in grammar, in the use of certain words instead of others of similar meaning, and in changing the position of words in a sentence. The very worst manuscript, were it our only copy of the New Testament, would not pervert one christian doctrine or precept. By all the *omissions* and all the *additions* contained in all the manuscripts, no fact, no doctrine, no duty, presented in our authorized version, is rendered either obscure or doubtful. The diversity of readings is ample proof that our present manuscripts were made from *various* copies in ancient times; while the inconsiderable importance of this diversity of readings shows how nearly those copies conformed to the original scriptures, and how little difference would be seen between our present New Testament and the autographs of its writers, could they be now collated. No ancient book has preserved its text so uncorrupt as those of the New Testament. None is attended with so many means of detecting an inaccurate reading. A common reader, could he compare the various manuscripts, would be sensible of no more difference among them than among the several copies of his English Bible, which have been printed during the last two hundred years.

The uncorrupt preservation of the text of the New Testament is also evident from its agreement with the *numerous quotations in the works of early christian writers, and with those ancient translations which are now extant.* In the remaining books of the fathers of the first three centuries, quotations from the New Testament are so abundant, that almost the whole of the sacred text could be gathered from those sources. Excepting some six or seven verses, the genuineness of which is not perfectly settled, there is an exact agreement, in all material respects, between those quotations and the corresponding parts of our New Testament. The same confirmation, though still more satisfactory, is derived from *ancient versions.* We possess, in various languages, versions of the New Testament, reaching as far back as the early part of the second century. The Mæso Gothic version, discovered by Mai in 1817, and made by Ulphilas, bishop of the Mæso Goths, in the year 370, of which only fragments were possessed before, has the same text as ours. The old Syriac version, called *Peshito,* is considered by some of the best Syriac scholars to have been made before the close of the first century. It was certainly in existence and general use before the close of the second. Though never brought into contact with our copies of the New Testament, because not known in Europe till the sixteenth century; though handed down by a line of tradition perfectly independent of, and unknown to, that by which our Greek Testament was received; yet, when the two came to be compared, the text of the one was almost an exact version of the text of the other. The difference was altogether unimportant. So clearly and impressively has Divine Providence attested the integrity of our beloved scriptures.

It is now high time we had relieved your attention. You will allow me to proceed, in the subsequent lectures, on the belief that the authenticity and integrity of the New Testament have been satisfactorily proved. But let us not separate without acknowledging, in thankfulness of heart, our debt of gratitude to Him who, on a subject of such unspeakable importance, has given us such abundant reason for complete conviction. He has made the great truth, for which we have been contending, like "*the round world, so sure, that it cannot be moved.*"

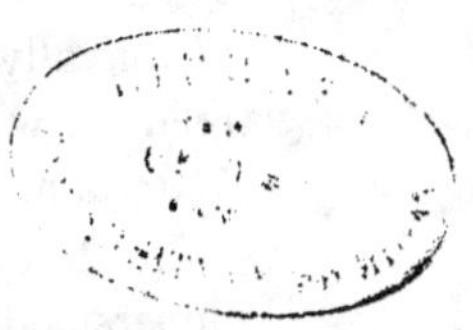

LECTURE IV.

CREDIBILITY OF THE GOSPEL HISTORY.

In the last two lectures our attention was occupied with the authenticity and integrity of the New Testament. A body of proof was presented, of such variety and conclusiveness, as should cause us to feel that, in taking these important points for granted in our subsequent course, we assume nothing which every candid mind should not acknowledge to have been satisfactorily established. You will allow me, therefore, to treat the books of the New Testament as needing no further argument to prove that they were written in the age to which they are ascribed, and by the authors whose names they bear.

But it should be remembered, that a book may be *authentic*, and yet not *credible.* It may have been written indeed by the reputed author, and yet its narrative may not be worthy of confidence. This, I say, is a possible case. Examples illustrating it are not numerous. So generally do authentic histories prove to be true, that when we have ascertained a book to have been composed by the individual whose name is on it, we have a strong presumptive argument for the truth of all the conspicuous and important features in its narrative. But inasmuch as these two things are not always associated, an important question remains to be determined, before we can open the New Testament as *the book* of the life and religion of the Lord Jesus Christ, and worthy of entire reliance, as an account of what was done and taught by himself and his apostles. Does the New Testament contain a true history of events connected with the ministry of

Jesus and his primitive disciples, so that we may receive as historically accurate whatever is related therein? This refers to what is usually called the *credibility of the gospel history*, and expresses the subject of our present lecture.

But lest the bearing of my remarks should not be distinctly understood, I will endeavour to state the subject still more precisely. Observe then; it is not the inspiration of the gospel history, or that it was written by holy men as they were moved by the Holy Ghost, that we shall seek to prove this evening; nor that it contains a revelation from God; nor that its doctrines are true; nor that any of its facts were miraculous; these are subjects which it would be premature to introduce at present. All at which we now aim, is to furnish conclusive evidence that the gospel history *is true*, in the same sense as Marshall's Life of Washington is true—that what it relates, as matter of fact, is worthy of entire reliance as matter of fact, independently of all inferences or doctrines with which it may be connected.

How do we prove the credibility of the gospel history? I answer: precisely as you would ascertain the credibility of any other history. Though, as in the case of authenticity, we are ready to produce a variety and an abundance of evidence, far exceeding what the best established and the most unquestionable books of ancient profane history can pretend to, still the nature of the evidence is the same in one case as the other. The fact that one history is called sacred, and the other profane; that in one book, the actions of a holy and extraordinary philanthropist, named Jesus, are related; and in another the actions of a wicked and extraordinary man-slayer, named Cæsar, are related; occasions not the least difference in the nature of the evidence by which the credibility of both must be ascertained.

Here it would be perfectly safe and reasonable to rest the question of credibility upon the proof arrived at in the last lecture. Although it does not follow, in all cases, that to

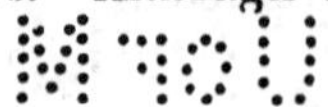

prove a book authentic, is to prove it credible also, with regard to its principal events, yet in the case before us, the fact that the books of the New Testament were written in the first century of christianity, and by the apostles and original disciples of Christ, is complete evidence that, in respect to the main events of the gospel history, they are true. If one should write a romance, calling it the memoir of some well known and distinguished personage, and publish it, not as grave, credible biography, but under the character of a novel, the authenticity of the work would have no connexion with its truth. But should he issue a book professing to be the true biography of Washington; should he vouch in every way for its truth, and stake his reputation upon its accuracy, in the midst of a generation familiar with the life of that noble man, and still containing some who were his companions and the eye-witnesses of many of his deeds, it would be reasonably inferred that, unless the author were an idiot or a madman, his work must be correct, at least, in the great mass of its statements and in all its conspicuous events. He must be aware that, under such circumstances, no important narrative without truth could escape detection. The fact, therefore, that he has published, in the midst of this generation, what he expects to be received as a correct biography of Washington, is sufficient warrant that, however inaccurate it may be in minute details, and however deficient in many respects of good writing and useful history, we may safely receive its principal narratives. Such a thing cannot be produced as a book published in the age to which its events are said to have occurred, and among the people to whose minds those events are said to have been familiar; a book which its author gravely avowed, and defended, as true and accurate; and yet in its principal narratives, in its prominent characters and occurrences, was not in accordance with fact. Men have too much sense, if not too much honesty, to attempt such a Quixotic adventure; especially when character and worldly interests are committed by the falsehood. But there is no book, to which this remark is so applicable as the New Testament. Not only was it published in the age in which the events related are asserted to have occurred, and among the people to whom they are said to have been notorious; but in an age and among a people awake to the whole subject of its history; determined to sift its correctness to the uttermost; capable of the severest scrutiny, and anxious to take advantage of the smallest inaccuracy. This the writers were perfectly aware of. They must have known that in the brevity of the history; in the fewness of its principal facts; in the great prominence and notoriety of each; in the few persons to whom they belong, as their leading agents; in the few places and the confined region in which they are said to have occurred; and in the brief space of time within which they were all embraced; their adversaries possessed advantages for investigation which nothing but bold and plain truth could confront, and no fiction could possibly elude. That, in the face of all these advantages, they did publish, and stake their characters and lives upon the correctness of their narratives, is a full warrant that they published truth. This argument can only be escaped by charging the writers of the New Testament with a degree of idiocy or madness, which the eminent wisdom and excellence of their works prove to have been impossible. I venture to say, that should the same argument be alleged with equal force in behalf of any other ancient book of history, its credibility, as to the main events related would be considered, independently of any other evidence, as placed beyond a reasonable suspicion.

Here, then, we might proceed to open the New Testament as a book of correct narrative; certified that, because *authentic*, it is therefore, as to all important matters of fact, *credible*. But we are not restricted to a single method of proof. The subject is compassed about with a cloud of witnesses. We take up another and broader plan of argument, the force of which none can mistake.

Let me ask by what sort of evidence you would feel assured of the credibility of any history, professing to relate events of a passed age? Suppose you should discover a volume hitherto concealed, professing to have been written by some well known individual of the Augustan age, and to contain a narrative of events in the personal history and domestic life of Augustus Cæsar. You would first examine into its authenticity. That settled, you would inquire into the credibility of its narrative. The first question would be, did the writer possess every advantage of knowing the events in the personal history of Augustus? May I depend on the sufficiency of his knowledge? Now he may not have lived with Augustus, and yet his knowledge may have been perfectly adequate. But your mind would be fully satisfied on this head, should it appear that the writer was not only a contemporary, but that he was domesticated with Augustus; conversed familiarly with him, lived at his table, assisted at his councils, accompanied him on his journeys.

The question of adequate knowledge being thus at rest, another would remain—*May I depend on the honesty of the writer?* In ordinary cases, you would be satisfied if nothing appeared in the book itself, or in the testimony of contemporaneous writings, impeaching his honesty. But your satisfaction would be much increased should you discover, in the style and spirit of the narrative, in its simplicity, modesty, and freedom of manner, in the circumstantial character of its details and the frequency of its allusions to time, place, and persons, those internal features of honesty, which it is so extremely difficult, if not impossible, to counterfeit. Your confidence would grow exceedingly if, on a comparison of the book with other well established histories of the same times, you should discover, not only that there is no contradiction in any particular, but that all its allusions to the customs, institutions, prejudices, and political events of the times, are abundantly confirmed from other sources. This would set the honesty of the writer in a very favourable light.

But suppose that, at this stage, you should discover three other books, upon the same subject; each evidently written by a person in the family and confidence of Augustus, or else with equally favourable opportunities of knowing him; each evidently an independent work, and having all the inward and outward marks of truth before detailed. Suppose, that on comparing these four histories together, you find that, while each contains some minor facts which the others do not, and relates, what all contain in common, in its own style and language, there is no disagreement among them; but on the contrary, the most perfect confirmation, one of another. Surely, after this, no further evidence could be demanded of the veracity of all those historians. But still, though you would have no right to require, you might perhaps discover additional evidence. You might search collateral history for the private characters of those writers; and how would it heighten your satisfaction to find that universally they were esteemed beyond reproach, even by their personal opponents. You might also inquire what motive they could have had for deception; and how conclusive would it seem in their favour to discover that, so far from any suspicion of such a motive attaching to them, they had undertaken to publish what they did, with the certainty of sacrificing every thing earthly, and actually plunged themselves by it into poverty, contempt, and suffering. One can hardly imagine stronger evidence of truth. None could, with any reason, require it.

But yet there might be additional evidence. These historians, perhaps, had many and bitter personal adversaries. How did *they* treat their books? The books were published during the lifetime of many who had seen Augustus, and had witnessed the principal events described: they were published in the very places where those events took place, and in the midst of thousands who knew all about them. How, then, did their *enemies* treat these histories? Now, should you discover that the personal adversaries of these four writers, however disposed, were unable to deny, but on the contrary acknowledged, assumed, and reasoned upon their narratives as true; and furthermore, that the thousands who had witnessed the principal events recorded, never contradicted those narratives, but in numerous instances afforded all the confirmation they were capable of; I am sure you would think the whole evidence for the credibility of those four histories, not only conclusive, but singularly and wonderfully so.

I have thus sketched a mass of evidence, and a variety of adequate evidence, which, were the half of it required for any book of ancient history but the Bible, would bring its credibility into utter condemnation. If a book, with all this in its favour, ought not to be believed, historical truth, or the possibility of ascertaining it, must be given up. But who would think of resisting such evidence? What would be thought of the intellect, not to speak of the candour of the man, who, with all this before him, should take up the memoirs of the life of Augustus Cæsar, as above supposed, and not feel that it were the absurdest folly to question the accuracy of their statements? In laying out this sketch, I have exhibited a general view of the evidence for the credibility of the gospel history. In proceeding, now, to more particular details, I hope to show you that every branch of the evidence I have glanced at, however vain to seek it in favour of any other ancient history, can be cited in attestation of the credibility of that in the New Testament.

From the brief view we have taken of the evidence which may be brought for the credibility of any historical document, it appears that the great points to be made out in favour of the writer are these two—*competent knowledge* and *trust-*

worthy honesty. Did he know enough to write a true account? and then, was he honest enough to be unable to write any other than a true account? Establish these, and the book is established—the question is closed. Let us take this plan as to the history before us. We have several independent writings containing the gospel history. Let us select that of St. John, and try the question first upon it. We begin, then, with this most important inquiry:

I. Had the writer of this book *sufficient opportunities of possessing adequate knowledge as to those matters of fact which he has related?* I do not suppose that much array of argument can be necessary to prove that he had every opportunity. It is to be first considered that the amount of knowledge required to enable John, or either of the other evangelists, to give an accurate account of so much of the life of Christ and of the transactions connected with his cause, as he has embraced in his narrative, was not very considerable. The gospel history is contained in a small space. Twenty-nine or thirty pages, of a common family Bible, comprise the whole of what John has related. It is a plain straight forward account of a very simple intelligible train of events. There are no labyrinths of historical truth to trace out—no perplexed involutions of circumstances to unravel. Consequently, when you consider that John, by the testimony of all tradition, as well as that of the gospel history, was a member of the household of Christ—admitted into his most unreserved and affectionate intercourse—the disciple whom he specially loved—who accompanied him in all his journeyings, followed him into his retirements, stood beneath his cross, and was a constant companion of the other disciples, and a witness of their actions—you will readily grant that John must have possessed all desirable opportunities of knowing, and must actually have known the gospel history so perfectly as to be fully competent to write an accurate account. I shall therefore refrain from any further remarks upon this branch of the argument, and shall pass to the second, in entire confidence that I leave no mind in any reasonable doubt of the *adequateness of our historian's knowledge.*

The second and the main question to be pursued is this: Have we reason to rely with implicit confidence upon the honesty of this historian? Believing him to have known enough to relate the truth, may we also believe that he was too honest to relate any thing but the truth? This is a fair and plain question. Prove the negative, and John's history must be given up. Prove the affirmative, and it "is worthy of all acceptation." We begin the argument for the affirmative.

II. *There is abundant evidence that the writers of the gospel history were too honest to relate any thing but truth.*

We will apply, in the first place, to the history itself. There are certain characteristic marks of historical honesty, which can hardly be counterfeited to any extent, and always produce a favourable impression. Take up the history written by St. John. I call your attention to the obvious fact that;

1st. Its narrative is in a very high degree *circumstantial.* A false witness will not need to be cautioned against the introduction of many minute circumstances into his statement. The more he connects it with the particulars of time, and place, and persons, so as to locate his facts and bring in living men as associated with them, the more does he multiply the probability of detection. He gives the cross-examination every advantage. It would be impossible for a false statement, abounding in such details, and at the same time exciting general interest in the neighbourhood where, and soon after, they are alleged to have occurred, to escape exposure. Consequently, when we take up a narrative thus minutely circumstantial, and which we are sure did excite among all classes, where its events are located, the very highest and most scrutinizing interest, and that, too, within a short time after the period to which the events are referred; we always feel impressed with a strong persuasion that the writer had the consciousness of truth and the fearlessness of honesty. It is evident that he had no disposition, and therefore no cause, to shun the closest investigation. On the other hand, if you take up any books professing to be histories of events within the reach and investigation of those among whom they were first published, but yet in a great measure untrue, you will find a great deficiency of such minute details of time, place, and persons, as would serve to test their faithfulness. Compare them with the histories of the Peloponnesian and Gallic wars, by Thucydides and Julius Cæsar, and you will see directly how strong a feature of true narrative, in distinction from whatever is in a great degree invented, is a circumstantial detail of minute particulars.

Generality is the cloak of fiction. Minuteness is the natural manner of truth, in proportion to the importance and interest of the subject. Such is the precise manner and continual evidence of the honesty of St. John. His history is full of the most minute circumstances of time, place, and persons. Does he record, for example, the resuscitation of Lazarus? He tells the name of the village, and describes the particular spot where the event occurred. He gives the names of some of the principal individuals who were present; mentions many unbelieving Jews as eye-witnesses; states the precise object for which they had come to the place; what they did and said; the time the body had been buried; how the sepulchre was constructed and closed; the impression which the event made upon the Jews; how they were divided in opinion in consequence of it; the particular expressions of one whose name is given; the subsequent conduct of the Jews in regard to Lazarus. This, you perceive, is being very circumstantial. It is only a specimen of the general character of St. John's Gospel. It looks very much as if the writer was not afraid of any thing the people of Bethany, or the survivors of those who had been present at the tomb of Lazarus, or the children of any of them, might have to say with regard to the resurrection. Now, when you consider that John's history was widely circulated while many were yet living, who, had these events never been, in Bethany, must have known it; and among a people, who, in addition to every facility, had every desire to find out the least departure from truth, I think you will acknowledge that the circumstantial character of this book is very strong evidence that the author must have written in the confidence of truth.

2d. Another striking evidence, to the same point, is seen in this, that the author exhibits no consciousness of narrating any thing, about which, as a matter of notorious fact, there was the smallest doubt. He takes no pains, evinces no thought of attempting, to convince his reader of the truth of what he relates. On the contrary, the whole narrative is conducted with the manner and aspect of one who takes for granted the entire notoriety of his statements. He comes before the public as one familiarly known, needing no account of himself or of his pretensions to universal confidence. He goes straight forward with his story, delivering the least and the most wonderful relations in the same simple and unembarrassed manner of ease and confidence, which nothing but an assurance of unimpeachable consistency can explain. Nothing is said to account for what might seem inexplicable; to defend what would probably be cavilled at; to anticipate objections which one feeling himself on questionable ground, would naturally look for. The writer seems to be conscious that, with regard to those for whom especially he wrote, all this were needless. He is willing to commit his simple statement alone, undefended, unvarnished, into the hands of friend or foe.

Nothing is more remarkable in this connexion than that, while he could not have been ignorant that he was relating many very extraordinary and wonderful events, he shows no wonder in his own mind, and seems to expect no wonder among his readers. This looks exceedingly like one who writes, not of extraordinary events, just contrived in his own imagination, but of extraordinary events which, whatever the wonder they excited when first known, are now perfectly notorious, not only to himself, but to all his readers. It is one thing to relate a series of astonishing occurrences which we feel are perfectly new to the readers, and a very different thing to relate the same to those who have long since been familiarly acquainted with their prominent particulars, and desire only a more circumstantial and confidential account. In the former case, the writer would naturally, and almost necessarily, betray in his style and the whole texture of his statement an expectation of the wonder and probable incredulity of his readers. In the latter, he would deliver his narrative as if he were thinking only of an accurate detail of truth, without particular reference to whether it was astonishing, or the contrary. Thus it is with St. John. There is no appearance of his having felt as if any of his Gospel would be new, or excite any new emotions of wonder in his readers. The marvellous works of Christ were, at that time, notorious. When first heard of, they excited universal astonishment. "His fame went abroad, and all the people were amazed." But so much time had now elapsed, that emotions of wonder had subsided, under the influence of repetition and familiarity. In striking consistency with this is the whole aspect of St. John's narrative. He goes directly forward in the relation of events, in themselves exceedingly impressive and astonishing, exhibiting no sign of any astonishment in his own mind, anticipating none in his contemporaneous readers. How is this to be explained? One can discover no plausible explanation but in the supposition that he was conscious of recording events, with which, in their chief particulars, the public mind had been entirely familiarized. This may deservedly be considered a strong indication of truth.

3d. I see another plain evidence, to the same point, in *the minute accuracy which marks all the allusions of this narrative to the manners, customs, opinions, political events, and other circumstances of the times.* The situation of Judea, in the time of the Saviour, was such as to bring it frequently under the eye of the profane writers of that age. From them we derive a great many particulars, illustrating the several modifications in the civil and religious institutions of the Jews, by their subjection to Rome. And hus we have a great many points of comparison between the gospel history and the other histories of the same times. The former contains innumerable references to the peculiarities then existing in the Jewish state—its laws, courts, punishments—as well as to the opinions, prejudices, and customs then prevailing. This was dangerous ground for the inventor of a story. The continual fluctuations in public affairs; the numerous and complex changes in the supreme officers of Judea and the neighbouring provinces; as well as in the boundaries and character of their governments, within the period embraced in the gospel history, must have added greatly to the difficulty of an inventor of a narrative located in such circumstances, and filled with allusions to them. We have a Jewish historian of the same age, with which to confront the gospel history. Josephus has furnished us with a full and minute account of those internal affairs of the Jews, both civil and religious, to which allusions are made in the gospel history. It would be evidently very far beyond the limits of a lecture, to attempt a proof that all the minutest allusions in our sacred history are not only uncontradicted, but wherever the same things are spoken of, are positively confirmed by the secular authority to which we have referred. But we assert it as a fact, well known to every student of the gospel history, and of which any who have the disposition to examine the question, may easily be satisfied. Now it seems to me it would have been next to impossible for the inventor of a story, exciting such general and intense interest, branching out into such circumstantial details, and connected, at so many points, with the peculiarities of the times, to tread upon ground so covered with snares, without being caught.

4th. Hitherto we have directed your attention to the gospel history as furnished by only one of its witnesses. But suppose you should unexpectedly discover in the ruins of Herculaneum three distinct writings, heretofore entirely unknown, but containing the most satisfactory evidence of authenticity, and evidently written in the first century of christianity, by three several and independent authors, each possessed of the best opportunities of knowledge. And suppose that in every one of them there should be found a history of Christ and his Gospel; what an uncommon opportunity would it seem of trying the accuracy of this book of St. John. Even if these three newly discovered authors were bad men; yet if their statements should agree with his, it would determine the accuracy of his history. But if it should appear that they were all good men, how much more complete would be their confirmation. Suppose, however, it should turn out that these three writers were not only good men, but, like St. John, disciples of Christ and ministers of his Gospel, what effect would their concurrent testimony then have upon his accuracy? Would it be diminished in conclusiveness by the discovery of their christian character? I believe that, in the minds of multitudes, it would; but most unjustly. Precisely the contrary *should* be the consequence. If four of the chief officers in Napoleon's staff had published memoirs of his life, I venture to say that the concurrence of their several statements instead of having its evidence weakened, because they were all attached to Napoleon and admitted to his domestic circle, would be greatly strengthened, in your estimation, by that very circumstance, inasmuch as it would ensure the accuracy of their knowledge, without impeaching their integrity. But some seem to suppose that the laws regulating the force of testimony are all changed as soon as the matter of fact, in question, is removed from the department of profane to that of sacred history.

How much has been made of the testimony of the Roman historian, *Tacitus*, to some of the chief facts of the gospel history. It is the testimony of a Heathen, and, therefore, supposed to be incomparably valuable. Now suppose that Tacitus the Heathen had not only been persuaded of the facts he has related, but had been so deeply impressed with the belief of them as to have renounced heathenism and embraced the christian faith, and then published the history we now possess—who does not know that, with the infidel, and with many a believer, his testimony would have greatly suffered in practical force? No reason for this can be given, except that we have a vague idea that a Christian in the cause of christianity must be an interested witness. To be sure he is interested. But is his testimony the less valuable?

A scientific man, bearing testimony to a phenomenon in natural history, is an interested witness, because he is devoted to science, but his testimony is not the less valuable. A good man, bearing testimony to the character of another good man, is an interested witness, because he is the friend of virtue and of all good men, but his testimony is not the less valuable. In this, and no other sense, were the original disciples interested witnesses. They were interested in christianity, only so far as they believed it true. Suppose them to have known it to be untrue, and you cannot imagine the least jot or tittle of interest they could have had in it In such a case, on the contrary, the current of all their interests and prepossessions would run directly and powerfully in opposition to christianity. This then, being all the way in which they can be regarded as interested, the force of their testimony, so far from being in the least impaired, is greatly enhanced by the consideration. The bare fact that any primitive writer, bearing witness to events related by St. John, was not a Heathen, or a Jew, but a Christian, is the very thing that should be regarded as completing his testimony. Is the evidence of Tacitus, who relates such events, but remained a Heathen, any thing like so strong; as if we could say, it is the evidence of Tacitus, who was a Heathen, but believed those events so firmly that he became a Christian? If a man speak well to me of the virtues of a certain medicine, but does not use it himself, is his opinion half so weighty as if he were to receive it into his own vitals, and administer it in his family? Would it be reasonable, in this case, to refuse his testimony, because you might denominate him an interested witness?

I have thus enlarged upon this head, because I am going to present you with the concurrent testimony of seven ancient writers, in confirmation of the accuracy of the gospel history, as given by St. John. They are writers whose testimony has this particular value, that, whereas once they were Jews and enemies to the gospel, they were afterwards converted to its belief and service; became Christians, and *as Christians* wrote, and gave every practical evidence that what they wrote they believed. Of these, three composed regular histories of the life and labours of Christ, similar in object to that of John. One of them, beside a memoir of Christ, has carried on the subsequent history of christianity, under the name of the Acts of the Apostles. Four others composed various letters to different individuals, or bodies of Christians, in which they allude continually to events related in the narratives of the former. Now all these several writings are perfectly independent, each of the rest. We have them bound up in one volume, and are apt to overlook the fact that they are as independent productions as if they had never been in contact with one another. Written by various authors in widely remote countries, in all parts of the first century from its forty-first to its ninety-seventh year, in as many different styles and methods as they had writers; these productions cannot, with the least reason, be suspected of having been composed in concert. Of the competency of the knowledge of each writer, we can have no more doubt than in the case of St. John. In each of their histories we see the same *circumstantiality*, the same striking internal characteristics of honesty as we have already noticed in that of the other evangelist. Now, let us divest ourselves of the delusion so apt to arise out of the thought that they are christian witnesses; and as if this were a question as to the truth of a history of Pythagoras, by one of his disciples, and these other writers were also contemporaneous disciples of Pythagoras, let us bring them face to face, and see how they agree. Here, then, we have four independent histories of the life of Christ, all of them by his contemporaries, besides the other documents we have mentioned. Now, "it is an extraordinary and singular fact that no history since the commencement of the world has been written by so great a number of the companions and friends of an illustrious person, as that of our Saviour. One contemporary history is a rarity—two is a coincidence scarcely known—four is, so far as appears, unparalleled."* We have therefore, an unequalled opportunity of coming at the truth. We compare our several histories. If we find them contradictory, our confidence declines. If they bear a systematic, particular, and yet comprehensive resemblance, we must suspect collusion. But we perceive neither the contradiction nor the resemblance. We see great variety. What one relates, another sometimes

* Wilson's Lectures.

leaves out. They differ in arrangement, in minuteness, and sometimes as to fact, in such manner that the reader might be alarmed at first view, lest there should be found a contradiction; while such is the actual agreement, that all difficulties vanish before a strict investigation; and, down to the utmost minuteness of statement, their mutual support is undiminished by a single opposing representation. The attempts of infidels to make out the appearance of a contradiction, show to what shifts they have been driven, and how accurate is the concurrence. Now this unfailing agreement of four several, independent, and contemporaneous historians—each so circumstantial—each so full of allusions to the events, and institutions, and customs of the times—and none contradicted by any evidence whatever—is as convincing an evidence of the honest accuracy of all, as any mind should require. Were the gospel history untrue, such evidence would have been morally impossible. It is peculiar to that history. No other can plead it, to any similar extent. And here we feel that we might safely leave the question of credibility. But there are two or three points remaining, which must not be left unnoticed.

Should I occupy enough of your time to take any thing like a full view of the whole of this argument, I should here introduce the uncontradicted acknowledgment of Jewish and Heathen enemies of the gospel, to the purity and integrity of the primitive disciples of Christ; the strong evidence of their having possessed these virtues, exhibited in the peculiarly modest and humble manner in which the evangelists speak of themselves, never concealing or excusing what might make exceedingly against them, but always mentioning what might seem humiliating or honourable to themselves in the same plain, simple way as they relate any other matter of fact. We should also introduce the variety of incidental confirmations obtained from profane writers, and from coins, of various particulars contained in the gospel history. We should cite especially the testimony of Tacitus to the time and the fact of the Saviour's crucifixion; as well as the records called the Acts of Pilate, bearing witness to the same event, and appealed to by early christian writers as notoriously laid up among the papers of the Roman senate. But since we have not room for every thing, we must dispense with these particulars.*

Let it be remembered that we are still employed upon the honesty of the writers of the gospel history. Suppose, then, for a moment, that they were not honest in their statements—that they knew they were endeavouring to pass off a downright imposition upon the world. We will not speak of their intellect in such a case, but of their motive. Now, it would be difficult to suppose that any man could devote himself to the diligent promotion of such an imposture without some very particular motive. Much more that, without such motive, the eight various writers concerned in the New Testament should have united in the plan. What motive could they have had? If impostors, they were bad men; their motive, therefore, must have been bad. It must have been to advance themselves, either in wealth, honour, or power. Take either, or all of these objects, and here, then, is the case you have. Four historians, with four other writers of the New Testament—all, but one of them, poor unlearned men—undertake to persuade the world that certain great events took place before the eyes of thousands in Judea and Galilee, which none in those regions ever saw or heard of, and *they* know, perfectly well, did never occur. They see beforehand that the attempt to make Jews and Heathens believe these things will occasion to themselves all manner of disgrace and persecution. Nevertheless, so fond are they of their contrivance, that though it is bitterly opposed by all the habits prejudices, dispositions, and philosophy—all the powers and

* See Horne's Introd. vol. i.

institutions of all people—they submit cheerfully to misery and contempt—they take joyfully the spoiling of their goods—they willingly endure to be counted as fools and the offscouring of all things—yea, they march thankfully to death out of a mere desire to propagate a story which they all know is a downright fabrication. At every step of their progress they see and feel, that instead of any worldly advantage, they are daily loading themselves with ruin. At any moment they can turn about and renounce their effort, and retrieve their losses; and yet, with perfect unanimity, these eight, with thousands of others equally aware of the deception, persist most resolutely in their career of ignominy and suffering. Not the slightest confession, even under torture and the strong allurements of reward, escapes the lips of any. Not the least hesitation is shown when to each is offered the choice of recantation or death. He that can believe such a case of fraud and folly as this, can believe any thing. He believes a miracle infinitely more difficult of credit than any in the gospel history. I charge him with the most superstitious and besotted credulity. In getting to such a belief, he has to trample over all the laws of nature and of reasoning. Then on what an unassailable rock does the honesty of the writers of the New Testament stand, if it can be attacked only at such sacrifices. How evident it is, not only that they could have had no motive to deceive, but that in all their self-devotion and sacrifices they gave the strongest possible evidence of having published what they solemnly believed was true.*

Now, if I have produced satisfactory proof from all the unquestionable marks of honesty in the gospel history;

* "We cannot make use (says Hume) of a more convincing argument" (in proof of honesty) "than to prove that the actions ascribed to any persons are contrary to the course of nature, and that no human motives, in such circumstances could ever induce them to such a conduct." *Philosophical Essays.*

from the concurrence of profane historians with many of its facts; from their being contradicted by none; from the unprecedented harmony of eight independent writers in their minutest events and allusions; from the impossibility of supposing any motive to deception, and from the sacrifices the apostles endured in the promotion of christianity; if from these sources I have satisfactorily shown that the writers of the gospel history could not have intended to record any thing but truth—then, having previously ascertained that they must have known whether what they wrote was true or false, we have those two requisites which ensure the credibility of any history—*knowledge* and *honesty*. This shuts up the question. But it is not the whole strength of the argument. A question may be shut up and locked; but then it may have bolts and bars besides. The truth of the gospel history is not only sealed, but sealed seven-fold.

It has all the testimony that could possibly have been expected, in the nature of things, from the enemies of christianity. It would have been unreasonable to expect that a Heathen or Jew would come forward with a detailed statement to acknowledge the events narrated by the evangelists. We have not this; but we have much better. We have the confession of the whole nation of Jews and of all the Greeks to the same point. None ever ventured in any publication to deny the statements of the evangelists. Unquestionably they would have done it, every where, had they been able. When Luke published in Jerusalem, that a man lame from the birth was healed by Peter and John, while sitting, begging, at the gate of the temple, and that a great multitude came together on account of the wonderful deed; had the Jews of Jerusalem been able to deny it, would their persecuting enmity have permitted them to be silent? Be it remembered that the gospel history was published in the places where its events are said to have occurred—in the lifetime of many enemies who are said to have seen them. Now it is certain that no adversaries either in Judea, or Greece, or Rome, rested their opposition to the gospel, in any degree, on the denial of these events. What is the consequence? They could not deny them. What is the meaning of this silence? Being interpreted, it is nothing less than a universal testimony from all Jews and Heathens, who were capable of knowing any thing of the matter, that these things were so. But they did not stop here. Tacitus, the Roman historian, positively asserts some of the chief events of the gospel.* Celsus, a bitter antagonist of christianity, in the second century;† Porphyry, a learned as well as earnest opposer, in the third;‡ and Julian, the apostate emperor, in the next century;§ all acknowledge not only the authenticity of the New Testament books, but, so far as they refer to them, the historical correctness of their narratives, even as to the most extraordinary particulars, not excluding the miracles of Christ. But we have stronger witness still.

About thirty-two years after the crucifixion, took place the first Roman persecution, under Nero. The number of Christians discovered in the one city of Rome, and condemned, is called by Tacitus "a *vast multitude*."‖ Of course they must have been exceedingly numerous in all other places taken together. These but a few years before were all either *Jews* or *Heathens*. Many resided in Jerusalem, Capernaum, Antioch, Philippi, Ephesus, Corinth, &c. By the time of this persecution, all the Gospels, but one, as well as the Acts of the apostles, had been published. The events recorded in these books are said to have taken place before the eyes of the people of the cities just mentioned. It was an easy thing for those people to ascertain whether they, or their neighbours, or parents, had seen them. What

---

* Lardner, iii. 611. † Ib. iv. 121—130; 133, 4. ‡ Ib. 234—8. § Ib. 341 2.
‖ Tac. Annal., lib. xv. c. 44. Lardner, iii. 610—14.

did they do? They came forward in great multitudes; they threw off judaism; threw off paganism; espoused the gospel, and suffered unto death, sooner than renounce it. This was but thirty-three years after the events recorded of Christ; it was in the life-time of Paul. I say, therefore, that every Christian of those days was a witness—the strongest witness—far more impressive in his attestation than any enemy could have been, to the shining, powerful truth of the gospel history. "We are compassed about," therefore, "with *a great cloud of witnesses;*" witnesses who did not just acknowledge these things, and still remain what they were before; but witnesses adding to their acknowledgment the testimony of their conversion; the evidence of their lives, which were wholly devoted to these things; the seals of ten thousand martyrdoms, endured solely on account of their perfect assurance of these things.

Now consider a moment, and see the *utter impossibility* that the gospel history should have gained such currency for a single year, had it not been notoriously true. In about eight years after the crucifixion, Matthew publishes his Gospel among the Jews. He tells the people of Jerusalem that, only eight years from that time, while a great multitude of them were witnessing the crucifixion of our Lord Jesus, there was darkness over the whole land, from twelve to three o'clock in the afternoon, and "the veil of the temple was rent in twain, and the earth did quake, and the rocks rent." Suppose all this to have been a fabrication; would Jerusalem have held her peace? could a book of such barefaced untruth have lived an hour?

The book of the Acts of the Apostles was published about thirty years after the ascension of Christ, and was immediately circulated among the churches, and open to the perusal of the enemies of christianity. It is related in the second chapter of that work, that on the day of Pentecost, soon after the death of Christ when a great multitude, collected from all parts of the earth, were assembled at Jerusalem, a deep impression of astonishment was produced on the public mind by a rumour of certain miraculous events in the company of the apostles, so that "the multitude came together and were confounded, because that every man heard them speak in his own language." Parthians, and Medes, and Elamites, and Cretes, and Arabians; dwellers in all countries; men of every speech, were amazed at hearing those Galileans, who were well known to have learned no other tongue than that of Palestine, speaking in all varieties of foreign languages, the wonderful works of God. Such is the relation in the Acts of the Apostles. How could a writer, in his senses, attempt to pass it upon his readers had it not been notorious that such things had actually occurred? The lapse of thirty years could not have so obliterated every recollection of that feast; or so swept the world of surviving witnesses, as to prevent the certainty, that wherever this book should circulate it would meet with persons capable of remembering or of ascertaining whether these things were so. Had not the fact of the apostles having spoken in the presence of thousands, in various tongues, been undeniable, witnesses innumerable would have arisen against the book that related it. Had no such event occurred, the Acts of the Apostles could have gone into no part of the world without finding those who would stand up and declare that they were at the feast referred to, and saw nothing and heard nothing of the marvellous things declared by its author. I say, therefore, the fact that the gospel history was received, loved, and read, every where among Christians; that it has outlived all the withering of time, and all the weapons of enemies; that Jews could not gainsay it, nor Heathens resist it; that eighteen centuries of scrutiny and trial have only added new assurance to its truth, is one which reduces the supposition of imposture to a perfect and ridiculous absurdity. Therefore was it not in the power of such modern infidels as Hobbes, and Chub, and Bolingbroke, to deny the point in question. The latter, as an example of the others, speaking of John and Matthew, acknowledges that "they recorded the doctrines of Christ in the very words in which he taught them; and they were careful to mention the several occasions on which he delivered them to his disciples or others. If, therefore, Plato and Xenophon tell us, with a good deal of certainty, what Socrates taught, these two evangelists seem to tell us, with much more, what the Saviour taught, and commanded them to teach."

Here I think we may safely leave the question of credibility. So conclusive and certain have seemed to my mind the several consecutive arguments to which you have listened, that instead of feeling at each step as if any candid hearer would wait for additional proof, I have felt not unfrequently as if I were tiring your attention with an unnecessary accumulation. Why this heaping of argument upon argument, one may say, when from the very outset of the question, from the certain authenticity of the Gospels, united with their internal evidence, we have a proof of credibility with which any rational mind should be perfectly satisfied? We acknowledge the reasonableness of the inquiry. If the history under consideration related to the life of Alexander the Great and his generals, instead of that of the meek and lowly Jesus and his apostles, who would think it necessary to go into all this detail of evidence to establish its truth? That it contained no internal marks of dishonesty; that it was uncontradicted by contemporaneous writers and by other histories of the same times; that it had been received, ever since, as a true account; would be considered an ample warrant of its historical correctness. Few, if any, profane histories, can produce more positive proof of credibility than this. Try them by the scale on which the gospel history is measured; require them to present one half of the weight of evidence which infidels demand, and Christians bring in support of the sacred narrative; and you must exclude them from all claim to the confidence of their readers. We might speak of the unfairness of requiring so much more in proof of a history because its character is sacred, and its facts are connected with religion. I see not that the inferences arising from an event, are entitled to any influence in changing the amount of evidence necessary to its proof. Whether an evangelist be worthy of dependence, when he relates the works of Jesus, is a question of testimony to be determined by the same degree of proof as should satisfy us as to the accuracy and honesty of any other writer, on any other subject of history. But we have no disposition to complain that so much has been demanded in evidence of the gospel narrative. It has only served to quicken the investigations of the friends of truth, and to exhibit, with a more impressive assurance, those great events, on which all that is precious in a Christian's faith is founded. It has showed, not only how amply, but how wonderfully the God of truth and grace has made the anchor of our hope to be sure and steadfast. It teaches how, in the hands of Divine Wisdom, the wrath of man is made subsidiary to the praise of God; how the fiery darts of the wicked are not only broken against the shield of faith, but made the means of increasing the light by which the Christian is guided, and often of carrying back confusion into the ranks of the enemy. It should lead the believer to adore, with admiring gratitude, the goodness of Him, who, for the sake of those that love Him, causes all the schemes and assaults of unbelievers to work together for good; making it more and more manifest, by the defeat of every new attack, that this is "the true light"—"the shining light, which shineth more and more unto the perfect day."

Had we time, or were it needful, to enter upon a particular view of the authenticity and credibility of the Old Testament volume, this would be the place for the argument

But we have room only to advert to it. The connexion between the truth of the christian scriptures and that of the Jewish is so obvious and essential; the dispensation of Christ so continually assumes the divine authority of that of Moses, and is so evidently built on its foundations; the writings of the apostles so frequently quote and refer to the law and the prophets, as authentic, credible, and inspired scriptures; the argument for the books of the Old Testament is so parallel, in its mode and means, to that for the books of the New; and the cavils of sceptics, in relation to the former, are so similar in objection, principle, and reasoning, to those with which they assail the latter; that in having established the authenticity and credibility of the one, we may be fairly said to have done the same, in outline, for the character of the other. Certain we are, that one who is intelligently convinced of the authenticity and credibility of the New Testament, will not halt between two opinions as to the writings of Moses and the prophets, but will read them as assuredly the writings of those whose names they bear; and deserving, in relation to all matters of fact, the character of credible scriptures.

LECTURE V.

MIRACLES.

Our last lecture was on the CREDIBILITY OF THE GOSPEL HISTORY. In a previous one, we ascertained the AUTHENTICITY of the books in which it is contained. If the evidence adduced in proof of both these fundamental articles appeared as satisfactory to the hearers, as to the speaker, we are then prepared to open the New Testament with the assurance that the books it contains were written by those original disciples whose names they bear; and that we may confidently depend on the historical correctness of their statements. The seals, therefore, of the volume are now unloosed. Immediately on inspecting the contents, it appears that the grand and continual reference is to Jesus Christ, as a Teacher and Saviour sent from God, to communicate personally, and by his apostles, a revelation of truth and duty to man. This revelation, the New Testament professes to contain. Now, the grand question is, *what are the evidences that the religion contained in the New Testament is a divine revelation?*

When an ambassador from a foreign power presents himself at our seat of government, charged with certain communications from his sovereign, he first exhibits his credentials of appointment. These being satisfactory, whatever he may communicate, in his official character, is received with as much reliance as if it were heard from the lips of his sovereign himself. It is treated as a revelation of the mind or will of that sovereign. In the New Testament we read that our Lord Jesus Christ appeared among men as an ambassa dor from God, charged with certain important proposals to the world. Before we can be justified in receiving them as a divine revelation, we must know the credentials of the ambassador; we must have sufficient evidence that he was sent of God. Furnish this, and we are bound to receive his communications, as confidently as if they should be heard directly from the throne of the Most High. Thus the Jews said to him: "What sign showest thou, that we may see and believe thee? What dost thou work?"* The Saviour, admitting the propriety of the demand, appealed to his *works*, as his credentials. "The works that I do, they bear witness of me.") On another occasion, he called up his miracles. "The blind (said he) receive their sight, the lame walk, the lepers are cleansed, the deaf hear, and the dead are raised up."† As if he had said: "Such works can only be done by the direct and supernatural interposition of the power of God. They are done at my word and will. They are therefore a perfect attestation that God is with me, and that my claim to your confidence as His ambassador is true." Nicodemus understood this, and expressed no other than the plain dictate of common sense, when he said to Jesus: "We know that thou art a teacher come from God, for no man can do these miracles which thou doest except God be with him."‡ The credentials of the apostles, as subordinate agents of divine revelation, are expressed in like manner. "God also bearing them witness, both with signs and wonders, and with divers miracles, and gifts of the Holy Ghost."§ None can question the absolute certainty of such credentials. This has been acknowledged even by the most famous advocates of infidelity. Woolston says: "I believe it will be granted on all hands that the restoring a person indisputably dead to life is a stupendous miracle, and that two or three such miracles, well attested and credibly reported, are enough to

---

* John, vi. 30—ii. 18. † Mat. xi. 5. ‡ John, iii. 2. § Heb. ii. 4

conciliate the belief that the author of them was a divine agent, and invested with the power of God."* Make good, therefore, the evidence that the Saviour and his apostles wrought miracles in attestation of their divine mission, and the christian religion, as contained in the New Testament, and taught by them, must be a divine revelation.

Our way, therefore, is plain. We must inquire into the evidence on which it can be established, *that the Saviour and his apostles did work miracles.* To this inquiry we should proceed immediately, were it not for the peculiar circumstances which meet us in the way. The adversaries of the gospel have had wit enough to see that either the evidence of miracles must be overthrown, or they must surrender the contest. Unable to meet the direct and abounding testimony by which the wonderful works of Christ and his apostles are proved, they have taken position and entrenched themselves upon the advanced and desperate ground of the insufficiency of any testimony to prove a miracle. Thus have we a redoubt in our way, commanding the whole field of controversy, which, though easily carried when properly assailed, would be of great damage, if left in our rear. The present lecture will be occupied, therefore, with the discussion of certain preliminary subjects, anticipating a direct application to the evidence of miracles, in our next. We commence with the following proposition.

I. *There is nothing unreasonable or improbable in the idea of a miracle being wrought in proof of a divine revelation.* I know not but that all persons, of ordinary information, have a sufficiently correct idea of what is meant by a miracle, without the aid of a definition. No one would mistake the restoration of sight to the blind, by the use of human skill, however wonderful it might be considered, for

---

* Scheme of Literal Prophecy, pp. 321, 322.

a miracle. No one could mistake the sudden communication of sight to one born blind at the mere word of another, without any intervening cause, for any thing else than a miracle. The former result, though astonishing, would be *according to the common course of nature*, or to what are called *the laws* of nature. The latter would be *beyond, or different from those laws*. One would be a natural, the other a supernatural event, or a *miracle*.*

Now the idea of a revelation from God, and the idea of a miracle to attest the divine commission of those who make it, are essentially connected. If one or more individuals be sent to communicate the revelation, they must prove their mission by some credentials. What can their credentials be but miracles? The necessity of these will be evident from a little consideration. They can appeal to but three sorts of proof; the internal excellence and fitness of their communications; their own integrity and judgment; and the miraculous works attendant on their ministry. With regard to the two former, it is manifest that, in the most favourable circumstances, they would need too much time, and evidence, and discrimination, for their own establishment; and would always remain of a character too uncertain to permit their being used with any effect in proof of a divine revelation. They would answer well as auxiliaries; but would require something of a much more positive nature to sustain the chief burden of proof. The claim to be received as a messenger of God, for the purpose of making a revelation to the world, could never be substantiated on such grounds. Evidence is needed which all minds may appreciate. It must be something that has only to be seen, to be understood and acknowledged. When a plenipotentiary presents himself at the seat of government, intrusted with certain communications from a foreign power, of great importance on both

* See Gregory's Letters, i. 167.

sides, and requiring to be immediately acted upon, it would not answer for him to plead, in evidence of his delegated authority, that his personal integrity is unimpeached, and his communications are such as might be expected from his government. The time for action would be lost while such proof was being proved. He must exhibit credentials which carry on their face the direct evidence of his commission. He must show the broad seal of his sovereign stamped upon their hand writing. So must an ambassador from God. What then can he show but miracles? What else can set to his communications the seal of God? "In fact, the very idea of a revelation includes that of miracles. A revelation *cannot* be made but by a miraculous interposition of Deity."*

So that the idea of miracles can be unreasonable or improbable only so far as it is unreasonable or improbable that God should commission one or more persons to make a revelation of his truth and will. That such a revelation was needed in the world at the time when Christ appeared, can be denied only by asserting that the additional light now possessed, in consequence of the gospel, is superfluous and useless. This denial can only be maintained by showing that the world, sunk in idolatry, vice, and darkness, as it was universally before the gospel came, had all the knowledge of God, and all the assurance of his will, and of the retributions of a future state, that were important to its happiness. A matter of proof which I suppose no one here imagines to be possible. Then if it cannot be shown that a revelation was not needed; it cannot be proved that the idea of a revelation, from a God of infinite goodness and mercy, was either unreasonable or improbable. But a revelation can be attested only by miracles. They are inseparable. Consequently, in the idea of miracles being wrought

* Gregory's Letters.

n proof of divine revelation, there is nothing either unreasonable or improbable.

It would not be difficult to show, that in the circumstances of the world at the christian era, a revelation was not only probable but necessary; and, by manifest consequence, that miracles, as its necessary attestations, were also not only probable but necessary. Having thus endeavoured to show that there is no presumptive evidence against a miracle, except as it lies equally against a revelation; and that the one is probable, in proportion as the other may be expected; let us proceed to our second proposition.

II. *If miracles were wrought in attestation of the mission of Christ and his apostles, they can be rendered credible to us by no other evidence than that of testimony.* There are various descriptions of evidence, as *the evidence of sense—the evidence of mathematical demonstration—the evidence of testimony.* Each of these has its own department of subjects. A question of morals cannot be demonstrated by mathematics, or proved by the senses. A question of historical fact can be settled only by testimony. It might as well be put to the tests of chemistry, as to have applied to it either the evidence of mathematical demonstration, or of the senses.

Not only is there a separate department for each of these species of evidence; but each is sufficient, in its appropriate place, for the complete establishment of truth. By this I mean, that when the quantity of an angle is proved by mathematical demonstration, we have a result of no more practical confidence than when the existence of this house is proved by the senses, or that of the city of London is proved by testimony. *Proof* in either case is the foundation of entire belief. We are just as certain that such a man as Napoleon once lived, as that any proposition in geometry is true—though one is a matter of testimony, the other of demonstration. We are quite as sure that arsenic is poisonous, as that food is nutritious—though one is, to most of us at least, a matter of testimony only; while the other is, to all, a matter of sense. We are perfectly certain of all these things.

It is likely that some minds are led into erroneous notions of the comparative conclusiveness of testimony on one side, and that of mathematical demonstration and of the senses on the other, on account of the technical name by which the former is distinguished in philosophical discussions.* It is called *probable* evidence. It would seem to some as if, because *probable*, it must be less satisfactory than the other kinds; since in common speech, what is merely probable is not *certain*. But in philosophical language, the word *probable* is used, not in distinction from *certain* evidence, but simply from that which is sensible or demonstrative, without reference to the measure of certainty attached to it. Thus, our belief that the sun will rise to-morrow, or that we are all to die, or that London was once visited with a dreadful plague, is founded on what is called *probable* evidence; though we should be suspected of lunacy did we question the propriety of acting upon it with perfect assurance. Such, then, being the sufficiency of testimony to convey a perfect assurance of any thing in its appropriate sphere, however distant in point of time or place; I return to the proposition that if miracles were wrought by Christ and his apostles, they *can be rendered credible to us, of the nineteenth century, by no other evidence than that of testimony.* Mathematical evidence is evidently inapplicable to the question. It is a matter of fact belonging to another century, and therefore intangible by sense. Nothing remains but testimony. This is perfectly appropriate to the question. If, therefore, the gospel miracles are true, they must be substantiated by testimony, or not at all. We proceed to the next proposition.

* Stewart's Phil. ii. p. 179.

III. *Miracles are capable of being proved by testimony.* This I consider as true and obvious as that miracles are capable of being proved by the evidence of the senses. That a certain person was dead and buried yesterday; and that he is alive and walking the streets to-day; the senses are perfectly competent to decide. I never heard of this being questioned. But if I and twenty others saw these facts, is there no way of making them credible to my neighbour who did not see them? Will it be pretended, that if twenty men of unquestionable honesty and intelligence, should solemnly and by every means of conviction in their power, assure me that they saw the man dead, buried, and in corruption, I would have no sufficient reason to believe their assertion? Will it be pretended, that if the same men should in the same way assure me, that subsequently they saw the same man alive, and conversed with him; I would have no reason to believe their assertion? I think there are none among us who could avoid belief in such a case. It would evidently be a case of miracle, believed on testimony; and to maintain that it would be believed without reason, and that no conceivable addition of honest testimony could furnish reason for the belief of those two simple facts, that the man was dead yesterday and is alive to-day, would seem an absurdity too gross to be touched by argument.

Here I should leave the mattter, confident in the common sense of my hearers, were it not that the very absurdity, in view, has been so mystified with the drugs of false philosophy, so disguised under the dress of logical forms and ceremonies, and so followed, in its circulation, with the influence of one of the chief names in modern scepticism, as to perplex many minds unaccustomed to the entanglements of sophistry. The principle that no conceivable amount of testimony can prove a miracle, with David Hume for its original champion, has been eagerly adopted by the many whose convenience makes them unbelievers but whose convenience it would not suit to attempt an honest, manly answer to the abounding testimony by which the miracles of the gospel are proved. A labour-saving machine was wanted, by which the whole business of silencing the inconvenient variety and troublesome multitude of christian evidences might be done at once, as well by the ignorant as the learned. Hume invented it. Any body can work it. It is not necessary, any more, that a man should study the Bible, to refute its claims. He may never have seen it; but if he can only retain in his memory these few talismanic words, "*No testimony can prove a miracle*," it is enough. At the rubbing of this marvellous lamp, the fabric of christianity passes away. The terrible genii of the gospel mysteries dissolve in air. Like a similar assertion, and equally philosophical doctrine of the same writer, that there is no external world—that this house is nothing but an idea, built not of matter, but only of mind—this happy invention of sceptical ingenuity digs so far below the foundations of all truth and common sense, that the man whose convenience bids him use it, may feel assured that not many advocates of christianity will descend low enough to spoil him of his consolation.

A brief attention to this matter will not be out of place at present.

The argument of the writer referred to, is abridged, in the Encyclopedia Britannica, as follows: "Our belief of any fact from the testimony of eye-witnesses is derived from no other principle than our experience of the veracity of human testimony. If the fact attested be miraculous, there arises a contest of two opposite experiences, or proof against proof. Now a miracle is a violation of the laws of nature; and as a firm and unalterable experience has established these laws, the proof against a miracle, from the very nature of the fact, is as complete as any argument from experience can possibly be imagined; and if so, it is an undeniable consequence that it cannot be surmounted by any proof whatever, derived from human testimony."

Now all this is very conclusive, provided we admit its premises. The grand hinge of the whole is this, that our belief in testimony is founded on no other principle than OUR EXPERIENCE OF THE VERACITY OF HUMAN TESTIMONY. Hence the reasoning is, that a miracle being, in the author's estimation, contrary to experience, opposes and contradicts the very foundation of its evidence, and therefore destroys itself. But let me ask, admitting that a miracle is contrary to experience, (which is not true,) *what experience* is it contrary to? The argument requires that it should be contrary to our experience *of the veracity of human testimony.* To say merely that it is contrary to experience of some sort, without specifying this particular sort, does not touch the question. It is its contrariety to that particular kind of experience, on which our faith in testimony (according to Hume) is built, that must destroy the credibility of a miracle, if it is to be destroyed at all. But this, it would be ridiculous to assert. So far from miracles being inconsistent with our experience of the veracity of human testimony; the truth is directly on the other side. Deny that miracles were ever wrought, and your whole experience of the truth of testimony is directly and violently opposed.

But again—*Is our belief in testimony founded in our experience of its veracity?* Prove that it is not, and the whole argument of our author is undermined. The proof is easy. None depend more absolutely upon testimony than those whose experience is almost a nullity. Children are perfect believers in its veracity. All writers on the philosophy of the mind, but the one before us, consider it an original principle of nature that we should rely on testimony, until there is proof, either of suspicious competency to know, or of suspicious honesty to speak, the truth. This principle is necessary to human nature, long before any experience can be gathered up. Without it, how could children begin to learn? How could they avoid poison, or receive wholesome food, if they must wait for an experience of the veracity of their parents, and nurses, and teachers, before they can believe what they testify? The plain truth is, that instead of experience being our whole dependence for the credibility of testimony, it is just the school that makes us sometimes suspicious of that credibility. It teaches us that testimony may be false, and furnishes the characteristics by which we may distinguish between that which is suspicious, and that which may be confidently relied on. We deny, therefore, and with evident reason, the whole foundation of the argument we are considering.

But again. Another essential hinge, in this argument, is the assertion that a miracle, being, as the author defines it, "a violation of the laws of nature," *is contrary to experience.* Here we might deny that a miracle is a violation of the laws of nature. It is only a *deviation* from those laws, or from the customary mode of the divine operations. But, waving this, what is meant by a miracle being *contrary to experience?* Have we, or others ever experienced the *opposite* of any of the miracles of Christ? I cannot conceive how this could be, unless we had been on the spot when the miracle is said to have taken place, as when Lazarus is said to have risen from the dead; and instead of seeing him rise, had seen him continue dead. That is the only way in which I can conceive of opposition between experience and a miracle. The resurrection of Lazarus is not contrary to my experience, any more than a volcano is contrary to it. All I can say of either, in this respect, is, that I have never experienced it. It is *beyond,* not *in opposition to,* my experience.

But when our author asserts that miracles are contrary *to experience,* what are we to understand? Does he mean one's own *personal* experience? or the experience of *all* *mankind?* If the former, then it would follow that testimony can render no event credible to us which we have not personally experienced. But this would be too sweeping, even for the most absolute scepticism. On this ground, a native of the torrid zone might refuse the testimony of the rest of the world in evidence of the fact that water in winter is so congealed that we can drive our carriages upon its surface. He need only say, "It is contrary to my experience. I have never seen it, and therefore no testimony can make it credible." *

But does our author mean to be understood as affirming that miracles are contrary to the *experience of all mankind?* His argument will then stand as follows: 'Belief in testimony is founded on experience. But miracles are contrary to the experience of all mankind. They contradict, therefore, the credibility of testimony, and cannot be proved by it.' But this is a manifest assumption of the whole question. Whether miracles are contrary to the experience of all mankind, is the precise point in debate. We assert that mankind, in different ages and places, have experienced them. Our author is at liberty, if he pleases, to assert the contrary. But it is too much to expect us to receive his assertion until it is proved. And if his argument cannot be sustained without thus taking for granted, in one of its premises, what it seeks to demonstrate in the conclusion, its correctness is certainly very suspicious.

The admission of the principle on which the argument under consideration is founded, would lead to perfect absurdity. "There was a time when no one was acquainted with the laws of magnetism; these suspend in many instances the laws of gravity; nor can I see, upon the principle in question, how the rest of mankind could have

* On Hume's argument, in general, see the references in Horne's Introd., vol. i. p. 243

credited the testimony of their first discoverer; and yet to have rejected it, would have been to reject the truth. But that a piece of iron should ascend gradually from the earth, and fly at last with an increasing rapidity through the air, and, attaching itself to another piece of iron ore, should remain suspended, in opposition to the action of its gravity, is consonant to the laws of nature. I grant it; but there was a time when it was contrary, I say not to the laws of nature, but to the uniform experience of all preceding ages and countries; and at the particular point of time, the testimony of an individual or of a dozen individuals, who should have reported themselves eye-witnesses of such a fact, ought, according to the argumentation (of Mr. Hume) to have been received as fabulous. And what are those laws of nature, which, according to this writer, can never be suspended? Are they not different to different men, according to the diversities of their comprehension and knowledge? And if any one of them (that, for instance, which rules the operations of magnetism or electricity) should have been known to you, or to me alone, whilst all the rest of the world were unacquainted with it; the effects of it would have been new and unheard of in the annals, and contrary to the experience, of mankind, and therefore ought not in your opinion to have been believed."* If this be the legitimate result of the principle in question; if no testimony could have rendered the phenomena of magnetism credible, in the dawn of knowledge on that subject, because they were contrary to experience; it is evident that a certain truth in Hume's principle would have been, in that case, directly in opposition. But whether the experience of mankind be opposed by phenomena above the laws of nature—*miracles*—or by phenomena which, though in reality according to those laws, are perfectly new, and, to all human view, incon-

* Bishop Watson.

sistent with the established order of nature, is of no consequence to the argument. Experience is opposed in both cases alike. It cannot be less absurd in one than in the other, to maintain, that because the phenomena have never been experienced, no testimony can make them credible.

But if the argument of Hume, with all its assumptions, and false statements, and equivocal expressions, were true; it would prove not only that miracles cannot be proved by testimony, but that they cannot be proved at all. Now, that it is possible for God to work a miracle, none will deny. Consequently, that it is possible that the miracles related in the New Testament are true, none will deny. Suppose them to be true, how can they be proved to us? If testimony will not do, what remains? Mathematical evidence—the evidence of the senses—are perfectly inapplicable. But there is no other description of evidence. If, therefore, those miracles are to be proved to us, it must be done by some species of evidence not now in existence, entirely foreign to the laws of nature. In other words, it must be miraculous. Miracle must be brought to prove miracle. And since no testimony, according to the principle we are considering, can prove a miracle, the very miracle which is brought in proof of those in the New Testament, must itself be proved by another before it can be believed by any who did not see it. But what an absurdity is here! If Jesus did open the eyes of the blind, who can maintain that God has no way of giving all generations reason to believe it without an unceasing series of miracles in all places, for the purpose?

There is but one way of evading this extreme and absurd conclusion. It must be denied that we have any reason to believe that God can work a miracle. For as long as it is acknowledged to be *possible* that God, by the apostles, did work miracles, the possibility of His making them credible to us, without other miracles to prove them, and by the natural means of human testimony, must also be acknowledged:

the latter, to say the least of it, being no greater effort of power than the former. To this necessity, the sagacity of our philosopher was not blind. Nor does he scruple at embracing it, rather than give up his favourite discovery. Speaking of some alleged miracles, he writes: "What have we to oppose to such a cloud of witnesses, but the absolute impossibility or miraculous nature of the event?" In this sentence, it is evident that "*absolute impossibility*," and "*miraculous nature*," are used as equivalent expressions. But elsewhere he endeavours to persuade us that there is no reason to suppose that a miracle is possible with God. "Though the Being (he says) to whom the miracle is ascribed, be, in this case, Almighty, it does not, on that account, become a whit more probable; since it is impossible for us to know the attributes or actions of such a Being, otherwise than from the experience which we have of his productions, in the usual course of nature." This brings us directly to atheism. The argument is thus. We know the attributes of God only by the experience of his works in the usual course of nature. But, according to our philosopher, we have no experience of a miracle among those works. Consequently, we have no knowledge that there is any divine attribute by which God can produce a miracle. Now, besides the folly of denying the possibility of a miracle, because nothing like it is found in the usual course of nature, when a miracle, by its definition, is *out* of the usual course of nature; we have here *the plain denial of the omnipotence of God.* For if we have no reason to believe that God can produce an event differing from and above the ordinary course of nature, we have no reason to suppose that he is Almighty; or that he is the Sovereign of Nature; or that He created, and preserves, and governs, all things. The nature and majesty of God are denied by this argument. It is atheism. There is no stopping place for consistency between the first principle of the essay of Hume, and the last step in the denial of God with the abyss of darkness for ever. Hume, accordingly, had no belief in the being of God. If he did not positively deny it, he could not assert that he believed it. He was a poor, blind, groping compound of contradictions. He was literally "without God and without hope;" "doting about questions and strifes of words;" and rejecting life and immortality out of deference to a paltry quibble, which common sense is ashamed of. "An unfortunate disposition to doubt every thing," said Lord Charlemont, one of his particular friends and admirers, "seemed interwoven with the nature of Hume, and never was there, I am convinced, a more thorough and sincere sceptic. He seemed not to be certain even of his own present existence, and could not, therefore, be expected to entertain any settled opinion respecting his future state."

But it was very needless for our author to give himself so much intellectual effort as must have been required for the invention of this short and easy method of undermining the evidences of Christianity, when he had previously produced a much shorter and easier plan. He had already proved, in his estimation, that there is no external world—nothing but ideas; consequently there can be no external miracles—nothing but miraculous ideas. Why not hold to this? It was certainly just as reasonable; just as consistent with philosophy and common sense, as the idea that no testimony can prove a miracle.

But our sweeping sceptic was not quite so well satisfied with his arguments against all testimony and all sense, as would at first appear. Speaking of his speculations, he says: "they have so wrought upon me, and heated my brain, that I am ready to reject all belief and reasoning, and can look upon no opinion even as more probable or likely than another. Where am I, or what? From what causes do I derive my existence, and to what condition shall I return? Whose favour shall I court, and whose anger must

I dread? What beings surround me, and on whom have I any influence, or who have any influence on me? I am confounded with all these questions, and begin to fancy myself in the most deplorable condition imaginable, environed with the deepest darkness, and utterly deprived of the use of every member and faculty." A sad confession this of the satisfaction of what he calls "*the calm, though obscure regions of philosophy.*"

But he proceeds: "Most fortunately it happens that since reason is incapable of dispelling these clouds, nature herself suffices to that purpose, and cures me of this philosophical melancholy and delirium, either by relaxing this bent of mind, or by some avocation and lively impression of my senses, which obliterates all these chimeras. I dine, I play a game of back-gammon, I converse and am merry with my friends; and when, after three or four hours amusement, I would return to these speculations, they appear so cold, and strained, and ridiculous, that I cannot find in my heart to enter into them any farther." A sad exhibition this of the dignity and consolations of scepticism. But if Mr. Hume was sometimes constrained to look upon his own speculations as strained and ridiculous, we may be pardoned if they appear to us in the same aspect. Indeed, it was more than he could do, to write consistently with them, for any length of time. His own common sense insisted, sometimes, on the privilege of speech; so that, after all the show of reasoning to which we have been attending; after having asserted that "*a miracle, supported by any human testimony, is more properly a subject of derision than of argument,*" we find him apparently coming to himself, and making the following most singular acknowledgment: "*I own there may possibly be miracles of such a kind as to admit of proof from human testimony.*" He then states an imaginary case of miraculous occurrence, attested by a measure of proof, which, he says, philosophers ought to receive as certain testimony. But how is this? Has he entirely abandoned his ground? One would think so. But mark his method of escape. We quote his words: "But should this miracle be ascribed to a new system of religion, men in all ages have been so imposed on by ridiculous stories of that kind, that this very circumstance would be a full proof of the cheat." Here, evidently, the whole ground is changed. Miracles are no more considered as incapable of proof by testimony. They are no more set at nought because contrary to experience. It is admitted they may be proved by testimony, whether with object or without it, except when the object is religion. It is nothing, therefore, in the nature of a miracle, but only in its application, that renders it incredible. This is indeed a change. A miracle may be proved any where but in the service of a revelation from God. But why? Because, says our author, "men in all ages have been so imposed on by ridiculous stories of that kind." Now, besides that it is untrue that any religion, but that of the Bible, ever attempted to set up its claims by the credentials of miracles, this is utter trifling. After all the metaphysical parade to which we have been attending; are we brought to this, that, because some men have been knaves and fools, therefore all must be such? Can we believe in the sincerity of none, because hypocrites have been many? Must we refuse belief in any accounts of physical phenomena, because men in all ages have been imposed on by ridiculous accounts of such things? Must we decline accepting any notes issued by our banks, because men have so often been imposed on by counterfeit currency? On the contrary, counterfeit currency is positive proof that there is such a thing as a sound and honest currency. And in like manner, the fact of spurious pretensions to miracles, so far from being a reason for rejecting all accounts of miracles, is a strong presumptive proof that some of them are true. An argument which finds itself constrained to seek refuge under the shadow of such a position as this, must indeed have been reduced to an extremity.

We have dwelt on this desperate effort of the most noted and acute sceptic of modern times, much longer than was called for by any thing either difficult or important in itself, because it affords a very strong presumptive proof of the impossibility, by any force of talent or skilfulness of manœuvre, of breaking the solid mass of testimony by which the miracles of the gospel are defended. Such a mind, as that of the historian of England, would never have descended to the absurdity of denying the credibility of any testimony in proof of a miracle, had it not been that all his efforts to pick a flaw in the testimony of those of Christianity had utterly failed. Show me a man endeavouring to pick his way through the stone wall of a prison, and I need not be told that he is shut up, and has despaired of escape by the door.

The pains which all sceptics have taken to escape from being shut up to the faith of Christ, adopting every other conceivable method than the one simple and equitable plan of refuting the direct evidences of christianity, should be considered unequivocable proof that there is a force in those evidences which their enemies dare not encounter face to face—something that persuades the bold champion of infidelity that in this warfare, "*discretion is the better part of valour.*"

But we cannot relinquish this division of our lecture, without pausing to draw a lesson from the scepticism of Hume. That he was a learned and very ingenious writer none can deny. That he was much more amiable and less unexemplary in his temper and habits than infidel champions generally are, we have no disposition to question. But these commendations only render his case the more affecting, and his insidious sophistry the more dangerous. The pride of reason was his master. The praise of a philosopher was his idol; to doubt what others believed, his habitual tendency; to maintain a paradox against the world, his prevailing ambition. Under the influence of these dispositions, the very fact that the religion of Christ was a revelation, requiring him to sit at its feet and *learn*, instead of a theory, flattering the sufficiency of his own powers to *discover* truth, was its condemnation. The more it possessed the sanction of ages and of the greatest minds, the more did it rouse him to its rejection. The imposing multitude and weight of its evidences were the strongest stimulants of his unbelief. He first denied the miracles of the gospel, and then set his wits to contrive some grand argument by which all the testimony in their favour might be undermined. He reasoned himself almost out of his own existence, and surrounded himself with impenetrable darkness. The present was all contradiction, the future all "an enigma," to his mind. Poor, unhappy, philosopher! How little his learning could do in the search of truth, for want of humility! How easily can all human knowledge, and all mortal wisdom, become foolishness, when the wise man leans to his own understanding, instead of acknowledging and seeking God in all his ways! That Hume was accustomed to pray for guidance in his investigations of truth, it is impossible to suppose. The great fountain of light being thus denied, God gave him up to the devices and desires of his own heart. Verily, "He taketh the wise in their own craftiness." Thus, most justly, did our philosopher meet with darkness in the day-time, and was permitted to grope in the noonday as in the night. One just view of himself as a sinner would have refuted and broke up his whole system of proud unbelief. I have known a good deal, by experience, of the conflict which infidels maintain behind the entrenchments of Hume and other champions of their cause; I have known also something, personally, of conversions among such people, and it has often astonished me to see how immediately a whole system of well jointed infidelity tumbles to pieces; how entirely the most darling argument against the gospel is changed into folly, and given to the winds, as soon as one realizes that he is a sinner, and must stand before God in judgment.

IV. Let us pass to our fourth proposition. *The testimony in proof of the miracles of the gospel has not diminished in force by the increase of age.* It is not an uncommon idea that the transmission of remote events, by successive testimony, from generation to generation, weakens their evidence in proportion to the time. It is supposed, that had we lived in the fourth instead of the nineteenth century, we should have possessed the testimonial evidence of the christian miracles in much greater force than it is now enjoyed. But we deny that there is any reason for this supposition. Mere *oral tradition* must weaken with age. But written testimony cannot suffer loss as long as the genuineness of the document containing it is unimpaired, and the character of the witnesses is substantiated. For example: suppose it be recorded on the minutes of the Young Men's Society of New York, that on the 13th day of January, 1832, this lecture was delivered to its members, on the Evidences of Christianity, and those minutes be laid up among its records; and the society exist from generation to generation, keeping a regular account of its transactions, for 400 years; and at the end of that time, some one, searching into its early papers, should read the minutes of the above event; the evidence of the fact would be considered as conclusive, as if, instead of 400 years, only 50 had elapsed since its occurrence. The event would be as certain as the genuineness of the record, and would have no reference to the age of either. Let the society continue 1000 years, and its records being still preserved uncorrupted, the evidence will remain undiminished. We rely upon the testimony in proof of the invasion of Britain by Julius Cæsar, or of Italy by Hannibal, with quite as much confidence as we read of the wars of Charles the First in England. And if our present accounts of those widely remote events shall be preserved to the end of the world, the confidence of our posterity at that time in their historical correctness, *cæteris paribus*, will be as complete as ours. Indeed, it is only with regard to the facts related in the Bible that men ever talk of any diminution, by the lapse of years, in the credibility of testimony. But with how little reason is evident when you remember that a matter of historical fact is of the same nature in regard to testimony, whether it be found between the covers of the Bible, or those of a Roman historian. For precisely the same reason that the event of this lecture, recorded in the minutes of the Young Men's Society, would retain its evidence unimpaired as long as the Society and its minutes should exist together, does the testimony to the great events of primitive christianity continue to this day unabated.*

The christian church is also a society which was in existence when the events recorded in its scriptures occurred. Its principal institutions are founded upon them. Our New Testament books are its records, which, like those of any other institution of past ages, have been handed down from generation to generation. The members of the christian church have died from age to age, but the church, the society, the living keeper of these records, the librarian of the scriptures, has never died. The passing away of the several individuals who, since the commencement of christianity, have belonged to this society, has no more to do with the permanence of the institution itself, than have the rapid changes in the particles of the human body, with the permanence of the man. There is a personal identity in the midst of continual change. The man of seventy is the very identical man that he was at twenty, though many

* Gregory's Letters.

times have the particles composing his body been entirely changed. Thus the christian church in her nineteenth century is the same identical society that existed under that name in the days of the apostles, though so many generations of members have lived and died. She is as capable of remembering the events of her youth, as we are of remembering the events of ours. The records made by her members in testimony of those events, and in the age of their occurrence, having been preserved in her possession with the greatest vigilance and the most zealous attachment, are as certain evidence at present, as when they were written, of the facts related therein. She has been reading those records in her places of worship, in all parts of the world, ever since they were written; and she knows as well that they have preserved their personal identity, and, in all important respects, their uncorrupt, unmutilated character, as any of us can know that our family bibles are the same now as when they were purchased. Thus, I think, we are warranted in considering our proposition sustained, that *the testimony in proof of the miracles of the gospel has not diminished in force by the increase of age.**

V. We proceed to our last proposition, *that, in being called to examine the credibility of the gospel miracles by the evidence of testimony, we are more favourably situated in regard to moral probation and discipline, than if we had been enabled to judge of them by sensible evidence.* This will appear from the consideration, that evidence obtained by investigation, and appreciated by reflection, is more consistent with the state of probation, and of moral discipline and responsibility in which we are placed, than evidence forced upon us by the involuntary agency of the senses.

We are under trial and discipline, as well as to our understanding, as our conduct. We are responsible as well for

---

* Wilson's Lectures.

what we believe, as what we do. Precisely the same causes that would persuade a man to immoral practice, may persuade him to immoral principle. The same disposition that would induce him to disobey the precepts, may lead him to deny the doctrines and evidences of the gospel. It is therefore his trial, in part, whether in forming his opinion of religious truth, he will so resist evil example and prejudice and so deny himself the influence of all sinful inclinations and partialities, as to enter with honest candour upon the investigation of what he ought to believe and do, with a full determination to embrace the truth wherever it may appear. Now, with the nature and responsibility of this probationary condition, the evidence of testimony in proof of the christian miracles is specially consistent. Did those miracles appear before us, as once for special reasons they did before multitudes, forcibly arresting our senses; not only compelling attention, but almost compelling submission, by the palpable and amazing evidences attending them; it is evident that there would remain comparatively but little room for any freedom of mind or will; and consequently for any moral probation. Liberty of will and of decision would be suspended in proportion to the degree in which the senses should be directly and impressively addressed. But the miracles of the gospel addressing, not our senses, but our minds, through the medium of testimony, possess a degree of evidence which, while amply sufficient to satisfy all who examine it with suitable impartiality, is not so overcoming but that one may reject it, if he choose; not so irresistible, but that persons of indolence and indifference, or of pride and prejudice—persons who examine to refute it, more than to ascertain its truth, or whose habits and dispositions set them in direct opposition to the holiness of the gospel—may receive their reward in being allowed to continue unconvinced. They are thus dealt with in a way peculiarly consistent with their character as moral and accountable agents.

The exercise of an active solicitude for the discovery of truth thus presented, and of a fair, impartial consideration of its evidence before conviction, is as truly an exercise of morality; as much an act of moral discipline and of a correct temper of mind, as a correct religious practice would be in one already convinced. It is also as really an exhibition of immorality and dissoluteness to manifest a spirit of indifference, or of prejudice, or aversion, in relation to a matter of such infinite importance, as if one should display the same spirit in regard to the most necessary duties of moral living. "Thus, that religion is not intuitively true, but a matter of deduction and inference; that a conviction of its truth is not forced upon every one, but is left to be by some collected with a heedful attention to premises; this as much constitutes religious probation; as much affords opportunity for right and wrong behaviour, as any thing whatever." * It tests the heart of the inquirer.

But to illustrate our doctrine, take the case of one who is disposed to put religion away from him; who comes to its evidences with a decided wish that it may appear untrue, and examines them under strong aversions and prejudices. Suppose him suddenly arrested by the sight of a miracle wrought in his presence, so that in spite of all his dislikes and evil dispositions, he cannot escape believing. Take then the case of another, bearing a precisely similar character, who, having no evidence but that of testimony, is obliged, either to discipline his mind into a frame for candid, honest investigation; or else hazard the consequences of an inquiry conducted under the influence of habits and tempers directly hostile to the clear view and impartial acknowledgment of truth. Suppose him to choose the latter alternative, and that he is permitted, in reward for this voluntary perversion of his judgment, to continue in unbelief. I ask which of these

* Butler's Analogy, p. ii. c. vi.

individuals is treated in a way most consistent with his condition as a moral and accountable agent?*

But besides the greater adaptation to a probationary state, there is greater spiritual profit in the way by which we of latter days must arrive at the truth of the miracles of the gospel. Take the case of two Christians; let one be a disciple of these days, and the other, Thomas, one of the apostles. They are equally convinced of the Saviour's resurrection, but by different means; Thomas by the force of sight and touch; the other, by a careful, honest examination of the testimony we now possess. Which, in becoming a disciple, expressed the greater love of the truth? Which, the greater readiness to receive and submit to it? Thomas had

---

* "If (says Butler) there are any persons who never set themselves heartily and in earnest to be informed in religion; if there are any who secretly wish it may not prove true, and are less attentive to evidence than to difficulties, and more to objections than to what is said in answer to them—these persons will scarce be thought in a likely way of seeing the evidence of religion, though it were most certainly true, and capable of being ever so fully proved. If any accustom themselves to consider this subject usually in the way of mirth, or sport; if they attend to forms and representations, and inadequate manners of expression, instead of the real things intended by them, (for signs often can be no more than inadequately expressive of the things signified), or if they substitute human errors in the room of divine truth—why may not all, or any of these things, hinder some men from seeing that evidence which really is seen by others, as a like turn of mind, with respect to matters of common speculation and practice, does, we find by experience, hinder them from attaining that knowledge and right understanding, in matters of common speculation and practice, which more fair and attentive minds can attain to? And in general, levity, carelessness, passion, and prejudice, do hinder us from being rightly informed with respect to common things; and they may in like manner, and *perhaps in some farther providential manner*, with respect to moral and religious subjects; hinder evidence from being laid before us, and from being seen when it is. The scripture does declare that every one *shall not understand*. And it makes no difference by what providential conduct this comes to pass; whether the evidence of christianity was originally and with design, put, and left, so that those who are desirous of evading moral obligations, should not see it, and that honest-minded persons should; or whether it comes to pass by any other means."

Butler's Analogy, p. ii. c. vi.

only to open his eyes, and reach forth his hand; the other pursued a course of candid, patient, serious reflection. Thomas required for his conviction that the Saviour should stand before him, and say: "Be not faithless, but believing." The other went forth seeking "the truth as it is in Jesus," through all the reasoning and objections; all the patient consideration and study, which circumstances placed in his way, not demanding to be constrained by the arrest of his senses, but prepared to submit as soon as the testimony was sufficient. Now it is plain that in this case there is a simplicity of heart; a love of truth; a candour in its pursuit, and a willingness to bow to it at all cost, such as are by no means implied in the conviction of Thomas. It is plain, also, that the moral discipline to which the former was subjected—and the state of mind involved in the mode by which he came at the truth, are far more conducive to his happiness, and afford a much higher promise of steadfast and elevated attachment to the service of the truth, than if, like Thomas, it could be said of him: "Because thou hast *seen*, thou hast believed." So that we may now acknowledge the truth of those words, "Blessed are they that have not seen, and yet have believed; and may repeat our proposition, that *in having to try the credibility of the gospel miracles by the evidence of testimony, we are more favourably situated, in a very important sense, than had we been present to judge them by the evidence of our senses.**

From the whole truth exhibited in this lecture, we are called to adore the wisdom of God. "His ways are not as our ways; neither his thoughts as our thoughts." Why, in such a momentous business as that of religion (demands some weak mortal), was not truth rendered intuitively certain, so that the most careless could not mistake? Why (asks another) should such tremendous matters be necessarily

---

* See Saurin, on Obscure Faith.

settled by investigation and argument; by the weight of testimony, and the records of distant ages; instead of bringing them at once to the test of every one's experience? "*Show us a sign!*" is still the requisition of multitudes, who, if they must believe, desire to do it without trouble; but would much rather be excused from both. God is infinitely wiser. "He knoweth whereof we are made." He has dignified us with reason, as well as sense; and made us capable of *learning* by reflection and study, as well as of *knowing* by instinct and necessity. He deals with us as rational beings. He makes us responsible for the use of our minds, as well as of our limbs. He requires the obedience of the will, the labour of our thoughts, and the pains-taking of all our intellectual and moral faculties, in order that we may know and serve him as becometh our natures. To this end, He has so constructed religion, and delivered to us its evidences, that whoever is sufficiently interested in His will to bestow his best thoughts, and affections, and efforts, upon the work of its discovery, truly desirous of knowing that he may embrace it, and earnestly looking up to God for protection against prejudice, and for guidance in the way of light, will certainly come to the knowledge of the truth, whatever the grade of his intellect, and will arrive at it by a way most wisely adapted to make him hold fast and obey it. On the other hand, God has so framed the gospel, and set before us its credentials, that whether one will believe or not, is left to his free and voluntary choice; his probationary character is inviolate; his reason and his will are perfectly responsible. If he desire not to believe; if his heart revolt against the gospel on account of the humility, and repentance, and holiness, and self-denial, it demands of him; if he study its nature and evidence carelessly, proudly, and partially; if he consult more the objector than the advocate, and try to invent reasons for unbelief more than arguments for the contrary: if he love vice, and would retain his sins; he may easily convince himself against the claims of the gospel. God has left unclosed many avenues by which such a man may escape into infidelity. He is wisely punished by being permitted to go in thereat. God may justly take him at his word, and condemn him to the darkness and final misery of rejecting what he investigated so unjustly. It is the wisdom of God that His truth does not, in offering conviction to such examiners, afford at the same time, encouragement to such unworthiness.

LECTURE VI.

MIRACLES.

Our last lecture was occupied in settling certain preliminaries, for the purpose of being enabled, in this, to enter directly upon the work of weighing the testimony to the miracles of Christ and his apostles. The question to which we now proceed may be stated thus: The Lord Jesus Christ claimed to be received as a teacher, come from God for the purpose of communicating a divine revelation. His apostles claimed to be received as his inspired and divinely commissioned agents in publishing that revelation. All appealed to miracles, as the credentials of their embassy. None can deny that such credentials, plainly ascertained, are certain proof of the sanction of God. The appeal to them is, therefore, unquestionably fair. The point, then, which remains to be determined, is: *Have we satisfactory evidence that genuine miracles were wrought by the Lord Jesus Christ and his apostles?*

In answer to this question, we might proceed on a plan of argument which would occupy but a few moments. In the lecture preceding the last, we ascertained the credibility of the gospel history; in other words, that we have the strongest reason to rely implicitly on the narratives contained therein, as to all matters of fact. Now it is there related, that on a certain occasion our Saviour was followed by five thousand men, into a desert place, where they were an hungered—that all the food in his possession was five barley loaves, and a few small fishes—that of these he commanded his disciples to distribute to the multitude; and after they had all eaten and were filled, the fragments remaining were much more, in quantity, than the original loaves and fishes. These are plain statements, related in the gospel as unquestionable facts. The gospel history being credible, they must be true. To call that a credible history, and then suppose it unworthy of reliance in such prominent particulars, would be absurd. But these facts constitute a miracle. There must have been a miraculous multiplication of the loaves and fishes. Consequently, in having proved the credibility of the Gospel history, we have proved that in this case a miracle was wrought.

Thus might we proceed with regard to a great variety of other statements, as to the works of Christ and his apostles; and I fully believe that, in strict justice, nothing more ought to be required in evidence of the gospel miracles, than what has been already adduced in proof of the credibility of the narratives contained in the New Testament. But inasmuch as our object is not merely to exhibit a sound and conclusive argument, such as ought to satisfy every mind, but so to present the great variety and abundance of proof in support of christianity, that no attentive candid mind can help being satisfied, we will adopt a broader plan.

Before proceeding any further, let it be remarked, that *the religion of the Bible is the only one which, in its first introduction, appealed to miracles for evidence of the divine authority of its teachers.* Under the religion of the Bible I include the dispensation of Moses and that of Christ, as exhibiting essentially the same religion; though more largely and clearly revealed under the latter than under the former. Both dispensations were introduced and sanctioned by miracles. Now, I know, it is a common supposition, that the same mode of attestation was resorted to by all the false religions that ever gained acceptance in the world; and that this was the chief cause of their ascendency in the public mind. But the truth is, that no religion, except that of the Bible, was ever set up by appeal to miracles as the credentials of its founder. We speak of miracles which are capable of being witnessed and investigated by others. It is not asserted that many wonderful things, of a miraculous nature, have not been pretended to and boasted among the disciples of sundry false religions. The annals of paganism abound with relations of auguries, and oracles, and apparitions. many miraculous, not to say ridiculous, marvels are asserted of Mohammed. But the remark is applicable to all of these things, and is of great importance in connexion with our present object, that they were asserted not as *proofs* of religions appealing to them for credentials, but only as *appendages* of religions already set up, and received on considerations entirely independent of *their* truth or falsehood. It was the credit and influence of the established religion which gave them all their currency; and not *their evidence* which established the religion with which they were respectively connected. The prodigies of heathenism, unaccompanied as they were by any pretence of proof, had no manner of reference to the setting up of a new system of faith, or of a teacher pretending to a divine commission. Miraculous stories were published of Mohammed by writers of six and eight centuries after his death; but no such pretensions were made by himself. On the contrary, he expressly disclaimed miraculous powers. In the Koran it is written of him: "*Nothing hindered us from sending thee with miracles, except that the former nations have charged them with imposture.*" Again: "*They say, unless a sign be sent down unto him from his Lord, we will not believe · answer, signs are in the power of God alone, and I am no more than a public preacher. Is it not sufficient for them that we have sent down unto them the book of the Koran, to be read unto them?*" We grant that Mohammed did give out to the credulity of his followers a few marvellous doings; but they were such as cannot be included under the title of *sensible* miracles, inasmuch as he always took the discreet precaution of having no witness but himself, entirely avoiding the hazardous experiment of resting the evidence of his divine mission upon the testimony of any eyes more disinterested than his own.

But how can it be accounted for, that one of such high pretensions—aware, as he was, of the success which miracles had obtained for the gospel in times past—should have neglected so powerful a means of proselyting the world? It was not for want of importunity on the part of others; for his opposers were constantly teazing him with their demands on this head. It was not because he could anticipate no favourable influence from a well-sustained pretension to miracles; for his adversaries assured him, even by oaths, that on the evidence of one such sign they would own his claims. Nor was it that Mohammed was too honest. The marvellous tales of the nocturnal visits of Gabriel; of his own night-journey; and of the transmission, from time to time, of parcels of the uncreated book from heaven, prove what this impostor was capable of attempting when allured by a prospect of success. Nor was it that this unequalled adventurer was deficient in an unusual degree of craft and address for the management of bold imposture. His whole biography would refute such an opinion. Nor was it that he was surrounded with a people peculiarly prepared, by knowledge and cultivated discernment, for the detection of such frauds. The age was one of the darkest in the annals of man, and his country, one of the darkest of that age. Nor could it have been that his cause needed no such auxiliary; for the fruits of his labour, during the first three years, were only fourteen disciples; and in ten years his cause had not advanced beyond, and had made but little progress within, the walls of Mecca. Then if Mohammed was neither too honest to attempt the forgery of miracles, nor too unskilful to manage it with cunning and address; if his cause needed it, and his enemies demanded it, and the bar-

barity of the people and age favoured it; no earthly reason can be given for his having disclaimed the attempt, except that he considered it too difficult and hazardous; too certain of detection, even among a barbarous, credulous, and superstitious race. The religion of the Bible is the only one that ever ventured on such evidence in proof of divine original. This single fact, united with the well known truth that, however her miracles may have been derided and suspected by enemies, none ever pretended to have discovered an imposition, is strong presumptive evidence that they had a reality which no human device could rival—a truth which no human scrutiny could alarm.

In coming, therefore, to our present examination, we should feel that the religion of the Bible stands alone, not only as to the wisdom and grandeur of her communications, but equally so as to the boldness of her evidence; the sublimity of her credentials; and the godlike dignity with which she cometh to the light, that her deeds "may be made manifest that they are wrought in God."

We proceed to the testimony connected with the miracles of Christ.

I. We observe, in the first place, that supposing the works related of the Lord Jesus to have actually occurred, many of them *must have been genuine miracles*. They cannot be ascribed to natural causes. If five thousand men were fed, when all the food to feed them with, prior to the act of Jesus, was a few loaves and fishes; if the centurion's servant was healed, at the word of Jesus, while the latter was nowhere within the sight, or hearing, or knowledge, of that servant; if the man born blind was made to see by no other physical act than that of Jesus putting clay on his eyes, and his washing it off in the pool of Siloam; if Lazarus, having been dead four days, did come forth from the sepulchre, at the word of Jesus; then we have facts for which no natural causes can account. They are unquestionable miracles. and we are forced to the alternative of either denying, in the face of all evidence, the truth of the statements contained in the gospel history; or else acknowledging that miracles, in the fullest sense, were wrought at the word of Christ.

II. The miracles of Christ were such as could at once be brought *to the test of the senses.* It is an essential requisite to a rational belief in miraculous agency, that one be presented with facts of such a nature as that the senses of those present could easily decide upon their reality and their supernatural character. Now, that the senses of the most ignorant were as competent as those of the most learned; that the senses of any man or woman in Judea were perfectly competent to decide whether the son of the widow of Nain, having been dead and carried out to be buried, did arise and sit up at the word of Christ, and continue thereafter to reside, a living man, in Nain; that any one's senses were perfectly competent to judge whether thousands of men were fed with a few loaves and fishes, or the blind received their sight, or the lepers were cleansed, or those, notoriously lame from their birth, were enabled to walk at the bidding of Christ, it would be folly to doubt.

III. The miracles of Christ were performed for the most part *in the most public manner.* It is the detracting circumstance of all the most plausible pretensions to miracles, exclusive of those of the scriptures, that they were done in a corner, or in the presence only of those already inclined to believe them, or under favour of circumstances calculated to prevent a free examination. Just the contrary is the fact with regard to a great portion of the wonderful works of Christ. Not only were they accessible to the senses of witnesses; but to the senses of multitudes of witnesses, of witnesses of the most eager and violent enmity to the claims of Jesus; witnesses of all ranks and classes in society—the learned and mighty, as well as the ignorant and feeble—the scribes and Pharisees, the priest and the centurion, as well as the publicans and beggars. It was in the synagogues, in the streets, in the open fields, surrounded by thousands—in the midst of Jerusalem, and at the time of the great annual festivals, when an immense concourse of Jews, from all parts of the world, crowded the holy city, that almost all of the mighty works of Jesus were performed. In this way, as in other ways, he could say to his persecutors, "*I spake openly to the world.*"

His miracles were wrought upon subjects so numerous, in so many places, and in such circumstances, as that *none could suspect the cases to have been previously selected and prepared.* What the condition of the subject had been before the miracle, thousands knew, and all could easily ascertain. What it was, for a long time after the miracle, was equally notorious. Those who were cured of blindness, or leprosy, or lameness, or palsy, or who had been raised from the dead, did not die immediately after, nor hide themselves from public inspection; but continued to go in and out among the people, as living examples of the power of Christ. The grave of Lazarus was surrounded with unbelieving Jews. They saw him come forth. They had as much opportunity, as disposition, to find out whether it was Lazarus or some one else; whether the man was alive, or only *pretending* to be alive. Instead of being immediately snatched from their view, he was seated some time after as one of the guests at a supper, in Bethany; and so well known was the fact, that "much people of the Jews" came to the place to have a sight of one who had been raised from the dead. "The chief priests consulted that they might put him to death, because that, by reason of him, many of the Jews went away and believed on Jesus."

IV. The miracles of Christ and his apostles were *very numerous, and of great variety.* It has been a characteristic of all cases of imposture, that the wonderful works pretended to were but few in number, and of great sameness

The sect of the Jansenists, in the church of Rome, pretended to miracles at the tomb, and by the posthumous intercessions, of the Abbê Paris. But, besides the want of evidence that any of the facts recorded were miraculous, they were neither numerous nor various. Could this be said of the works of Christ, it would deprive them of one of the most palpable evidences of the fearless integrity in which they were wrought. But his history is full of miraculous works. Besides about forty that are related at large, we frequently meet with such accounts as this: "*His fame went throughout all Syria, and they brought unto him all sick people that were taken with divers diseases and torments, and those which were possessed with devils, and those which were lunatic, and those that had the palsy, and he healed them.*" Similar declarations are made as to the miracles of the apostles. As, for example, in Acts, v. 16: "There came also a multitude out of the cities round about unto Jerusalem, bringing sick folks, and them which were vexed with unclean spirits; and they were healed every one."

But the miracles of the Saviour and his apostles were also of *great variety.* It was not disease of one or two classes only that Jesus removed, but disease of all kinds. Not diseases only, but all kinds of human calamity, departed at his will. Even death surrendered his captives at his command. The blind from their birth; the hopeless leper; those that were lame from the womb; those that had long been bowed down with infirmity; the withered, the palsied, the insane—all were alike delivered of their affliction. On two occasions, thousands were fed with a mere pittance of food. Thrice, beside the instance of his own resurrection, did Jesus raise the dead. A corresponding variety characterizes the works of his apostles.

V. It is a matter of great importance to remark, that amidst all this variety, the success in every instance was *instantaneous* and *complete.* The sick were perfectly healed.

The deaf, and blind, and lame, were perfectly delivered from their infirmities; the leper was entirely cleansed; the dead arose, not merely to life, but to health and strength. These effects were as immediate as they were perfect. No sooner was the voice spoken, or the thing done, that was required of the applicant, than all was finished. Did Jesus say, "Let there be light? *there was light;* let there be health? *there was health.* He left no time for second causes to operate—no room for human means to intervene. "He spake, and it was done. He commanded, and it stood fast."

VI. There is no evidence of an attempt, on the part of Christ or his apostles, to perform a miracle in which they were accused of having failed. It is notoriously true of the wonderful works ascribed to the tomb of the Abbé Paris, for example, that the cases in which any beneficial effects resulted to the applicants were very inconsiderable in number, compared with those in which there was a manifest and total failure. But although the ministry of Christ lasted between three and four years, during which he was continually resorted to by multitudes, with a great variety of cases, seeking his miraculous aid; and although the ministry of his apostles continued many years longer, during which time they are said to have been attested by "*divers miracles,*" no case is mentioned in which an attempt was unsuccessful, or in which an applicant was denied. The language of the history in relation to the multitudes that applied to Christ is continually, "*he healed them* ALL." The enemies of the gospel, who were eye-witnesses of these applicants, did never maintain that the power of Christ, or of his disciples, was exerted unsuccessfully in a single instance. Had such an event taken place, would they not have discovered it? Had they discovered it, would they not have proclaimed it far and wide? Would any of the books, written against christianity in the first centuries, have omitted so important a fact? The total absence of all insinuation of such a thing in the whole controversy between the primitive Christians and their adversaries, is certain evidence that an unsuccessful attempt was never made, and that an unsuccessful applicant was not known.*

Now, on the supposition that the miraculous doings recorded in the gospel were all a cheat, *what a miracle is here!* That all was contrivance, and imposture, and accident, and yet not an enemy ever detected an instance of failure; that the machinery was never out of place, out of time, or out of order; that it was equally successful in all cases, equally ready at all seasons, always invisible, yet always at hand, and always instantaneously effectual—what a *miracle!* Who is the man of weak credulity?—the believer or the infidel?

VII. The *length of time, during which* the Saviour and his apostles professed to perform miracles, should be specially considered. Seventy years elapsed between the commencement of the ministry of Christ and the death of the last of the apostles. During all this interval, the miraculous gifts, in question, were exercised. Now, as every repetition in case of imposture multiplies the dangers of detection, and every extension of time makes it the more difficult to keep up the confederated plan, it is no inconsiderable evidence of the genuineness of the miracles of the gospel, that they continued to be wrought and inspected during a period of so many years, and yet so securely.

This consideration is the more important when you reflect that the miracles were not confined to one or two places; were not wrought in little villages, or among the poor and ignorant only—but that the scenes of most of them were in

* The case mentioned in Mat. xvii. 14—21, would have been an example of failure, had the narrative ended with the inability of the disciples. But the Master performed what they, being as yet in their noviciate, had attempted in vain.

the chief cities of the Roman empire. Instead of remaining together in one place, or moving together wherever they desired to produce an impression, and then confining themselves to such places as might be most easily deceived; the apostles, with singular folly, on the supposition that they were confederated for an imposture, separated to all parts of the world. They went alone to the most populous, polished and enlightened cities. They put themselves in the most public places of those cities; thus making combination impossible, and rendering their success, as mere counterfeiters perfectly miraculous.

VIII. We have the most perfect certainty that the miracles of the gospel underwent, at the time they were wrought, and for a long time after, the most rigid examination from those who had every opportunity of scrutinizing their character. Forged miracles may pass current, where power and authority, or the favourable dispositions of the people protect them from too close an inspection. But let the power of the magistrate, the authority of public opinion, and the partialities of those concerned, be once leagued in opposition, and the imposture cannot escape. Such was the league against the miracles in question. Never was the power of the state in more perfect alliance with public opinion, or more zealously supported by all the envy, hatred, and malice, of which popular feeling is capable, than when it set its face against the gospel. Not only were these miracles exposed, by their great publicity, to universal examination, but they were of such a nature that any mind was capable of examining them. Not only did they present themselves to the wise and the great, in the chief places of concourse, and in the great cities of the world; but they were such as necessarily provoked every description of scrutiny. Being performed in avowed support of a religion which could not be successful without destroying the whole hierarchy of the Jews, and advancing its victories over the ruins of heathenism; they roused at once into united and stern opposition, all the civil power of the governments; all the enmity of Jewish and Pagan priesthoods; all the partialities, and prejudices, and national attachments, of all people. The enmity of the scribes and Pharisees; of the doctors, and lawyers, and priests, of the Jews, must have been fired with peculiar indignation. As miracles multiplied and disciples increased, the deepest interest must have been awakened in relation to them among all classes of society. This we know to have been the case. Hence it is certain that they did not escape the most thorough examination; that all the ingenuity and diligence of contemporaries and eye-witnesses, animated by the strongest motives, and favoured by every conceivable advantage, were enlisted in the trial; and this, not for a day, or a week, or a month, but as long as miracles were professed, and a hope of detection remained.

IX. It is a matter deserving of special remembrance, that the adversaries of the gospel were placed in the most favourable circumstances for a thorough investigation of the reality of its miracles, by *their being published and appealed to immediately after, and in the very places where, they occurred.* The miracles ascribed to the founder of the society of Jesuits are sufficiently answered by the fact that, during his life, and for many years after his death, nothing was heard of them. Those of Francis Xavier, one of the first disciples of Loyola, are deficient in evidence, because, having been wrought (as it is stated) in the far distant East, they were first published in the western world; and the narratives, if they ever reached the places to which they relate, could not have been known there till long after the opportunity of a close investigation had passed away, and must have been published among a people too indifferent to be at the pains of inquiring into their truth or falsehood. But the miracles of the gospel were published immediately after, and in the very places of, their occurrence. It is true, indeed, that the earliest gospel, that of St. Matthew, is not by any supposed to have been published earlier than the seventh or eighth year after the death of Christ. Supposing this to have been the first publication of the miracles, it was sufficiently near their date to afford every reasonable opportunity of investigation.

But we know from the gospel history, that during the three years of the Saviour's ministry, and all the while the apostles laboured, their miracles were notorious. The scribes and Pharisees met in council on the subject. Many, unable to deny them, ascribed them to demoniacal power. Herod, when he heard of them, said: "This is John the Baptist; he is risen from the dead; and therefore mighty works do show forth themselves in him."* The fame of the miracles of Jesus, at the beginning of his ministry, "went throughout all Syria," so that multitudes, with all kinds of afflictions, flocked to him from all quarters to be healed, and, when healed, returned to publish still more widely the works of their deliverer.† The raising of Lazarus was so widely published in Bethany, where it took place, and in the region round about, that, in a few days, "much people of the Jews came, not for Jesus' sake only, but that they might see Lazarus also, whom he had raised from the dead."‡ When, at the word of Peter and John, the impotent man, at the gate of the temple, had been made whole, they immediately published the miracle on the spot, to the multitude of Jerusalem; appealing to it in evidence of the power of their Lord. "His name (said they), through faith in his name, hath made this man strong, whom ye see and know: yea, the faith which is by him, hath given him *this perfect soundness in the presence of you all.*"§ Only about fifty days was Jesus risen from the dead, when his disciples began to proclaim every where, and first at Jerusalem, among those

* Mat. xiv. 1 and 2. † Ib. iv. 23—25. ‡ John, xii. 9. § Acts, iii. 16.

who slew him and had set the guard at the sepulchre, this chief of miracles. They appealed to it in every discourse; challenged every examination; defied all contradiction. All the miracles of Christ, they declared before the very people whom they asserted to have witnessed them. "Ye men of Israel, hear these words (said Peter); Jesus of Nazareth, a man approved of God among you by miracles, and wonders, and signs, which God did by him *in the midst of you, as ye yourselves also know.*"* How eminently this bold and immediate publication must have aided, as well as stimulated, the investigation of the enemies of the gospel, furnishing those, who had every disposition, and all power, and all intelligence and cunning, *with every opportunity* to try the minutest circumstance, and ferret out every clue to the detection of imposture, I need not show.

X. Now consider, *who the agents were, whose works were obliged to stand such trials.* Had they been men of learning, of power, of wealth, accustomed to any thing that was calculated to furnish them for the work of imposing upon mankind, the case would not be quite so strong. But, on the supposition that Christ was a mere man and pretender, what was he or what were his apostles, by education or standing in society, that they should be qualified for such an unparalleled effort of ingenuity and concealment? Is there any miracle more marvellous than that which is involved in the idea of a poor and unlearned individual of Nazareth, followed by twelve obscure, unlettered Jews, for the most part accustomed to nothing but their nets and fishing-boats, having practised such a system of imposture, under such circumstances of risk and exposure, without an individual among their numerous enemies to discover their secret, or detect the deceit?

XI. Consider, moreover, that notwithstanding all that

* Acts, ii. 22.

was done to entice and intimidate the early Christians who were eye-witnesses of what Jesus or his apostles wrought, *none were induced to confess themselves deceived; or that they had seen any thing but truth in those miraculous gifts, by which they had been persuaded to embrace the gospel.* It is not asserted that none who professed to be converted from judaism or paganism to christianity, ever renounced the cause of Christ. The persecution of enemies was sometimes successful in forcing their victims to forsake the gospel, and do sacrifice to idols, rather than be burned at the stake, or thrown to wild beasts. But the case cannot be brought of one such unhappy deserter, whether man or woman, having been persuaded to *bear witness against the christian miracles.* A convert, after having united himself to the apostles; been received to the fellowship of the church; and become an agent in advancing its cause; must have become acquainted with its secrets. He must have often looked behind the scenes, and had many opportunities of knowing the hidden machinery by which the imposition, if any existed, was carried on. Had the evidence of contrivance and forgery been ever seen by the primitive christians; those who deserted the cause had every motive to divulge it. Their own indignation at having been deceived; the rewards which they might have expected from the enemies of christianity, would have been sufficiently persuasive. That none ever went a step further than simply to give up the profession of the gospel, through fear of torture; that none ever turned round upon the apostles by whose miracles they had been convinced, and charged them with fraud; is absolutely inexplicable on any other supposition than their thorough conviction that fraud did not exist.

This evidence is specially strong in the case of Judas Iscariot. He was one of the twelve who always companied with Jesus. He was the treasurer of the family—admitted to every opportunity of knowing whatever secrets may have belonged to the works of Christ. That he knew *what* and *where* the imposition was, if any existed in the gospel miracles, cannot be doubted. That he was treacherous enough to betray it, is manifest from his having betrayed the Master himself. That he had every inducement to do so, none can question who knows how precious the chief priests and Pharisees would have considered such a disclosure. Did he come forward with any such thing? He delivers up the person of Christ; does he accuse his character?—deny his works?—expose his cause? The Saviour is arraigned before his powerful enemies—witnesses are called. Where is Judas? False witnesses are brought. Where is Judas? Has he nothing to say against him whom he has already sold for thirty pieces of silver? The enemies of Christ cannot be ignorant of the importance of such a witness; nor can he be ignorant of the gain that would accrue from his delivering such testimony. But he is not there. The Jews never pretended to have obtained any accusation from that traitor. Not a word is spoken, in all the controversy with primitive adversaries, about the treachery of Judas as having turned to their advantage. On the contrary, it is written in the gospel history, and was never denied by those men, that he not only abstained from any accusation, but in the strongest possible manner confessed the truth and excellence of Jesus and his cause. Under the stings of conscience, and in spite of the covetousness of his disposition, he went and delivered up the money he had received for his iniquity into the hands of those who had paid it. Nor was this all. He was constrained to confess to the chief priests and elders, whose wrath he knew it would inflame to the uttermost, saying: "*I have sinned in that I have betrayed the innocent blood.*" "*And he cast down the pieces of silver in the temple, and departed, and went and hanged himself.*"* Stronger

---

* Mat. xxvii. 3, 4, 5.

evidence of truth and righteousness, it is impossible for any works or any cause to possess.

XII. Having considered in another place the character of the individuals by whom the miracles of the gospel were performed, it is important now to remark the character *of the miracles themselves.* Either they were real miracles, or false. If false, the individuals who performed them could not, by any excess of infatuation, have supposed them true. They must, therefore, have been the deliberate asserters of a divine commission, which they knew had not been given them; and the persevering exhibiters of credentials which they knew were forgeries. Hence it is not possible that they could have been honest men; much less, good men. And inasmuch as they must have acted from some motive and with some object in view, and we cannot suppose that such impostors would be sacrificing themselves merely out of a benevolent disposition to promote the happiness of their fellow-creatures and relieve their woes; it must have been some object of ambition or of gain which they were pursuing. We do not pause now to show what perfect idiots they must have been to select such a scheme out of ambitious or pecuniary motives. But since, on the supposition that their works were fictitious, we can imagine no other, the question arises, how do these miracles correspond with the idea that the agents were impostors, and their motives ambitious or covetous?

Now I maintain, that considering how many and various are the miracles recorded in the New Testament, in what various circumstances and by what various agents they were performed, and that not for a month or year only, but many years, in full assemblages of enemies; it would have been quite miraculous, supposing them false, had they been in every instance garnished with a concealment so perfect, that nothing low, or mean, or undignified—nothing betraying the spirit of designing, ambitious, or covetous men—should ever have been manifested. Take up the accounts of any confessedly fictitious miracles, in any age or country, and you will soon detect the hand-writing of the spirit and motives that produced them. But most singularly—contrary to all experience and all law, on the assumption that the miracles of Christ and his apostles were fictitious, you discover nothing in them but what is entirely worthy of the majesty, holiness, justice, and goodness of that God, by whose power they professed to be wrought. The most perfect correspondence appears between the exalted and holy character and office in which the Saviour and his apostles claimed to be received, and the works by which their claim was sustained. Propriety, dignity, disinterestedness, benevolence of the loveliest spirit, and compassion of the tenderest sensibility, distinguished them. Not the least trace is marked on them of any ambitious or other suspicious motive. Though the Lord Jesus and his apostles were compassed about with reproachful and persecuting enemies, you discern nothing vindictive or resentful. Though always in personal poverty, "*despised and rejected of men*," their miracles discover nothing ostentatious—nothing to gratify curiosity—no anxiety for repute—no aim at wealth or temporal power. While feeding the hungry by thousands, Jesus continued in poverty. While, as the good Shepherd, ever following the lost sheep through suffering and want, that he might administer to their necessities, he showed no sign of any care for himself. Now, if Jesus and his apostles did not work miracles in truth; if their high claims were false, and they consequently were prosecuting a scheme of imposture with selfish purposes, either of ambition or gain; there is something in all this singularly unaccountable—very unlike the laws of nature—exceedingly miraculous.

XIII. But that the miracles of the gospel were not fictitious, but genuine and undeniable, we have the *plainest and strongest confession from the primitive adversaries of Christ and his cause.* In the first place; we have a very conclusive and impressive confession, though silent, from the whole Jewish nation and the whole Gentile world. It consists in this unquestionable fact, that no individual among them ever detected, or was publicly supposed to have detected, an imposture. You are to remember that these miracles were addressed to the senses; performed in open daylight; with all possible publicity; that they were exceedingly numerous and various; wrought by many different agents; in many and remote countries; before citizens of the most enlightened cities, and in the most enlightened age of the Roman empire; that those of the Apostles did not cease until nearly seventy years from their commencement, during all which time they must have endured the very closest scrutiny that the combined forces of learning, enmity, and political authority, could institute. You are to remember, also, what kind of men were those who performed them, and that the accounts of them which we now possess were published far and wide in the very places where the works were done, and among the very people who are said to have witnessed them. You are to remember, for example, the miracle of the gift of tongues on the day of Pentecost in Jerusalem, how it was published abroad in Jerusalem and the whole empire, that, on that day, an immense multitude of people of all languages were amazed at hearing the twelve apostles, who were well known as unlettered Jews, preaching the gospel in so many different languages, that all, whether Cretes, Arabians, Mesopotamians, or of any other name, all heard, in their respective tongues, the wonderful works of God. You are to consider, that in publishing an account of this astonishing transaction, as was done by the apostles in all their preaching, and a few years afterwards, by Luke in the Acts of the Apostles; an open, honest appeal was made to all the hundreds of thousands who had been assembled on that day in Jerusalem, to come forth and deny that these things did then and there occur. Hence was every possible facility afforded for the detection of imposture. Without a miracle for its concealment, it could not have escaped. Had there been a detection with regard to but one of all the miracles, we should have heard of it. Judea, and Greece, and Rome, would have rung with the news. The books of Jewish and Heathen adversaries would have reiterated its publication in illuminated pages and golden capitals. All the generations of succeeding adversaries would have quoted it as one of the dearest bequests of classic antiquity. Is there any such thing? I sound the inquiry through the whole region of Jewish, and Grecian, and Roman history, and I hear nothing in answer, but the echo of my own voice: "*Is there any such thing?*" I must answer it myself. There is no such thing, in all that has come to us from antiquity, as even a pretence to the detection of imposture in the gospel miracles.

This I think you will join me in considering a very impressive and conclusive confession, though a silent one, from the whole Jewish nation and Gentile world, to the undeniable reality of the miracles of Christ and his apostles. It is all the evidence we could with any reason expect from enemies. When Deists bid us produce the testimony of enemies, as well as friends, it is perfectly unreasonable to require that we should find enemies, in those days of bitter hostility to christianity, positively acknowledging that it was attested by miracles. That they did not deny it; that Jews and Gentiles; that the Mosaic and the Pagan priesthoods; that the Pharisees of Jerusalem, and the philosophers of Corinth, and Ephesus, and Rome, were silent, on this head, one would suppose, is a great deal to get from such adversaries.

But we can go further. Unreasonable, as it is, to demand more positive testimony from enemies, we can meet the demand. Having, in a previous lecture, ascertained the credibility of the gospel history, we may now appeal to it for the acknowledgment of enemies. Peter on the day of Pentecost assumed the fact that the multitudes of Israel, to whom he was speaking, acknowledged that Jesus of Nazareth had approved himself among them *by "miracles, and wonders, and signs."** "*This man doeth many miracles,*'† was the confession of the chief priests and Pharisees, in council, relative to Jesus. "*What shall we do to them?* (said the Jewish rulers, in relation to Peter and John) *For that indeed a notable miracle has been done by them is manifest to all them that dwell in Jerusalem, and we cannot deny it.*"‡ You know that the only way of escape the Jewish rulers could find, while they could not deny the miracles, was to ascribe them to magic, or the power of demons. "*He casteth out devils by Beelzebub,*" &c. But we have similar testimony, without recourse to the scriptures. The Jewish rabbies, in the Talmud, acknowledge these miracles, and pretend that they were wrought by magic, or by the power attendant upon a certain use of the name Jehovah, called *tetragrammaton*, which, they pretend, Jesus stole out of the temple.§ But we have positive testimony also from Heathens. Celsus, who wrote in the latter part of the second century, not only allows the principal facts of the gospel history, but acknowledges *that Christ wrought miracles*, by which he engaged great multitudes to adhere to him as the Messiah. That these miracles were really performed, so far from denying, he tries to account for by ascribing them to magic, which (he says) Christ learned in Egypt.‖

---

* Acts, ii. 22. † John, xi. 47. ‡ Acts, iv. 16.

§ Quod Christus per hoc nomen quoque miracula sua ediderit, probavit ante multos annos Purchetus. Ejus tamen fabulæ illustrandæ causa, hoc addo, quod apud Talmudicus reperi. Ut Christus in ea historia refertur descriptum Shemhamphorasch (id est, nomen expositum, quod est ipsum nomen יהוה), inclusisse in discissam cutem pedis, et ex templo eduxisse, ut sic per ejus vim miracula postmodum ediderit. *Buxtorf*

‖ Lardner, iv. 129—130.

Hierocles, president of Bythinia, and a persecutor of Christians, in a work written against christianity, does not deny the miracles of Christ, but compares them with those which he pretended had been wrought a long time before, by one Apollonius, of Tyanea, a heathen, complaining at the same time that Christians made so much ado about the works of Jesus, as to worship him for God.*

Julian, the emperor, in the fourth century, acknowledges the miracles of Christ, and contents himself with trying to depreciate their importance. "Jesus," he says, "did nothing worthy of fame, unless any one can suppose that curing the lame and the blind, and exorcising demons in the villages of Bethsaida, are some of the greatest works." He acknowledges that Jesus had a sovereign power over impure spirits, and that he walked on the surface of the deep.† Now, it is a matter of no little wonder, to say the least of it, that in this nineteenth century, men should be so sagacious as to discover that Christ and his apostles did not attest their claims and doctrines with miraculous powers, when learned sagacious, and sufficiently hostile unbelievers of the earliest centuries of christianity, having opportunities for discovering the state of the case such as they cannot pretend to, were constrained to acknowledge precisely the contrary. I marvel that Celsus, and Porphyry, and Hierocles, and Julian, and the Scribes, and Pharisees, can rest in their graves, when such reflections are cast upon the zeal and talents with which they searched for imposture in the works of Christ.

XIV. But we have even better testimony than that of enemies. Had Celsus found himself not only unable to deny the miracles of Christ, but persuaded, by the mere force of their truth, to renounce heathenism, and consecrate his life, in the face of persecution and death, to the service of the gospel, would not his testimony have been greatly increased

* Lardner, iv. 254. † Lardner, vol. iv. 332—342.

in importance? Would not the very fact of his becoming a Christian, under the power of evidence, be the consideration which, instead of injuring his testimony as that of a friend, would have given it peculiar force as that of a friend *who was once an enemy?* Then if I find cases precisely corresponding with this—if I present you with hundreds and thousands of such cases, and tens of thousands—will you not own that their positive testimony is far stronger than even that of the adversaries whom we have cited, and the strongest of which in the nature of things we could be possessed? I find precisely such cases in the apostles of Christ They are regarded as interested witnesses, because they were friends. But what made them friends? Were they not men like others? Jews, like others? Consider Paul, once a fierce persecutor of Christians! What made him a friend? Consider the three thousand, converted from bitter, persecuting Judaism to the faith of Christ, on the day of Pentecost. What made friends and disciples of them? Was it that they expected any earthly honours or gains from taking up the cross of a crucified Master, in whose wonderful works they did not believe? Was it that they coveted reproach, enjoyed suffering, and loved death? or because, by careful consideration, they were so convinced that the miracles of Christ, especially that of his rising from the dead, were true, that no certainty of persecution, no sacrifices of property, character, friends, or life, were sufficient to prevent them from confessing him before men? To these add the hundreds of thousands, who, during the ministry of the apostles, from having been Jews or Heathens, and enemies of the gospel, became its devoted followers and heroic confessors. They bore witness, by word and deed, in torture and death, to the great fact that the miracles of Christ were true. And what is their testimony worth? What possible motive can you assign for the total change which took place in all their habits, attachments, manners, and affections, when they became Christians, other than that of deep, solemn conviction? To suppose they were not convinced, is to suppose that they made the most tremendous sacrifices, not only without motive, but in direct opposition to the most powerful motives of the human breast. They well knew the poverty, and persecution, and martyrdom, to which they exposed themselves. Why, then, did they become Christians? When afterwards pursued as the off-scouring of all things, and pests of the world; when no name was so odious as that of Christian; when to bring those who bore it to torture was universally accounted meritorious; when it was the study of magistrates and soldiers to invent new modes of tormenting them; when thousands of all ranks and ages were daily slain for the testimony of Jesus, who, by the act of a moment, could have stilled the storm to perfect peace; why did they persist and die? To pretend to explain their steadfastness, except on the supposition of their having firmly believed what they professed, were perfectly absurd. But did they not know? Living in the same age with the apostles; living in the very places where the miracles were performed; they, if any on earth, must have possessed the opportunity of discovering the truth with regard to them. We have, then, the impressive fact of hundreds of thousands of the adversaries of the gospel, *in the first century of Christianity*, Jews, and Greeks, and Romans, many of whom had been persecutors of Christians, bearing the most positive testimony to, what they had every opportunity of investigating, the reality of the miracles of Christ; and sealing their testimony in the renouncing of all that was dear to them by birth, habit, or education, and embracing christianity at the expense of the keenest reproach and the most painful death. Testimony stronger or more undeniable than this, I cannot imagine. If this be not sufficient to prove a plain matter of fact, such for example as that Lazarus was seen alive after he was known to have been dead; then farewell all history and all knowledge. Nothing can be reasonably believed, except on evidence of sense, and hardly then, after rejecting this.

We have now arrayed as many of the materials of the argument for the gospel miracles as our time would permit. It only remains that we put them together into one view, so as to enable you to appreciate their united strength. I know not how to do this in a better way, than to take the supposition that all the miracles of Christ and of his apostles were fictions, and consequently their authors, deliberate deceivers; and then consider how far the supposition will carry us. Let us do so. You understand the supposition. What must be believed by those who will maintain it?

They must believe that Jesus and his apostles, being obscure, unlettered Jews, without a single circumstance to give them influence, were so perfectly silly and mad as to flatter themselves that *they* could set up a scheme of religion, which, though in utter contradiction to the habits, passions, prejudices, and institutions, of all the world, should succeed in overturning the religious systems and institutions of the most enlightened nations; and yet that, with this unacountable infatuation, they were so singularly wise, as to maintain, throughout all the miracles which they professed to work in proof of their system, the most perfect consistency with the dignity and disinterestedness of the office they assumed, and with the majesty, holiness, and goodness of that God in whose name they professed to come.

They must believe that Jesus and his apostles were so wicked, as to attempt an imposture which involved not only continual dishonesty, but downright blasphemy, and this from motives of mere ambition or avarice; and yet that during the space of seventy years they kept up such an invariable show of eminent goodness and disinterestedness, as in all their works to manifest not the smallest appearance of selfishness or any evil design; but, on the contrary, the utmost evidence of self-denial, of self-humiliation, of purity, of holiness, of the tenderest compassion, and the most laborious benevolence; so that even their enemies never brought inconsistency to their charge.

They must believe the apostles to have been so strangely in love, either with wealth, or honour, or power, or something else, to be willing, even out of their obscurity and weakness, as to seek it by such a desperate scheme as that of christianity; and yet that, when honours were offered, they earnestly refused them; when they saw the triumph of their enemies in the crucifixion of Christ, and that nothing awaited his followers but disgrace, poverty, and persecution, they persisted in advocating the cause of their fallen leader; and when the storms of persecution grew darker and darker, and ruin and death were the certain consequences of perseverance, and one word of confession would have saved them, such was their infatuated attachment to this scheme of imposture, such their singular devotion to self, to honour, or wealth, or power, or something else, that they drove on from suffering to suffering, from shame to shame, ending at last their pursuit in a bitter death, with the full belief, as Jews, that in eternity they should be condemned to an awful retribution for their whole career.

They must believe that while the apostles were so utterly destitute of common ingenuity that they selected precisely that kind of credential which it was the most difficult to forge, and instead of seeking, as other impostors would have done, private, or confined, or solitary places, for their miracles, chose those of the greatest resort and publicity, and then placed and left their miracles directly under the senses of the multitude; that while they had so little contrivance that instead of selecting a few masked friends, or the most ignorant of the populace for witnesses, they seemed rather to prefer having hardly any witnesses but enemies, and those frequently of the highest, most literate, and powerful classes;

that while so utterly wanting in the common cunning of impostors, that instead of keeping their doings to one or a few places, they performed them any where, upon any subjects, however suddenly or confusedly presented, and, instead of ceasing when they had done a few with success, continued the hazard for many years, in innumerable instances, and while they were widely separated from one another; I say it must be believed, that Christ and his apostles, with all these evidences of extraordinary idiocy or lunacy, were yet so wonderfully ingenious, wary, and wise; so singularly skilled in imposture; so learned in human nature and the world; such a marvellous match for the combined efforts of the wise, and mighty, and diligent, of Judea, and Greece, and Rome; laid their plans so deeply; concerted their movements so skilfully; kept their secrets so closely; carried on the whole complicated plot for many years so consistently, that though ever watched while together and while separated; continually scrutinized by all sorts of witnesses and of enemies; none could ever detect the least flaw in their pretensions; none could discover that the blind did not see; the lame did not walk; the dead did not rise. On the contrary, the people of Bethany were so deceived as actually to believe that they daily saw one of their townsmen, whom they knew to have died, living and eating among them. The people of Jerusalem were so deceived as to believe, that they saw a man whom they knew to have been lame from his birth, daily walking among them perfectly well. The five thousand were fully persuaded that they did all eat and were filled with a few loaves and fishes. The people of Syria were so tricked as really to believe that their multitudes of sick with divers diseases and torments, whom they had brought to Jesus, went home with them perfectly well, without an exception. Yea, the whole Jewish and Heathen world was so imposed upon by these unlettered, simple, despised, persecuted Jews, as tacitly to confess the genuineness of their miracles. Philosophers and rabbies, when they attacked christianity, did not deny it; several of them positively, in their books, acknowledged it; and hundreds of thousands in the age of the apostles, out of the most polished cities and most respectable classes, were so entirely taken captive and spell-bound by the magic scheme of these weak men, that they forsook all and took joyfully the spoiling of their goods, and yielded themselves to fire and sword and wild beasts, rather than not confess and follow Christ.

Such are the wonderful things; such the violations of the laws of nature and of common sense; such the wicked and contradictory miracles which necessarily follow as true, as soon as the miracles of christianity are rejected as false. Now, tell me on which side the charge of credulity lies with the greatest weight. Now, give the reason why our modern unbelievers, instead of meeting the testimony of the gospel miracles in front, are so conscientiously scrupulous never to know any thing about it, and always expend their ingenuity in ridiculing the dignity, or in picking out what they would represent as inconsistencies in the books, of scripture. Now explain the singular phenomenon that the grand high-priest of modern infidelity should have invented the convenient principle which sceptical philosophy had ever before so painfully sighed after, *that no testimony can prove a miracle.* Ah! yes. It was his only hope. The testimony of the christian miracles is perfect. It is so overwhleming, that if there be any difficulty about them, it arises from the very brightness of their evidence itself. It is almost inconceivable that such works, wrought so publicly and frequently, and with such incontrovertible marks of a divine hand, should not have made more converts; that all who beheld them did not yield at once to the great Teacher whom they attested, and espouse his cause. But the explanation is not difficult. The human heart is depraved enough for the most desperate rejection of such a master as the Lord Jesus. Men will go to the greatest lengths of folly and unbelief to gratify their passions, foster their pride, retain their prejudices, and escape the necessity of making sacrifices for conscience's sake. The truth that so many Jews and Heathens, with this blaze of testimony before them, did not submit to the gospel, is not so astonishing as what is seen every day among ourselves: persons believing the New Testament, and that Christ is the only Saviour of sinners—that eternal blessedness awaits those who follow him, and eternal wo those who neglect his salvation—and yet, for all practical ends, as unmoved by these truths as if they were fables—as little engaged in the service of Christ as if they had never heard his name.

But we must conclude. I trust you will henceforth allow me to consider the miracles of the gospel as proved to be genuine. If so, we must consider the credentials of Christ and his apostles as acknowledged. They were therefore what they professed to be, divinely commissioned and inspired teachers. God was with them. What they published as a revelation from God, we are consequently bound to *receive* as a revelation from God. That publication is contained in the New Testament. We have already ascertained the authenticity and credibility of the New Testament as containing it. We cease, therefore, this evening, with the conclusion that the religion published in the New Testament is a revelation from God.

May the greatest and best of all the works of the Lord Jesus be wrought in all of us; even the blessed work of his grace, awakening the sinner from spiritual death; changing, exalting, purifying all the affections of his depraved nature; opening the eyes of his understanding to behold the glory of God; leading him, in repentance and faith, to the cross for pardon and peace; shedding abroad in his heart the spirit of divine love; and causing him to rejoice in the blessed assurance of a crown of glory that fadeth not away!

LECTURE VII.

PROPHECY.

HAVING shown the genuineness of the miracles recorded in the New Testament, in attestation of the divine mission of the Saviour and his apostles; we are now to take up the subject of prophecy. But while proceeding to this additional source of evidence, it is important to be observed, that we do so, not because we consider the reasoning in proof of christianity, as a divine revelation, to which you have already listened, in any sense incomplete. Had our course of lectures been terminated with the last, the argument would have been brought to an incontrovertible issue. Having made out the great point that genuine miracles were wrought by the Saviour and his apostles, in attestation of the divine authority of what they did and taught; we have established, by necessary consequence, the great truth that Jesus Christ was a teacher come from God, and that the New Testament, as an authentic publication of the religion taught by him, is to be received as containing a divine revelation of truth and duty. One line of evidence, therefore—one road leading to the scriptures, as the great central fountain of divine truth, we have travelled over; and it has set us down beside the water of life. Now, if this were the only road, it would be amply sufficient. The loftiest intellect need not be ashamed; the weakest need not fear to walk therein.* But God has not only furnished us with the plainest, but with the most various and abundant evidence.

* A celebrated infidel once acknowledged that even atheism would be refuted by the proof of a single miracle of the gospel. Spinoza declared that

And since the object of these lectures is not only to prove the divine authority of the gospel, but also to give you an idea of the diversified character of the many ways by which the proof may be established; we propose now to return from the position we have reached by the argument of our last lecture, and endeavour to arrive at it again by a route entirely different. We take up the prophecies, recorded in the scriptures, and shall endeavour to produce from them satisfactory and impressive evidence that in the Bible we have divine inspiration, and in Jesus Christ a teacher sent of God.

What is a prophecy, according to the sense of scripture, and as we are now about to consider it? It is a declaration of future events, such as no human wisdom or forecast is sufficient to make; depending on a knowledge of the innumerable contingencies of human affairs, which belongs exclusively to the omniscience of God; so that, from its very nature, prophecy must be divine revelation. "*The prophecy came not in old time by the will of man; but holy men of God spake as they were moved by the Holy Ghost.*"

A prophecy, considered in itself, separately from its fulfilment, is no evidence of revelation. But as soon as fulfilled, it is complete. The hand of God in it, is then attested. The evidence that the person by whom it was uttered was under the influence of the spirit of divine omniscience, is finished. Then prophecy takes the place of miracle, and becomes at once the highest and most unquestionable proof, not only that the individual who declared it was the agent of communicating, in that particular, a divine revelation; but also that a divine sanction is impressed upon that whole

---

he would have broken his atheistic system to pieces, and embraced without repugnance the ordinary faith of Christians, could he have been persuaded of the resurrection of Lazarus from the dead! Was it not a foresight of the arguments that would necessarily result from the proof of this miracle that prevented him from being persuaded of its truth?

system of religion with which his prophecies may be connected.* "Future contingencies, such, for example, as those which relate to the rise and fall of nations and states not yet in existence, or to the minute concerns of individuals not yet born, are secrets which it is evident no man or angel can penetrate, their causes being indeterminate, their relations with other things fluctuating and unknown. It follows, therefore, that the prediction of such contingent events cannot otherwise than proceed from God; and farther, since God cannot without a violation of His perfect holiness and rectitude, visibly aid delusion and wickedness, the inference is equally cogent and necessary, that the accomplishment of predictions delivered by those who profess divine authority amounts to a full proof that they really possess the authority they assume. Other arguments may be evaded; other evidence may not convince. Strange effects (though not miraculous ones) may be produced by other than divine power."† But this can only be evaded by refusing to behold it, and only counterfeited by him who is ingenious enough to borrow omniscience in aid of imposture. "To declare a thing shall come to be, long before it is in being (says Justin Martyr); and then to bring about the accomplishment of that very thing, according to the same declaration; this, or nothing, is the work of God."

There are considerations connected with this particular source of evidence, which render it specially interesting and valuable.

Prophecy furnishes an argument, *the force of which is continually growing*. The argument began, when first a single prophecy was fulfilled. It increased more and more, as predictions and fulfilments multiplied. In the age of the

---

* "All prophecies (says Hume) are real miracles, and as such only, can be admitted as proofs of any revelation."—*Philosophical Essays.*

† Gregory's Letters.

apostles, it was a powerful, as well as favourite weapon in proof of the gospel. But during that period, many new predictions were published, and many ancient ones remained to be accomplished. The argument, consequently, was not yet at its height. It has been growing ever since, as one century after another has rolled out an additional fulfilment, or completed and enlarged those already advanced. We, in the present age, enjoy an expanse, and variety, and completeness of prophetic evidence far exceeding those which the chart of history presented to St. Paul. There is to us, a voice from the silent solitudes where Babylon and Tyre once stood in pride, and reigned in power; from the modern history of the prostrate Egypt; from the wonderful annals and present condition of the Jewish race; from the desolate state of the holy land and adjoining countries; from the rise and present aspect of the mystic Babylon—which the primitive christians had not the privilege of hearing. The force of this argument is yet to grow continually. A few years hence, in all probability, will exhibit it invested with a brightness and glory, compared with which, all present evidence will seem but as morning twilight. The end of the world will be its full maturity. Prophecy having begun with the history of sin, extends to the completion of its tragedy; and not till the blazing of the great conflagration when "the earth and all that is therein shall be burned up," will its every prediction be fulfilled; or the fulness of glory with which it was designed to show the truth of God in the gospel of his Son, be made to appear.

Now it is this continual growing of prophetic evidence that makes it so peculiarly valuable. The argument derived from miracles, though it could never have been more conclusive than it is to us, was certainly more impressive to those who saw the miracles, or who lived in the age in which they were wrought. And it is very difficult for most persons to distinguish between the conclusiveness and the impressiveness of evidence. Because the lapse of centuries, by removing the christian miracles far from us, has diminished the sensible effect they would otherwise have had upon our minds, it is very generally supposed that the same cause has enfeebled the evidence on which their genuineness is maintained. This idea, though unfounded entirely, is too natural, to those who do not think deeply, to be easily removed. But with regard to the evidence arising from prophecy, it cannot exist. Predictions, now in progress of fulfilment, are miracles which centuries can only render more certain and impressive. If there was a peculiar privilege conferred on those who saw, in the miracles of Christ, manifest to sense, the wonderful works of God's *omnipotence;* there is also a similar privilege conferred on us, who, in consequence of the ever increasing fulfilment of prophecy, may see in the scriptures, more brilliantly illuminated than ever, the hand-writing of God's *omniscience.*

There is another peculiarity in much of the evidence from prophecy, which renders it peculiarly valuable. *It is evidence before our eyes, addressed to our senses.* By this we do not mean that the evidence arising from the miracles of Christ and his apostles would be any more conclusive, however much it would be increased in its *impression* on our minds, did we behold the miracles, instead of reading of them in well attested history. We believe, on the contrary, that this description of evidence, as addressed to us, is perfect. But still there is, and perhaps ever will be, a class of minds that, like the disciple Thomas, will require to see before they will believe. Either their indifference or sluggishness prevents them from pursuing a line of argument that would carry them back amidst the testimonies of antiquity; or else their willing scepticism, by ingenious sophistry, would shield them from all the evidence derived from miraculous agency, by the assumption that no testimony can prove a miracle. The utter fallacy of this position, we trust, was satisfactorily shown in a preceding lecture. But here are evidences with which, were it true, it could have no connexion. God, in his infinite wisdom and mercy, has provided for all classes of mind, and all descriptions of infidelity; so that all unbelievers may be without excuse. The argument from prophecy may be rendered brief enough for the most sluggish—tangible enough for the most obstinate opposers of historical testimony. They have only to read in the Bible the predictions with regard to the once proud cities of Babylon and Tyre, or the once powerful empire of Egypt, and then to open their ears to the accounts which almost every wind conveys, or go and see for themselves the obscure remnants of the ruins of those cities, and of that once mighty empire; they have only to read in the books of Moses, what, 3300 years ago, was foretold of the history of the Jewish people; and then to lift up their eyes, and behold the present condition and the notorious peculiarities of that wonderful race; to see that the prophecies of the Bible have been plainly and most particularly fulfilled—fulfilled in a manner which no human sagacity could have foreseen, which no human power could have brought to pass; and consequently that the authors of those prophecies were inspired men, and the religion they taught was the word of God. In these and various other examples, which might be adduced, of the present and visible fulfilment of prophecy, the miracles of the Jewish and Christian dispensations are in fact continued among us. "Men are sometimes disposed to think that if they could see a miracle wrought in their own sight, they would believe the gospel without delay, and obey it unreservedly. They know not their own hearts. '*If they believe not Moses and the prophets, neither would they believe though one rose from the dead.*' But in the whole range of prophecy now fulfilling before their eyes, they have in fact a series of divine interpositions, not precisely of the nature of miracles, in the sense of brief, and instant, and visible sus pensions of the laws of nature, but evidently so in the sense of supernatural interference, in the rise and fall of cities, and nations, and empires; in the arrangement of times and circumstances; in that wonderful display of infinite foreknowledge and infinite power, apparent in the control of the wills of unnumbered free and accountable agents to a certain result."*

In our last lecture we stated that the religion of the Bible is the only one which, on its first introduction, appealed to miracles in evidence of the divine authority of its teachers. We make a similar remark, with still more evident truth, with regard to prophecy. The sublime appeal of men, professing to be commissioned of God, to the events of thousands of years thereafter, as witnesses of their truth; the moral grandeur of that appeal, which, after having deposited in the hands of nations, a prediction of minute transactions, which the innumerable contingencies of a long retinue of centuries are to bring out, stakes its whole cause upon a perfect fulfilment, thus resting itself singly upon the omniscience and omnipotence of God, and separating to an infinite distance all possibility of human support; this is a dignity to which nothing but the inspiration of the scriptures can pretend; a noble daring on which nothing else was ever known to venture. The corruptions of christianity, as existing in the church of Rome, have attempted to prop up their feeble foundations on the credit of miracles, easily refuted indeed, but widely boasted of. But prophecy, even the effrontery of that "man of sin," "whose coming (saith St. Paul) is with all deceivableness of unrighteousness," has never pretended to. Although Mohammed did not profess to support his pretensions by miracles, and the Koran expressly concedes that miraculous power was not given him; yet his followers, hundreds of years after his death, related many miracles as having been performed

* Wilson's Lectures.

under his hand. But that Mohammed, though styled the prophet of God, never declared a *prophecy*, on the fulfilment of which he rested his claims to inspirations, none ever asserted.

The history of pagan nations, indeed, abounds with stories of auguries, and oracles, and detached predictions; but it was with no reference to the establishment of paganism that they were uttered. On the contrary, the fact that paganism was established already gave them all their reverence. But what an immeasurable distance separates all the pretended oracles of paganism, from the dignity of the prophecies in the Bible. The avowed end of the former was to satisfy some trivial curiosity, or aid the designs of some military or political leader. The influence of intimidation or of bribery produced them. They were never spontaneous. The oracles were careful to take advantage of the security of silence, until obliged to speak in answer to a direct appeal. Then they never uttered a syllable without getting time for preparation. Inquiries were rendered as difficult and as expensive as possible, in order, not only to enrich the oracles, but to diminish the occasions of exposure. Every inquiry must be attended with numerous and minute ceremonies on the part of the applicant, as well as the prophet; in order that omissions or mismanagements might afford frequent excuses for the failure of the response, without implicating the inspiration of its author. The god was not always in a humour to be consulted. "*Either he was talking, or he was pursuing, or he was in a journey, or peradventure he was sleeping, and must be awakened.*" This afforded a very convenient opportunity of putting off a difficult case. "Omens were to be taken, and auguries examined, which, if unfavourable in any particular, either precluded the inquiry for the present, or required further lustrations, ceremonies, and sacrifices, to purify the person who had consulted, and render him fit to receive an answer from the gods, or to bring their wayward deities to a temper suitable to the inquiry."* When no means of evasion remained, the answers given were either so ambiguous as to suit any alternative, or so obscure as to require a second oracle to explain them. When the prediction failed, there was no want of subterfuges by which to maintain the credit of the oracle. It was conveniently discovered, either that the gods were averse to the inquirer, or that he had not been in a proper state for the consultation, or that some indispensable ceremony had been omitted or mismanaged. But all these precautions and artifices were not sufficient to prevent those oracles from falling into utter contempt with the more enlightened heathens.† Who could think of comparing such pitiful mockeries of divine omniscience with the dignified, and sublime, and holy prophecies which are spread out so openly and widely in the scriptures? To point out the particulars in which the prophets of the Bible were distinguished above all the oracles of the Pagans, were to suppose a measure of ignorance among my hearers, as to the most conspicuous features of the scriptures, with which I cannot believe them chargeable. But our assertion remains, and deserves to be repeated, that neither in the rise, nor in the progressive advancement of any religion, but that of the Bible, have prophecies been professed or appealed to; in evidence of its truth. This single fact, that all other religions have shrunk from attempting such dangerous ground; that notwithstanding the boldness with which other descriptions of evidence have been counterfeited among Pagans and Mohammedans, and in support of the corruptions of popery, all have kept aloof from this; and yet that this very evidence, so extremely hazardous—so certain of ultimate exposure in case of imposition—is every where professed in the Bible, and forms the golden chain that holds all its parts together,

---

* Nare's View of Prophecy.

† Stillingfleet's Orig. Sacræ, l. 2, c. 8, p. 221.

and by which it spans the world, touching at once its beginning and ending, the first and the last; this, I say, independently of the question of fulfilment, is a strong presumptive argument that the Bible contains something of great importance which no other religion possessed; something to warrant it in venturing where nothing but Divine Omniscience is able to tread; in other words, that its writers *were holy men, who "spake as they were moved by the Holy Ghost."*

The overpowering weight of the evidence from prophecy, and the moral grandeur with which it attests the inspiration of God and the Messiahship of Christ, can only be appreciated by a full view of the immense scheme and the vast extent of the prophecies in the Bible. Their record occupies a large portion of the scriptures. In the third chapter of the Bible, it begins; in the last, it ends. Its spirit arose with the fall of man in Eden; its predictions will only end with his perfect recovery in heaven. During the progress of more than four thousand years, the scheme of prophecy was continually opening; its predictions were continually multiplying; its grand object and purpose were continually becoming more distinct and luminous. The spirit of prophecy first uttered its voice when as yet our fallen parents had not been expelled the garden of innocence. Cain heard in it the warning of his punishment. Enoch continued its declarations. Noah transmitted its strain. Abraham's whole life was guided and encouraged by its inspirations. Isaac was the child, as well as the instrument of prophetic communication. Jacob with his last breath foretold the future history of his twelve sons in their generations, and the reign of a lawgiver in Judah till Shiloh should come. The harp of prophecy remained in silence, while the posterity of Jacob remained in Egyptian bondage; but no sooner was Israel free, than the Spirit again breathed upon its strings, and in the hand of Moses it spake of the great Prophet who was to come to the church, and sketched the Jewish history, with wonderful minuteness, down even to the present and far future times. Between Moses and David, lived Samuel, a prophet of the Lord. Immediately after him, began what may be styled, with emphatic distinction, "*the age of prophecy.*" It opened with the elevated and sublime poetry of David. It advanced with the stern ministry of honoured Elijah. As he went up in the flaming chariot, translated to heaven, his mantle descended upon the "man of God" Elisha. Among the minor prophets who carried on the spirit of this age of seers, were Hosea, Amos, and Micah. Then followed Isaiah, as full of the spirit of the gospel, as of the spirit of prophecy; and Jeremiah, overflowing as well with tender lamentation for the affliction of Israel, as with the sublimest predictions of the days when the Lord would heal and comfort them; then Ezekiel, with as many visions of the future, as the eyes in his mysterious wheels, prophecying "in the midst of the valley which was filled with bones." Ezekiel connected in his person the age of prophecy with that of the captivity of Judah. Daniel succeeded him, and beside the prophetic interpretation of the hand-writing on the wall, foretold the succession of the four powerful monarchies, and the feeble rising and ultimate dominion of the fifth, and determined the time when the daily sacrifice would cease, and *Messiah be cut off—not for himself.* Haggai and Zechariah continued the prophetic strain, after the return of Judah from captivity. Malachi terminated the line of Old Testament prophets and the canon of Old Testament scriptures, with the sublime annunciation of one who was to come, in the spirit and power of Elijah, to prepare the way of the Lord. Again the harp of prophecy was silent as during the bondage of Egypt, until "that Prophet" like unto, but infinitely greater than, Moses arose. JESUS, the great object of prophecy from the beginning—himself "*the spirit of prophecy;*" —foretold, besides his own death and resurrection, the calamities that should befall Jerusalem, as well as the utter destruction of the Jewish state. Paul followed his Master's steps, as well in the walks of prophecy, as of martyrdom, forewarning the church of "that man of sin, the son of perdition, whose coming is after the working of Satan, with all power, and signs, and lying wonders."* John closed the succession of prophecy, and the canon of scripture together, with predictions, the awful sublimity of which no pen can rival, and the wonderful expanse of which, nothing but the events of all future time can measure.

Thus have we a train of holy men, reaching from the earliest age of mankind, through a period of more than four thousand years, and extending their prediction to the world's end. I see in them the utmost variety—as well as to condition and character, as to the ages in which they lived—*princes, patriarchs, priests, legislators, shepherds, fishermen.* Exceedingly various in natural qualifications, in education, habits, and employments; they wrote in various styles, but each as he was moved by the Holy Ghost. Now when, in connexion with this variety in the prophets themselves, I consider the vast variety and extent of the subjects on which their predictions are employed, embracing not only the history of the Jews for many centuries, but that also of the minor nations immediately around, with that of the more remote empires of Egypt, and Assyria, and Chaldea, and Persia, and Macedon, and Rome; when I consider that in this immense vastness of extent, so great is their minuteness of detail, that sundry particular events and features in their destruction, not only of the city of Jerusalem, but also of Nineveh, and Babylon, and Tyre, are predicted with the most graphic and striking precision; when, in the midst of such wonderful diversity of authors, ages, circumstances, and of subjects, from the downfall of an empire, to the

* 2 Thess. ii. 3—9.

tumbling of a wall, I perceive not the smallest inconsistency or collision, but, on the contrary, the utmost harmony, as well of execution as of purpose and of spirit—the whole array of prophecy, from first to last, bearing down and concentrating upon one grand object—*the testimony of Jesus—the rise, progress, and eternal accomplishment of his plan of redeeming love;* in a word, when I behold a scheme so vast, as to embrace all time, and yet so minute that it can detail the events of an hour; so general that, in a few lines, it predicts the history of the four mightiest empires, and yet so particular that chapters are devoted to the history of one individual; so diversified in its materials, as to be made up of contributions from men of all ages and minds, during a period of four thousand years; and yet so identical that one spirit and one grand, harmonious purpose animate the whole; when I compare all this, arrayed, as it is, in the richest poetry and loftiest eloquence that eye of man ever read, with whatever else in the world ever pretended to the praise of prophecy; I behold a grandeur of conception —a sublimity of design—an all-controlling power of execution—a unity and self-depending supremacy of mind which bespeak the omniscience and omnipotence of Him who "*was, and is, and is to come, the Almighty.*" I say nothing yet of the fulfilment of any portion of this stupendous plan; I only say, look at the plan itself in all its comprehensiveness and minuteness, and tell me if it be not utterly at variance with all human experience, and in itself perfectly incredible, that imposture should have conceived such a scheme, or should ever have dared to commit its cause to a venture that could only succeed by a continuance of miraculous fortune through all ages of the world. Consider the plan itself, the various minds that carried on the succession of its several predictions, forming a line of holy men from the earliest periods of antediluvian history, down to the last of the apostles of Christ; see how they all agree in spirit and purpose, while yet so different in character and circumstances; see how they all unite in testifying of Christ, so that, as the last of them said, "*the testimony of Jesus is the Spirit of prophecy*;" then tell me how imposture can be supposed to have wrought, unexposed, for so many thousands of years; how it could have chosen its agents out of forty centuries—out of circumstances so disadvantageous, and bid them embrace such an immense range of subjects for their predictions, and yet without any inconsistency, or want of harmony, or any thing incompatible with the idea of one all-pervading mind having regulated the whole. I do not now say that so much as one prophecy has been fulfilled. I only say, and I challenge all denial, that not a single prediction in the whole succession can be shown to have failed; or to have been contradicted by the times or events to which it referred. I only assert that, while many of the prophecies remain unfulfilled, because the times they relate to have not arrived; a very great number must have either been fulfilled already, or have utterly failed; and yet no unbeliever could ever put his hand on that portion of history which contradicted the truth of any. I ask you to remember this important and undeniable fact, and then say whether it is not most impressive evidence that another mind than that of man was the author of the prophecies of the Bible; whether it can be supposed possible in the nature of things that human ingenuity could have contrived a volume of predictions—reaching so far—extending so widely—telling so much—assuming such particularity, without having been contradicted by a single event in the history of nearly six thousand years.

We now enter upon the question of fulfilment. I undertake to show that the history of the world has wonderfully responded to the prophecies of the Bible, and echoed back to the holy men who uttered them, a complete assurance that they "spake as they were moved by the Holy Ghost. But where shall I begin? It were easier to write a volume on this one subject, than to compress the matter within our necessary limits, so as to do it any tolerable justice. Selecting some insulated portions of the train of prophecy, we must content ourselves with exhibiting their accomplishment as specimens of the whole. To this, the remainder of the present lecture, and the whole of the next, will be devoted.

As an example of minute prediction and singular fulfilment, compare Jeremiah, xxxiv. 2 and 3, with Ezekiel, xii. 13. In the former scripture, it was foretold by one prophet, that Zedekiah, the king of Judah, should be delivered into the hand of the king of Babylon, and behold his eyes, and speak with him mouth to mouth, and *go to Babylon.* In the latter, it was foretold by another prophet, that Zedekiah *should not see Babylon,* though he should die there. But is there not a contradiction here? How could Zedekiah be taken to Babylon, and behold her king, and die there, and yet never see the city? The history of the kings of Judah, written without any design of pointing out the fulfilment of prophecy, fully explains the difficulty. Zedekiah was delivered into the hands of the king of Babylon, and beheld his eyes, and spake with him mouth to mouth; not, however, at Babylon, but at Riblah. *There his eyes were put out* by command of his captor. In this state, he went to Babylon, and died there, *having never seen the city of his captivity.*

Another example of wonderful minuteness is found in the prophecies of the fall and destruction of Babylon. We can notice only a small part of them. "It shall never be inhabited, neither shall it be dwelt in, (said the prophet,) from generation to generation. Neither shall the Arabian pitch tent there, neither shall the shepherds make their fold there. But wild beasts of the desert shall lie there, and the houses shall be full of doleful creatures; and owls shall dwell there, and satyrs shal' dance there, and the wild beasts of the desert shall cry in their desolate houses, and dragons in their pleasant palaces."* "I will also make it a possession for the bittern, and pools of water: and I will sweep it with the besom of destruction, saith the Lord of hosts." These words were uttered when Babylon was "the glory of kingdoms, the beauty of the Chaldees' excellency," about 160 years before she was brought down. "How hath the golden city ceased!" "Her pomp is brought down to the grave." Sixteen centuries have passed since her foundations were inhabited by a human being. Deterred by superstitious fears of evil spirits, which are said to haunt the place where she stood, and by the more rational dread of reptiles and wild beasts, the wandering Arab never pitches his tent there. In a plain once famous for the richness of its pasture, the shepherds make no fold. Reptiles, bats, and "doleful creatures"—jackals, hyenas, and lions—inhabit the holes, and caverns, and marshes, of the desolate city. In the fourth century, Babylon was a hunting ground for the Persian monarchs. By the annual overflowing of the Euphrates, pools of stagnant water are left in the hollow places of the ancient site, by which morasses have been formed, so that Babylon has indeed become a *possession for the bittern, and pools of water.* It has been *swept with the besom of destruction.* The fertile plain of Shinar, renowned for its ancient abundance, is an uninterrupted desert, strewed with the confused ruins of Grecian, Roman, and Arabian towns. A modern traveller, in his "*search after the walls of Babylon,*" describes "a mass of solid wall, about thirty feet in length, by twelve or fifteen in thickness," as the only part of them that can now be discovered.† Thus, according to the words of the prophet, is she *cast up as heaps, destroyed utterly; nothing of her is left.*‡

Tyre was once the emporium of the world, "the theatre

* Is. xiii. 20 21, 22. † Buckingham's Travels ‡ Jer. l. 26.

of an immense commerce and navigation, the nursery of arts and science, and the city of perhaps the most industrious and active people ever known."* *Situate at the entry of the sea, she was a merchant of the people for many isles. All nations were her merchants in all sorts of things. The ships of Tarshish did sing of her in the market; and she was replenished and made very glorious in the midst of the seas.*"† It was of this mistress of princes, that Ezekiel prophesied in the name of the Lord: "I will scrape her dust from her, and make her *like the top of a rock. It shall be a place for the spreading of nets in the midst of the sea.*"‡ How singularly particular! She was not only to be utterly destroyed, but the use that would be made of her site, and the kind of men who would inhabit it were pointed out more than a thousand years before her complete destruction. How precise the fulfilment! Shaw, in his book of travels, describes the port of Tyre as so choked up, that the boats *of the fishermen, who now and then come to the place, and dry their nets upon its rocks and ruins*, can hardly enter.§ Bruce describes the site of Tyre as "a rock whereon fishers dry their nets." But the testimony of the infidel, Volney, is more valuable. "The whole village of Tyre contains only fifty or sixty poor families, who live obscurely on the produce of their little ground and a *trifling fishery*."‖

Egypt, the most ancient, was also the most powerful and wealthy of kingdoms. But a prophecy went forth against her while yet she was in all her pomp and pride, that *the pride of her power should come down; that her land and all that was therein should be made waste by the hand of strangers; that there should be no more a prince of the land of Egypt, and the sceptre of Egypt should depart away.*¶

---

* Volney's Travels. † Ezek. xxvii. ‡ Ib. xxvi. 4, 5.
§ Shaw's Travels, ii. p. 31. ‖ Travels, ii. p. 212.
¶ Ezek. xxx. 6, 12, 13.—Zech. x. 11.

How universally this once fertile country, the granary of the world, has been wasted, and her innumerable cities have been buried; how remarkably the hand of strangers has done it, and how deplorably the remnant of this populous nation is now, and has been for many centuries, under slavery, and ignorance, and poverty, and rapine, and every crime, I need not describe. The most remarkable portion of the prophecy is that which declares that there shall be "no more a prince of the land of Egypt." From the conquest of the Persians, about 350 years before Christ, to the present day, the sceptre of Egypt has been broken; she has been governed by strangers; every effort to raise an Egyptian to the throne has been defeated. Out of the mouth of Volney, the Lord has caused to be declared the fulfilment of His word. Of Egypt, that most unwilling agent in establishing the truth of scripture writes: "Deprived, twenty-three centuries ago, of her natural proprietors, she has seen her fertile fields successively a prey to the Persians, the Macedonians, the Romans, the Greeks, the Arabs, the Georgians, and at length the race of Tartars, distinguished by the name of Ottoman Turks. The Mamalukes, purchased as slaves and introduced as soldiers, soon usurped the power, and elected a leader. If their first establishment was a singular event, their continuance is not less extraordinary. They are replaced by slaves brought from their original country. The system of oppression is methodical. Every thing the traveller sees or hears reminds him he is in the country of slavery and tyranny."*

Among the most interesting fulfilments of prophecy, are those discovered in the present condition of the country and cities of Judea. For a very striking view of them, the reader is referred to Keith on Prophecy, a valuable work lately republished in this country. But there is one predic-

* Travels, ii. p. 74, 103, 110, 198.

tion in this department which I cannot pass over. After describing the divine judgments upon the land, the prophet adds: "The generation to come of your children, *and the stranger that shall come from a far land*, shall say, when they see the plagues of that land, and the sickness which the Lord hath laid upon it: '*Wherefore hath the Lord done thus unto this land? What meaneth the heat of this great anger?*'"* About three thousand years after these words were written, a famous traveller, a scoffer at the scriptures, walks through this smitten country. He is a *stranger from a far land.* Deeply impressed with the aspect of all things around him, and in all probability entirely ignorant of the prophecy he is about to fulfil, he exclaims: "Good God! from whence proceed such melancholy revolutions? For what cause is the fortune of these countries *so strikingly changed?* Why are so many cities destroyed? Why is not that ancient population reproduced and perpetuated." "I wandered over the country. I traversed the provinces. I enumerated the kingdoms of Damascus and Idumea, of Jerusalem and Samaria. This Syria, said I to myself, now almost depopulated, then contained a hundred flourishing cities, and abounded with towns, villages, and hamlets. What are become of so many productions of the hands of man?"† &c.

No prophecies deserve more of the attention of the student of scripture than those concerning the Jews, which are scattered from one end of the Bible to the other. Their wonderful accomplishment is in every one's view. We can only glance at some of the many particulars which they embrace. Three thousand two hundred years ago, it was written by Moses: "The Lord shall scatter thee among all people, from the one end of the earth even unto the other; and among these nations shalt thou find no ease, neither shall the sole of thy foot have rest; and thou shalt become an

* Deut. xxix. 22, 24. † Volney's Ruins, c. ii. p. 8.

astonishment, a proverb, and a by-word among all the nations whither the Lord shall lead thee; and thou shalt be only oppressed and crushed alway; and the Lord will make thy plagues wonderful, and the plague of thy seed, even great plagues and of long continuance."* But notwithstanding all this, the Jews were not to be destroyed without recovery. "Yet for all that (saith the prophet), when they be in the land of their enemies, I will not cast them away, neither will I abhor them to destroy them utterly."† "I will make a full end of all the nations whither I have driven thee, but I will not make a full end of thee."‡ "For the children of Israel shall abide many days without a king, and without a prince, and without a sacrifice, and without an image, and without an ephod, and without teraphim: afterwards shall the children of Israel return, and seek the Lord their God, and David their king; and shall fear the Lord and his goodness in the latter days."§

There is nothing in the history of nations so unaccountable, on human principles, as the destruction and the preservation of the Jews. "Scattered among all nations;" where are they not? Citizens of the world, and yet citizens of no country in the world; in what habitable part of the world is not the Jew familiarly known? He has wandered every where, and is still every where a wanderer. One characteristic of this wonderful race is written over all their history, from their dispersion to the present time. Among the nations, *they have found no ease, nor rest to the soles of their feet.* Banished from city to city, and from country to country; always insecure in their dwelling places, and liable to be suddenly driven away whenever the bigotry, or avarice, or cruelty of rulers demanded a sacrifice; a late decree of the Russian Empire has proclaimed to the world that

---

* Deut. xxviii. † Lev. xxvi. 44. ‡ Jer. xlvi. 27, 28.
§ Hosea, iii. 4, 5.

their banishments have not yet ceased. Never certain of permission to remain, it is the notorious peculiarity of this people, as a body, that they live in habitual readiness to remove. In this condition of universal affliction, how singular it is that among all people the Jew is "*an astonishment, a proverb, a by-word.*" Such is not the case with any other people. Among Christians, Heathens, and Mohammedans, from England to China, and thence to America, the cunning, the avarice, the riches of the Jew are proverbial. And how wonderful have been their plagues! The heart sickens at the history of their persecutions, and massacres, and im prisonments, and slavery. All nations have united to oppress them. All means have been employed to exterminate them. Robbed of property; bereaved of children; buried in the dungeons of the inquisition, or burned at the stake of deplorable bigotry; no people ever suffered the hundredth part of their calamities, and still they live! It was prophecied that, as a nation, they should be restored; consequently they were not only to be kept alive, but unmingled with the nations, every where a distinct race, and capable of being selected and gathered out of all the world, when the time for their restoration should arrive. The fulfilment of this, forms the most astonishing part of the whole prophecy. For nearly eighteen hundred years, they have been scattered and mixed up among all people; they have had no temple, no sacrifice, no prince, no genealogies, no certain dwelling places. Forbidden to be governed by their own laws; to choose their own magistrates; to maintain any common policy; every ordinary bond of national union and preservation has been wanting; whatever influences of local attachment, or of language, or manners, or government, have been found necessary to the preservation of other nations, have been denied to them; all the influences of internal depression and outward violence which have ever destroyed and blotted out the nations of the earth, have been at work with unprecedented strength, for nearly eighteen centuries, upon the nation of Israel; and still the Jews are a people—a distinct people—a numerous people, unassimilated with any nation, though mixed up with all nations. Their peculiarites are undiminished. Their national identity is unbroken. Though scattered upon all winds, they are perfectly capable of being again gathered into one mass. Though divided into the smallest particles by numerous solvents, they have resisted all affinities, and may be traced, unchanged, in the most confused mixtures of human beings. The laws of nature have been suspended in their case. It is not merely that a stream has held on its way through the waters of a lake, without losing the colour and characteristic marks of its own current; but that a mighty river, having plunged from a mountain height into the depth of the ocean, and been separated into its component drops, and thus scattered to the ends of the world, and blown about by all winds, during almost eighteen centuries, is still capable of being disunited from the waters of the ocean; its minutest drops, having never been assimilated to any other, are still distinct, unchanged, and ready to be gathered, waiting the voice that shall call again the outcasts of Israel and the dispersed of Judah. Mean while, where are the nations among whom the Jews were scattered? Has not the Lord, according to his word, *made a full end of them?** While Israel has stood unconsumed in the fiery furnace, where are the nations that kindled its flames? Where the Assyrians and the Chaldeans? Their name is almost forgotten. Their existence is known only to history. Where is the empire of the Egyptians? The Macedonians destroyed it, and a descendant of its ancient race cannot be distinguished among the strangers that have ever since possessed its territory. Where are they of Macedon? The Roman sword subdued their kingdom, and their posterity

* Jer. xlvi. 28.

are mingled inseparably among the confused population of Greece and Turkey. Where is the nation of ancient Rome, the last conquerors of the Jews, and the proud destroyers of Jerusalem? The Goths rolled their flood over its pride. Another nation inhabits the ancient city. Even the language of her former people is dead. The Goths! where are they? The Jews! where are they not? They witnessed the glory of Egypt, and of Babylon, and of Nineveh; they were in mature age at the birth of Macedon and of Rome; mighty kingdoms have risen and perished since they began to be scattered and enslaved; and now they traverse the ruins of all, the same people as when they left Judea, preserving in themselves a monument of the days of Moses and the Pharaohs, as unchanged as the pyramids of Memphis, which they are reputed to have built. You may call upon the ends of the earth, and will call in vain for one living representative of those powerful nations of antiquity, by whom the people of Israel were successively oppressed; but should the voice which is hereafter to gather that people out of all lands, be now heard from Mount Zion, calling for the children of Abraham, no less than four millions would instantly answer to the name, each bearing in himself unquestionable proofs of that noble lineage.

What is this but miracle? Connected with the prophecy which it fulfils, it is double miracle. Whether testimony can ever establish the credibility of a miracle, is of no importance here. This one is obvious to every man's senses. All nations are its eye-witnesses.

Among the most striking and comprehensive, and yet particular prophecies, are those of Daniel. The history of the four great empires of Chaldea, Persia, Macedon, and Rome, is embraced in his predictions. We mention these, not that we intend to trace out their fulfilment, but merely, in passing, to insert a remarkable testimony concerning them from one of the most learned expositors of the prophetic scriptures, and another from the most learned and acute of the ancient opposers of christianity. Bishop Newton, speaking of that portion of Daniel's prophecies which relates to the kingdoms of Egypt and Syria, from the death of Alexander the Great to the time of Antiochus Epiphanes, a period of 148 years, remarks: "There is not so complete and regular a series of their kings—there is not so concise and comprehensive an account of their affairs—to be found in any author of those times. The prophecy is really more perfect than any history. No one historian hath related so many circumstances, and in such exact order of time, as the prophet hath foretold them; so that it was necessary to have recourse to several authors, Greek and Roman, Jewish and Christian, and to collect here something from one, and to collect there something from another, for the better explaining and illustrating the great variety of particulars contained in this prophecy."* Thus far, the testimony of a learned friend of Christianity. The corresponding testimony of a learned enemy, we have in the celebrated Porphyry, of the third century, to whom the exact correspondence between the predictions and the events was so convincing, that he could not pretend to deny it. He rather laboured to confirm it; and from the very exactness of the fulfilment, forged his only weapon of defence, in the assertion that the prophecy could not have been written by Daniel, but must have been written by some one in Judea, in the time of Antiochus Epiphanes.† Others after him have asserted the same thing, not only without any proof, but contrary to all the proofs which can be had in cases of this nature. They preferred the denial of the plainest historical evidence of the time when the prophecy was written, to the acknowledgment that its author must have written "*by inspiration of God.*" Paine, however, whose willing-

* Newton on Prophecy, ii. 149. † Lardner, iv. 211.

ness to escape the argument from prophecy cannot be questioned, and who was probably ignorant of what Porphyry had acknowledged as to the correspondence between the words of this prophet and those of subsequent history, confessed the authenticity of the book of Daniel. Here, then, we have one famous infidel acknowledging that the prophecy was written at the time and by the man to whom it is ascribed; and another, verifying the exactness of its fulfilment in the history of a subsequent age. Paine denied the fulfilment; Porphyry, the authenticity. Porphyry acknowledged the fulfilment; Paine, the authenticity. "*He taketh the wise in their own craftiness.*"

I now call your attention to the prophecies concerning our Lord Jesus Christ. They are scattered every where throughout the prophetic portions of the Bible. "To him bear *all* the prophets witness." None of them could lay down the pen of inspiration till they had written something, directly or indirectly, of Jesus.

1. The first class of these predictions consists of those which relate *to the time and circumstances of the advent of Christ.* Daniel, A. C. 556, determined the year of his coming, when 490 years should be accomplished from the going forth of the command to rebuild Jerusalem. Jacob, more than a thousand years before Daniel, had said it would be when the sceptre was departing from Judah, and a lawgiver from between his feet.* Haggai and Isaiah declared that it would be before the destruction of Jerusalem, and during the existence of the second temple.† Micah designated Bethlehem Ephratah as his birth-place.‡ Many prophecies predicted that he should come, not only of the stock of Judah, but of the stem of Jesse.§ Isaiah and Malachi spake of the messenger who should go before him, in the spirit and power of Elijah, to prepare his way.‖

* Gen. xlix. 10. † Is. xl. 9—xli. 27.—Hag. ii. 6—8. ‡ Mic. v. 2.
§ Is. xi. 1. ‖ Is. xl. 3.—Mal. iii. 1—iv. 5.

2. The next class of predictions, concerning our Lord, contains those which speak of his *life, sufferings, death, resurrection, and the increase of his kingdom.* These are so numerous and particular, and so familiar to most readers of the Bible, that we shall content ourselves with a rapid summary. They predicted that Christ, or Messiah, would be born of a virgin;* that he should enter Jerusalem on the foal of an ass;† that in his manner of teaching he should be characterized by special gentleness and compassion;‡ that he would be distinguished as wise "to speak a word in season to him that is weary;"§ that he should blind the eyes of the learned and proud,‖ and preach good tidings to the poor and despised; that under his ministry the lame should be made to walk, the deaf to hear, the blind to see, the dumb to speak, the captive to be loosed, and the dead raised up;¶ that he should teach the perfect way, and be the instructer of the Gentiles;** that he should be a sacrifice for sin, be rejected of the Jews, who themselves should be rejected of God;†† "that the kings of the earth and all people should worship him;‡‡ but that the people who rejected him should continue a distinct people, and yet be scattered over all nations, and wander about without princes, without sacrifices, without an altar, without prophets, looking for deliverance and not finding it, till a very distant period.§§

The correspondence between the several particulars related of the death of Christ, and the predictions scattered through the Bible, is extremely striking. The evangelists, in this respect are but echoes of the prophets. I can give but a rapid sketch. These predictions include the treachery and awful end of Judas;‖‖ the precise sum of money for which

---

* Is. vii. 14. † Zech. ix. 9. ‡ Is. xlii. 1, 2, 3. § Is. l. 4.
‖ Is. v. 15. ¶ Is. xxxv. 5, 6—ix. 2. ** Is. xlii. 6.
†† Is. liii.—viii. 14, 15. ‡‡ Is. lx. 10, 11, 12, &c.—liii. 12.
§§ Jer. xxxi. 36.—Hos. iii. 4, 5. ‖‖ Ps. xli. 9—lv. 12, 13 14, 15

he betrayed his Master; and the use to which it was put.* They specify not only the sufferings of Christ, but of what they should consist. That his back should be given to the smiters, his face to shame and spitting;† that he should be put to death by a mode which would cause his hands and his feet to be pierced; that he should be wounded, bruised, and scourged;‡ that, in his death, he should be numbered with transgressors,§ and in his sufferings, have gall and vinegar given him to drink;‖ that his persecutors should laugh him to scorn, and shake their heads, reviling him, and saying: "He trusted in the Lord that he would deliver him; let him deliver him."¶ Although it was the custom to break the bones of those who were crucified, and although the bones of the thieves crucified with him, were broken, yet it was predicted that "not a bone of him should be broken;"** and moreover, that his garments should be divided, and lots cast for his vesture;†† that while he should "make his grave with the wicked," as he did in being buried like the wicked companions of his death, under the general leave for taking down their bodies from the cross, he should at the same time make his grave "with the rich," as was done when they buried him in the sepulchre of Joseph of Arimathea.‡‡ I might enumerate many more details of prophecy centering upon the life and death of Christ. What have been mentioned are abundantly sufficient for our present argument. I have only recited a concise list of the predictions. I cannot suppose any of you so unacquainted with the history of Christ as not to be able, familiarly, to refer to all those passages in his life and death by which they were minutely and wonder-

* Zech. xi. 12, 13. † Is. l. 6. ‡ Zech. xii. 10.—Ps. xxii. 16.
§ Is. liii. 4, 5, 8, and 12. ‖ Ps. lxix. 21. ¶ Ps. xxii. 7, 8.
** Numb. ix. 12.—Ex. xii. 46.—Ps. xxxiv. 20. †† Ps. xxii. 18.
‡‡ Is. liii. 9.—The translation of this verse in Lowth's Isaiah is much more to the point than that of the common text: "And his grave was *appointed* with the wicked; but with the rich man was his tomb."

fully fulfilled. Now, consider that no question is raised by any one, whether these predictions were made and published several centuries before the birth of Christ. The enemies of Christ, his crucifiers, have been the librarians of these writings.* The Jews preserved them for us, with sacred care, for many hundreds of years. They were translated. from Hebrew into Greek, at least two hundred years before Christ. The Jews then understood them to refer to the Messiah, as we do now; and it was on account of some of them that a general expectation of the speedy coming of Messiah, prevailed so widely in Judea at the time of the public appearance of Christ.

That all these particulars were most remarkably combined in the person, character, works, sufferings, and burial of the Lord Jesus, I need not say. If the predictions did not ori ginally refer to him, and only happened to be accomplished in him, it would be reasonable to suppose that out of the innumerable millions of men that have lived since they were published, some other individual, if not hundreds, would have appeared, exhibiting the same correspondence. Where is the record of such an event? Can the person be mentioned, in whom there was even an approximation to the fulfilment exhibited in the history of Jesus? I need not say, that no one ever pretended to be able to find such a person. These prophecies describe a combination of gentleness with power; merit with ignominy; benevolence with contempt; they bring together details of ancestry, of family, of

* Augustine, in the fourth century, spoke very often of the great advantage which Christians had in their arguments for the truth of the gospel, from the subsistence and dispersion of the Jewish people, who every where bear testimony to the antiquity and genuineness of the books of the Old Testament; so that none could say they were afterwards forged by Christians. He therefore calls the Jews the librarians of the Christians; he compares them to servants that carry books for the use of children of noble families; or that carry a chest or bag of evidence for a disputant.—*Lardner*, ii. 598

birth, of time, of works, of sufferings, of death, which it were ridiculous to pretend have been united in any individual whose name is in the annals of man, except the *Son of man, Christ Jesus.*

But it may be said, that among these predictions, there are some which human design might have brought to pass. It may be suggested, that a band of men undertaking to pro mote an imposture, and having these predictions before them, might have selected for their leader one who had been born at Bethlehem, of the lineage of David, and might have ordered his appearance at the precise time of the prophecy. Let this be supposed, and let us overlook the fact that no possible motive can be assigned that could induce a band of impostors to desire the setting up of such a cause as that of Christ; still, how would imposture contrive to unite in its leader the fulfilment of prophecies which, on one hand, foretold him as eminent for wisdom and benevolence; and on the other, for shame and suffering? How, on this supposition, could all those predictions have been accomplished which relate to the agonies of the cross? Would a deceiver seek crucifixion for the sake of fulfilling prophecy? How was it managed that one should betray him; and afterwards, out of remorse, hang himself? How was it contrived that the enemies of Christ should measure the price of his blood at the exact sum predicted; and then, that the mercenary traitor should return it to them again, and they should use it in purchase of the predicted potter's field? How did imposture so artfully combine in its cause all the persecutors of Christ, that, without any design to advance its interests, they should have chosen precisely that mode of execution; those expressions of contempt; those instruments of torture; those companions of his sufferings; that mixture for his drink; that severity to his body, while he was alive, and that forbearance to it after he was dead, which, if they had been anxious to prove him the true Messiah, foretold in the scriptures, would have composed the most effectual means they could possibly employ? Most evidently, the bitter adversaries of christianity—not its friends—brought out the demonstration that Jesus was he to whom gave all the prophets witness.

And now is there any possible escape from the absolute necessity of acknowledging that the Spirit of God was in the writers of the Bible, and that this Spirit has testified of Jesus? Will any one pretend that in the idea of *chance* there is any explanation of the coincidences which have been mentioned? It will not be useless to spend a moment on this matter of chance. It is conceivable that a prediction, uttered at a venture, confining its terms to but one event, and expressing that in a general way, may happen to result so plausibly as to seem like a genuine prophecy. But only let it descend to the minutiæ of time, place, and incidents, and it is evident that the possibility of its success, by a fortuitous concurrence of events, will become extremely desperate. Hence the oracles of heathen antiquity always took good care to confine their predictions to one or two particulars, and to express them in the most general and ambiguous terms. Hence, in the whole range of history, except the prophecies of the scriptures, there is not a single instance of a prediction, expressed in unequivocal language, and descending to any minuteness, which bears the slightest claim to the praise of fulfilment. But to set this in a more impressive light, I will quote a few sentences from one of the most scientific laymen of the present day. "Suppose (says Olinthus Gregory) that instead of the spirit of prophecy, breathing more or less in every book of scripture, predicting events relative to a great variety of general topics, and delivering besides almost innumerable characteristics of the Messiah, all meeting in the person of Jesus; there had been only *ten* men in ancient times who pretended to be prophets, each of whom exhibited only *five* independent criteria as to place, government, concomitant events, doctrine taught, effects of doctrine, character, sufferings, or death; the meeting of all which in one person should prove the reality of their calling as prophets, and of his mission in the character they have assigned him: suppose, moreover, that all events were left to *chance* merely, and we were to compute, from the principles employed by mathematicians in the investigation of such subjects, the probability of these *fifty* independent circumstances happening *at all*. Assume that there is, according to the technical phrase, an *equal chance* for the happening or the failure of any one of the specified particulars; then the probability against the occurrence of all the particulars in *any* way, is, that of the fiftieth power of two to unity; that is, the probability is greater than *eleven hundred and twenty-five millions of millions* to one, that all these circumstances do not turn up even at distinct periods."* But this calculation, you must observe, specifies no particular period for these things to take place; but allows, from the time of uttering the predictions, to the end of the world, for all the fifty particulars to occur. But if a time be fixed, at or near which they must happen, the immense improbability that they will take place exceeds all the power of numbers to express. This, moreover, is on the supposition of every thing being under the disposal of that fiction of unbelief, a *blind chance*. How infinite does the improbability appear, when it is remembered that "all events are under the control of a Being of matchless wisdom, power, and goodness, who hates fraud and deception; who must especially hate it when attempted under his name and authority." This is enough, one would think, to silence for ever all pleas of *chance*, as furnishing an unbeliever the least opportunity of escape from the evidence of prophecy. What then is the conclusion to which, by the considerations presented in this lecture, we are authorized to come?

---

* Gregory's Letters.

First: That in the Bible, there is a great variety of prophecy relative to the Messiah, which has been so remarkably fulfilled in Jesus Christ, and so entirely unfulfilled in any other individual of whom we have any history, that the correspondence necessarily proves the predictions to have been given by inspiration of God, and Jesus Christ to be the person to whom that inspiration, in the uttering of those predictions, referred.

Secondly: That the Bible, in thus containing genuine prophecies scattered through its several books, contains a *revelation from God*, and exhibits numerous and wide-spread impressions of the seal of divine authority.

Lastly: That Jesus Christ, being thus pointed out and honoured by the Spirit of God, breathing on the lips of holy men, who in various centuries before his coming concurred in rendering him their testimony, as they were moved by the Holy Ghost, was and is to come, no other than what he said—the Son of God—the Saviour of sinners—"King of kings and Lord of lords."

"Behold (saith He) I come quickly: blessed is he that keepeth the sayings of the prophecy of this book." "He that confesseth me before men, him will I also confess before my Father who is in heaven." But "how shall we escape if we neglect so great salvation?"

LECTURE VIII.

PROPHECY.

Our blessed Lord was a prophet, as well as the grand subject of prophecy. Not only did he possess omnipotence to call up the dead from the sepulchre, but omniscience also to bring forth from the darkness of the future what to uninspired man lies as secret as the mysteries of death. By prophecy, as well as miracles, he established the divinity of his mission. In the latter, his appeal was to the senses of eye-witnesses: "*The works that I do, they bear witness of me.*" In the former, it was to the testimony of subsequent history: "*Now I tell you before it come to pass, that when it is come to pass, ye may believe that I am he.*" He predicted not only his own sufferings, and death, and resurrection, but the manner and circumstances attending them; the treachery of Judas; the denial of Peter; the particulars of his ignominious treatment in the council of the Jews, and under the hands of Pilate and his soldiers. He foretold the rapid spread of the gospel; the persecutions of his disciples; the precise manner of Peter's martyrdom; the continuance of John till after the destruction of Jerusalem; the rejection of the Jews, and the bringing of the Gentiles into the church of God.

But none of our Saviour's prophecies are more impressive than those concerning the destruction of Jerusalem, contained in the Gospels of Mark and Luke; but most at large in the twenty-fourth chapter of Matthew. These we select as the subject of our consideration at present; believing we shall be enabled to show, by most impressive evidence, that Jesus did indeed possess the spirit of prophecy, and consequently was divinely commissioned in setting up the faith of the gospel.

There is but one preliminary question to be answered, at the commencement of this investigation: *Is it well ascertained that these prophecies were published before the destruction of Jerusalem?*

This has been already settled, in our lecture on the subject of authenticity; in which it was shown that the several books of the New Testament were written in the age to which they are referred, and by the men whose names they bear. It will be sufficient to state in this place, that of the three evangelists who have related these prophecies, Matthew and Mark are well ascertained to have died, and there is good reason to suppose that Luke also was dead, before the destruction of Jerusalem.

The Gospel of Matthew, which contains the most complete account of the predictions in question, is commonly acknowledged to have been written first. Its date is about the eighth year after the death of Christ. The destruction of Jerusalem being in the seventieth year of the christian era, the prophecies in relation to it were published by Matthew about thirty years, and were declared by our Saviour about thirty-seven years, before their fulfilment. Several years elapsed, also, between the publication of the same prophecies by Mark and Luke, and the events to which they relate. John, the only one of the four evangelists that lived and wrote subsequently to the ruin of the holy city, is the only one that omits an account of the predictions concerning it But we have the most satisfactory evidence that no suspicion of an *ex post facto* origin can justly attach to these prophecies, in the important fact, that although familiarly quoted by the early christian writers as striking evidence of the prophetic character of Jesus, we read of no writer against christianity in the primitive centuries having attempted to paralyze the argument by maintaining that they were not published till Jerusalem was destroyed. If enemies, so near the events predicted, had nothing to say; will any deny us the privilege of proceeding in our present investigation un embarrassed by any question on this head?*

There is a history of the destruction of Jerusalem, which, if it had been composed for the express purpose of attesting the complete accomplishment of our Lord's predictions, could have hardly been made more appropriate to our present object. It was written by an eye-witness of the tragedy; a learned witness; a witness who, having been first an eminent leader among the troops of Judea, and then a prisoner to the Roman commander, and continually kept about his person for the sake of his services, cannot be accused of having written without accurate information. His book was composed at Rome; and having been presented by the author to the emperor Vespasian, and to his son Titus, who had commanded at the siege of Jerusalem, the latter not only desired its publication, but subscribed his own hand in confirmation of its correctness. It was also presented to, and approved by, several Jews, who had been present at the scenes described.† We could not desire a more complete attestation of the fulfilment of our Saviour's prophecies than this book affords. And yet the writer was a Jew to the day of his death, and consequently an enemy of christianity, and could have had no design in favour of the prophetic spirit of its founder. I speak of Josephus. It is remarkable that one of the most minute prophecies in the Bible should have, from an enemy, the most minute of histories to show its fulfilment. No great event in profane history is related with so much attention to all the particulars connected with it, as is the destruction of Jerusalem by this Jewish writer. When we consider these things, and remember the extraordinary manner in which Josephus was several times protected from almost inevitable death, we may clearly discern the hand of a wise Providence,

---

* On this subject, see some excellent remarks in Paley's Evidences, Part ii. c. i.

† Josephus' Life, § 65, p. 23.—Contr. Apion b. i. § 9

preparing the way of the gospel. A witness was preserved and chosen of God, to write an account of the divine judgments upon Jerusalem, whose testimony neither Jews nor Heathens could deny or suspect. We proceed to compare his statements with the prophecies in question.

I. Let us begin with those events which the Saviour foretold as *signs* of approaching desolation. Thus it is written: "*Take heed that no man deceive you, for many shall come in my name, saying, I am Christ, and shall deceive many.*"* Here are two distinct predictions. *Many pretenders to the character of the Messiah*, and *their success in deceiving many*. As the prophecy draws nearer to the chief event, it enlarges on this particular sign: "*There shall arise false Christs and false prophets, and shall show great signs and wonders.*" Here it is intimated, that as the great catastrophe should approach, these deceivers would multiply; and that they would pretend to signs and miracles. The very places where they would appear, and whither they would lead their followers, are also pointed out. "*If they shall say unto you, Behold he is in the desert; go not forth: Behold he is in the secret chambers; believe it not.*"†

Now it is worthy of note, that, until the day when these words were uttered, there had been no events in Jewish history in any manner corresponding with those which they describe. Two years, however, had not elapsed before their fulfilment began. Simon Magus, very soon after the crucifixion, was heard boasting himself as the son of God; deceiving the people of Samaria with sorceries; *to whom they all gave heed, saying this man is the great power of God.*‡ Another, named Dositheus, a Samaritan, pretended that he was the Christ foretold by Moses. In about the tenth year after the death of Christ, appeared one Theudas, who assured the people that he was a prophet, promising to show a miracle in dividing the waters of Jordan.§ "By such speeches,"

---

* Mat. xxiv. 4, 5. † Ib. xxiv. 26. ‡ Acts, viii. 9, 10.

§ The impostor, mentioned above, must not be confounded with him of the

says Josephus, in the very words of the prophecy, "*he deceived many*."* As we approach nearer the final event, (A. D. 55.), these deceivers multiply. "The country was filled with impostors who deceived the people," and "persuaded them to follow them into the *wilderness*; where, as they said, they should see manifest wonders and signs."† Not only were the people thus seduced into the *deserts*, but also into "the *secret chambers*." The inner apartments of the temple were the secret chambers referred to in the prophecy. Josephus relates that a great multitude whom the Roman soldiers destroyed in the "*cloisters*" of the temple, had been led there by a false prophet, who had made a public proclamation, that very day, that God commanded them to get upon the temple, and that there they would receive miraculous signs for their deliverance. At that crisis, "there was a great number of false prophets."‡ Thus have we have all the particulars of the prophecy, so far as it has been quoted: —*Many false Christs and prophets, deceiving many*; pretending to *signs and wonders*; leading their followers into the *deserts and secret chambers*; and *multiplying as the destruction drew near*.

II. "*Ye shall hear of wars and rumours of wars: see that ye be not troubled: for all these things must come to*

same name, spoken of by Gamaliel, Acts, v. 36. There were two noted characters of the name of Theudas. The one referred to by Gamaliel appeared about thirty years prior to the time of the council which that learned Pharisee addressed. But he was a mere insurrectionist, making no pretension to any of the honours of that great prophet whom the Jews were expecting. The person referred to in the text, appeared in Judea in the time of Cuspius Fadus, the governor, and professed to be inspired, to be a prophet, and to have the gift of miracles. Judas of Galilee, or the Gaulonite, mentioned also by Gamaliel, was a political partizan, in opposition to the enrolment made by Cyrenius in Judea, whose doctrine was that the Jews were free, and should acknowledge no dominion but that of God. Neither he, nor the elder Theudas, can with any propriety be numbered among "false Christs," or "false Prophets," such as the Saviour spoke of in the prophecy under consideration. See Lardner, i. 221—225.

* Josephus' Antiquities of the Jews, b. 20. c. v. 1. † Ib. c. viii. 5.

‡ Josephus' Wars of the Jews, b. 6. c. v. § 2 and 3.

pass, but the end is not yet. For nation shall rise against nation, and kingdom against kingdom."* At this time, the Jews were at peace among themselves, and with all nations. To human view there was so little reason to expect a war, that even some years after when the emperor Caligula ordered his statue to be set up in the temple, and there was danger of slaughter, on account of the resistance of the Jews, Josephus remarks that "some of them could not believe the stories that spoke of a war."† Nevertheless, such became in a short time *the rumour of war*, that the fields remained uncultivated on account of the public anxiety. The country was soon filled with violence. In Alexandria, Cæsarea, Damascus, Ptolemais, Tyre, and almost every other city in which many Jews and Heathens were mingled, fierce contentions arose, and dreadful slaughter ensued. In the words of the Jewish historian: "The disorders all over Syria were terrible. For every city was divided into parties armed against each other; and the safety of the one depended on the destruction of the other. The days were spent in slaughter, and the nights in terrors."‡ In addition to these calamities, the Jewish nation rebelled against the Romans; Italy was convulsed with contentions for the empire; and, as a proof of the troublous and warlike character of the period, within the brief space of two years four emperors of Rome suffered death.§

III. Another class of signs was predicted, as follows: "*There shall be famines, and pestilences, and earthquakes, in divers places.*"‖ These, together with the signs previously mentioned, the Saviour said would be "*the beginning of sorrows.*" There came a famine not long before the war, which extended all over the country of the Jews, and lasted with severity for several years.¶ Both before and after this there were famines in Italy, which are mentioned by histo-

* Mat. xxiv. 6, 7. † Wars, &c. b. 2. c. x. § 1.
‡ Wars, &c., b. 2. c. xviii. § 1 and 2. § Keith on Prophecy.
‖ Mat. xxiv. 7, 8. ¶ Acts xi. 25—30. Ant. b. 20, c. ii. 6; c [illegible]

rians of those days.* *Pestilences* raged in various places, as the full time for Jerusalem's cup of trembling drew nigh.† Josephus speaks of one at Babylon. Five years before the destruction of the holy city, there was a great mortality at Rome, while various parts of the empire were visited with similar calamities. *Earthquakes* were also among the signs of the times. Of these, the heathen historians, Tacitus, Suetonius, Philostratus, &c., speak of many. Crete, Italy, Asia Minor, and Judea, were visited at different times, and some of them repeatedly, with earthquakes.‡ Josephus describes one, in Judea, as so extraordinary in its awfulness, that "any one (he remarks) might easily conjecture that these wonders foreshowed some grand calamities that were coming."§

IV. To the signs already mentioned, we find, in Luke's account of these prophecies, the addition of "*fearful sights, and great signs from heaven.*" These sights and signs Josephus sets himself to the work of narrating, with as much particularity as if he had been specially bent upon making good the words of Christ. He relates that just before the desolating war, "a star resembling a sword stood over the city, and a comet that continued a whole year." At the feast of unleavened bread, and "at the ninth hour of the night, so great a light shone round the altar and the holy house, that it appeared to be bright daytime; which light lasted for half an hour." "The eastern gate of the inner court of the temple, which was of brass and vastly heavy, and had been with difficulty shut by twenty men, and had bolts fastened very deep into the firm floor, was seen to be opened of its own accord about the sixth hour of the night." This, the learned of Jerusalem understood as a signal of approaching desolation. Moreover, "before sun-setting, chariots and troops of soldiers, in their armour, were seen running about among the clouds and surrounding cities."

* Ant. b. 3. c. xv. 3. † Lardner, iii. 499. ‡ Ib. iii. 499.
§ Wars, &c., b. 4. c. iv. § 5.

"At the feast of Pentecost, as the priests were going by night into the inner court of the temple, they felt a quaking, and heard a great noise, and after that they heard the sound as of a multitude, saying: 'Let us remove hence.'" But the sign which Josephus considered the most impressive, was that of a man named Jesus, who, four years before the war, at a time of entire peace, having come to the feast of tabernacles, began suddenly to cry aloud: "A voice from the east—a voice from the west—a voice from the four winds—a voice against Jerusalem and the holy house—a voice against the bridegrooms and the brides; and a voice against the whole people." With this cry he went through all the city, day and night. No severity of punishment; no acts of kindness could silence this voice. He spoke neither good nor ill to any, whether they gave him food or scourging. For seven years and five months, his solemn cry continued; until its warning was just about to be fulfilled. A little while before the city was taken, as he was going round upon the wall, he cried with his utmost force: "Wo, wo to the city again, and to the people, and to the holy house;" and just as he added, "wo to myself also," a stone from one of the engines killed him immediately.*

However incredible the narrative of these signs may seem to some, it is not a little in its confirmation that the Roman historian, Tacitus, speaking of the same time and place, says: "There were many prodigies presignifying their ruin, which were not to be averted by all the sacrifices and vows of that people. Armies were seen fighting in the air with brandished weapons. A fire fell upon the temple from the clouds. The doors of the temple were suddenly opened. At the same time there was a loud voice, declaring that the gods were removing, which was accompanied with a sound as of a multitude going out. All which things were supposed by some to portend great calamities."† Whether all these

* Wars, &c. b. 6, c. v. § 3.

† Lardner, iii. 613. Tacit. Hist. b. 5, c. ix.—xiii.

things did really take place, or whether some or all of them were not the conceits of superstitious and excited minds, I shall not discuss; nor is the question at all material to our present object. Certain it is that they were regarded as realities at the time, and consequently were in effect, "*fearful sights and great signs from heaven*" to the Jews, whatever they may have been in reality. It required as much of the spirit of prophecy to predict that the Jews should believe such things to have occurred, as to predict any thing else that did certainly occur. Whatever we may conclude, therefore, concerning the singularly concurrent testimony of the Jewish and Roman historians, the prophecy of the Saviour was most impressively fulfilled.

V. From the calamities of the nation and city, our Lord continued his prophecy to those of his own followers: "*Before all these, they shall lay their hands on you and persecute you, delivering you up to the synagogues and into prisons, being brought before kings and rulers for my name's sake.*"* "*They shall kill you; and ye shall be hated of all nations for my name's sake.*"† "*I will give you a mouth and wisdom, which all your adversaries shall not be able to gainsay nor resist.*"‡ For the proof of the accomplishment of all this, the Acts of the Apostles afford abundant evidence. Remember how Saul *made havoc of the church, entering into every house; punishing the christians in every synagogue, and persecuting them even unto strange cities.* Peter and John were *delivered to councils.* Paul was *brought before kings.* The former were also *imprisoned.* Paul and Silas were not only imprisoned but *beaten.*§ There was given them indeed *a wisdom, which their adversaries were not able to gainsay nor resist.* The very discourses of Peter that caused his persecution subdued thousands into obedience to the faith of Christ.‖ The murderers of Stephen

* Luke, xxi. 12. † Mat. xxiv. 9. ‡ Luke, xxi. 15.

§ Acts, viii. 3—xxvi. 10, 11.—iv. 5.—xviii. 12.—xxiv. and v.—iv. 3.

‖ Acts, ii. 41.

were *not able to resist the wisdom with which he spake.** The jailer that incarcerated Paul and Silas in the evening, was their convert before the morning.† Felix trembled, and Agrippa was almost persuaded to be a Christian, under the speech of Paul. Stephen and James were put to death. There is reason to believe that none of the original apostles or evangelists, but John, died a natural death. Christians were counted as the *fifth of the world*, being literally hated for the very name they bore. About six years before the destruction of Jerusalem, arose the tremendous persecution under Nero, when it was enough that any one was called by the name of Christian, to lead him to torture. Tacitus bears witness, not only to their exquisite sufferings, but also to the fact that they were held in universal hatred on account of their religion and name.‡

VI. "*Then shall many be offended, and shall betray one another, and hate one another; and because iniquity shall abound, the love of many shall wax cold.*"§ The apostle of the Gentiles, in his epistles, complains of Demas, and Phygellus, and Hermogenes, and many others in Asia, who turned away from him; and that when he first appeared at the bar of Nero, *no man stood with him, but all forsook him.*‖ And Tacitus speaking of the persecution by Nero, says: "*At first, those who were seized confessed their sect; and then, by their indication, a great multitude were convicted.*"¶

VII. Immediately after the prediction of the outward persecutions and internal defections by which the servants of Christ were to be troubled, there follows this remarkable prophecy: "*This gospel of the kingdom shall be preached in all the world, for a witness unto all nations; and then shall the end come.*"** The end, referred to, was that of the Jewish polity, which entirely ceased at the destruction of the Jewish metropolis and temple. Jesus prophesied that before

* Acts, vi. 10. † Acts, xvi. 32—4. ‡ Lardner, iii. 498. Tac. Ann. 15. c. 44.
§ Mat. xxiv. 10—12. ‖ 2 Tim. i. 15.—vi. 10.—iv. 16. ¶ Ann. b. xv.
** Mat. xxiv. 14.

this, that is, in forty years from the time when he uttered these words, the gospel would be preached in all the world. Of all that was then in futurity, what could have been more improbable, or to human view, more impossible than this? The gospel was then received but by a handful of unlettered Jews. In a few days after, its author was crucified as a malefactor; his disciples were scattered and discouraged; his enemies triumphant, and the gospel seemed at an end. When the infant church was gathered together in Jerusalem, immediately after the ascension of its Head, the number of the disciples that could be collected, was but one hundred and twenty. What, but the omniscience of God could have foreseen, that in less than forty years that church would be extended into all countries of the known world? But thus it came to pass: "It appears from the writers of the history of the church, that before the destruction of Jerusalem, the gospel was not only preached in the Lesser Asia, and Greece, and Italy, the great theatres of action then in the world, but was likewise propagated as far northward as Scythia, as far southward as Ethiopia, as far eastward as Parthia and India, as far westward as Spain and Britain."* The epistles of Paul, in the New Testament, were directed to churches then flourishing in Rome, Corinth, Galatia, Ephesus, Philippi, Colosse, and Thessalonica. In the Epistle to the Romans, he asserts that the christian faith was then (ten years before the end) "*spoken of throughout the world.*"† To the Colossians, about three years after, he asserts that "*the gospel had* (then) *been preached to every creature under heaven,*"‡ meaning that to all nations, without distinction, it had been published. Tacitus bears witness that, in the sixth year before the destruction of Jerusalem (Nero's persecution), the religion of Christ had not only extended over Judea, but through Rome also; and that its followers were then so numerous, that "*a vast multitude*" were apprehended and condemned to martyrdom.§ Thus, impossible as such an

* Newton, ii. 257. 8. † Rom. i. 18. ‡ Col. i. 23. § Tac. Ann. b. xv.

event must have seemed at the time when this prophecy was uttered, the end did not come until *the gospel of the kingdom of Christ was preached* "*in all the world.*" We know not which should be considered the most impressive evidence that God was with the gospel; *this wonderful fact*, brought to pass by such means, and in the face of such universal and deadly opposition; or the *prophetic eye* by which the Saviour predicted, in circumstances so unpromising, that thus it would be.

VIII. The next prophetic sign brings us almost to the awful catastrophe. "*When ye shall see Jerusalem compassed with armies;*" or, as the expression is in Matthew: "*When ye shall see the abomination of desolation stand in the holy place,*" "*then know that the desolation thereof is nigh.*" "*Then let them which be in Judea flee to the mountains: let him that is on the house-top not come down to take any thing out of his house: neither let him which is in the field return back to take his clothes.*"*

By *the abomination of desolation standing in the holy place*, Matthew expresses the same thing as when Luke speaks of Jerusalem being *compassed with armies.* The standards of the Roman armies had on them images to which idolatrous worship was paid, and which were therefore an abomination to the Jews. On this account, we read that a Roman general, when conducting his army through Judea towards Arabia, was besought by the principal Jews to lead it another way.† "Every idol and every image," says Chrysostom, "was called *an abomination* among the Jews." These idolatrous ensigns being connected with a desolating army, constituted them *the abomination of desolation;* and when the Roman army planted its standards around the holy city, the abomination of desolation literally stood *in the holy place*, or on holy ground. This the Saviour predicted. It was to be the signal to Christians that the desolation of Jerusalem was nigh. Then they were to escape with haste

* Luke xxi. 20. Mat. xxiv. 15 16, 17, 18.

* Ant. b. 18, c. vi. § 3.

to the mountains. The warning implied that, even after the city was encompassed with armies, they would have an opportunity of escape; but, at the same time, that the opportunity would be brief. All this came to pass. One would suppose that the Christians, in having delayed till the city was surrounded with a besieging host, would thus have waited till all escape was cut off. But a remarkable providence took care that they should await the sign, and yet obey the admonition to flee. Cestius Gallus, the Roman general, at the commencement of the war, besieged the city; took possession of the suburbs; encamped over against the royal palace; and might easily, Josephus says, have got within the walls, and won the city. Indeed "many of the principal men were about to open the gates to him." But although the abomination of desolation was thus in the holy place, the followers of Christ were there also. The time of the end, therefore, was not yet come. An opportunity must be found for them to flee. The Lord sees to this. Just as the city was ready to open its gates to the Roman chief, "he recalled his soldiers from the place—without having received any disgrace; and retired from the city, *without any reason in the world.*" This the Jewish historian expressly ascribes to a special interposition of Providence; though he knew not its object. It could be accounted for on no military or prudential considerations. Josephus relates that many principal men of Jerusalem embraced this opportunity to depart from the city as from a sinking ship.* A short time after, when the Roman armies were again approaching with the abomination of desolation towards the holy place, our historian states that *a great multitude fled to the mountains.*† Among these, were probably the disciples of Christ. But we learn more certainly from ecclesiastical historians, of the early centuries, that, at this crisis, all the followers of Christ took refuge in the mountainous regions beyond Jordan; thus obeying the prophetic warning of their Lord; so that there is nowhere any

* Wars b. 2. c. xx. § 1. † Ib. b. 4. c. viii. § 2.

mention of a single Christian having perished in the siege and destruction of Jerusalem.* But as the Saviour forewarned them: what they were to do, they had to do quickly. For as soon as Jerusalem was again encompassed with armies, it was surrounded entirely with a wall, so that, in the words of the historian, "*all hope of escaping was now cut off from the Jews*."†

Who the enemy would be, and the power, and fury, and universal spread of his desolations, the Saviour foretold, by the use of this proverbial expression: "*Wheresoever the carcass is, there will the eagles be gathered together*."‡ Prophecy often speaks a great deal in a few words. The carcass was the Jewish nation given over, as thoroughly corrupt and forsaken of God, to be devoured as by birds of prey. An army is distinguished by its banners. They constitute its characteristic insignia. The banners of the Roman army were surmounted by eagles—emblems of strength, of swiftness, and ferocity. By these the Saviour described it as that which would desolate Jerusalem. Literally, wherever the carcass was, these eagles were gathered. Josephus testifies that all parts of the land participated in the desolations of Jerusalem.§ The legions of Rome, like flocks of birds of prey, flew from city to city, spreading devastation and slaughter wherever they planted their standards. With eagle-swiftness, they descended upon the unprepared population; with eagle-strength, they triumphed over every opposition; with eagle-fierceness, they devoured and tore in pieces, sparing neither age nor sex, sending into hopeless slavery the few to whom the sword denied its mercy. The melancholy record of Jotapata relates that all its population were slain but infants and women. These were carried into bondage. The rest, forty thousand, were slaughtered. Joppa was demolished; the neighbouring villages were destroyed; the whole region was laid waste. Of all the population of

* Lardner, iii. 507. Newton, ii. p. 266. † Wars, b. 5, c. xii. § 2, 3.
‡ Mat. xxiv. 28. § Wars, b. 4, c. viii. § 1.

Gamala, two women alone escaped. Here, not even infants were spared the sword. Such was the extreme awfulness of the slaughter, that many Jews in preference threw their children, their wives, and themselves, from the hill, on which the citadel was built, into the deep abyss below. The number that perished thus, was computed at five thousand. These are but a few cases out of the many which illustrate the perfect accomplishment of the prediction before us.*

IX. But our Lord foretold not only the enemy by whom Jerusalem would be destroyed, but the means by which it would be taken. "*The days* (said he) *shall come upon thee that thine enemies shall cast a trench about thee, and compass thee round, and keep thee in on every side.*† A trench and a wall or embankment always go together in military operations. Both were certainly intended here. But it was exceedingly improbable that such a measure would be resorted to in the siege of Jerusalem. The nature of the ground, and the great extent of the city, rendered it extremely difficult. It had never been attempted in the previous sieges of the same place. It was not necessary, because, had the Roman general been content to wait a little, the famine and the contending factions within the city would soon have delivered it into his possession. After all, it was contrary to the advice of his chief men, and was adopted only because a more protracted siege would have been less

* How minutely were the enemy and his desolations described by Moses as much as one thousand five hundred years before the war! "The Lord shall bring a nation against thee from far, from the end of the earth, as swift as the eagle flieth; a nation whose tongue thou shalt not understand; a nation of fierce countenance, which shall not regard the person of the old, nor shew favour to the young: and he shall eat the fruit of thy cattle, and the fruit of thy land, until thou be destroyed: which also shall not leave thee either corn, wine, or oil, or the increase of thy kine, or flocks of thy sheep, until he have destroyed thee. And he shall besiege thee in all thy gates, until thy high and fenced walls come down, wherein thou trustedst, throughout all thy land; and he shall besiege thee in all thy gates throughout all thy land which the Lord thy God hath given thee. Deut. xxviii. 49—52.

† Luke, xix. 43.

glorious. The higher cause, however, was, that he was God's instrument unwittingly, to fulfil the words of Christ. Titus must confirm the prophetic character of Jesus. By building a wall about Jerusalem, he was to build up the defence of the gospel. The city was therefore literally compassed round, and its inhabitants were kept in on every side by a wall and trench, put up by the troops of Titus, and measuring about five miles in circumference. Josephus is very particular in stating precisely the direction of the wall in its whole circuit.*

X. "*These be the days of vengeance*," said the Lord; "*for then shall be great tribulation, such as was not from the beginning of the world to this time, nor ever shall be.*"† Days of vengeance, indeed, they were, when all that was written and threatened in Moses and the prophets was fulfilled. As if Josephus had written with the very words of the Saviour in view, he bears record, that in his opinion, "*no other city ever suffered such miseries; nor was there ever a generation more fruitful in wickedness, from the beginning of the world.*" "It appears to me, that the misfortunes of all men from the beginning of the world, if they be compared to these of the Jews, are not so considerable." "For in reality it was God who condemned the whole nation, and turned every course that was taken for their preservation to their destruction." It is impossible to describe the truth in this case. "The multitude of those who perished (says our historian) exceeded all the destructions that man or God ever brought on the world."‡ At the commencement of the siege, immense multitudes having come up from all parts of the country to the feast of the passover, *the nation*, literally, was crowded into Jerusalem; so that the city was supposed to have in it upwards of two million, seven hun dred thousand souls. The miseries endured by this impri

* Wars, &c. b. 5, c. xii. § 2. † Luke, xxi. 22.

‡ Wars, &c. b. 5, c. x. § 5.—Preface to Wars, § 4.—Wars, b. 6, c. viii § 4.—b. 6, c. ix. § 4.

soned multitude are minutely detailed in the history of the siege. Famine commenced, and numbered its thousands of unburied and loathsome victims. This destroyer raged so widely that the people devoured their shoes and girdles, the soldiers the leather on their shields. Wisps of old straw were turned into food. That which before they could not endure to see, they now consented to eat. United to these desolations were the remorseless cruelties of contending factions. The city was filled with robbers, who divided its population into parties, more destructive than all the soldiery of the besiegers. Filled with rage and instigated by hunger, they alike refused to be at peace with each other, or to capitulate to the common enemy. They robbed the temple; slew the priests at the altar; defiled the sanctuary with a sea of blood. To keep each other from food, they fired storehouses containing provisions for a siege of many years. Whenever any corn appeared, bands of robbers instantly seized it. They searched every house in which they suspected there was food. Parents snatched it from their children; children spoiled it from the mouths of their parents. There was a lady of high birth and much wealth, who had come from the country, and was kept in Jerusalem by the siege. All her effects, and all the food she had saved for herself and children, had been taken by the prowling bands that continually ranged the streets for prey. By imprecations and reproaches, she endeavoured in vain to provoke them to take her life as well as bread. At last she prepared a feast. Keen hunger found out a lamb. A mother's desperation slew and served it. Having consumed a part, the rest was concealed. The smell of food soon brought in the wolves. They threatened instant death unless she discovered it. With bitter irony she assured them that *a fine portion had been saved for them*, and then uncovered what remained of the lamb. *It was the half-eaten body of her infant son.* Struck motionless with horror, they would not partake of it. Then she upbraided them as pretending to more tenderness than a woman, and more compassion than a mother. All the city, and the whole Roman camp, were filled with astonishment at this horrid evidence of the reigning wretchedness; so that the dead were envied for having escaped the sight of such miseries.* But the wo went on. The prisoners taken in endeavouring to desert the city were nailed on crosses by the Roman soldiers, "some one way, some another, as it were in jest," around the outside of the walls, "till so great was the number, that room was wanting for crosses, and crosses were wanting for bodies."† Thus had the Jews, forty years before, crucified the Lord of glory without the walls, with cruel jesting and bitter mockery.‡ Those who continued within the city took refuge in caverns, aqueducts, sewers, and other secret places, to escape from one another. Titus, as he beheld the dead bodies that had been thrown from the walls into the valleys, "lifted up his hands to heaven, and called God to witness that this was not his doing."§ The number of those who perished during these "days of vengeance," is computed by Josephus at upwards of one million, three hundred thousand; and of these, one million, one hundred and fifty thousand were of Jerusalem, beside ninety-seven thousand carried into slavery, and an innumerable multitude who perished uncounted in various places, through famine, banishment, and other miseries.‖ Add to this destruction of life, the complete ruin of their holy city and magnificent temple, dearer to the Jews than

* How exactly did Moses, at least fifteen hundred years before, depict this very scene! He described even the rank, quality, and habits of the unhappy woman. "The tender and delicate woman among you, which would not adventure to set the sole of her foot upon the ground for delicateness and tenderness, her eye shall be evil toward the husband of her bosom, and toward her son, and toward her daughter, and toward her young one that cometh out from between her feet, and toward her children which she shall bear: for she shall eat them for want of all things secretly in the siege and straitness where with thine enemy shall distress thee in thy gates."—Deut. xxviii. 56, 57.

† Wars, &c. b. 6, c. iii. § 4.—b. 5, c. xi. § 1.

‡ "His blood be on us and on our children."

§ B. 5. c. xii. § 4. ‖ Lardner, iii 529.

life; add moreover the universal desolation and almost depopulation of Judea; and you will find no difficulty in interpreting the Saviour's prediction of "*a tribulation such as was not from the beginning of the world.*" It was when our compassionate Redeemer had all this in full prospect that "he beheld the city" from the mount of Olives, "and wept over it, saying, if thou hadst known, even thou, in this thy day, the things that make for thy peace, but now they are hid from thine eyes."* How did the anticipation of all this misery affect him, when, as he was going to his cross. he turned to the women who wept and wailed because of him, and said: "Daughters of Jerusalem, weep not for me, but weep for yourselves and your children; for behold the days are coming, in the which they will say, Blessed are the barren and the wombs that never bare, and the paps which never gave suck. Then shall they begin to say to the mountains, fall on us, and to the hills, cover us!"† Who can help reflecting here upon that solemn question, "*What shall the end be of them that obey not the gospel of God?*"

XI. We come now to the work of destruction, which forms the most remarkable particular in this wonderful prophecy. The ruin of the city was foretold in these words: "*They shall lay thee even with the ground, and thy children within thee: and they shall not leave in thee one stone upon another that shall not be thrown down.*"‡ The ruin of the temple was foretold as follows. As the disciples were showing to Jesus the stupendous buildings of the temple, he answered: "*Verily I say unto you, there shall not be left here one stone upon another that shall not be thrown down.*"§ Most wonderfully was the spirit of prophecy manifested in these words. Every thing conspired to make the events appear improbable, and to prevent their occurrence, when the time predicted had arrived. Jerusalem was surrounded with three massive walls of immense strength, rendering its

* Luke, xix. 42. † Luke, xxiii. 28, 29, 30. ‡ Luke, xix. 44.
§ Matthew, xxiv. 2.

garrison almost unassailable. except by famine, or pestilence, or internal discord.* Never were men more perfectly devoted to the defence of a city than those of Jerusalem. None cared for life at the expense of her ruin. The garrison was ten times the number of the besiegers. It was, therefore, exceedingly improbable that the city would even be entered by the Romans. Such was the testimony of Titus, as he looked around upon its towers. "We have certainly," said he, "had God for our helper in this war. It is God who has ejected the Jews out of these fortifications. For what could the hands of men, or any machines, do towards throwing down such fortifications."† But it was equally improbable, even if the city were taken, that such complete destruction would be made of all therein. Think of the difficulty of completely destroying such an immense extent of triple wall, and of buildings within. Think of the temple! What a pile to be laid low! Its walls enclosed more than nineteen acres; that of the eastern front rose to a height of nearly eight hundred feet from its base in the valley beneath. In this, and the other walls, the stones were immense, the largest measuring sixty-five feet in length, eight in height, and ten in breadth. How great the difficulty of a thorough levelling of such a structure, even under the instigation of the strongest motive! But what motive was likely to excite the Romans to such destruction? They prided themselves upon a veneration for the arts, and upon the sacred care with which, in all their conquests, the monuments of architectural taste were protected. The temple was emphatically such a monument. The immensity of its walls; its splendid gates and beautiful marble colonnades; the glory of its golden sanctuary; the grandeur of its whole appearance; and all

* Gibbon, speaking of the strength of Jerusalem at this time, says: "The craggy ground might supersede the necessity of fortifications, and her walls and towers would have fortified the most accessible plain."

Decline and Fall, vol. viii. c lviii. p. 144.

† Wars, b. 6, c. ix. § 1.

its associations of antiquity and of sacredness, constituted the temple of Jerusalem precisely such an object as Roman commanders had always gloried in preserving from the desolations of conquest. Even barbarians were used to spare such monuments in their march of devastation. Genseric, when, with his Moors and Vandals, he had sacked the city of Rome, spoiled her wealth and carried away the ornaments of her temples and capitol, but spared her noble structures;* and to this day, after all the scenes of war that have raged through her streets, the pillar of Trajan, the triumphal arch of Titus, the unmutilated Pantheon, and the noble Colisseum, with numerous other monuments of art, attest the ancient glory of the mistress of the world. How often have hostile armies filled the streets of Athens, and hordes of Gothic barbarians encamped amidst her sanctuaries; and yet the beautiful temple of Theseus is scarcely injured, as a model of architecture, and the Parthenon, though defaced and robbed, remains, a noble example still of the grandeur and purity of Athenian taste in the age of Phidias and Pericles. How improbable then must it have seemed to one beholding the temple in the days of our Lord, that Romans should lay it even with the ground. Much more improbable, had the cultivated taste, and the mild, amiable, and humane disposition of Titus, their commander, been anticipated. Still more improbable, when it is remembered how strongly he was bent upon saving the city and temple from destruction; how he employed all the means in his power to induce the Jews to surrender, before such extremities were necessary.† When he had reached the temple, and saw the danger it was in of being sacrificed to the obstinacy of its defenders and the rage of his own soldiers, he was "deeply affected," and appealed to the gods, to his army, and to the Jews, that he did not force them to defile the holy house. "If (said he) you will change the place whereon you will fight, no Roman

* Gibbon, v. 5.

† Wars, &c., b. 5, c. viii. § 1.—c. ix. § 2.—c. xi. § 2.—b. 6, c. ii. § 1.

shall either come near your sanctuary, or offer any affront to it; nay, I will endeavour to preserve your holy house whether you will or not."* But the Lord of that temple had said: "*Behold your house is left unto you desolate.*" God would not suffer the prophetic words of his son *to return unto him void.* Now, therefore, even the authority of Titus was of no avail with his troops. Now the discipline of the Roman legion was broken up that all that was written might be fulfilled. When the fire first reached the temple, their commander despatched a force to extinguish it. As it broke out again, he again used his authority to save the edifice. A soldier, disobeying the will of his general, threw fire into the golden window of the inner sanctuary. At this, Titus, followed by all his chief officers, rushed to the place, and by voice, and gesture, and force, exerted himself most earnestly to prevail with his troops to spare the building. He ordered a centurion to punish the disobedient. But neither his threatenings nor persuasions could arrest their fury. At last, a soldier taking advantage of his absence, when he had gone out of the sanctuary to restrain the others, "threw fire upon the holy gate in the dark; whereby the flame burst out from within the holy house immediately."† And thus was it devoured by the fire. And now orders were given to demolish to the foundation the whole city and temple. Nothing was spared of the former but three towers, and so much of the wall as was required for a shelter to the garrison to be stationed there. "As for all the rest of the whole circumference of the city, it was so thoroughly laid even with the ground, by those who dug it up to the foundation, that there was nothing left to make those who came thither believe it had ever been inhabited."‡ In quest of plunder, the soldiers literally turned up the ground on which the city and temple had stood, searching the sewers and aqueducts. Last of all, it is related by the Jewish Talmud and Maimonides, that

* Wars, b. 6, c. ii. § 4. † Wars, b. 6, c. iv. § 2, 3, 4, 5, &c.
‡ Wars, b. 7, c. i. § 1.

a captain of the army of Titus (Terentius Rufus), "did with a ploughshare tear up the foundations of the temple."* "A ploughshare," says Gibbon, "was drawn over the consecrated ground, as a sign of perpetual interdiction." Thus literally fulfilling that prophecy of Micah: "Therefore shall Zion, for your sakes, be ploughed as a field, and Jerusalem become heaps, and the mountain of the house as the high places of the forest."† How forcibly is the perfect fulfilment of the Saviour's prediction illustrated in the speech of Eleazer to a remnant of Jews in the city of Masada: "Where is now that great city, fortified by so many walls, and fortresses, and towers; which could hardly contain the instruments prepared for the war, and had so many ten thousands of men to defend it? Demolished to the very foundations; and hath nothing left but the camp of the destroyers among its ruins; some unfortunate old men also lie upon the ashes of the temple, and a few women are there preserved alive, by the enemy, for our bitter shame and reproach."‡

XII. But the prophecy of our Lord did not end with the destruction of the city and of the civil and ecclesiastical polity of the Jews. His omniscient eye followed the unhappy race in their subsequent dispersions and afflictions. "*They shall fall by the edge of the sword, and shall be led away captive into all nations.*"§ How many fell by the edge of the sword, in fulfilment of these words, I need not state. Blood flowed through the streets of Jerusalem like a river. But many who escaped the sword were led away captive into various parts of the earth. Before the city was taken, it is related that an "*immense number*" of deserters, having fallen into the hands of the besiegers, were sold "with their wives and children."‖ Besides ninety-seven thousand, who went into slavery from Jerusalem alone, there were sent from Tarichea to Nero, six thousand choice young men, while thirty thousand, from the same place, were sold. Similar convoys of slaves were

* Whitby on Mat. xxiv. 2. † Mich. iii. 12. ‡ Wars, b. 7, c. viii. § 7.
§ Luke, xxi. 24. ‖ Wars, b. 6, c. viii. § 2.

marched from many other desolated towns. Of the captives from Jerusalem, the tall and handsome were carried to Rome to grace the triumphal entry of Titus. Of the remainder, many were sent as slaves to the public works in Egypt; but the greater number were distributed through the Roman provinces, literally "*into all nations*," to be slain by gladiators, or exposed to wild beasts in the shows of the amphitheatre. From that time to the present, the history of all the nations of Europe, Asia, and Africa, is filled with testimonies to the prophetic spirit of him, who, when Jerusalem was in peace and strength, predicted the approaching and yet existing calamities of her sons. In what country of the world, as then known, have they not been persecuted and enslaved?

But in addition to the captivity of the people, "*Jerusalem* (saith the Lord) *shall be trodden down of the Gentiles until the times of the Gentiles be fulfilled.*" It is well ascertained, by corresponding passages of the Bible, that by this expression, *the times of the Gentiles being fulfilled*, was intended the universal ingathering of the nations to the faith of Christ. This has not yet arrived. Jerusalem is therefore still trodden down of the Gentiles, just as she has been, ever since the ploughshare of the Roman desolation was first driven over the ruins of her temple. The hand of Providence, in the uninterrupted fulfilment of this prediction down to the present time, is wonderfully manifest. Two things are specially to be noted in the prophecy: First, that *the Jews were never to be re-established* in Jerusalem; and secondly, that it was not only to be in possession of, but to be "*trodden down of the Gentiles*," until the times of the Gentiles should be fulfilled. That the Jews have never been re-established in Jerusalem since its destruction, has not been owing to any want of desperate effort on their part; nor because the power of the Gentiles has not been vigorously employed in their behalf. In about sixty-four years after their almost total expulsion from Judea, under the conquest of Titus; Jerusalem was partially rebuilt by the emperor Adrian. A Roman colony was settled there, and all Jews were forbidden, on pain of death, to enter therein, or even to look at the city from a distance. Soon after this, the Jews revolted with great fury, and made a powerful effort to recover their city from the heathen. They were not subdued again without great loss to the Romans, and immense slaughter among themselves.

In the reign of Constantine the Great, their effort was repeated, and terminated as before, in perfect defeat, with increased massacre and oppression. But in the person of the nephew of Constantine, their zeal for the rebuilding of their temple was associated with the determination of the emperor Julian to overthrow christianity; and between the power of a Roman sovereign with a victorious army at his feet, and the exulting enthusiasm of the whole remnant of the Jewish people, a union was formed for the single object of rearing up the temple with its ancient ritual, and of planting around it a numerous colony of Jews, which, to all human judgment, bore the assurance of complete success. The grand object of Julian was to convert "the success of his undertaking into a specious argument against the faith of prophecy, and the truth of revelation."* A decree was issued to his friend Alypius, that the temple of Jerusalem should be restored in its pristine beauty. To the energies of Alypius, was joined the support of the governor of Palestine. At the call of the emperor, the Jews from all the provinces of the empire assembled in triumphant exultation on the hills of Zion. Their wealth, strength, time, even their most delicate females, were devoted with the utmost enthusiasm to the preparation of the ground, covered then with rubbish and ruins. But was the temple rebuilt? The foundations were not entirely laid! Why? Was force deficient? or zeal, or wealth, or perseverance, when Roman power and Jewish desperation were associated? Nothing was lacking. "Yet (says Gibbon) the joint efforts of power and enthusiasm were unsuccessful, and the ground of the Jewish temple still continued to exhibit the

* Gibbon.

same edifying spectacle of ruin and desolation." There was an unseen hand, which neither Jews nor emperors could overcome. The simple account of the defeat of this threatening enterprise of infidelity is thus given by a heathen historian of the day, a soldier in the service, and a philosopher in the principles of Julian. "Whilst Alypius, assisted by the governor of the province, urged with vigour and diligence the execution of the work, horrible balls of fire breaking out near the foundation, with frequent and reiterated attacks, rendered the place, from time to time, inaccessible to the scorched and blasted workmen; and the victorious element continuing in this manner obstinately and resolutely bent, as it were, to drive them to a distance, the undertaking was abandoned."* "*Such authority should satisfy a believing, and must astonish an incredulous mind*," acknowledges even the sceptical Gibbon. *He* cannot but own that "an earthquake, a whirlwind, and a fiery eruption, which overturned and scattered the new foundations of the temple, are attested, with some variations, by contemporary and respectable evidence." One writer, who published an account of this wonderful catastrophe, in the very year of its occurrence, boldly declared, says Gibbon, *that its preternatural character was not disputed, even by the infidels of the day.*† Another speaks of it thus: "We are witnesses of it; for it happened in our time, not long ago. And now, if you should go to Jerusalem, you may see the foundations open; and if you inquire the reason, you will hear no other than that just mentioned."‡

Whether this attempt of Julian was defeated by miraculous interposition, is a question which our present object does not require us to argue.§ Two things are certain. First: That the power and wealth of the Gentiles were united with the

* Ammianus Marcellinus. † Gibbon's Dec. and Fall, vol. iii. chap. xxiii.

‡ Chrysostom. See Lardner, iv. 324.

§ See the miraculous character of this event very ably advocated in Bishop Warburton's Julian.

devoted enthusiasm of the Jews, to defeat the prophecy of Christ, by rebuilding the temple, and by re-establishing its ritual, and by reorganizing a Jewish population as possessors of Jerusalem. Secondly: That contrary to all expectation, when nothing was lacking for the work, and none in the world lifted a finger against it, it was suddenly abandoned, on account of sundry alarming and singular phenomena bursting from the original site of the temple, by which even the fanaticism of the Jews was deterred, and the enmity of Julian to the gospel, defeated. These undeniable facts are sufficient to show, with impressive evidence, the hand of God, protecting the prophetic character of our Lord. When, in connexion with these, you consider the great anxiety so universally felt among the Jews of all centuries, to enjoy the privilege of living and dying in Jerusalem; that no risk of life, or sacrifice of property, would be thought too great for the purpose of once more setting up the gates and altars of the holy city; that the nation is now as numerous as at any period of its ancient glory; and yet that during almost the whole period since the destruction of Jerusalem, so entirely have Jews been prevented from living on her foundations, that they have had to purchase, dearly, the permission to come within sight of her nills; and to this day are taxed and oppressed to the dust, as the cost of being allowed to walk her streets, and look, at a distance, upon her mount Moriah; you will acknowledge that the prediction of our Saviour, in reference to their exclusion from Jerusalem, has been not only most strikingly fulfilled, but fulfilled in spite of the most powerful causes and efforts for its defeat.

But it was predicted that Jerusalem should not only be possessed by the Gentiles, but "*trodden down*" by them, till their times should be fulfilled. What the soldiers of Titus did, has already been stated. From that time, during sixty-four years, a Roman garrison alone inhabited the ruins. At the end of these years, the city was rebuilt by the emperor Adrian, under the name of *Œlia;* a Roman colony was planted there; all Jews were banished on pain of death; every measure was used to destroy sacred recollections, and desecrate what were esteemed as holy places. The city was consecrated to Jupiter Capitolinus; a temple was erected to the pagan god, over the sepulchre of Jesus, a statue of Venus was set up on mount Calvary; and the figure of a swine, placed in marble on the gate that looked towards Bethlehem. Jerusalem continued in possession of the Roman emperors till subdued in the year 637 A. D. by the Saracens. The king of Persia had, in the mean while, besieged and plundered it, but his dominion was too short-lived to claim an exception from this statement.* In the hands of Mohammedans, sometimes of Arabian, sometimes of Turkish, and sometimes of Egyptian origin, it continued to be literally trampled down and desecrated, during a period of more than four hundred years; when having been taken by the crusaders, its government was assumed by one of their leaders, and Christians alone were allowed to dwell therein. Only about eighty-eight years elapsed, however, before the crescent of Mohammed was again planted upon the hill of Zion; where to this day, it has remained, with a single trifling exception, undisturbed either by Jew or Christian. During the seven centuries of this uninterrupted dominion of Mahommedanism, Jerusalem has been captured and recaptured, again and again by the various contending families and factions of the followers of the Arabian prophet. The desolations of war; the marches of contending hosts, have indeed "*trodden down*" her melancholy hills. In the sixteenth century, when Selim, the ninth emperor of the Turks, visited the city, it lay, just as it had been seen by the famous Tamerlane more than one hundred years before, "miserably deformed and ruined," inhabited only by a few Christians, who paid a large tribute to the sultan of Egypt for the possession of the holy sepulchre."† Its condition still, is thus stated by

* Gibbon's Decline and Fall, vol. vi. p. 206, c. xlvi.

† Newton on Prophecy, ii. 319—334.

a recent traveller: "At every step, coming out of the city, the heart is reminded of that prophecy, accomplished to the letter: '*Jerusalem shall be trodden down of the Gentiles.*' All the streets are wretchedness; and the houses of the Jews more especially (the people who once held a sceptre on this mountain of holiness) are as dunghills." "No expression could have been invented more descriptive of the visible state of Jerusalem, than this single phrase, '*trodden down.*'"* "Not a creature is to be seen in the streets," says another traveller, "not a creature at the gates, except, now and then, a peasant gliding through the gloom, concealing under his garments the fruits of his labour, lest he should be robbed of his hard earnings by the rapacious soldier. The only noise heard from time to time, in the city, is the galloping of the steed of the desert."† "The Jerusalem of sacred history is, in fact, no more. Not a vestige remains of the capital of David and Solomon; not a monument of Jewish times is standing. The very course of the walls is changed, and the boundaries of the ancient city are become doubtful."‡

Thus, during a period of seventeen hundred and sixty years, have the captivities, and dispersions, and oppressions of the Jewish people, together with the desolate condition of their city and temple, most signally attested the prophetic character of our Lord. And shall we not hence be confident that what remains of his prediction will be accomplished? Will not *the times of the Gentiles be fulfilled*? Will not Jerusalem continue, until then, to be *trodden down of the Gentiles*? And then, will it not cease to be subject to them? And does not the expression of the prophecy imply that it will be again rebuilt and possessed by the Jews in the day when "all Israel shall be saved?" "For what reason can we believe that, though they are dispersed among all nations, yet by a constant miracle, they are kept distinct from all, but for the further manifestation of God's purposes towards

* Jowett's Researches, p. 200. † Chateaubriand.
‡ Modern Traveller, Palestine, 75.

them? The prophecies have been accomplished to the greatest exactness, in the destruction of their city, and its continuing still subject to strangers; in the dispersion of their people, and their living still separate from all people; and why should not the remaining parts of the same prophecies be as fully accomplished in their restoration, at the proper season, *when the times* of the Gentiles shall be fulfilled?"*

We have now exhibited the exact fulfilment of all the particulars of this remarkable prophecy, with one exception. The Lord specified the *time* of those great events which he so minutely foretold. "*This generation shall not pass away till all these things be fulfilled.*" Forty years had not elapsed from the date of this prediction, before all things referred to in it had taken place.

And now let me add but a few words in conclusion.

No charge can be brought against the prophecy which we have been exhibiting, on the score of obscurity or ambiguousness of expression. It is expressed in the plainest terms, and admits of but one interpretation. Nothing can be said in detraction from its claim to inspiration, on the ground of its being general in its expression. It is singularly particular, as well as comprehensive. Nothing can be said in denial of the complete correspondence between these various predictions and the history of the times and places to which they refer. We have drawn the evidence from sources which cannot be suspected of any partiality to the prophetic character of Jesus. The History of the Wars of the Jews by Josephus, the Jewish priest; the Annals by Tacitus, a Roman consul; and the History of the Decline and Fall of the Roman Empire by Gibbon, the English sceptic, are all the vouchers we require. What, then, is the alternative to which the student of prophecy is reduced? He must either acknowledge that Jesus was possessed of the spirit of genuine prophecy; or that he was so sagacious as to be able to fore tell all these particulars, when no one else could see any sign

---

* Newton, ii. 336.

of them; or that the Gospels containing these predictions were written after the events. The first the sceptic is resolved at all hazards to deny; the second he cannot suppose; the last he must assert or give up his cause. For the same reason, therefore, that the heathen Porphyry, when he could not deny the strict correspondence between the prophecies of Daniel and the subsequent history of Egypt and Syria, rather than confess that Daniel was a prophet, contradicted every principle of historical testimony for the sake of pretending that he must have written after the occurrence of what he foretold. So have some modern Porphyries been driven to assert that the Evangelists who relate this prophecy of Jerusalem must have written after the city was destroyed.* I need not say that the only reason pretended to in support of this assertion is the very thing we have been labouring to show, *the strict agreement between the prophecy and the event.* Their argument is neither more nor less than the following: If these words were written before the destruction of Jerusalem, Jesus was a genuine prophet. But we will not believe him to have been a genuine prophet. Therefore these words were not written before the destruction of Jerusalem. A conclusion as shameless as it is senseless; as opposite to the faith of all history as to the rules of all sound criticism, and the opinion of the learned of all ages. It shows the strength of the argument from prophecy, as well as the infatuated obstinacy with which the human heart is capable of resisting whatever would bind it to the obedience of Christ.

But let us not forget that the destruction of Jerusalem, with its signs and tribulations, is set in the scriptures as a type of an unspeakably more awful and momentous event—THE END OF THE WORLD. A day cometh when "the sun shall be darkened, and the moon shall not give her light, and the stars shall fall from heaven, and the powers of the heavens shall be shaken: And then shall appear the sign of the

* Voltaire.—Watson's Ap. for Bible, 169.

son of man in heaven: and then shall all the tribes of the earth mourn, and they shall see the Son of man coming in the clouds of heaven with power and great glory. And he shall send his angels with a great sound of a trumpet, and they shall gather together his elect from the four winds, from one end of heaven to the other."* When that day shall arise on the world, knoweth no man. One thing we know, that it will find us just as death shall find us. Death, to each of us, will be virtually the coming of the Son of man. Then our eternal state will be sealed. Therefore doth wisdom utter her voice: O ye sons of men, prepare to meet your God! for in such an hour as ye think not the Son of man cometh. Watch! walk as children of light. Embrace the promises of the gospel, and live by faith in Christ Jesus the Lord! "Blessed is that servant whom his Lord, when he cometh, shall find so doing."

POSTSCRIPT.

The following remarks on the subject of *chance*, in connexion with prophecy, though in a measure anticipated in the quotation from Dr. Gregory, at the end of the last lecture, are too valuable to be omitted, and constitute a most appropriate supplement to all that has been said on this most interesting branch of the evidences of christianity. They have been kindly prepared, at the request of the author, by a friend and parishioner, who finds no incompatibility between a supreme devotion of himself to the faith and service of Christ, and an eminent proficiency in mathematical and other human sciences.

"The argument from the fulfilment of prophecy, which appears so strong and conclusive in its *affirmative* aspect, is no less so when the negative mode of reasoning is adopted. We may waive, for example, the idea of a divine intelligence operating in the annunciation and fulfilment of prophecy, and attempt to account for the facts mentioned in some other way. But upon what other principle can we account for them? The prophetic scheme is evidently too vast and multifarious for *human* agency; and this excluded, there remains only the hypothesis of *chance*—the negation of all intelligence, human and divine. The law of events, under this supposition, is the same as that by which probabilities are calculated in some of the pursuits and occupations of life; and an argument on this point, therefore, resolves itself into a mere application of the theory of probabilities to the subjects of prophecy. If it result from such application that the fulfilment was an event to be calculated upon with some degree of reasonableness, independently of any intelligent

* Mat. xxiv. 29, 30, 31

supervision, then are we at liberty to adopt the philosophy of chance; but otherwise we are bound to reject it.

"The laws of chance, applicable to the case, may be briefly stated as follows: When circumstances seem to determine an event *equally*, in two different ways, the chances are said to be *equal;* and the expectation of either result is expressed, with evident truth, by the fraction 1-2. But when the determining circumstances are *unequally* divided, so that any proportion, more or less than half of the whole number, operates in favour of a particular result, the chance of that result is expressed by the corresponding fraction. If a ball, for example, is to be drawn from a bag containing equal numbers of white and black, the probability of a white one being drawn is expressed numerically by 1-2; but if there be only *one fifth* of the whole number *white*, the ratio of expectation will be 1-5, and so for any other proportion: and this is the general law of *simple* probability.

"The probability of a joint occurrence, when two independent events are expected, is determined by the *product* of their simple ratios; for there must evidently be, in this case, a whole range of possible results, *as regards one event*, corresponding to each possible result of *the other;* and by a parity of reasoning, the same truth is made evident for any number of events jointly considered. If balls, for example, are to be drawn concurrently from two or more bags, containing different proportions of black and white, the probability of the whole result being *white* will be found in the compound ratio of all those proportions: thus, if one contains 1-2 white, another 1-5th, another 1-8th, and another 1-10th, there will be one chance in 800 that, in drawing one ball from each, the whole four will be white; and this is the general law of *compound probability*.

"With these premises let us open the book of prophecy, and select an example from among the various remarkable events there predicted. We choose one of so extraordinary a character as to place it among the most improbable events (humanly speaking) of any age or nation; but to be quite sure that we do not over-estimate it, we suppose it to have an *equal* chance of general fulfilment; expressed, as we have said, by the fraction 1-2. This does not, however, include the particularities of time and place, both of which are comprehended in the terms of the prediction. With regard to *time*, we observe, that as there is no natural circumstance to determine the event spoken of to one age or period more than another, the probability of exact fulfilment in this respect must be inversely as the whole number of ages in which it might have taken place. *This*, if we allow forty years for the average duration of an age, is about sixty; and the fraction 1-60th, therefore, expresses the contingency of time in the case supposed. With regard to *place*, the probability of exact fulfilment is evidently determined by the relation of the locality named to the whole world. This, in the case referred to, is not greater than that of *one to* 100,000; and the fraction 1-100,000, therefore, is the numerical factor for this element of probability. Combining these three ratios, we obtain an aggregate of no less than *twelve millions* of chances against the *fulfilment of the assumed event at the time and place* designated; and this event is the personal appearance of Jesus Christ upon earth as the Saviour of the world.

"Remarkably associated with this appearance in many ancient predictions, was the continuance of the Jewish dominion, and of the temple at Jerusalem; the joint contingency of which, according to the principles explained, cannot be rated at less than 1-340th. A multitude of predictions are found, also, in various parts of scripture, relative to extraordinary particulars in the life, character, and death, of our Saviour, as well as with reference to the political and social aspect of the times in which he appeared. Many of them are so nearly miraculous in their nature, or so minute and circumstantial in their details, as almost to preclude the idea of chance in any sense. And we are very sure, therefore, that we do not assume too much in assigning to *twenty* of them an average equal chance of non-occurrence. Proceeding upon this ground, we find the probability of their joint occurrence opposed by a disparity of *more than a million* of chances *to one;* and it results from the combination of all the ratios thus found, that the advent of our Saviour, in all its characteristic circumstances and relations, could not have been calculated upon as a matter of fortuitous occurrence, with more than *one* in *four thousand millions of millions* of chances. The term *probability* can scarcely be applied with propriety to a case so very remote; but the argument does not stop here.

"Our Saviour, at a time when all the calculations of human forethought were diametrically opposed to him, predicted the general dissemination of his gospel, and the consummation of prophecy with regard to the destruction of Jerusalem, in the short space of a single generation: and so it turned out. By the laws of probability, neither event had, at the utmost, more than *one* chance in *ninety* of occurring at that particular time; and there was, therefore, only *one* in 8,100 of their joint occurrence.

"The predictions relative to the siege of Jerusalem, the subjugation of Judea, and the dispersion and subsequent condition of the Jews, present many particulars equally remarkable in character and fulfilment. We select twenty four, which have severally a degree of probability not greater than 1-2, and the result is an aggregate of nearly seventeen millions of chances opposed to their joint occurrence.

"The predictions of the Old and New Testament relative to the state and condition of the church in various ages, and its influence upon the moral and political welfare of mankind, furnish another class of particulars which have been singularly verified. The individual probability of most of them would be much less than 1-2; but we concede this, and limit ourselves to twelve points, the aggregate contingency of which is about 1-4000th.

"Finally, the prophecies of the Old Testament relative to the Gentile nations around Judea, and the great empires Nineveh, Babylon, Tyre, Egypt, &c., present about fifty particulars worthy of notice in this calculation. To avoid, however, all possibility of error, we consider only half that number, from which we deduce the expectation of their united fulfilment in about the ratio of *one* to thirty-three millions.

"There remains still a vast number of correlative and circumstantial details, not reducible to any of the foregoing heads, which are found scattered through the pages of scripture, and furnish a "thick array" of corroborative evidence for the affirmative view of the subject; but we need not fear to waive the use of them in the present calculation. The composition of the ratios already determined gives an aggregate which it requires nearly forty places of figures to enumerate, and which the utmost powers of the human mind may vainly attempt to appreciate. If we should even assume a *single grain of sand* for the numerator of the fraction, the whole globe of the earth, repeated many millions of times, would scarcely suffice for its denominator; and such is the extreme improbability of any consistent fulfilment of the scriptural prophecies on the principles of chance.

"It will not be objected to this calculation that it regards the different subjects of prophecy as parts of one and the same system; for although they were in fact uttered by different prophets and in diffierent ages of the world, they are all united by a common subject; and that with a degree of consistency and harmony scarcely less wonderful than the fulfilment itself."

LECTURE IX.

THE PROPAGATION OF CHRISTIANITY.

There is a peculiarity in the argument for the divine authority of christianity, which we cannot but notice in the commencement of this lecture. While the several parts unite with the utmost harmony and prodigious strength in the construction of one grand system of evidence; each is a perfect argument in itself, and capable of furnishing, had we nothing else on which to depend, an ample support for the whole fabric of christianity. We speak of the several parts composing that general division to which these lectures are restricted—*the external evidence*—such as *the miracles; the prophecies;* and that on which we are now about to enter, *the propagation of christianity.* The two former have been discussed. We praise the subject, not the lecturer, in saying that we have not only established on solid ground the genuineness of the miracles of the gospel, and the prophetic attestation to the divine mission of our Lord; but that, in having done thus, we have *twice finished* the proof of christianity, as a divine revelation. It was complete when we had shown that Jesus and his apostles were attended by the credentials of genuine miracles. It was commenced again and completed a second time, and by a course of argument entirely different, when we had shown that Jesus was a prophet, as well as the great subject of prophecy. We are now to begin anew, hoping to prove a third time, and by a course of evidence entirely different from either of the preceding, that the Gospel of Christ is none other than "*the glorious Gospel of the blessed God.*" Our argument will be drawn from the rapid propagation of the gospel, in contrast with the difficulties it had to overcome.

It was only forty days after the resurrection of Christ, that he delivered to his little band of apostles the parting charge: "*Go into all the world, and preach the gospel to every creature.*" "*Go, teach* (or disciple) *all nations, baptizing them in the name of the Father, and of the Son, and of the Holy Ghost.*" In other words; Go, carry the war of the truth into the midst of its enemies; think not your work completed till you have planted the cross upon the high places of the heathen, and have gathered together my elect "from the four winds, from one end of heaven to the other." Such was the work intrusted to those few, unlearned, despised disciples, who formed almost the whole strength of the christian church in the day when their beloved Master was received out of their sight, and ascended into heaven. Now let us consider in the first division of this lecture:

I. THE DIFFICULTIES *they had to surmount in executing this command.* Be it remarked,

1st. In the first place, that *the idea of propagating a new religion*, to the exclusion of every other, was at that time a perfect novelty to all mankind, with the exception of, perhaps, a few individuals of the Jews, specially enlightened in the prophetic declarations of the Old Testament scriptures. The Jewish religion was, indeed, sufficiently exclusive; but in its external organization it was neither designed nor adapted for extensive promulgation. Nothing could have been more perfectly foreign to all the reigning opinions, prejudices, and dispositions of that insulated nation, in the days of the apostles, than the thought of attempting to convert even a single city of the Gentiles to their unsocial system of religion. Their zeal was indeed extremely energetic in behalf of whatever involved the security and honour of their faith; but, in regard to other nations, it was the zeal of jealousy to keep them at a great distance, rather than of invitation to bring them to a participation in their superior privileges.

The charge of the Saviour to his apostles was, if possible, still more novel to the Gentiles than the Jews. Heathenism had never been propagated from place to place. In its innumerable forms, it had grown up out of the depraved dispositions of human nature, all over the world; as thorns and thistles, though never sown by the husbandman, are found every where on the face of the earth. Without a creed, it was without principle; and therefore had nothing to contend for but the privilege of assuming any form, worshipping any idol, practising any ritual, and pursuing any absurdity, which the craft of the priesthood, or the superstitions and vices of the people might select. It never was imagined by any description of Pagans that all other forms of religion were not as good, for the people observing them, as theirs was for them; or that any dictate of kindness or common sense should lead them to attempt the subversion of the gods of their neighbours, for the sake of establishing their own in their stead. So that nothing could have been more perfectly new, surprising, or offensive to the whole Gentile world, than the duty laid upon the first advocates of christianity, to go into all nations, asserting the exclusive claims of the gospel, denouncing the validity of all other religions, and labouring to bring over every creature to the single faith of Christ. Had christianity been content to *stand*, without urging its right to stand *alone*, the heathen nations might have allowed it as much toleration as they were accustomed to yield to the various systems of idolatry among themselves. An altar would, perhaps, have been vouchsafed, in many an idol temple, to the Christian's God; and an image, in honour of Christ, might have been permitted a place among the divinities of the Pantheon. But its character being rigidly exclusive, and yet its spirit universally benevolent, the apostles must have seen at once that they were charged with a work not only perfectly new, but which would necessarily bring them into conflict with all the institutions, passions, customs, prejudices, and powers of all nations of the world.*

* A religion, under which all men could unite with one another, appeared to the ancients an impossibility. "A man must be very weak (said Celsus),

2d. But the difficulties to be surmounted by the apostles were not confined to the novelty of their enterprise, and the exclusiveness of their faith. In the whole character of the gospel, *as a system of religious doctrine, and a rule of heart and life*, there was a barrier in the way of its progress, which to human wisdom and power would have rendered their cause perfectly desperate. To propagate any religion at the expense of every other, would have been to them, in their own strength, destitute as they were of all earthly auxiliaries, a hopeless task; but to propagate the religion of the gospel, was unspeakably more difficult. A system of doctrine partaking, in the least degree, of any of its characteristic qualities, was a thing entirely unimagined among the Heathen, and scarcely thought of, by one in ten thousand of the degenerate posterity of Abraham. Religion, among the Gentiles, was a creature of the state; it consisted exclusively in the outward circumstance of temples, and altars, and images, and priests, and sacrifices, and festivals, and lustrations. It multiplied its objects of worship at the pleasure of the civil authorities; taught no system of doctrine, recognised no system of morality, required nothing of the heart, committed the life of man to unlimited discretion, and allowed any one to stand perfectly well with the gods, on the trifling condition of a little show of respect for their worship, to whatever extent he indulged in the worst passions and lowest propensities of his nature. Heathen religion, in all its forms, was the most perfect contrast to every thing spiritual, holy, humbling, self-denying. Nothing could have been more foreign to every habit of thought, in the mind of a native of Greece or Rome, than the scripture doctrine of the nature and guilt of sin, of repentance, conversion, faith, love, meekness, and purity of heart. Their languages had scarcely expressions sufficiently approximated to these subjects to admit of their explanation without the coinage of new words

to imagine that Greeks and barbarians, in Asia, Europe, and Lybia, can ever unite under the same system of religion."

for the purpose. And in many respects the whole race of the Jews, degenerate as they were in the time of the apostles, were as little prepared for a spiritual, heart-searching religion, as any people of the Gentiles.

Then imagine the incipient effort of the disciples of Christ to gain over the nations to the obedience of the gospel. What could they say to them by way of conciliation, of all their systems of religion and habits of living, to which, from time immemorial, they had been accustomed? Nothing but unqualified, uncompromising reprobation. What could they offer as a substitute, and with what recommendations could they propose it? *The unity of God*, to the extermination of all idolatry; *the fall of man and his entire ruin and condemnation by sin*, to the utter subversion of all their proud conceit of their own merit, and of the dignity of their degraded nature; *the necessity of a new heart, including repentance and holiness, and humility, and the diligent pursuit of all godliness of living*, to the complete breaking up of all their philosophy; the mortification of all their pride, and the direct prohibition of all those unbridled passions and odious vices which then held such universal dominion in the world. It was no aid to the work of the apostles, that, besides the above unwelcome truths and requisitions, the gospel stipulated for a habit of secret prayer, a life of faith; a heart animated with patience, gentleness, forgiveness, and benevolence, to all mankind; and, above all, a single reliance for peace with God upon the death and intercession of One who had been crucified as a malefactor, despised and rejected even by the despised nation of the Jews.

It is easy to perceive from this brief sketch of some of the peculiarities of the gospel, in contrast with all that was loved, and practised, and gloried in by the nations of the earth, that while a new religion, willing to make terms with the habits and corruptions of men, might, if aided by the fascinations of eloquence, the enticements of worldly interest, and the arm of secular power, have gained some advancement

Christianity, with its uncompromising spirit; its holy require ments, and its twelve unlettered and despised apostles for its whole earthly strength, must have perished in its infancy, had not the "Mighty Ruler of the universe" been its friend.

3d. From what has been said, it is manifest that the enterprise of the apostles must have arrayed against it *all the influence of every priesthood* both among Jews and Heathens. In the beginning of christianity the priests of the Jews were not only very numerous and degenerate, but exceedingly influential in their nation. They were, in reality, the nobility of Judea. The power of the magistracy was, in a great measure, in their hands. The people were educated under their charge. They held the reins of public opinion, and headed all the great public movements of the community. What tremendous resistance they were capable of making to the advancement of christianity; how bitterly they replied to those claims which pronounced the dissolution of their priesthood, and the termination of their authority; and with what deadly concert they persecuted its blessed Author, thinking they had put also his gospel, when they had put his person to the cross, I need not remind you.

We turn to the *priests of the Gentiles*. The enterprise of the apostles was directly at war with their dignities, their influence, and their gains. What resistance *they* were capable of making, is obvious from a consideration of the extensive establishment, the high official dignity, the wealth, the political influence, and the superstitious veneration, attached, in the first years of christianity, to a heathen priesthood. "The religion of the nations," says Gibbon, "was not merely a speculative doctrine, professed in the schools or preached in the temples. The innumerable deities and rites of polytheism were closely interwoven with every circumstance of business or pleasure, of public or of private life; and it seemed impossible to escape the observance of them without, at the same time, renouncing the commerce of mankind. The important transactions of peace and war were prepared or concluded by solemn sacrifices, in which the magistrate, the senator, and the soldier were obliged to participate." The Roman senate was always held in a temple or consecrated place. Before commencing business, every senator performed an act of homage to the gods of the nation. The several colleges of the sacerdotal order, in the single city of Rome—the fifteen Pontiffs; the fifteen Augurs; the fifteen keepers of the Sibylline books; the six Vestals; the seven Epuli; the Flamens; the confraternities of the Salians and Lupercalians, &c., furnish an idea of the strong establishment of the priesthood in an empire that embraced the known world. The dignity of their sacred character was protected, as well by the laws as the manners of the country. "Their robes of purple, chariots of state, and sumptuous entertainments, attracted the admiration of the people; and they received from the consecrated lands and public revenue an ample stipend, which liberally supported the splendour of the priesthood, and all the expenses of the religious worship of the state." The great men of Rome, after their consulships and military triumphs, aspired to the place of pontiff or of augur. Cicero confesses that the latter was the supreme object of his wishes. Pliny was animated with a similar ambition. Tacitus, the historian, after his prætorship, was a member of the sacerdotal order. The fifteen priests, composing the college of pontiffs, were distinguished as the companions of their sovereign. And as an evidence of what accommodations paganism must have had in Rome in the days of her glory; the number of its temples and chapels, remaining in the three hundred and eightieth year after the birth of Christ, when, for more than three centuries, christianity had been thinning the ranks of its votaries, and for sixty years had been the established religion of the empire, was *four hundred and twenty-four*.* In connexion with all this organization and deep rooted power of heathenism: consider its various tribes of subordinate agents and interested

* Gibbon, vol. iv. c. xxviii.

allies; the diviners, augurs, and managers of oracles, with all the attendants and assistants belonging to the temples of a countless variety of idols; the trades whose craft was sustained by the patronage of image-worship, such as statuaries, shrine-mongers, sacrifice-sellers, incense-merchants; consider the great festivals and games by which heathenism flattered the dispositions of the people, and enlisted all classes and all countries in its support—the Circensian and other grand exhibitions among the Romans; the Pythian, Nemean, Isthmian, and Olympic games, celebrated with great pomp and splendour in almost every Grecian city of Europe and Asia —the pride of the people, the delight of all the lovers of pleasure or of fame, intimately associated with, and specially patronised by the religion of idols; and therefore directly attacked by all the efforts of christianity. Then say, what must have been the immense force in which the several priesthoods of all heathen nations were capable of uniting among themselves, and with the priests of the Jews, in the common cause of crushing a religion by whose doctrines none of them could be tolerated. That with all their various contingents, they did unite, consenting in this one object, if in little else, of smothering christianity in her cradle, or of drowning her in the blood of her disciples, all history assures us. How she survived their efforts; how the fishermen of Galilee could have overcome their whole array without the help of God, is a problem which infidelity only shows its own weakness by attempting to solve.

4th. But *the authority of the magistrate* was united with the influence of heathen and Jewish priesthoods in zealous hostility to the gospel. In all countries, the support of the religion of the state was the duty of the magistrate. Toleration, among the most civilized heathens, much as it has been eulogized by infidels, allowed of no religion that would not permit entire communion, on the part of its followers, in the worship appointed by the state. On this condition it countenanced the utmost latitude of belief and practice.* But to refuse conformity with the national rites, and worship to the national gods, was an offence unpardonable, not only to the gods, but to the civil authority. This it was that excited so much wonder among the Gentiles, and nerved the secular arm with such deadly offence against the disciples of Christ. "*Keep yourselves from idols*" was a precept that met the pagan Greek and Roman whenever he beheld a Christian. "What can be the reason (said a Roman prefect to an Alexandrian bishop) why you may not still adore that God of yours, supposing him to be a God, in conjunction with our Gods?" "*We worship no other God,*" was the Christian's answer;† a declaration which, from the sword of a heathen magistrate, could have no forbearance, and being every where received as a characteristic principle of the gospel, called out the whole power of the civil governments of the Gentiles to unite with their priesthoods in its destruction.

5th. To these associated powers, were added *the prejudices and passions of all the people.* These, among the Gentiles, were powerful, not only in favour of their own idolatries, but especially in aversion to a religion originating among Jews; still more to a religion advocated by Jews who were despised and persecuted by their own despised countrymen; and yet a great deal more to a religion so spiritual and holy, so utterly at war with vice and idolatry, as that of the gospel.

See, in the Epistle to the Romans, a picture from the pencil of a master, of the fierce passions, the vicious debasements, which universally characterized the Gentile nations in the days of St. Paul. "Filled with all unrighteousness, fornica-

* "The Athenian notion of toleration is well described by Socrates, and much resembles the opinion on that subject that many entertain, even in our own times. 'It appears to me, says Socrates, that the Athenians do not greatly care what sentiments a man holds, *provided he keeps them to himself but if he attempts* to instruct others, then they are indignant.'"

Douglas on Errors, &c. 212

† Euseb. Hist. Eccl. vii. c. xi.

tion, wickedness, covetousness, maliciousness; full of envy, murder, debate, deceit, malignity; whisperers, backbiters, haters of God, despiteful, proud, boasters, inventers of evil things, disobedient to parents, without understanding, covenant-breakers, without natural affection, implacable, unmerciful: Who, knowing the judgment of God, that they which commit such things are worthy of death, not only do the same, but have pleasure in them that do them."* This de scription is borne out, to the letter, by the testimonies of heathen writers. Paul has furnished a picture of the morals of his own nation corresponding with it in all essential features. What, then, could the gospel, with all its holy duties and spiritual doctrines, encounter in such a world, but a most violent opposition from the whole mass of the people?

6th. But the *wisdom and pride of the heathen philophers* were by no means the least formidable enemies with which the gospel had to contend. Their sects, though numerous and exceedingly various, were all agreed in proudly trusting in themselves that they were wise, and despising others. Their published opinions; their private speculations; their personal immorality; made them irreconcilable adversaries of christianity. It went up into their schools, and called their wisdom foolishness, and rebuked their self-conceit. It "came not with excellency of speech," or "the enticing words of man's wisdom," "doting (as they did) about questions and strifes of words;" but *knowing nothing among men save Jesus Christ and him crucified*, it just bade them repent, be converted, become as little children, and believe in a crucified Saviour for peace with God. This was, indeed, "*to the Greek foolishness.*" "*What will this babbler say?*" "*He seemeth to be a setter forth of strange gods,*" were the taunting words of certain of the Epicureans and Stoics when they encountered St. Paul. Mockery was the natural expression of their minds "when they heard of the resurrection of the

* Rom. i. 29—32.

dead."* The apostles, therefore, in attempting to propagate the gospel among the Gentiles, were opposed by all the wit, and learning, and sophistry; all the pride and jealousy, and malice, of every sect of philosophers. And how formidable was this hostility, is obvious, from the great credit, superior even to that of the priests, among the higher classes of society, which those sects had obtained. "Whoever pretended to learning or virtue was their disciple; the greatest magistrates, generals, kings, ranged themselves under their discipline, were trained up in their schools, and professed the opinions they taught."†

7th. In connexion with these powerful adversaries, consider *the character of the age* in which the apostles undertook the propagation of christianity. It was distinguished as one of profound *peace* among the nations, when the minds of men were peculiarly capable of deliberately investigating the claims of the gospel; it was the Augustan age, when philosophy thronged the cities with her disciples, and every description of polite literature was in the highest cultivation. Its peculiar feature was directly the reverse of credulity. No age of the world, before or since, was so extensively characterized by *scepticism*. While the great mass of the plebeians were superstitiously given to idolatry, the patricians were no less corrupted with opinions which went to the denial of all religion. Among the various schools which then divided the learned of the Roman empire; those which declared openly against the most fundamental truths of religion were much the most numerous. Of this description were the *Epicureans*‡ and *Academics;* the former maintaining that the soul was *mortal*, and that, *if gods there were, they took no car of human affairs;* the latter, that to arrive at truth was im possible; that, "*whether the gods existed or not; whether the soul was mortal or immortal; virtue preferable to vice,*

* Acts, xvii. 18—32. † Lyttletons's Conversion of St. Paul.

‡ Cicero complains that of all sects of philosophers, this made the most remarkable progress and gained the most adherents. *De Finibus.*

or vice to virtue;" could not be ascertained. These two sects, the one atheist, the other too sceptical even to believe in atheism, were the most numerous of all others in the age of the apostles, and were particularly encouraged by the liberality of the rich and the protection of the powerful.* From this prevalence of philosophy "falsely so called," the age was distinguished for curious and bold inquiry; the learned every where, like those of Athens, *spending their time in little else but either to tell or to hear some new thing.*† It was, also, for the same reason, an age of special contempt for whatever claimed to be received as supernatural. While every city, through the influence of the priests and magistrates, was wholly given to idolatry, so far as the multitude and the external aspect of all classes were concerned; yet, in the inner schools of philosophy and the private opinions of the educated, it was almost entirely pervaded with scepticism. Add to this, its necessary companion, the universal prevalence of unprecedented luxury and dissoluteness of living; and you will have a true outline of the character of the age in which the apostles, by "the foolishness of preaching," knowing "nothing among men save Jesus Christ and him crucified," were to "destroy the wisdom of the wise," and convert whole nations to christianity.

Most evidently, was the age peculiarly and entirely unpropitious. Nothing, on human calculation, could have been more certain of utter rejection and contempt, at such a time, than the simplicity, spirituality, and holiness of the gospel; especially its two cardinal points, *humble repentance and submissive faith.*

8th. Consider, next, *to whom the propagation of the gospel was committed.* Who were they that received the commission, "Go preach the gospel to every creature," and "make disciples of all nations?" Men, adapted to such a mighty work in no single qualification, except to show, in their weakness, that their success was altogether of God!

* Mosheim's Hist., part I. § xxi.

† Acts, xvii.

They were neither philosophers, nor orators, nor educated men. They were from a class of mankind denominated by the ruling nations, *barbarians;* they were of that nation among the barbarians, whom all the rest of the world particularly despised; they were of that portion of the nation, which was least esteemed by its own members. They were poor, without the least worldly consideration or influence They were acquainted with no craft but that of publicans and fishermen. They had never learned any language but that of Galilee, and yet they were to preach to people of all languages. Such were the men whose work it was to assault the high and fenced walls of Judaism; to break the power of heathenism, though entrenched in the vices of the people; upheld by the craft of their priesthoods; defended by the power of all nations; and sanctioned by the traditions of immemorial ages. Such were the men who were to go into the proud schools of philosophy; show their wisdom to be foolishness; teach their teachers; bring out captives to the humble faith of the crucified Nazarene; and baptize them in the name of the Father, and the Son, and the Holy Ghost.

9th. Consider *the circumstances of depression and discouragement* in which they commenced this work. The enemies of their Master had just succeeded in putting him to the shame of the cross, under accusation of capital guilt. Their taunting language to the agonizing victim: "*Come down from the cross, if thou be the Son of God,*" shows what a death-blow they supposed themselves to have given to his cause. All his disciples had forsaken him and fled. The stone upon the mouth of his sepulchre was not heavier than the weight upon their hearts, when they beheld him dead and buried. After a few days, they assembled together again in Jerusalem, when an upper room contained the whole congregation of those that believed in Christ. Their cause was universally supposed to have died with its Master. The fact that he had not been saved by the power of God from the disgrace of crucifixion, was regarded every where as a perfect answer to all his claims. Such was the beginning of the propagation of the gospel. These were the desperate circumstances in which the unfriended, unprotected, ridiculed apostles were to set up their banner. What could *they* do?

10th. Consider *the mode they adopted.* They sought no favour from worldly influence; courted no human indulgence; waited for no earthly approbation; paid as little deference to rank, or wealth, or human learning, as to poverty and meanness. They spake as men having authority; as ambassadors, commissioned from a throne, and sustained by a power before which, they had a right to demand that priests, and philosophers, and kings, should submit. "Not with enticing words of man's wisdom," did they seek to advance their cause; but in simple reliance upon "the demonstration of the Spirit." Instead of selecting such doctrines as would best conciliate their hearers, and concealing the rest; they fixed their preaching most emphatically on what they knew was the special topic of derision and mockery both to Jew and Greek: *glorying in nothing save in the cross of Christ.* Instead of seeking retired and ignorant people as the subjects of their efforts; instead of *a double doctrine,* as the philosophers had—one thing for the world, another for their disciples—a part for the novice—the whole only for the initiated—they kept back nothing, any where; declaring boldly the whole gospel in the most public places and before the greatest enemies. "Jesus and the resurrection," were preached as freely to Epicureans and Stoics in Athens, as to publicans and sinners in Jerusalem. Instead of accommodating their declarations in any degree to the vainglorious and vicious characters of those whom they addressed; they declared the wrath of God to be "revealed from heaven against all ungodliness and unrighteousness of men." To every soul that would be a Christian, they issued the requirement, "depart from iniquity," "crucify the flesh, with its affections and lusts," and be willing to be esteemed a fool and persecuted to death for Christ's sake. Such was the mode selected by these powerless Galileans, by which to subdue the fierce opposition of the proud, self-righteous Jews, and to make Christians out of Greeks and Romans, alike devoted to degrading vices, and puffed up with the conceit of superior wisdom.

11th. Now let us see in what manner the attempt to propagate christianity was received. It was met every where by the most strenuous hostility, and *the fiercest persecution* From the first discourse of the apostles, down to the three hundred and fifth year of the christian era, persecution never entirely ceased, while its more public and general onsets followed one another in such close succession, that the church had hardly time to bury her dead before she was called to prepare more candidates, by thousands at a time, for the tortures and triumphs of martyrdom. The preaching of the apostles began at Jerusalem, and there also persecution began. Saul hunted Christians with the appetite of a bloodhound. Stephen was the first victim. Soon the brethren were scattered far and wide by the fury of the storm. James was slain with the sword; Peter, imprisoned for execution; Paul, scourged and stoned, and pursued so continually that, in every city, bonds and afflictions awaited him. Whatever Jewish hate, goaded on by a jealous priesthood, could do, was put in requisition to crush the cause. All the devices that Roman governors, seconded by the superstitions and passions of the several nations of heathenism, could employ, were united in the one business of driving back the advancing cause of Christ. His disciples were calumniated as atheists; enemies of man; murderers and devourers of their own children; and as guilty of the most loathsome and horrible practices.* Instruments of torture were exhausted. Jews and Gentiles, soldiers, slaves, governors, and emperors, racked

* "The Atheists," was the universal name for Christians. To the charge of dire hostility to all religion, was added that of combined rebellion against all law and all mankind. "*Irreligiosi in Cæsares, hostes Cæsarum, hostes populi Romani*," was their universal character, among their enemies.

their ingenuity to find out new ways of tempting Christians to unfaithfulness, and, when they were steadfast, of increasing their agonies without hastening their death. Every province, and city, and village, was a scene of martyrdom. The great principle of the ruling powers was, that this "superstition," as they called it, *must at all hazards be put down.* "In a short time, the punishments of death were so common, that, as related by the writers of those times, no famine, pestilence, or war, ever consumed more men at a time." The edict of Trajan, commanding the presidents to inflict capital punishment on all who would not renounce christianity, was never abrogated while heathenism reigned in Rome.* What persecution was in the heart of the empire, it was also in Africa, Persia, Arabia, Capadocia, Mesopotamia, Nicomedia, Phrygia, and in almost every place where the christian name was known. "Those who suffered for the cause of Christ, men, women, youths of both sexes, were so numerous as to be estimated only in the mass." "In torments they stood stronger than their tormentors; their bruised and mangled limbs proving too hard for the instruments with which their flesh was racked and pulled from them; the blows, however often repeated, could not conquer their impregnable faith; even though they not only sliced and tore off the flesh, but raked into their very bowels." Such is the description given by one of those who thus endured to the end.† The strong language in the Epistle to the Hebrews is eminently applicable. Some "were tortured, not accepting deliverance; others had trial of cruel mockings and scourgings, yea, moreover of bonds and imprisonment: they were stoned, they were sawn asunder, were tempted, were slain with the sword: they wandered about in sheep-skins, and goat-skins; being destitute, afflicted, tormented: they wandered in deserts, and in mountains, and in dens and caves of the earth."‡

Christians were often the victims of popular fury, as well as of public edicts and imperial authority. Every odious

* Lardner, iv. 300. † Cyprian. ‡ Heb. xi. 35—38.

slander was propagated against them for the purpose of instigating the rage of the populace. The evidence of abject slaves or of persons forced by torture to testify as an in censed community desired, was used to justify the most dreadful explosions of vulgar hate. Did a drought occur? It was a proverbial explanation, that "if God refused rain, the Christians were in fault." Did the Nile refuse its annual irrigation, or the Tiber overflow its banks? Did earthquake, or famine, or any other public calamity, excite the popular mind? A ready cause was in every mouth; *the anger of the gods on account of the increase of christianity!* A ready sacrifice to propitiate the offended deities was immediately resorted to; *the slaughter of the Christians!* How the better informed of society endeavoured to stimulate the mob to these hecatombs of innocent victims, may be judged from the fact, that "Porphyry, a man who wished to be accounted a philosopher, found a cause for the inveteracy of an infectious and desolating sickness in this, that Esculapius could not exert any effectual influence on the earth in consequence of the prevalence of christianity."*

Such, then, were the obstacles which opposed the propagation of the gospel. Who, in their anticipation, must not have said: "If this cause be of man, it must come to naught?" Either it must die a natural death in the obscurity of its birth, or be torn to pieces at the first onset of its foes, or else it must be of God,—protected and advanced by His power.

Before proceeding to speak of the success of the apostles, we may deduce, from the premises we have established, a conclusive proof of the power by which they acted.

It is certain that they understood the difficulties, and anticipated the dangers, of their work. As men of ordinary understanding, they must have foreseen, while, by the predictions of Christ, they were distinctly apprised of, the obstacles and perils they would encounter. Nevertheless, with a perfect knowledge of their own weakness, they undertook

* Neander's Ch. Hist.

to propagate the gospel among all nations. Why? What was there in reproach and beggary, in racks and prisons, in wild beasts and flames, so inviting? Must they not have been sincere in their professions? Could any thing short of a thorough belief that Jesus was risen, and had promised to be with them in all their labours, have induced them to undertake such an enterprise? It is impossible, without ridiculous absurdity, to question their entire persuasion of this. But is this a proof that Jesus *was* risen, and that, in divine power, he was with them? We do not pretend that in general, the fact of the advocates of a doctrine being *convinced*, is valid *evidence*, of its truth. But in the case of the apostles it should be thus regarded, inasmuch as *they could not have been deceived.* Whether Jesus wrought genuine miracles or not; whether he had appeared to them "at sundry times and in divers manners" after his burial; whether he had eaten with them, conversed with them, journeyed with them, during the space of forty days subsequent to his death; whether they heard and saw him, at the end of those days, solemnly give them their charge to propagate the gospel, and the promise of his presence and power wherever they should go; *they must have known.* Consequently, when, with such undeniable knowledge and unquestionable sincerity, they went into all the world preaching Jesus and the resurrection, neither deceived nor wishing to deceive, the evidence was perfect that they laboured in the service of truth; that their faith stood not "*in the wisdom of men, but in the power of God.*"

II. Let us now consider THE SUCCESS OF THE APOSTLES IN EXECUTING THEIR MASTER'S CHARGE. On the fiftieth day after his death they commenced. Beginning in Jerusalem, the very furnace of persecution, they first set up their banner in the midst of those who had been first in the crucifixion of Jesus, and were all elate with the triumph of that tragedy No assemblage could have been more possessed of dispositions perfectly at war with their message, than that to which they made their first address. And what was the tenor of the address? "Jesus of Nazareth (said Peter), being delivered by the determinate counsel and foreknowledge of God, ye have taken, and by wicked hands have crucified and slain; whom God hath raised up. Therefore let all the house of Israel know assuredly that God hath made that same Jesus, whom ye have crucified, both Lord and Christ." One would have supposed that the same hands that had rioted in the blood of his Master, would now have wreaked their enmity in that of this daring and, to all human view, most impolitic apostle. But what ensued? *Three thousand souls* were that day added to the infant church.* In a few days the number was increased to *five thousand*;† and in the space of about a year and a half, though the gospel was preached only in Jerusalem and its vicinity, "multitudes, both of men and women," and "*a great company of the priests, were obedient to the faith*."‡ Now, the converts being driven, by a fierce persecution, from Jerusalem, "went every where preaching the word;" and in less than three years churches were gathered "throughout all Judea, Galilee, and Samaria, and were multiplied."§ About two years after this, or seven from the beginning of the work, the gospel was first preached to the Gentiles; and such was the success, that before thirty years had elapsed from the death of Christ, his church had spread throughout Judea, Galilee, and Samaria; through almost all the numerous districts of the lesser Asia; through Greece and the islands of the Ægean sea, the sea-coast of Africa, and even into Italy and Rome. The number of converts in the several cities, respectively, is described by the expressions, "*a great number*," "*great multitudes*," "*much people*." What an extensive impression had been made, is obvious from the outcry of the opposers at Thessalonica, "that they, *who had turned the world upside down*, were come hither also." Demetrius, an enemy, complained of Paul that, "not only at Ephesus, but also *throughout all*

* Acts, ii. 41. † Acts, iv. 4. ‡ Acts, v. 14; vi. 7. § Acts, viii. 4; ix. 13.

Asia, he had persuaded and turned away much people."[*] In the mean while, Jerusalem, the chief seat of Jewish rancour, continued the metropolis of the gospel, having in it *many tens of thousands of believers.*[†] These accounts are taken from the book of the Acts of the Apostles; but as this book is almost confined to the labours of Paul and his immediate companions, saying very little of the other apostles, it is very certain that the view we have given of the propagation of the gospel, during the first thirty years, is very incomplete. In the thirtieth year after the beginning of the work, the terrible persecution under Nero kindled its fires; then Christians had become so numerous at Rome, that, by the testimony of Tacitus, "*a great multitude*" were seized. In forty years more, as we are told in a celebrated letter from Pliny, the Roman governor of Pontus and Bythinia, christianity had *long* subsisted in these provinces, though so remote from Judea. "Many of all ages, and of *every rank*, of both sexes likewise," were accused to Pliny of being Christians. What he calls "the *contagion* of this superstition" (thus forcibly describing the irresistible and rapid spread of christianity), had "seized not cities only, but the less towns also, and the open country," so that the heathen temples "were almost forsaken," few victims were purchased for sacrifice, and "a long intermission of the sacred solemnities had taken place."[‡] Justin Martyr, who wrote about thirty years after Pliny, and one hundred after the gospel was first preached to the Gentiles, thus describes the extent of christianity in his time: "There is not a nation, either Greek or barbarian, or of any other name, even of those who wander in tribes and live in tents, among whom prayers and thanksgivings are not offered to the Father and Creator of the universe by the name of the crucified Jesus." Clemens Alexandrinus, a few years after, thus writes: "The philosophers were confined to Greece, and to their particular retainers;

* See Paley's Evidences. † Acts, xxi. 20. "Ποσαι μυριαδες."

‡ Lardner, iv. 13—15.

but the doctrine of the Master of christianity did not remain in Judea, but is spread throughout the whole world, in every nation, and village, and city, converting both whole houses and separate individuals, having already brought over to the truth not a few of the philosophers themselves. If the Greek philosophy be prohibited, it immediately vanishes; whereas, from the first preaching of our doctrine, kings and tyrants, governors and presidents, with their whole train and with the populace on their side, have endeavoured, with their whole might, to exterminate it, yet doth it flourish more and more."

There is no reason for diminishing the wonder which this rapid success of the gospel so necessarily excites, by the supposition that all these conversions, or the greater part of them, were little more than a change of profession and name; the substitution of a christian church, for a heathen temple—a mere transition from one system of religious ceremonial to another. In times of fierce persecution the reality of a conversion is tried "*as by fire.*" There was little during the first three hundred years of christianity to encourage a profession of its faith, except so far as the heart had become sufficiently devoted to its holy and self-denying duties, to be willing to suffer on their account the loss of all things. Mere cold assent and dead formality were not likely to put themselves in the way of being torn by wild beasts, or buried in the mines. The change wrought in the converts was, for the most part and notoriously, a change of heart and of life, as well as an entire change of opinion. The striking alteration in those who embraced the gospel, bore a powerful attestation to its divine authority Philosophers complained that men improved but little, in goodness, under their instructions; while Paul could say to the Christians of Corinth, a city famous for the profligacy of its inhabitants, "*Such were some of you: but ye are washed, ye are sanctified, ye are justified in the name of the Lord Jesus, and by the Spirit of our God.*" "The doctrine of

Christ," says a writer of those times, "did convert the most wicked persons who embraced it from all their debaucheries, to the practice of all virtues."* So remarkable was the difference between the Christians and those whom they had once resembled, that Origen, defending their faith against the attacks of Celsus, challenges a comparison between their moral character and that of any other societies in the world. Even the sceptic Gibbon unites in this testimony. Speaking of these early converts, he says: "As they emerged from sin and superstition to the glorious hope of immortality, they resolved to devote themselves to a life not only of virtue, but of penitence. The desire of perfection became the ruling passion of their soul." "Their serious and sequestered life, averse to the gay luxury of the age, inured them to chastity, temperance, economy, and all the sober and domestic virtues. The contempt of the world exercised them in the habits of humility, meekness, and patience. The more they were persecuted, the more closely they adhered to each other. Their mutual charity and unsuspecting confidence has been remarked by infidels, and was too often abused by perfidious friends. Even their faults, or rather their errors, were derived from an excess of virtue."† From all these authorities, it is evident that the propagation of the gospel was not only of great rapidity, but of great power in transforming the hearts and lives of the multitudes who embraced it.

In connexion with the moral power and vast extent of this work; it should be considered, that among those who were brought to the obedience of Christ, were men of all classes, from the most obscure and ignorant, to the most elevated and learned. In the New Testament, we read of an eminent counsellor, and of a chief ruler, and of a great company of priests, and of two centurions of the Roman army, and of a proconsul of Cyprus, and of a member of the Areopagus at Athens, and even of certain of the house-

* Origen cont. Celsum.

† Gibbon, ii. xv. 138—9.

hold of the emperor Nero, as having been converted to the faith. Many of the converts were highly esteemed for talents and attainments. Such was Justin Martyr, who, while a heathen, was conversant with all the schools of philosophy. Such was Pantænus, who, before his conversion, was a philosopher of the school of the Stoics, and whose instructions in human learning at Alexandria, after he became a Christian, were much frequented by students of various characters. Such also was Origen, whose reputation for learning was so great, that not only Christians, but philosophers flocked to his lectures upon mathematics and philosophy, as well as on the scriptures. Even the noted Porphyry did not refrain from a high eulogium upon the learning of Origen.* It may help to convey some notion of the character and quality of many early Christians; of their learning and their labours; to notice the christian *writers* who flourished in these ages. St. Jerome's catalogue contains one hundred and twenty writers previous to the year 360 from the death of Christ. The catalogue is thus introduced: "Let those who say the church has had no philosophers, nor eloquent and learned men, observe who and what they were who founded, established, and adorned it."† Pliny, in his celebrated letter to Trajan, written about sixty-three years after the gospel began to be preached to the Gentiles, expressly states that, in the provinces of Pontus and Bythinia, *many of all ranks* were accused to him of the crime of being Christians.‡

---

* Stillingfleet's Orig. Sac. 273—4. † See Paley, 346.

‡ The early advocates of christianity, in controversy with the heathen of Greece and Rome, were accustomed to dwell with great stress upon the argument from its propagation. Chrysostom, of the fourth century, writes: "The apostles of Christ were twelve, and they gained the whole world." "Zeno, Plato, Socrates, and many others, endeavoured to introduce a new course of life, but in vain; whereas Jesus Christ not only taught, but settled a new polity, or way of living, all over the world." "The doctrines and writings of fishermen, who were beaten and driven from society, and always lived in the midst of dangers, have been readily embraced by learned and unlearned, bondmen and free, kings and soldiers, Greeks and barbarians.'

We have now prepared the several facts that constitute the materials of our argument. Here is an unquestionable historical event.—The rapid and extensive spread of christianity over the whole Roman empire in less than seventy years from the outset of its preaching. Has any thing else of a like kind been known in the world? Did the learning and popularity of the ancient philosophers, powerfully aided by the favour of the great, and the peculiar character of the age, accomplish any thing in the least resembling the success of the apostles? It is a notorious fact that only one of them "ever dared to attack the base religion of the nation, and substitute better representations of God in its stead, although its absurdity was apparent to many of them. An attempt of this kind, having cost the bold Socrates his life, no others had resolution enough to offer such a sacrifice for the general good. To excuse their timidity in this respect, and give it the appearance of profound wisdom, they called to their aid the general principle that it is imprudent and injurious to let people see the whole truth at once; that it is not only necessary to spare sacred prejudices, but, in particular circumstances, an act of benevolence to deceive the great mass of the people. This was the unanimous opinion of almost all the ancient philosophical schools."* No further proof is needed that such men were incapable of effecting any thing approximating to the great moral revolution produced in the

"Though kings, and tyrants, and people strove to extinguish the spark of faith, such a flame of true religion arose as filled the whole world. If you go to India, and Scythia, and the utmost ends of the earth, you will every where find the doctrine of Christ enlightening the souls of men." Augustine, of the same century, speaking of the heathen philosophers, says: "If they were to live again, and should see the churches crowded, the temples forsaken, and men called from the love of temporal, fleeting things to the hope of eternal life and the possession of spiritual and heavenly blessings, and readily embracing them, provided they were really such as they are said to have been, perhaps they would say: 'These are things which we did not dare to say to the people; we rather gave way to their custom than endeavoured to draw them over to our best thoughts and apprehensions.'"

Lardner, ii. 614 and 597.

* Reinhard's Plan, n. 165. 6.

world by the power of the gospel. How different the apostles! boldly attacking all vice, superstition, and error, at all hazards, in all places, *not counting their lives dear unto them, so that they might "testify the gospel of the grace of God."* But where else shall we turn for a parallel to the work we have described? What efforts, independently of the gospel, were ever successful in the moral regeneration of whole communities of the superstitious and licentious?

The only event in the annals of time that has ever been supposed to bear any resemblance to the propagation of christianity, is the rapid progress of Mohammedanism. But a little reflection will show you that the single fact of its rapid and extensive progress is the only point of resemblance; while, in every thing else, there is direct opposition. The Koran based its cause upon no profession of miracles, and therefore had no detection to fear. The gospel rested all upon its repeated miracles, and, consequently, unless it had been true, would have been certain of detection. Mohammed was of the most powerful and honourable family in Mecca, the chief city of his nation; and though not rich by inheritance, became so by marriage. Jesus was of a family of poor and unknown inhabitants of an obscure village in Judea, and had not where to lay his head. Mohammed began his work among the rich and great. His first three years were consumed in attaching to his cause thirteen of the chief people of Mecca. Jesus commenced among the poor. During his three years of ministry on earth, twelve obscure Jews, many of them fishermen, all unlearned and powerless, were his chosen disciples. Of the first thirteen apostles of the Koran, all ultimately attained to riches and honours, to the command of armies, and the government of kingdoms Of the twelve apostles who commenced the propagation of the gospel, all attained to the utmost poverty, contempt, and ignominy; and all, but one, to a violent death on account of their cause. The age, when Mohammed set up his banner, was eminently propitious to his enterprise. "Nothing can equal the ignorance and darkness that reigned in this century."* Science, philosophy, and theology, had every where declined into almost nothingness. The age when the apostles of Christ began their work was eminently unpropitious to any cause but that of God. *It was the Augustan age.* Mohammedanism took its rise in an interior town of Arabia, among a barbarous people, and its first conquests were among the rudest and least enlightened of the most ignorant regions of the world. Christianity arose in the splendid metropolis of a populous and intelligent nation, and achieved her earliest victories in some of the most polished and enlightened cities of the world. In the town of Mecca, where Mohammed opened his mission, there was no established religion to contend with. In the city of Jerusalem, where Jesus and his apostles began their work of love, an established religion was powerfully fortified within the triple wall of priest, magistrate, and people, and defended by all the powers and passions of the nation. When the prophet of Arabia appeared, his cause was favoured by the feuds that prevailed among the Arab tribes around him, and by the bitter dissensions and cruel animosities then reigning among various sects of degenerate Christians; dissensions that filled the greater part of the east with such enormities as rendered the very name of christianity odious to many. When the great Prophet of christianity appeared, the temple of Janus was shut, in token of universal peace, so that all the schools of philosophy, all sects of superstition, and all the powers and animosities of the nations were free to combine against his gospel. Mohammed attempted to conciliate the prevailing religion of the empire, by preaching to the ignorant generation of Christians that his religion was no other than what had been originally their own. The unity of God, the prophetic character of the patriarchs and prophets of the Old Testament, and the divine mission of Jesus, he carefully and artfully asserted; pretending to restore

---

* Mosheim.

the purity, instead of attacking the foundations, of the religion they had taught. This was politic. The apostles, on the other hand, attacked, boldly, and unsparingly, the religion of all the world. While asserting the essential principles of the religion of Moses, they aimed directly at the subversion of its, then, degenerate institutions; and, as to all Gentile nations, pretended to nothing but uncompromising opposition. This certainly was any thing but politic. Mohammed, while he required nothing of his followers that called for self-denial,* expressly sanctioned and promoted their strongest passions. Impurity, revenge, ambition, pride, were his cardinal and honoured indulgences. Thus he enticed human nature. I need not say that the requisitions and allurements proclaimed by the apostles of Christ were precisely the contrary. But thus they repelled human nature.

Even, with all these advantages in his favour, Mohammed, at the end of the first twelve years of his enterprise, had not extended his cause beyond the walls of Mecca, and had gained but few disciples within them, because his efforts had been confined to *persuasion.* While christianity with all its disadvantages, in half the time from the beginning of the ministry of Christ, could number more than ten thousand disciples in Jerusalem, and churches throughout all Judea, and Galilee, and Samaria; and yet her efforts were also confined to *persuasion.* But Mohammed, after twelve years experience, discovered that, even with all his indulgence to passion and pride, some argument much more cogent than that of persuasion was necessary to convince the nations. This was found at the edge of the sword. He sounded the trump of war; promised the spoils of nations, the fairest of the captives, and the most luxurious arbour in Paradise, to those who would join his standard. Then, proselytes were multiplied. The roving Arabs, converted to the faith for the

* The prohibition of wine, the fast of Ramadan, and the pilgrimage to Mecca, were no part of Mohammedanism until several years after its commencement, when military successes had completely established its authority

sake of the plunder, flocked to his cause. Death or conversion was the only choice of the idolater. "The Koran, the tribute, or the sword," was vouchsafed to Jews and Christians. Henceforward the demon of Mohammedanism was always seated on the hilt of the sword, and made its way by force and slaughter. How and why, it prevailed both rapidly and extensively from this time, I am as little bound to explain, as to account for the martial prowess of Napoleon, or of the Goths and Vandals. It was the success of the warrior, not of the prophet.

But I may not leave this subject, without turning what to some may have seemed almost parallel to the success of the gospel, into an auxiliary illustration of its superhuman power. It is a strong fact, in evidence that God was on the side of the apostles, that when they had every thing on earth to contend with, they succeeded, by mere efforts of persuasion, in subduing kingdoms, and bringing innumerable multitudes to holiness of life; while Mohammed and his apostles, in the most favourable circumstances, were confined, as long as they used no weapon but that of persuasion, to a few followers, and, had they never taken the sword, would probably never have been heard of beyond the sands of Arabia.

But should it still be contended that the success of the apostles may be accounted for without reference to supernatural aid; let the question be answered why, when the same human means have since been employed in so many instances, nothing even approximating to the same results has ever ensued. Jews are found at present as numerous as ever. Some of the strongest obstacles which opposed the success of the gospel among them, in the apostolic age, do not now exist. They have no religious establishment; no regular priesthood; no power to persecute. Christianity, on the other hand, is established. Instead of appearing to the Jew as a thing of yesterday, advocated but by a few obscure men, as she did of old; she now presents herself under the sanction of eighteen centuries, illustrated by the learning of her disciples, professed by all civilized nations. It cannot be said that less human effort, in the aggregate, has been employed for the conversion of the Jews, than was used by the twelve apostles. Much more money has been expended; much more learning has been devoted; much more human power has been exerted; many more individuals have been employed. The same gospel has been preached. The same arguments have been urged. And why should not corresponding effects appear? "There is reason to think that there were more Jews converted by the apostles in one day, than have since been won over in the last thousand years."* The simple explanation is and must be, that the great power of God was with the apostles for the establishment of the truth, in a degree far greater than that in which it is now vouchsafed to his ministers in promoting the wide extension of the truth.

From the Jews turn to the heathens. There is no reason to believe that the heathenism of the present day is any more opposed to the propagation of christianity, than that of the world in the age of the apostles. Instead of twelve, there are hundreds of labourers in this field—men of education, talent, indefatigable zeal, undaunted devotion. The art of printing has furnished them with facilities of which the apostles, unless it be conceded that they possessed the miraculous gift of tongues, were entirely destitute. The scriptures are now circulated in full; while in the days of St. Paul, the canon being incomplete, they were circulated only in parts. In addition to all this, christianity is recommended among many heathen nations, by the political importance of the countries from which its preachers have gone, and in some, by the actual co-operation of christian powers ruling in the midst of pagan institutions. With these important advantages; what is the success of present efforts among the heathen? Enough, indeed, to reward all the zeal expended in their support; enough to show that still the power of God is with the gospel,

* Bryant on the Truth of Christianity.

and that ample encouragement is given for all the increase of effort which Christians can ever bestow on the heathen; but nothing comparable with the success of the apostles. Paul was instrumental in converting more heathens, in thirty years, than all modern missionaries in the last five hundred. Explain this fact! It is absurd to attempt it, in view of all the circumstances of the case, except you admit the solution given by Paul himself—"I have planted, and Apollos watered; *but God gave the increase.*" Without this grand truth, "*God gave the increase;*" christianity would have perished on the cross of its founder.

I have now set before you a miracle, the evidence of which no eye can be too blind to see: *Christianity universally propagated; and yet propagated by no earthly influence but that of the apostles.* This is the miracle. It is as directly contrary to the laws of nature and to universal experience, as if, at the word of man, the desert of Arabia should bud and blossom like a fruitful garden, or the sepulchre give up its dead. As long as this one fact, the propagation of christianity, shall remain; the gospel will be supported by a pillar of evidence which infidels can only remove by taking away the foundation of all inductive evidence, and bringing down the whole temple of human knowledge to their own destruction.

Now, in conclusion, let us see what an *unbeliever* must *believe* in consistency with his profession. He must believe that the apostles were either such weak-minded men as to imagine that their crucified Master had been with them, from time to time, during forty days after his burial, had conversed with them, and eaten with them, and that they had every sensible evidence of his resurrection, while in truth he had not been near them, but was still in his sepulchre; or else that they were so wicked and deceitful as to go all over the world preaching that he was risen from the dead, when they knew it was a gross fabrication. Suppose the unbeliever to choose the latter of these alternatives. Then he believes, not only that those men were so singularly attached to this untruth as to give themselves up to all manner of disgrace, and persecution, and labour, for the sake of making all the world believe it, knowing that their own destruction could be the only consequence; but also, what is still more singular, that when they plunged, immediately at the outset of their ministry, into an immense multitude of those who, having lately crucified the Saviour, were full of enmity to his disciples; they succeeded, without learning, eloquence, power, or a single conceivable motive, in making three thousand of them believe that he, whom they had seen on the cross, was indeed alive again; and believe it so fully, as to renounce every thing, and be willing to suffer any thing, for the sake of it, and this on the very spot where the guards that had kept the sepulchre were at hand to tell what was become of the body of Jesus. He must believe, moreover, that although in attempting to propagate a new religion to the exclusion of every other, they were undertaking what was entirely new, and opposed to the views of all nations; although the doctrines they preached were resisted by all the influence of the several priesthoods; all the power of the several governments; all the passions, habits, and prejudices of the people; and all the wit and pride of the philosophers of all nations; although the age was such as insured to their fabrications the most intelligent examination, with the strongest possible disposition to detect them; although, in themselves, these infatuated men were directly the reverse of what such resistance demanded, and, when they commenced, were surrounded by circumstances of the most depressing kind, and by opposers specially exulting in the confidence of their destruction; although the mode they adopted was of all others most calculated to expose their own weakness and dishonesty, and to imbitter the enmity and increase the contempt of their opposers, so that they encountered every where the most tremendous persecutions, till torture and death were almost synonymous with the name of Christian; although they had nothing to propose, to Jew or Gentile, as a matter of faith, but what the wisdom of the world ridiculed, and the vice of the world hated, and all men were united in despising; although they had nothing earthly with which to tempt any one to receive their fabrication, except the necessity of an entire change in all his habits and dispositions, and an assurance that tribulations and persecutions must be his portion: Yet when philosophers, with all their learning, and rank, and subtlety, and veneration, could produce no effect on the public mind, these obscure Galileans obtained such influence, throughout the whole extent of the Roman empire, and especially in the most enlightened cities, that, in thirty years, what they themselves (by the supposition) did not believe, they made hundreds of thousands of all classes, philosophers, senators, governors, priests, soldiers, as well as plebeians, believe, and maintain unto death; yea, they planted this doctrine of their own invention so deeply that all the persecutions of three hundred years could not root it up; they established the gospel so permanently that in three hundred years it was the established religion of an empire co-extensive with the known world, and continues still the religion of all civilized nations. This, says the unbeliever, they did simply by their own wit and industry; and yet, he well knows that, preachers of the gospel, with incomparably more learning, with equal industry, in far greater numbers, and in circumstances immeasurably more propitious, have attempted to do something of the same kind among heathen nations, and could never even approximate to their success. Still the apostles had no help but that of their own ingenuity and diligence! Such is the belief of the unbeliever. To escape acknowledging that the apostles were aided by miraculous assistance, he makes them to have possessed in themselves miraculous ability. To get rid of one miracle in the work, he has to make twelve miracles out of the twelve agents of the work. The Christian takes a far different course. "Paul planted, Apollos watered, but *God gave the increase." The weapons of their warfare were not carnal, but mighty through God, to the pulling down of strong holds.* To which solution, philosophy or common sense would award the prize of rational decision, it is easy to determine.

The argument from the propagation of christianity is not yet complete. Satisfactory already, it is yet to receive an immense accession of strength. "The wilderness and the solitary place," the immense regions of Pagan and Mohammedan desolation, shall yet be glad for the blessings of the gospel, and "the desert rejoice and blossom as the rose." Every nation and kindred shall be brought "into captivity to the obedience of Christ," for the word hath gone forth out of the mouth of the Lord: "I will give thee the heathen for thine inheritance, and the uttermost parts of the earth for thy possession." How should every heart respond *Amen!* and pray: "Thy kingdom come; thy will be done on earth as it is in heaven!"

LECTURE X.

THE FRUITS OF CHRISTIANITY.

In our preceding lectures, we have followed the currents of three independent arguments, each of which was found sufficient to conduct us to a complete proof of the divine authority of the gospel of Christ. That, to which we now proceed, is especially capable of being "known and read of all men," and deserves to be ranked in the highest class of the evidences of christianity. Our blessed Lord, speaking of false pretenders to divine revelation, delivered the following rule, by which they might be distinguished: "*Ye shall know them by their fruits. Do men gather grapes of thorns, or figs of thistles? Even so every good tree bringeth forth good fruit; but a corrupt tree bringeth forth evil fruit. Wherefore by their fruits ye shall know them.*" This is a test universally approved of, and necessarily employed. Its influence on our judgment is unavoidable; and when properly applied, its results are certain. The goodness of a tree cannot be doubted, while we know the excellence of its fruit. No more reason have we to question the holy character and divine origin of religion, while its legitimate effects on the lives and hearts of its genuine disciples are holy. We may come to an erroneous conclusion by judging erroneously of the fruit; by ascribing effects to causes which did not produce them; by charging upon religion a train of consequences of which it was only the incidental occasion, instead of the natural cause. But these are errors in the application, and independent of the correctness of the test. Whenever you have ascertained the true results of any system of doctrine, you have found a plain and certain expression of its intrinsic character. It is good in proportion as the fruit is good. If its fruit be godly, it must itself be of God.

Let infidelity be always tried by this equitable rule, so as to receive the full credit of all the evils which may easily be found to have grown upon its branches; let it be stripped of all those adventitious circumstances of a favourable kind for which it is indebted to the surrounding influence of christianity; and few eyes will fail to see that the root is one of bitterness, and the tree fit only to be cut down as a cumberer of the ground. If men would judge christianity also, by the fair application of this rule, carefully separating from her genuine productions all those of which, however enemies may love to lay them to her charge, she is only the innocent occasion; it would require but little discernment to be convinced of her heavenly origin, and of the duty of all to spread the knowledge and acceptance of her divine revelation. Such will be the object of the present lecture. Christianity may be known by its fruits. Christians are desirous that their faith should be judged by this test, as well as by every other that is just and equal. We set out, therefore, with this question: *What are the fruits of Christianity?* In the examination of this subject, we will consider,

I. THE EFFECTS OF CHRISTIANITY ON SOCIETY IN GENERAL.

II. ITS EFFECTS ON THE CHARACTER AND HAPPINESS OF GENUINE DISCIPLES.

Reserving the latter of these divisions for another lecture, we devote our attention at present exclusively to the former.

In proceeding to illustrate *the beneficial effects of christianity on society in general,* I know of no way so direct as to consider in what condition the countries now blessed with its influence would have remained, had they been left to the several forms of religion under which they had previously subsisted. Let us take a brief survey of the moral state of the ancient world in the age when the preaching of the cross effected its wonderful revolution in the whole fabric of society. And that we may not be accused of unfairness, let us take into view, not the more distant and uncivilized provinces, but those chief central states, where all the light and moral vigour of the heathen world were concentrated. Let our survey be confined to the society of Italy and Greece, where philosophy held her court, and literature and the arts were cultivated with the utmost devotion and success. Unfortunately for the interests of truth, the history of Greece and Rome has fallen, for the most part, into the hands of writers much more concerned with their intellectual and martial prowess, than their moral attainments and social virtues; so that while the reader is occupied in admiring the acuteness of their schoolmen, the taste of their poets, the perfection of their arts, and the warlike character of their soldiery, he is seldom called to look within the enclosures of society, and inquire how they lived, what manner of men they were in their families, in their social relations, in their moral principles, and their private habits.

A certain eminent writer, who lived in the age to which we refer, addressing the people of Rome, describes the heathen population of the civilized world as given up to the vilest, most unnatural, and beastly affections; filled with all unrighteousness and degrading wickedness; full of envy, murder, deceit, malignity; disobedient to parents; covenant-breakers, without natural affection, implacable, unmerciful, not only committing such things as were worthy of death, but having pleasure in them that did them. Such, according to St. Paul, were the polished Grecians and the sterner Romans.*

1st. Consider *their religion.* "Professing themselves to be wise, they became fools, and changed the glory of the uncorruptible God into an image made like to corruptible man, and to birds and four-footed beasts, and creeping things."† Deities were multiplied till there was a god for every thing, and any thing answered for a god. Athens was

* Rom. i. 29—32. † Rom. i. 22, 23.

full of statues dedicated to different deities; those of various countries being so crowded together, that it was said to be "easier to find a god than a man." There was the god Caius Cæsar, and the god Augustus Cæsar, and the god Lucius Cæsar, and the goddess Julia, the profligate daughter of Augustus, to whom the rulers of Athens ascribed the title of *Providence.* The senate of the Areopagus, and that of the six hundred, erected her statue, and enacted her divinity; an altar having been consecrated many years before, to "*the Unknown God.*" Rome exceeded Athens in the number of her gods, only by having, as the mistress of the world, all nations to collect from, and all forms of paganism to countenance. "The deities of a thousand groves and a thousand streams possessed, in peace, their local and respective influence; nor could the Roman, who deprecated the wrath of the Tiber, deride the Egyptian who presented his offering to the beneficent genius of the Nile. Every virtue and even vice acquired its divine representative; every art and profession its patron, whose attributes in the most distant ages and countries, were uniformly derived from the character of their peculiar votaries. It was the custom (of the Romans) to tempt the protectors of besieged cities by the promise of more distinguished honours than they possessed in their native country. Rome gradually became the common temple of her subjects, and the freedom of the city was bestowed on all the gods of mankind."* "In this mania for foreign gods, the nobles and the emperors themselves set the most corrupting examples. Germanicus and Agrippina devoted themselves especially to Egyptian gods. So also Vespasian. Nero served all gods with the exception of the Dea Syra. Marcus Aurelius caused the priests of all foreign gods and nations to be assembled in order to implore aid for the Roman empire against the incursions of the Marcomanni. Commodus caused himself to be initiated into the mysteries of the Egyptian Isis and the Persian Mithras. Severus worshipped

* Gibbon's Dec. and Fall, i. 32, 35, 36.

especially the Egyptian Serapis; Caracalla chiefly the Egyptian Isis; and Heliogabalus the Syrian deities; though he was desirous of becoming a priest of the Jewish, Samaritan, and Christian religions."*

The traditions of the principal divinities of the ancient heathen are a true guide to the vices of their worship. What the gods were said to have been in their lives, their worshippers were actually in their service. "It is a shame," said one who knew them well, "even to speak of those things which were done of them in secret." The chief oracles of the heathens appointed human sacrifices; so that not only the barbarians, but even the Athenians, Lacedæmonians, and Romans, were accustomed to worship idols in the blood of their fellow-creatures. What must have been the state of public morals when gods were patrons of vice, and their rites encouraged both cruelty and obsceneness, it is easier to imagine than describe. "Eusebius is compelled to use language when describing the height of wickedness and impurity which the *worship* of the heathens attained, such as no virtuous man can read without shuddering." The gods were entreated, by costly offerings, on splendid altars, to favour the indulgence of unnatural lusts; the perpetration of murders; the robbery of the orphan and the widow. Seneca exclaims: "How great is now the madness of men! They lisp the most abominable prayers in the ears of the gods. And if *a man* is found listening, they are silent. What a man ought not to hear, they do not blush to rehearse to God."† Well might St. Paul describe them as "*given up to uncleanness through the lusts of their own hearts.*"‡

2d. Consider *the spirit of cruelty* that reigned among those people. It was not solely owing to the madness and depravity of a Tiberius, a Caligula, a Nero, or a Caracalla, that a cruel and sanguinary spirit, in their day, was so universal. Had not the whole mass, the peasant, the soldier, the citizen, and

* Prof. Tholuck on Heathenism.—*Biblical Repository*,

† Epist. 10 ‡ See Potter's Antiquities, ii. 301.

he senator, as well as the prince, been foully tainted, the monstrous enormities of those vicious tyrants could never have been perpetrated. Such was the cruelty of Romans to their slaves, that it was not unusual to put the aged and useless to perish on an island in the Tiber; and some masters would even drown them, as food for the inhabitants of their fish-ponds.* Scenes of blood and slaughter were the public diversions of the people. Witness the shows of gladiators in the crowded amphitheatre, when to celebrate a birth-day or gratify a popular whim, crowds of captives were set to mutual slaughter, or else to contend with the fury of wild beasts. What must have been the moral sensibility of those nations, of which the most refined females delighted in such revolting cruelties, criticising the skill of the ferocious swordsman, and exclaiming with enthusiasm at the graceful stroke that opened the heart of the vanquished, and poured out his lifeblood upon the arena! † St. Paul describes the heathen community as *full of murder and malignity*. Hume, speaking of "the

* "The custom of exposing old, useless, or sick slaves on an island of the Tiber, there to starve, seems to have been pretty common in Rome; and whoever recovered after having been so exposed, had his liberty given him by an edict of the emperor Claudius." "The *ergastula*, or dungeons, where slaves in chains were forced to work, were very common all over Italy." "A chained slave for a porter, was usual in Rome, as appears from Ovid and other authors." The evidence of slaves "was always extorted by the most exquisite torments."—*Hume on the Populousness of Ancient Nations.*

† "Who," says Hume, "can read the accounts of the amphitheatrical entertainments without horror? or who is surprised that the emperors should treat people in the same way the people treated their inferiors? One's humanity is apt to renew the barbarous wish of Caligula, that the people had but one neck. A man could almost be pleased, by a single blow to put an end to such a race of monsters."—*Note to Essay on the Populousness of Ancient Nations.*

How Cicero, "*the mildest of all pagan philosophers and orators*," regarded with an inhuman approbation the cruelties above named, may be seen from his sayings, as quoted in Jortin's Discourses concerning the truth of the Christian Religion. He states that the supplications of a poor wretch begging his life, on the arena, only made the spectators, as a matter of course, the more violent against him, and the more set upon his death. See the Oration for Milo.

most illustrious period of Roman history," says that "at that time, the horrid practice of poisoning was so common, that during part of a season a prætor punished capitally for this crime above *three thousand persons* in a part of Italy, and found informations of this nature still multiplying upon him! So depraved in private life," adds the historian, "were that people whom in their history we so much admire."* *Murder* was in common practice among all classes. "Such," says Gibbon, "was the unhappy condition even of Roman emperors, that, whatever might be their conduct, their fate was commonly the same; almost every reign is closed by the same disgusting repetition of treason and murder." Suicide was not only extensively practised, but advocated as a right, and commended as virtuous. Seneca pleaded for it. Cicero was its advocate. Brutus, and Cassius, with many others, both defended and practised it. Cato is praised by Plutarch for having been his own murderer. These, in their day, were among the lights of the heathen world! What then, must have been the awful deeds of darkness among the more ignorant populace!

They were "*without natural affection.*" Nothing could exhibit, in a more appalling light, their utter annihilation of moral principle and natural affection, than the fact that "the exposition, that is, the murder of new born infants, was an allowed practice in almost all the states of Greece and Rome: even among the polite and civilized Athenians, the abandoning of one's child to hunger or to wild beasts was regarded without blame or censure."† "This practice," says Hume, "was very common; and is not spoken of by any author of those times with the horror it deserves, or scarcely even with disapprobation. Plutarch, the humane, good-natured Plutarch, mentions it as a merit in Attalus, king of Pergamus, that he murdered, or, if you will, exposed all his own children in order to leave his crown to the son of his brother, Eumenes. It was Solon, the most celebrated of the sages of Greece, that

* Essay on Politics. † Smith's Theory of Moral Sentiments.

gave parents permission by law to kill their children."* Philosophers supported the custom by argument. Aristotle thought it should be encouraged by the magistrates. Plato maintained the same inhuman doctrine. It was complained of, as a great singularity, that the laws of Thebes forbade the practice. In all the provinces, and especially in Italy, the crime was daily perpetrated. From one end to the other of the Roman empire was stained with the blood of murdered infants. Think of the state of domestic virtue, when such was a prevailing inhumanity of parents; and the learned defended it as wise; the magistrate countenanced it as useful; and public sentiment regarded it as innocent! Such was the power of a father by the Roman law, that his adult children might be sent to the mines, sold into slavery, or destroyed at his will; his daughter could be compelled, at his discretion, to forsake a husband whom he himself had approved, while his wife could be dismissed at pleasure; and for certain crimes, some of them of a very trivial nature, might be put to death. The authority of the father was that of a despot. The subjection of his family was that of slaves.

3d. But the Greeks and Romans were as notorious for their departure from the lowest grade of decency, as for their savage disruption of all the ties of natural affection. Sallust, speaking of the Roman youth in the time of Cicero, says: "Luxury, avarice, and pride, enslaved them; they wantoned in rapine and prodigality; undervalued their own, and coveted what belonged to others; trampled on modesty, friendship, and continence; confounded things divine and human, and threw off all manner of consideration and restraint." "Men and women laid aside all regard to chastity."* We cannot name the degrading crimes which in Greece were sanctioned by the public laws, and at Rome were practised, in the time of Seneca, without shame. It was considered a singular example in Athens, that the most

* Hume on the Populousness of Ancient Nations.

† Rose's Translation.

moral philosopher did not indulge in them. Even Cicero could speak, without any sign of disapprobation, of Cotta, an eminent Roman, as having owned an habitual addiction to the vileness we are alluding to, and as having quoted the authorities of ancient philosophers in its vindication. There was no species of degrading crime which had not its attempted justification in the written doctrines, and its shameless perpetration in the avowed practices, of the wise men, and such as are usually supposed to have been the *good* men, of the most civilized nations of antiquity. Quinctilian, speaking of the *philosophers* of the first century of the Christian era, says: "The most notorious vices are screened under that name; and they do not labour to maintain the character of philosophers by virtue and study, but conceal the most vicious lives under an austere look and singularity of dress."* Such, also, is the acknowledgment of Plutarch, with regard to the ancient philosophers in general. While he owns that they were generally noted for a certain infamous vice which we cannot name; he excuses them by the plea that they improved their minds at the same time that they corrupted their bodies. Lucian and others unite in this representation. Neither Seneca, nor Xenophon, nor Plato, nor Aristotle, nor even Socrates, whose morals have been extolled by infidels, as surpassing any thing in the Bible, is excepted from the revolting account of these writers. Granting that jealousy and calumny, among the ancients, included some of those illustrious names under a charge so degrading; what must have been the character of the great mass of the philosophers, when calumny durst venture so far?†

Such were the men whom our modern reformers would hold up to the public as patterns of virtue. "They opposed each other," says Voltaire, "in their dogmas; but in morality they were all agreed." "There has been no philosopher, in all antiquity, who has not been desirous of making men

* Quinctilian, Inst. Orat. † See M'Knight on Rom. i. 26, 27.

better." To the truth of the first assertion, we have no reason to object. In a sense directly opposite to that in which the writer intended it to be understood, they were indeed *in morality all agreed.* As to their unanimous desire of making men better, we can only say that they adopted the most singular means of effecting it. A Roman citizen, of the Augustan age, described them as those who, *being past feeling, had given themselves over unto lasciviousness to work all uncleanness with greediness.**

We have now exhibited some of the prominent features in the moral character of the society of Greece and Rome, in their most enlightened ages. From what has been stated, we may form a conception sufficiently accurate of the condition of things in all those departments of morality on which depends whatever is important to personal, domestic, and public happiness. We have been speaking of the most cultivated people of the ancient world. Unspeakably darker and more appalling would have been the picture, had we described the spirit, habits, and prevading crimes of any other pagan nations. But we are content that a fair repre-

---

* Among the philosophers of the time of Cicero, the *Cynics* were held in great repute, and were widely spread throughout the Roman empire. The wise man of this school "gave up all human relations towards mankind; contemned his country, his kindred, and the joys of wedded love, and sought his consolation in a self-complacent beastliness. One might see those beastly men half naked, moving about every where, with a great cudgel and a bread-bag, performing the animal necessities of their nature before the eyes of all; thrusting themselves, with extreme rudeness, among the multitudes, and there stepping forward as teachers of wisdom; not in a regular discourse, but with abrupt and broken language of vulgar sport and derision." And yet even the New Platonic philosophers greatly revered Cynicism, and represented Diogenes, its leader,as *a godlike man.*

Whoever may desire a more extended account of ancient, classic heathenism, in regard to its gross superstition, its disgusting sensuality, its obscene idols and ceremonies, its human sacrifices, its legalized cruelties, the odious vices of those who conformed to it, and its utter impotency for all purposes of moral improvement, is referred to an article, already quoted, on *the Nature and Influence of Heathenism*, by *Prof. Tholuck*, of *Halle, in Nos.* vi. and vii. *of the Biblical Repository, Andover.*

sentation of the best, should also be received as a good likeness of the worst communities of ancient heathenism.

We ask, what has become of all these deep rooted deformities? Look around upon the countries over which the influence of christianity has been exerted; those especially where the religion of Jesus has been enjoyed in the greatest purity, and cultivated with the truest devotion. Where are the remains of the abominations we have described! Crime remains indeed; but only in hidden dens. It shuns the light. Laws do not afford it countenance. Public sentiment drives it into concealment. What would the feeling of society now say to a show of gladiators; to the legalized exposure of infants by the hands of mothers; to the public, deliberate murder of worn out slaves; to the justification of suicide, and theft, and lying, and assassination, and the acknowledged practice of the most odious sensuality, by those who are looked up to as the moral teachers and examples of society? How would idolatry, with all its cruelties and obscenities; its profligate deities; its human sacrifices; its hidden mysteries of iniquity; and its public ritual of vice, affect the public mind, were its temples, and images, and lascivious ceremonies now set up in our cities? It is not enough to say that in countries where all these abominations once rioted without restraint and in full sympathy with the public taste, they have long since been driven away with abhorrence. Positive blessings, in every form and for every class of society, have risen up in their place. A measure of virtue which would have singled out an ancient philosopher as a wonderful exception to the rest of the world, is absolutely necessary at present to a character of ordinary decency. Benevolence, such as was not known in Greece or Rome, and had it appeared, would not have been comprehended, is now a matter of common, daily intercourse between man and man. An incalculable improvement has been effected in all departments of human affairs, from the administration of national government down to the most retired relations of the family circle. What rulers would have been remarkable once for *not doing*, the people would now expel them for attempting. A spirit of equity, moderation, and respect for the interests and happiness of the community, is required in the governments of countries under the influence of christianity, which was hardly conceived of by the nations of antiquity, and, if it ever appeared, was a marvellous exception to general rule. Laws, regenerated in their principles, are enacted in wisdom, and executed with a faithfulness unknown to the heathen. Instead of the despotic harshness with which a father was once permitted to rule his children and his wife, as his tools and slaves; universal sentiment demands it, as necessary even to decency, that he shall be kind to them as his own flesh, and as the rightful sharers in all his comforts. Women have been elevated from the rank of beasts of burden, to an equal participation in all the refinements and blessings of society. The condition of the dependant classes of the community has been raised from that of contempt, and oppression, and utter ignorance, to a level, in point of natural right, with all; while education shines upon their dwellings, and religion seeks their souls, as worthy of all sacrifices which christian benevolence can make for their salvation.

Efforts to provide for the sick, the destitute, the orphan, the widow, were unknown among the ancients. Rome, Athens, Corinth, contained no hospitals, no asylums, no public charities, no systems of gratuitous education. Such deeds of benevolence were impossible among a people who were accustomed to look upon all forms of human suffering with indifference, and to derive enthusiastic amusement from their promotion. In vain are the writings of their moralists examined for exhortations to any thing like an active concern for the poor or the ignorant. An orphan child was no object of public compassion in countries where orphans were daily and deliberately made, and left to perish by cold-blooded abandonment on the part of their parents.

But what new sympathies sprung up immediately where the gospel prevailed! It was made the duty of the whole christian community to provide for the stranger, the poor, the sick, the aged, the widow, and the orphan. For this one object, public contributions, at the time of divine service, were established, and private donations were multiplied. How much such benevolence was insisted on, may be judged from a passage of Tertullian, where, speaking of the impediments which a christian woman would encounter by marriage with a heathen, he says: "What heathen will suffer his wife, in visiting the brethren to go from street to street, into strangers', and even into the most miserable cottages? Who will suffer them to steal into prisons, to kiss the chains of martyrs? If a stranger-brother comes, what reception will he find in a stranger's house? If she has alms to bestow, the safe and the cellar are closed to her."

What the gospel effected, in promoting benevolence, and trampling down all the obstacles of selfishness and fear, when good was hardly to be done but at the cost of life, may be seen from the following representation of Dionysius, bishop of Alexandria, who had an opportunity of observing the contrast between heathens and Christians, when a terrible pestilence was raging in that city. "That pestilence appeared to the heathen as the most dreadful of all things, as that which left them no hope; not so, however, did it seem to us, but only a peculiar and practical trial. The greater part of our people, in the abundance of their brotherly love, did not spare themselves; and mutually attending to each other, they would visit the sick without fear, and ministering to them for the sake of Christ, they would cheerfully give up their life with them. Many died, after their care had restored others from the disease to health. The best among our brethren, some priests and deacons, and some who were celebrated among the laity, died in this manner, and such a death, the fruit of great piety and strong faith, is hardly inferior to martyrdom. Many who took the bodies of their christian brethren into their hands and bosoms, closed their mouth and eyes, and buried them with every attention, soon followed them in death. But with the heathen, matters stood quite differently; at the first symptom of sickness, they drove a man from their society; they tore themselves away from their dearest connexions; they threw the half dead into the streets, and left the dead unburied; endeavouring by all the means in their power to escape contagion, which, notwithstanding all their contrivances, it was very difficult for them to accomplish."

"In the same manner," writes Neander, from whose church history the above is taken, "the Christians of Carthage let the light of their love and christian conduct shine before the heathen in a pestilence which visited North Africa a little before, in the reign of Gallus. The heathen, out of cowardice, left the sick and the dying; the streets were full of corpses, which no man dared to bury; and avarice was the only passion which mastered the fear of death; for wicked men endeavoured to make a gain out of the misfortunes of their neighbours; and the heathen accused the Christians of being the cause of this calamity, as enemies of the gods, instead of being brought by it to the consciousness of their own guilt and corruption. But Cyprian required of his church that they should behold, in this desolating pestilence, a trial of their dispositions. 'How necessary is it, my dearest brethren,' he says to them, 'that this pestilence, which appears to bring horror and destruction, should prove the consciences of men! It will determine whether the healthy will take care of the sick, whether relations bear tender love one to another, and whether masters care for their sick servants.' That the Christians should show a spirit of mutual love among themselves, was not sufficient to satisfy a bishop who formed his notions after the model of the great Shepherd. He therefore called his church together, and addressed them thus: 'If we do good only to our own people, we do no more than publicans and heathens. But if we are the children of God, who makes his sun shine and his rain to descend upon the just and the unjust; who sheds abroad his blessings, not on his own alone, but even upon those whose thoughts are far from him; we must show this by our actions, endeavouring to become perfect as our Father in heaven is perfect, and blessing those who curse, and doing good to those who persecute us.' Encouraged by this paternal admonition, the members of the church addressed themselves to the work; the rich contributing money, and the poor their labour; so that in a short time the streets were cleared of the corpses who filled them, and the city saved from the dangers of a universal pestilence."*

That the spirit of primitive Christians is still the characteristic spirit of christianity, in regard to all works of charity, may easily be seen. Go where the gospel has attained the greatest supremacy, and behold how every form of human misery is met by the self denying diligence, and comforted by the munificence, of the benevolent. What conceivable method of removing distress, of preventing vice, and disseminating happiness, has not been put in operation? The whole Roman empire had not one benevolent institution. The single city of London counts her *three hundred!* And why is so little said or thought of them, except that the public mind has become so accustomed to the noblest efforts of benevolence, that they are now regarded almost as matters of course—the natural consequence of prevailing principles of brotherly kindness and charity?

It is not my design to exhibit any thing like a full length portrait of the contrast between the civilization of modern, and that of ancient nations. It is seen in all the relations of life; in the whole fabric of society, from the government of the family, to that of the state; from the tender cares of the cradle and the mother to the wide concerns of communities and rulers. Every thing has felt the change. Though not perfect, it is immense. Much remains to be done, but mighty

* Rose's translation of Neander's Ch. Hist.

improvements have been effected. Were the whole work undone · should the sun, which now enlightens the moral world, be commanded to go back, and suffer the classic paganism of Greece and Rome to resume its sway; every joint in the mechanism of society would groan with pain; every corner in the household of civilized beings would be filled with darkness; the transition from the arts and literature of England to those of Hottentots or New Zealanders, would not be greater than such a change from the moral elevation of the present age, to the highest refinements of the purest nations of antiquity.

Such is the fact. It remains to be accounted for. What produced this change? The religion of ancient heathens pleads "*not guilty*" to the charge. It had no reference to morals. The vilest crimes and the highest repute for piety were perfectly consistent with each other, among heathens of the Augustan age. It was no part of the business of their priests to teach men virtue. No religion but that of the Bible ever possessed or aimed at the power of reformation. Equally clear are the literature, and philosophy, and arts of antiquity from the imputation of this mighty revolution. Never did they prevail so extensively among the heathen, as in the first century of christianity; and never were they accompanied with such moral degradation. Philosophy had as little disposition, as ability to reform. Whatever light it may have possessed, it monopolized; holding its truth in unrighteousness, and studiously conforming its practice to the worst abominations. "Cicero declares that the ancient philosophers never reformed either themselves or their disciples; and that he knew not a single instance in which either th teacher or the disciple was made virtuous by their principles."*

---

* Dwight on Infidel Philosophy.

"In their writings and conversation, the philosophers of antiquity asserted the independent dignity of reason; but they resigned their actions to the commands of law and custom. Viewing with a smile of pity and indulgence the various errors of the vulgar, they diligently practised the ceremonies of their fathers, devoutly frequented the temples of the gods; and, sometimes conde-

But it may be supposed that, without any other cause than its own natural fluctuation, the moral condition of ancient nations may have taken a change, like the tides of the ocean, and begun to rise from the mere fact of being reduced to so low an ebb. Answer this by the present state of those nations that continued under the native influence of paganism. In which of them was such a thing ever known, as a reformation of public morals? Their unvaried history, from the days of Moses to the present, settles the matter, that heathenism has no power, but of progressive corruption; and, left to itself, can only reduce its votaries into deeper and deeper debasement. Then, if the vast improvement in question is neither the consequence of the religion, nor the philosophy, nor the arts, nor the literature, nor of any natural reaction in the moral state of the ancient heathen; to what other cause must it be assigned? History has but one answer. Reason has but one answer. Christianity alone; single-handed, persecuted christianity, by the agency of twelve obscure Jews, began the wonderful change, and under the favour of God, has accomplished its every step of advancement. Till such a thing as the religion of Christ appeared in the world, a reformation of heathen society was never dreamed of. Till Christians appeared among the Gentiles, none had ever adventured, none were ever disposed, to labour for the improvement of mankind. Christian writers were the first that dared to drag the abominations of classic antiquity to light, and brand them with the condemnation of truth and righteousness. The first christian emperor

---

scending to act a part on the theatre of superstition, they concealed the sentiments of an Atheist under the sacerdotal robes. It was indifferent to them what shape the folly of the multitude might choose to assume; and they approached, with the same inward contempt and the same external reverence, the altars of the Lybian, the Olympian, or the Capitoline Jupiter."—*Gibbon's History*, i. 34.

A sorry tribute, by a philosopher, to the benevolence and honesty of his ancient brethren. Paul would have drawn their picture with a darker pencil still Paul's Master would have named them "*hypocrites*," "*whited sepulchres*."

issued the first prohibition of inhuman practices and amusements, which many centuries had sanctioned. Till the gospel set up its churches and gathered its disciples, the gentile world had never seen such a spectacle as that of a society united by bands of love; shining in the beauty of holiness; animated with zeal to do good at the expense of self-denial and sacrifice.

How exclusively the happy effects of which we have been speaking are the fruit of christianity, is evident from the fact that, when you take up a map of the world and mark out the boundaries of christendom, you mark also the boundaries of all civilization and refinement; that as you approach the regions where the Bible is best known and most obeyed, you perceive a rapid increase of all the virtues, and charities, and blessings of which the society of man is capable; that the highest elevation of the human character is where christianity reigns in her purest form, and the blackest page in the history of Christendom, the page most polluted with vice, and red with cruelty and murder, is the record of the people who trampled down the institutions of the gospel, decreed the living God out of existence, and attempted to raise the deities of ancient paganism from the dead. That many individuals who deny the truth, and profess to be free from the influence of christianity, are decent men and far removed from the condition of the heathen in point of moral precept, as well as practice, is no evidence against our position. The light of christianity is all about them, and they cannot help seeing by its aid. They have learned christian truth from their childhood, and it cannot be unlearned. Do what they may, they cannot think or act without its influence. They may boast the sufficiency of their own reason, but they can no more exercise their reason without the aid of revelation, than they can breathe the air of spring without the fragrance of its flowers. "On all questions of morality and religion, the streams of thought have flowed through channels enriched with a celestial ore, whence they have derived the tincture to which they are indebted for their rarest and most salutary qualities."* What a community of deists would be without christianity, can only be known by remembering what deists were before christianity came into the world, and what they became, when in France they supposed they had almost banished her from the earth.

How remarkable are the confessions of infidels to the excellent fruit and indispensable influence of the gospel! Bolingbroke acknowledges, "that Constantine acted the part of a sound politician in protecting christianity, as it tended to give firmness and solidity to his empire, softened the ferocity of the army, and reformed the licentiousness of the provinces, and by infusing a spirit of moderation and submission to government, tended to extinguish those principles of avarice and ambition, injustice and violence, by which so many factions were formed." "No religion," says the same opposer of christianity, "ever appeared in the world whose natural tendency was so much directed to promote the peace and happiness of mankind. It makes right reason a law in every possible definition of the word. And therefore, even supposing it to have been purely a human invention, it had been the most amiable and the most useful invention that was ever imposed on mankind for their good." Thus even Rousseau: "If all were perfect Christians, individuals would do their duty; the people would be obedient to the laws; the magistrates incorrupt; and there would be neither vanity nor luxury in such a state." Such are the confessions of many other writers of the same class. And yet these men would run the ploughshare through the foundations of the church of Christ, so that one stone should not be left upon another. So much for the consistency, the virtue, and disinterested benevolence of infidelity; or rather so much for the contradiction between its head and its heart, its convictions and its vices.

I know of nothing, in the way of fact, more strikingly

* Robert Hall.

illustrative of the legitimate fruits of christianity; more completely in proof that all the social and moral blessings which civilized nations at present enjoy, are to be ascribed to her influence; and that what she once was, as a tree of life to the nations, she is now, and ever will be; than the history of the missions among the heathen, which protestant Christians are now sustaining. Here we have experiments of her power in all climates, over all habits and dispositions, and with all classes of mind. She has gone in among the ice-bound inhabitants of Greenland, whose intellect was as slow, and sleepy, and creeping, as the seals they lived on; and whose hearts were as barren and cold as their perpetual snows. She has entered among the inhabitants of the southern extreme of Africa, the Hottentots, the very lowest gradation of human nature, whose souls were supposed to be as incapable of enlightening and enlargement as the instincts of the vermin that covered them. She has tried her powers among the ferocious tribes of American Indians; upon warriors nourished with blood, and breathing a spirit of slaughter which no sufferings nor dangers could ever tame. She has lifted up her voice in the islands of the Pacific, among savages uniting with the most inhuman idolatry, the most beastly vices and unnatural cruelties; and from all this heterogeneous display of unshapen depravity, by the mere influence of her truth and love, she has led forth a multitude of disciples for the Lord Jesus, in whom are found precisely the same distinctive features of meekness, humility, love, and holiness. Look at the Sandwich, or the Society Islands! Within our own times were they universally pagan, having no altars but those of dæmons; no law but that of violence; no morals but those of unbridled passion. Theft was the most national art. Polygamy; crimes against nature; the murder of prisoners taken in war; the destruction of infants and the sacrificing of human victims, prevailed throughout their population. What is the change! Where are now their idols? In the museums of our missionary societies, as trophies of the victories of the cross; or cast "to the moles and the bats" by those who once adored them. The plan and mould of society have been recast. Laws, wisely enacted and well admistered, keep the peace and promote improvements. Crimes of all kinds are obliged to cease or go into concealment. Marriage has given parents new affection for their children, and their children new ties among each other. Benevolence, unknown before, has awakened a desire to go about doing good. The Sabbath is reverenced and widely kept for rest and worship. The arts of peace are cultivated where formerly the only art desired was that of war. The march of civilization is visible in all domestic comforts and private affairs; in agriculture, commerce, buildings, cleanliness, dress, manners, and government. Schools are spread through the islands, and education is eagerly sought by a large portion of the people of all ages and classes. Such are the fruits of christianity in our day. Nothing else could have produced such fruits. Just after infidelity had given the world a full length portrait, in the French revolution, of her power to tear down, and tear in pieces, and drown in blood, whatever is lovely and of good report; then christianity set out, on the opposite side of the world, to furnish a striking contrast, in the missions of the Pacific, of her benign influence to exterminate whatever is odious and depraved.*

* It is well known to the author that travellers and voyagers not unfrequently bring back reports of the effects of missionary labours in the regions they have visited, which stagger the minds of many sincere friends of foreign missions. The accounts of what those honoured and devoted servants of Christ, called missionaries, are doing, and of the advances which the gospel is making under their influence, may all be true; much more than they relate may be true; and yet it is very conceivable, yea, natural, that such men as our ordinary visiters of foreign lands should return from those regions, having neither seen nor heard any thing of the matter. Suppose a missionary were accomplishing, with his schools and his preaching, among a tribe of Indians in the centre of the state of New York, about as much as is reported of the American labourers in the island of Ceylon; how long might an intelligent traveller, with no interest in religion, no relish for its intelligence, no love for

Not only has the religion of the gospel produced such fruits, but the experiment of eighteen hundred years is perfect proof, that in proportion as it shall ever be possessed in

---

the society of its disciples, no knowledge of its journals—a man of fashion and gayety, mingling only with the literary and worldly-minded; how long might he reside in the fashionable circles of the city of New York, and sail up the Hudson, and stop at Saratoga, and visit Niagara, and yet know absolutely nothing of that diligent missionary and his usefulness? Men who have lived all their days in a city which abounds in religious institutions and christian labours, without having become sufficiently informed to give a stranger a correct account even of their respective characters, much less of their real usefulness, will touch at a port in the Sandwich islands, see the *port* population, go no further than the coast, inquire of none but the ungodly, and then come home and report that the missionaries have done nothing to civilize or convert the people. How should such men know? On their principles of judging, it might be reported, with equal reason, that christianity has secured no influence, and done no good, in the city of New York. An anecdote will illustrate how such authorities deserve to be regarded. A gentleman, not long since, returned to his native city in England, after having spent some three or four years in India. The pious people of his acquaintance (not considering the extent of the Indies, and his indifference to the cause of Christ) supposed that of course he had seen the missionary stations, and knew by his own observation all about the reported progress of religion in that country. They inquired of him the state of things in this respect. He assured them that the accounts they had read of missionary doings and successes in the East had no foundation—were mere traps to get contributions. He had been in India, and travelled extensively, and had seen nothing of any inroads upon heathenism, nor any changes among the people; had scarcely heard of the existence of missionary stations. The people were amazed! Much harm was doing; when a clergyman of the place, hearing of the matter, took an opportunity to converse with the traveller. Before disclosing his object, he said to him: "You are probably familiar with the national school system of instruction in this country. What do you think of it?" "Why no," answered the traveller, "I really am not acquainted with it." "But you doubtless know that there is such a system, and have probably seen its establishments, and heard much of its usefulness."—"Why no, I have never happened to do so, though I have a indistinct idea of the existence of such a system."—"Well," said the clergyman, "I will tell you. The national school system has been established for several years in England. Its schools are all over the country; its pupils are many hundreds of thousands; its influence is universally felt. It maintains more than one school in your immediate neighbourhood. Almost all your life has been spent in England, a small country, and yet you know nothing of these interesting facts. You have been a short time in the immense region of India, over which a few

native soundness, and have room and freedom to spread its roots and extend its branches, it will continue to bear such fruit, more and more abundantly and perfectly, to the end of time. This tree of life was planted to live through all ages, and spread its shadow over all nations. The trials it stood in its infancy; the fierce assaults of every species of enmity, which in every age of its subsequent growth have endeavoured in vain to destroy it, are evidences that, as no human power could have thus protected it, so no human opposition can hereafter prevent its increase; that it must grow, and spread, and blossom, till time shall be no more.

I am well aware, and I desire not to conceal, that it is very common with infidels to ascribe *wars*, *intrigues*, *bloodshed*, and *persecutions*, to the influence of christianity, and to assert that the world has been covered with slaughter by the hand of the gospel. The truth is, that whenever any evils, such as wars or persecutions, arise, though infidels by profession, or mere nominal christians, are at the bottom of them; though originated and carried on out of direct enmity to the gospel; yet, because the christian name is involved in the contest, infidels set down the whole to the account of a religion, which, nevertheless, their chief men confess, has a direct tendency *to make every body do his duty*,* and "*to promote the peace and happiness of mankind*."† But on the other hand, whenever any *good* is done in society, such as the banishment of the crimes and vices of heathenism; the promotion of virtue, peace, good laws, good institutions, benevolence, domestic and public happiness; then infidels have great difficulty in seeing how these blessings are connected with christianity, even though, by their own acknow-

---

missionary stations are scattered, as drops upon a desert; and because, in visiting a few prominent places, you heard or saw nothing of their influence upon the millions of heathen, you would persuade us that what we have read is all untrue. How much more should we believe that the national school system is a fable!" The traveller was silenced; the people were satisfied.

* Rousseau. † Bolingbroke.

ledgment, the life of Jesus "*showed at once what excellent creatures men would be, when under the influence and power of that gospel which he preached.*"*

It is freely granted that in countries called christian, great evils remain to be cured; their history abounds with wars, some of which have been on *account* of the christian religion, and have been accompanied with great slaughter and lasting enmities. But before these deplorable facts can justly be attributed to the influence of the peaceful and gentle religion of Jesus, a number of important questions, which we shall presently name, must be decided. By the confession of one of the most noted infidels: "We have in Christ an example of one who was just, honest, upright, and sincere, and above all, of a most gracious and benevolent temper and behaviour. One who did no wrong, no injury to any man; in whose mouth was no guile; who went about doing good, not only by his ministry, but also in curing all manner of diseases among the people. His life showed what excellent creatures men would be when under the influence and power of that gospel which he preached unto them."† But hear on this head the eloquence of the profligate Rousseau, venturing for once to speak the truth: "I will confess that the majesty of the scriptures strikes me with admiration, as the purity of the gospel has its influence on my heart. Peruse the works of our philosophers with all their pomp of diction; how contemptible are they compared with the scriptures! Is it possible that a book at once so simple and sublime should be merely the work of man? Is it possible that the sacred personage whose name it records, should be himself a mere man? What sweetness, what purity in his manner! What sublimity in his maxims! What profound wisdom in his discourses! Where is the man, where the philosopher, who could so live and so die without weakness and without ostentation? If the life and death of Socrates were those of a sage, the life

* Chubb's True Gospel, § viii. 55, 6.

† Chubb's True Gospel, § viii. 56, 57.

and death of Jesus were those of a God." Such are the confessions of a man whose vice and vanity constrained him to say: "*I cannot believe the gospel.*" No wonder, when at the same time he was saying in his heart, *I will not renounce my debaucheries.*

But such confessions abound in the writings of infidels, so that "the whole christian argument might be maintained on the admissions of one or other of the leading infidel writers, and no contest remain, unless, if it could then be called one, with the miserable, ignorant ferocity of Paine and his associates."*

On the ground of such acknowledgments, and of the acquaintance which any who ever read the New Testament must have with its principles and tendency, let the following questions be answered: Is there any tendency in the principles of the gospel to the enkindling of strife, hatred, war, or bloodshed? Was the character of its founder; were the characters of the apostles and primitive Christians among whom the native influence of christianity was most unequivocally exhibited, in any manner indicative of such a tendency in its principles? Is not the whole history of the purest ages of the gospel, as well as every page in the New Testament, directly in proof of the very opposite effect? Did not all the evils of war and national dissension prevail much more universally before the establishment of christianity, than they have done since? Is not the influence of this religion plainly visible in mitigating those horrors of war which she has not exterminated? And as to those which have continued to subsist, are they in direct consequence, or in spite of her influence; the fruit of the tree, or the poisonous weeds at its root, which oppose its growth? Are the men who have been concerned in promoting these evils, and who are called Christians, believed to have been *real* Christians? Do not infidels discriminate sufficiently between genuine and nominal religion, to understand that, in thus acting, they were departing

---

*Wilson's Lectures.

from the principles of the gospel, and proving that they were Christians but in name? "Have not the courts of princes, notwithstanding christianity may have been the professed religion of the land, been generally attended by a far greater proportion of deists, than of serious Christians; and have not public measures been directed by the counsels of the former, much more than by those of the latter? It is well known that great numbers among the nobility and gentry of every nation consider religion as suited only to vulgar minds; and therefore either wholly absent themselves from public worship, or attend but seldom, and then only to save appearances towards a national establishment. In other words, they are unbelievers. This is the description of men by which public affairs are commonly managed, and to which the good or the evil pertaining to them, so far as human agency is concerned, is to be attributed."*

It is a favourite manœuvre with infidels to charge christianity with all the persecutions on account of religion, and, at the same time, to speak in high terms of "the mild tolerance of the ancient heathens;" of "*the universal toleration of polytheism;*" of "the Roman princes beholding without concern a thousand forms of religion subsisting in peace under their gentle sway."† Better information on this subject is greatly needed in the community. Heathen toleration was any thing but virtuous, and much less universal than its modern eulogists would represent. It allowed all nations to establish whatever description of religion they pleased, provided each would acknowledge that all, in their several spheres, were equally good. But pagan nations required of every citizen conformity to the national idolatries. This yielded, he migh believe and be, whatever he pleased. This denied, immedi ately toleration ceased. Take a few examples. Stilpo was banished Athens, for affirming that the statue of Minerva, in the citadel, was no divinity, but only the work of the chisel of Phidias. Protagoras received a similar punishment for

* Fuller's Gospel its own Witness. † Gibbon.

this single sentence: "Whether there be gods or not, I have nothing to offer." Prodicus and his pupil, Socrates, suffered death for opinions at variance with the established idolatry of Athens. Alcibiades and Æschylus narrowly escaped a like end for a similar cause. Plato dissembled his opinions; and Aristotle fled his country, under the lash of *the mild and universal toleration of the Grecian mythology.* Cicero lays it down as a principle of legislation entirely conformable to the rights of the Roman state, that "no man shall have separate gods for himself; and no man shall worship by himself new or foreign gods, unless they have been publicly acknowledged by the laws of the state."* The speech, in Dion Cassius, which Mæcenas is said to have made to Augustus, may be considered a fair index of the prevailing sentiment of that polished age. "Honour the gods," says Mæcenas, "by all means, according to the customs of your country, and force others so to honour them. But those who are for ever introducing something foreign in these matters, hate and punish, not only for the sake of the gods, but also because they who introduce new divinities mislead many others into receiving foreign laws also. Suffer no man either to deny the gods, or to practise sorcery." Julius Paulus, the Roman civilian, gives the following as a leading feature of Roman law: "Those who introduced new religions, or such as were unknown in their tendency and nature, by which the minds of men might be agitated, were degraded if they belonged to the higher ranks, and if they were in a lower state, were punished with death." Under this legislation, many of the governors endeavoured to compromise with Christians, by allowing them to believe and honour what they pleased in their hearts, provided they would observe outwardly the religious ceremonies ordained by the state.†

Examples to the same effect, might be greatly multiplied. I have furnished enough to show in what sense the heathen princes "*beheld, without concern, a thousand forms of reli-*

* De Legibus, ii. 8.

† See Neander's Church History.

gion subsisting in peace under their gentle sway;" and how far Voltaire was accurately informed or honestly disposed, when boasting that the ancient Romans "never persecuted a single philosopher for his opinions from the time of Romulus till the popes got possession of their power."

It is willingly conceded that persecutions on account of religion were enormously increased immediately after the promulgation of christianity; inasmuch as nothing had ever before attacked the superstitions and vices of the heathen with her undaunted, uncompromising spirit. But did christianity persecute; or was she the object of persecution? Was Jesus the persecutor of Pilate? Did Paul persecute the worshippers of the Ephesian Diana, or the heathen of Iconium, or those who stoned him at Lystra? By whose intolerance was it, that, for three hundred years, the christian church was continually overflowed with the blood of her martyrs? Did the multitudes who perished for Christ's sake, under the paw of the lion, and the sword of the gladiator, and the screws of the rack—did they persecute the heathen priests, and people, and magistrates—Nero, and Trajan, and Diocletian—with their proconsuls, and governors, and executioners? I grant that in the lapse of centuries the guilt of persecution did attach to the church. Christian powers, and ministers, and people have, in various ages, been justly liable to this lamentable charge. But who does not know that the church, before ever she began to persecute, had manifestly degenerated from the purity of the gospel, and become deeply poisoned with the spirit of the world, having her chief places occupied by such men as infidels know were not influenced by vital christianity?* Who is so blind as not to see that wherever such evils have existed among

* The emperor Julian acknowledged that persecutions were the inventions of the later Christians; that neither Jesus, nor Paul, nor any other of the first preachers of the gospel, had taught men to kill others for being of a different religion, or for differing about lesser matters among themselves.—*Lardner*, iv. 337.

any people called Christians, they have been because those people had so little of the spirit of the gospel, and not because they had any of it? They have been directly the reverse of the religion professed by such persons; the fruits of their own native disposition, combined with the character of the ages they lived in, assimilating them thus far to infidels, who have always been persecutors in proportion to their power. True christianity desires but one favour: *liberty to preach "Jesus Christ and him crucified."* Her whole dependence is on "the demonstration of the Spirit." "*God giveth the increase.*"

We have now applied to christianity the test by which she claims to be proved; one universally employed as safe, and approved as just; *the tree is known by its fruits.* The religion of the gospel we have seen coming into the world at a period when every moral evil abounded. The grossest idolatry, attended with the most inhuman and indecent rites, prevailed among the most enlightened nations. Spectacles of slaughter and suffering constituted the public amusements. Parents without natural affection, children in slavery to their parents, and at the mercy of their displeasure, the female sex degraded to a rank of servile inferiority, murders and cruelties characterized the age. Vices of the most beastly kind were practised and avowed in the highest and most influential classes of society. What would now shame out of the world the most degraded of mankind, could then be acknowledged, even by a public teacher of morals, without reproach. Public opinion, the thermometer of public virtue, had no condemnation for habits not only against all the securities of domestic happiness and social welfare, but against every dictate of nature, and requiring for their permission the lowest debasement of the moral sense of the community. Among all the gentile nations, none possessed the benevolence to attempt, nothing had power to effect, the reformation of a world thus sunk in wretchedness, and paralyzed with vice. It was the era, indeed, of the world's wisdom; but of a wisdom by which the world knew not God. For centuries, had the wise men after the flesh been teaching, and writing, and boasting; and as long had every wo been increasing, and every school becoming more perplexed in its doctrines, and more abandoned in the practice of its disciples. No change, for the better, was hoped for from any human source. Then appeared "the wisdom of God." Christianity, uninvited, unwelcomed, rejected; christianity, persecuted as intrusive, despised as foolishness, ridiculed as weakness, commenced at this crisis the bold work of regenerating the world. Wherever she gained acceptation the face of society was renewed. Order, purity, benevolence, justice, mercy, every personal, domestic, and public virtue increased as her influence extended. Under her charge, immense communities of men and women were formed, who soon became famous in the world for their earnest self-denying benevolence, and their devotion to holiness. No sooner was christianity professed by the rulers of the Roman empire, than idolatry, with every unnatural crime and cruel amusement, was abolished from society, or compelled to deny its existence. In proportion as this religion has reigned in any age or country, there has been a manifest increase of all the blessings of civilization, all the arts of peace, all the virtues of individual character, all the securities of a wise and equitable government. Nothing has retarded the growth of these benefits but what has alike retarded the progress of christianity. No christian people have suffered on account of any evil, which christianity has not directly opposed. Present efforts to spread this holy religion among the heathen demonstrate that her natural force is not abated, nor her influence changed. What she did among the pagans of the first, she is accomplishing, though as yet by slower steps, among those of the nineteenth century. Such has been from the beginning; such is now; and such, we have every reason to believe, ever will be the fruit of christianity. By this she is known. By this let her claims to truth and divine original be judged. Every honest mind is capable of appreciating the evidence, and of applying the law. It is a case by itself. No party appears to claim the credit of what christianity ascribes to herself. Philosophy and the light of nature are joined to their idols and vices, and cannot come to the trial, and must therefore be excused. Infidelity was tried during the "Reign of Terror" in France, and received its sentence at the guillotine, and therefore cannot come. Either the blessings we have described must be adjudged, according to the plea, to the gospel of Christ, or pronounced to be effects without a cause. Do they belong to the gospel, or to nothing? We speak the language of every conscience and of all common sense when we say, *the gospel alone produced them, and the gospel alone could produce them;* and should the gospel be thoroughly conformed to in all the world, the whole world would be morally renovated, and all those physical evils which proceed from the vices of mankind would pass away.

What, then, is christianity? "Do men gather grapes of thorns, or figs of thistles?" "Can a corrupt tree bring forth good fruit?" This religion is either a truth or a fable; the revelation of God, or the wicked and blasphemous contrivance of man. If it be the work of human contrivance, it must be unspeakably offensive to God, inasmuch as it ascribes all its doctrines directly to His teaching; exalts its Founder to the dignity of the divine nature, calling him the Son of God, and making him equal to the Father in power and glory. Between its entire truth as a divine revelation, and its unparalleled audacity and impiety as a human imposture, there can be no middle ground. The unbeliever, in rejecting the former, must resort, if consistent, to the latter. Then let us see how much he is bound to believe in maintaining his position. He must believe that since the truth, according to his views, does not reside in christianity, it does reside in some or all of the systems of religion, or of philosophy, or of infidelity, to which christianity is opposed. His creed, therefore, is substantially the following: 'I believe that in proportion as the world has ever been committed to the influence of those antichristian systems among which the truth is to be found; it has been continually increasing in all moral degeneracy, having in it no spirit nor power of reformation. I believe, also, that in proportion as christianity, which should be regarded only as a human contrivance of the grossest blasphemy and impiety, has reigned in the hearts and lives of men; the world has been morally renovated, society humanized, benevolence invigorated, personal and public happiness extended and purified. Consequently, I believe that a God infinitely wise, holy, and true, has so constituted mankind, that for the improvement and well-being of society, we are under the necessity of believing and promoting what is not only false, but heinously offensive to Himself; truth must be concealed because we learn by experience that its currency can only be accompanied with the greatest evils to the morals, the peace, the whole interest of mankind; teachers of error and darkness must be depended upon as instruments of human elevation, while teachers of the truth should be discountenanced as capable of nothing but the unhinging of the whole frame-work of private and public welfare.' These, I say, are the articles of belief which, whether avowed or not, do lie wrapped up in the rejection of christianity. The proof of this assertion is in the lecture we are now closing. I need not say that it sets, in strong and shining relief, the truth of the gospel of our Lord Jesus Christ, as a revelation from Him who is the giver of every good and perfect gift. "For the preaching of the cross is to them that perish foolishness: but unto us which are saved it is the power of God. Where is the wise? Where is the disputer of this world? Hath not God made foolish the wisdom of this world? For after that in the wisdom of God, the world by wisdom knew not God, it pleased God by the foolishness of preaching to save them that believe; for the Jews require a sign, and the Greeks seek after wisdom: But we preach Christ crucified, unto the Jews a stumbling-block, and unto the Greeks foolishness: But unto them which are called, both Jews and Greeks, Christ, the power of God and the wisdom of God."*

---

* 1 Corinthians, i. 18—24.

LECTURE XI.

THE FRUITS OF CHRISTIANITY.

The rule by which christianity was tried in our last lecture, is as philosophical as it is scriptural. It is the rule of experiment, in distinction from all the whims of conjecture and ingenious theory, and has an application, as legitimate and conclusive, to the character of christianity, as to that of any tree, or food, or medicine. None can deny that the experiment of the religion of Christ has been varied sufficiently to put it to the fairest trial, and continued long enough to develope its most hidden qualities. Exposed to all extremes of physical and moral temperature; tried upon all descriptions of human beings; required to preserve its purity amidst all contagions; to display its energies under all conceivable burdens and bonds; to bear its fruit under the most blasting influences; and to stand against all possible combinations of enmity; sometimes subjected to the action of the fire, then of the rack, and then of the knife, of unrelenting persecutors; eighteen hundred years have measured out its trial, during which, whatever could be effected by science united with industry, malice united with power, or vigilance united with hypocrisy, has been done unceasingly to torture it into a confession or a display of something at variance with divine original. The trial, therefore, is sufficient. The tree has had time and ample opportunity to be known by its fruits. If it may not be finally tried by this rule, in the nineteenth century of its budding and bearing, the fault must be sought in the rule itself, not in the subject of inquiry.

In our last lecture we confined our attention to *the fruits of christianity in regard to society in general.* In the present we are to consider.

ITS FRUITS IN REGARD TO THE CHARACTER AND HAPPINESS OF ITS GENUINE DISCIPLES.

It is not without reflection that I introduce this subject into the department of *external evidence.* I am aware that it is generally considered as belonging exclusively to the class of arguments denominated *internal;* but I see not with what propriety. So far as any effects of christianity on individual disciples are incapable of being brought under the observation of others, being confined to the inward experience of the true believer, they are unquestionably *internal* in their character, and do not belong to our present department. But if they be such effects as witnesses can take knowledge of; if the proof of them may be seen and appreciated by those that are without, and who can look only on the outward appearance; I see not but they belong, as appropriately, to the external evidence, as any of the effects of christianity upon society at large. Without further vindication of a matter of mere classification, I proceed.

I. *The moral transformations which the gospel, in all ages, has notoriously wrought, and by unquestionable proofs, exhibited to the world, in the characters of those who have become its genuine disciples, cannot be accounted for, but on the supposition of a divine power accompanying its operation.*

To illustrate my meaning, let me describe what has been witnessed under the ministry of christianity so repeatedly, that hardly any who have been in the way of such things can have failed to become acquainted with apposite examples. Persons of all grades of society and of intellect, and of all degrees of enmity to the religion of Jesus; in circumstances the most unpropitious to its influence on their hearts; even while they were filled with the spirit of malice and persecution against its truth and disciples; have had their minds suddenly arrested by some simple expression of the Bible, or some unpretending statement of christian doctrine or experience; perhaps it dropped from the lips of a minister against whom, at that very time, they were nerved with anger; or was read in a Bible, or a little despised tract, that seemed accidentally to lie in their way, and at which, as if by accident they condescended to look. It told them nothing new; nothing but what they had often heard or read before without the smallest effect. And yet, without any argument to shake their ungodly principles, or special application, by any human being, of the word, thus heard or read, to their particular condition; they felt their minds seized upon by an influence from which no effort of infidel argument, nor struggle of pride, nor drowning of thought, nor exertion of courage, nor devices of company and amusement, could enable them to escape. A hand seemed to be upon them which all their efforts to shake it off only fastened with more painful power. They could get no peace of mind till they submitted to its arrest. They were induced to listen to the gospel of Christ, even while deeply conscious of a cordial opposition to its requirements. A conviction of sin and condemnation, such as they had ever derided, soon brought them to a posture of body and a spirit of supplication before God, in which, a short time before, they would not have been seen for the world. Soon they submitted to the claims of the gospel; became believers in Jesus; confessed him before men, and appeared, to all that had known them before,—*in what aspect?* As *new creatures!* Only a few days have elapsed since they were notorious scoffers, bold blasphemers, angry persecutors; of profligate habits, impure conversation, and hardened hearts, armed at all points against religion; immoveable, in their own estimation, by any thing christians could say, and regarded by almost all that knew them as utterly beyond conversion.

Now behold the change! It is a change not merely of belief, but of heart. Their whole moral nature has been recast; affections, desires, pleasures, tempers, conduct, have all become new. What each hated, a few days since, he now affectionately loves. What then he was devotedly fond of, he now sincerely detests. Prayer is his delight. Holiness he thirsts for. His old companions he pities and loves for their souls' sake; but their tastes, conversation, and habits, are loathsome to his heart. Feelings, recently obdurate, have become tender. A temper, long habituated to anger, and violence, and resentment, is now gentle, peaceful, and forgiving. Christians whose company and intercourse he lately could not abide, are now his dear and chosen companions, with whom he loves to think of dwelling for ever. The proud unbeliever is an humble disciple. The selfish profligate has become self-denied and exemplary, animated with a benevolent desire to do good. All these changes are so conspicuous to others; he has become, and continues to be, so manifestly a new man, in life and heart, that the ungodly are struck with the suddenness and extent of the transformation.

This is a drawing from life. That such cases have frequently occurred, and have been followed by all the permanent blessings of a holy life, in thousands of places, and before witnesses of all descriptions, it were a mockery of human testimony and of the faith of history to question. There is scarcely a faithful preacher of the gospel, whose ministry has not been blessed with such fruits. There is scarcely a village in this country, whose inhabitants cannot tell of many such examples. They began when christianity began. They have been repeated as pure christianity has been promoted and extended. Such a case was that of Saul of Tarsus. One moment he was a furious enemy of Jesus; learned, talented, proud; of high reputation; of brilliant prospects; the champion of Judea against the gospel of Christ; bearing the commission, and full of the spirit of a persecutor. The next, he was on his face on the ground, calling upon Jesus in the spirit of entire submission and deep repentance. In a few days, he was preaching Christ in the synagogues, at the risk of life, having made a total sacrifice of all earthly prospects and possessions, and given himself up to reproach, poverty and universal hatred, for the sake of the gospel. All his dispositions, affections, and habits, had in that short space undergone so complete a change, without any human agency, that he had become, and continued to be, directly the opposite of his former character. Many similar examples must have been included in those three thousand converts of the day of Pentecost, who although when the morning rose upon them they were filled with all the enmity of Jews and of crucifiers of Jesus, before the day was over, were bowed at the feet of the same Jesus, as his baptized disciples. So changed were they in every worldly disposition, that they "sold their possessions and goods, and parted them to all men as every man had need;" and all this under no human influence, but that of the preaching of men whom they began to hear with contempt, and of a doctrine to which they began to listen with the most rancorous aversion. How many thousand cases of the same kind would the domestic history of the first century of the gospel furnish! What volumes might be filled with similar examples, which the annals of christianity in the nineteenth century, and especially in this country, would exhibit! Who has attended to the blessed effects with which the distribution of tracts and bibles has been accompanied, and cannot call to mind instances in which the wonderful changes that were wrought in the Earl of Rochester, in Col. Gardiner, and in the once degraded, and afterwards excellent John Newton have in all important respects been equalled? Since I commenced the preparation of this lecture, a case in point has come to my view. Called from my study, to see a man who had come on business, I found in the parlour a well-dressed person, of respectable appearance, good manners, and sensible conversation—a stranger. After a little while, he looked at me earnestly, and said: "I think, sir, I have seen your face before."—"Probably," said I, supposing he had seen me in the pulpit. "Did you not once preach, in the receiving ship, at the navy-yard, on the prodigal son, sir?" "Yes." "Did you not afterwards go to a sailor sitting on his chest, and take his hand, and say, 'friend, do you love to read your Bible?'" "Yes." "I, sir, was that sailor; but then I knew nothing about the Bible or about God: I was a poor, ignorant, degraded sinner." I learned his history, in substance, as follows. He had been twenty-five years a sailor, and nearly all that time in the service of the British navy, indulging in all the extremes of a sailor's vices. Drunkenness, debauchery, profaneness made up his character. The fear of death, or hell, or God, had not entered his mind. Such was he, a sink of depravity, when an humble preacher of the Methodist denomination, one day, assembled a little congregation of sailors in the ship to which he was attached, and spoke on the text: "Behold, now is the accepted time; behold, now is the day of salvation." He listened, merely because the preacher was once a sailor. Soon it appeared to him that the latter saw and knew him, though he was sitting where he supposed himself concealed. Every word seemed to be meant for a description of him. To avoid being seen and marked, he several times changed his place, carefully getting behind the others. But wherever he went, the preacher seemed to follow him, and to describe his course of life, as if he knew it all. At length the discourse was ended; and the poor sailor, assured that he had been the single object of the speaker's labours, went up and seized his hand, and said: "Sir, I am the very man. That's just the life I have led. I am a poor miserable man; but I feel a desire to be good, and will thank you for some of your advice upon the subject." The preacher bade him *pray*. He answered, "I have never prayed in my life, but that I might be damned, as when I was swearing; and I don't know how to pray." He was instructed. It was a day or two after this, while his mind was anxious but unenlightened, that Providence led me to him, sitting on his chest. He said I showed him a verse of the Bible, as one that would guide him. I asked if he remembered which it was. "Yes, it was, '*Him that cometh unto me I will in no wise cast out*.'" Soon after this, his mind was comforted with a hope of salvation through Jesus Christ. His vices were all abandoned. He became, from that time, a new creature in all his dispositions and habits; took special care to be scrupulously attentive to every duty of his station; gained the confidence of his officers; and, having left the service, has continued ever since (more than three years) an exemplary member of society, and of the church of Christ. He is so entirely renewed, that no one could imagine, from his appearance or manners, that he had been, for twenty-five years, a drunken, abandoned sailor. This case I have selected only because it was at hand. It is by no means a solitary case. Nor is it any the worse for being taken from among the poor and ignorant. I know not that beastly vice is more susceptible of removal, or that habits of drunkenness, debauchery, and profaneness, are any more capable of being changed into those of soberness, purity, and prayer, for being seated in ignorance and poverty, than when associated with learning, rank, and opulence.

Now, be it remarked, that the reality of such cases is a matter of fact, which one may question with about as much reason as he might deny the best established phenomena in natural history. Be it remarked, also, that in all such effects, the individuals concerned have ascribed the total change in their hearts and lives to the direct influence of the word and Spirit of God, as set forth in the gospel of Jesus Christ. They have generally been able to tell the particular truth, or combination of scriptural truths, that awakened them from the death of sin, and led them to embrace the hope of Christ and the life or righteousness. Be it remarked, also, that among all the cases of such conversions in all ages, and regions, and circumstances, and with all varieties of character, there has been a wonderful identity. The same effects, essentially, have ensued under the application of the same gospel in the present century, as in the time of St. Paul; in modern Europe, as in ancient Greece and Rome; in Hindoostan, as in North America; among Hottentots, and the islanders of the South sea, and savages of our western borders, as among the polished inhabitants of New York or London. While all these varieties of age, climate, customs, and cultivation, give a natural and pleasing variety to what may be called, in a figure, the complexion, and costume, in which the conversion appears; the great change itself exhibits, under all circumstances, the same characteristic and inimitable features; insomuch that if you draw the likeness of a genuine convert to Christ in his chief peculiarities, as manifested in this country, and send it to Burmah, or to the Sandwich Islands, or to Caffre-land, or to Whampoa in China, or to Greenland, it will be considered a good likeness, in main points, of the dispositions, affections, tempers, habits, and life, produced by the converting power of the gospel in any of those widely differing regions. A genuine convert to Christ, in China, or in Africa, may come to this country, and find among genuine Christians here precisely his own feelings, tastes, sympathies, and labours, though he never saw an American or European before; and he will be more at home among their christian feelings, than he can be among the manners and dispositions of the people among whom he grew up and has always lived. Thus it is evident that, whatever be the cause of these universally similar effects, it must be the same cause, universally; the same in all ages, and in all parts of the world.

Now whether the gospel of Jesus Christ produced these great and invariably corresponding effects; or whether they proceeded from some other universal cause, of which none of the subjects were ever conscious, and which was never known where the gospel was not known, and never operates but under the name, and by means of, the gospel; no man of any philosophical pretensions is at liberty to doubt. He has precisely the same reason to be assured that the gospel, and nothing else on earth, is the cause of these admirable fruits; as that any medicine is the cause of a sick man's recovery to health; or that any vine, rather than a thorn-tree, produced the grapes obtained from its branches.

Then, since these effects unquestionably belong to the gospel, how are they to be accounted for? It will not do to put them aside, under the unceremonious imputation of fanaticism or enthusiastic excitement. Words are not reasons. Infidel cant is not philosophical argument. If the gospel be untrue; then, not only must these most excellent fruits be attributed to a corrupt tree, and these wholesome streams to a poisoned fountain; but it must be supposed that such sudden and entire transformations of human character, from the lowest debasement of nature, to the highest principles of virtue and purity, are nothing more than the results of human agency and natural means. But if this be the case; if a system of untruth in the hand of man has done all this, we have reason to expect that some other systems of doctrine, with the same agency, would be productive of equal effects. How then can it be accounted for, that nothing has ever been invented or heard of, in all the earth, to which any results of a like kind could be ascribed? Other causes have produced strong excitements, but no transformation of heart and life, from sin to holiness. Other means have improved the morals of men, by slow and in small degrees; but none ever took hold of a human wreck, and lifted him up out of the mire and dirt of his profligacy, and carried him at once across the wide gulf that separated him from pureness, and in a few days placed him in a new moral region, with a new heart, and, in all things, a new creature. How can this be explained, if the gospel be a human invention, and its effects of human production? Why should not infidels be capable, with all their wisdom and eloquence, of getting up a set of influences to rival these gospel wonders, and deprive Christians of this monopoly of the work of new creation and of holiness? How is it that in proportion as any church degenerates from the simplicity and purity of the gospel, it ceases to witness such changes in the people attendant on its preaching? It is nothing to say that many things called conversions eventuate in no good fruits, and are nothing more than the natural consequences of temporary excitement. This is freely granted. But you do not condemn a whole orchard, because some of the trees were not successfully grafted; nor all virtuous men, because some, under the profession of virtue, are mere pretenders. It is sufficient that thousands and thousands of these effects have been of the most radical and permanently beneficial character. Were they of human production, something of a corresponding kind would have appeared from other sources; by other hands than those of Christians; in other countries and ages than those enlightened by the Bible. Inasmuch as this has never occurred, we are fully warranted in concluding that *it could not;* consequently, that these effects are above the reach of human power. *To whom then shall we go but unto thee, O Lord!* who hast committed this treasure of the gospel to earthen vessels, to feeble men, to dispense it; "that the excellency of the power may be of God, and not of us." That we cannot comprehend in what manner the power of God operates in the hearts of men, to work such wonderful revolutions in their characters, is no valid objection to the matter of fact. "The wind bloweth where it listeth, and thou hearest the sound thereof, but canst not tell whence it cometh and whither it goeth." The phenomena of the winds are incomprehensible, and yet believed. "*So is every one that is born of the Spirit.*"

Now, I think we may be content to pass from the position with which we began—*that the moral transformations which the gospel, in all ages, has notoriously wrought, and, by unquestionable proofs, exhibited to the world, in the characters of those who have become its genuine disciples, cannot be accounted for, but on the supposition of a divine power accompanying its operations.*

II. We proceed to speak of the fruits of christianity, *as displayed in the lives of its genuine disciples, in contrast with those which notoriously characterize the lives of its opposers.* The virtues of true Christians have been the same in all ages of christianity. It was "with well doing" that, in the days of St. Paul, they were accustomed to silence their enemies. Having become free from sin, they became servants of righteousness, and had their fruit unto holiness. "Such were some of you," saith St. Paul to Christians of that famous brothel of all Greece, *the city of Corinth;* "Such were some of you (partakers in all vice); but ye are *washed*, but ye are sanctified, but ye are justified in the name of the Lord Jesus, and by the spirit of our God." The apostles could appeal to whole communities, for evidence of their blameless character. "Ye are witnesses and God also, how holily, and justly, and unblameably we behaved ourselves among you." Even by the testimony of the ancient and deadly enemies of the gospel, the lives of Christians had no parallel among any other people. The early defenders of the faith publicly challenged a scrutiny of their virtue. It was their remarkable steadfastness in resisting the allurements of vice, and their heroic patience, under all the tortures employed to break their attachment to holiness, that often excited the bitterest hatred of their enemies. Compare the purity, benevolence, and humility of the apostles, with those of any philosophers of antiquity, or any leaders in modern infidelity. Pliny, the Roman governor, in the first century, having investigated extensively, and even by torture, the moral character of the Christians, who filled the province over which he presided, declares, in his celebrated letter to Trajan, that he could discover nothing more against them than that "they were accustomed, on a stated day, to meet before daylight, and to repeat among themselves a hymn to Christ as to a god, and to bind themselves by an oath not to commit any wickedness; but, on the contrary, to abstain from thefts, robberies, and adulteries; also not to violate their promise, or deny a pledge; after which it was their custom to separate, and to meet again at a promiscuous, harmless meal." Gibbon fully sustains this testimony. By his description alone, the primitive Christians were lights of unequalled excellence in the midst of heathen darkness and depravity. What Christians were in primitive ages, they still remain, exactly in proportion as you have reason to believe their hearts to be engaged in their faith. To say in this country that any one is a true Christian, is at once to give a certificate that he is worthy of all confidence, and more than usually virtuous: we could not desire a more complete proof of *public opinion* as to the personal fruits of the gospel. The bare fact that there are hypocritical professors of the christian character; that bad men will put themselves to the self denial of endeavouring to act and seem like Christians, for the purpose of gaining confidence in their integrity, is a strong proof of the public estimation in which christian virtue is held, and of the genuine gold of which the character of a real disciple of Christ is composed. Men never counterfeit a spurious currency. Copper coin is too cheap to tempt a forgery. We never hear of the wicked putting on the mask of infidelity. to secure a character for honesty, soberness, chastity, faithfulness, and benevolence. If christian virtue were not in high repute, and much more current in society than any other, hypocrites would take care to choose a mask that would sit more pleasantly upon their vicious propensities; they would select a cloak that would less confine, and smother their sinful habits. It is notorious among us that no sooner do we hear of an individual that he has become a communicant in the church, than the presumption is that he is not only sober, honest, and of pure morality; but that he has adopted principles of a very elevated virtue and purity, and is more than ordinarily benevolent. Whence this, but from the general experience of what communicants are? What is it that makes a breach of truth and honesty, or an act of cruelty, or a violation of justice, or a departure from chastity or temperance, in a person professing to be a genuine Christian, so immediately and generally a matter of particular notice and surprise among all classes? Is it not because such occurrences are singular, and little expected? But they excite no surprise, and but little attention, when attached to those who reject christianity; because among such people they are neither singular nor unexpected.

Why is it that parents so universally prefer to have genuine Christians intrusted with the education of their children? that when places of trust and temptation are to be filled; when men have property to invest, or agents to engage, in a business requiring special inflexibility of uprightness, they feel it to be at once a heavy weight in the scale of a candidate, that he is a sincere and devoted Christian?* Who are the benevolent, disinterested, self-denied labourers in all good works? Where do the poor, and hungry, and outcast, apply for assistance with the most confidence of finding a sympathizing heart and a ready hand? Go around to all the noble institutions of charity; to the asylums for orphans, for widows, for the blind, for the deaf and dumb, for juvenile criminals; to the schools of gratuitous instruction. Take a list of those who give money, and time, and toil, for their support. What would become of them, were it not for the Christians associated in all their concerns? Who are they that tread the loathsome alleys, and dive into the wretched habitations

* The lecturer was once particularly struck with the evidence of this. He was connected with the military academy at West Point. Two offices of great importance to the discipline of the corps of cadets were to be filled from its own ranks. The order of the academy had suffered materially for want of officers in those places who would not swerve from duty out of deference to the public opinion, the persuasions or threatenings of their fellows. Two cadets were selected, who had recently become professors of religion. They were assailed with all manner of influence to induce them to relax in favour of certain indulgences to which a portion of the corps had been accustomed at the hands of their predecessors. I need not say they mildly, but firmly held to their duty. One day, as they were leading out the companies to which they were attached, for evening parade, I said to an officer of the institution who had been chiefly instrumental in their selection: "Why have you chosen these cadets for such places? One of them, indeed, has a fine soldierly appearance; but the other is just the contrary, and has nothing of the soldier about him." "Why (said he), the truth is, we required those who would do their duty without regard to the wishes and expectations of others or to the custom that has been prevalent in the corps; and we knew *they* would be firm." I never heard of this confidence being disappointed.

of vice and poverty, in crowded cities, in cold winter, hunting up the wretched subjects of disease and pollution, for the purpose of relieving and reclaiming them? Who put themselves to the painful work of begging for the poor, and after bearing all the extreme unpleasantness of such a task, finish their labour in the careful distribution of their hard earned alms, asking no recompense but that of doing good?

From Christians in general, turn your attention to their leaders. Is it not well known that when a minister of the gospel can be commended for nothing more than a moral life and unblemished honesty, it is considered a positive condemnation? To give him the highest praise that a Deist can pretend to, and then to say no more, is to leave his character under a taint. It is expected that he will be more than moral, and honest, and friendly. You look that he shall be holy; eminently pure; full of active benevolence, going about doing good. Prove that he is destitute of these distinguished virtues, and public opinion will adjudge him unworthy of his name and profession. That all ministers are not exemplary and devotedly holy men, only proves that the sacred office, like all others, is liable to be intruded on by the unworthy. Every body knows that such cases, instead of being favoured by the influence of christianity, are directly opposed to it. But subtract from the number of the ministers of the gospel, every one on whom the least suspicion of a want of virtue ever rested; leave none, but those who at any moment can obtain, from all that know them, the praise of being the excellent of the earth; and what a host will remain of men whose lives are conspicuous examples of inflexible integrity and of exalted principles of purity and holiness; whose daily strength is laid out in efforts to benefit their fellow-creatures; and around whom, at the bare mention of a charge implicating their characters, will be collected the widow, the fatherless, the stranger, with those who have been lifted up out of ignorance, or reclaimed from profligacy, or delivered from wretchedness, in grateful defence of their best earthly benefactors.

Now, for the sake of a contrast, let us turn to *the lives of infidels.* I do not deny that there are instances of such men, who have led what passes for a good moral life; men of fair dealing in business, and of sober, decent habits; whom public opinion, the customs of society, intellectual occupations, and prosperous circumstances, have preserved from the slavery of low propensities and criminal deeds. But what is there in such virtue, beyond a fair outside? Is it formed upon any foundation more meritorious than that of reputation, interest, and the expectation of society? Could you trust its purity in the presence of strong temptation? What would become of it, should interest, reputation, and human customs, withdraw their countenance, and preach a contrary practice? But we speak of infidels, *as a body.* The fact that a few are singled out and marked as sober, honest, moral men, only proves that such cases are exceptions to the character of the heterogeneous body with which they are associated. It is a general rule, that when you say of a man "he is an infidel," it is to say that he is not a moral man: not a benevolent man; not a person to engage in any self-denying labours for the purpose of doing good. This is public opinion, the result of a long experiment of infidelity. Its foundation may be seen in the whole history of criminal jurisprudence; in the records of our courts; the annals of our penitentiaries; the police of large cities; the inner chambers of the gambling house and the brothel. Cases of seduction, adultery, and suicide, are the authorities to which reference should be made for the fruits of infidelity, as generally exhibited.

A French writer, addressing Voltaire, asks him: "Will you dare assert that it is in philosophic families we are to look for models of filial respect, conjugal love, sincerity in friendship, or fidelity among domestics? Were you disposed to do so, would not your own conscience, your own experience, suppress the falsehood, even before your lips could utter it?" An anecdote in point is related by Fuller. A man of literary eminence, but an infidel, was accustomed to converse with a brother sceptic where they were necessarily heard by a pious but uneducated countryman. Afterwards, it came to pass that the educated infidel became an humble Christian. Feeling, now, a serious concern lest his conversation should have poisoned the mind of the countryman, he inquired if such was the fact. "By no means," answered the other; "it never made the least impression." "No impression! Why you must have known that we had read and thought on these things much more than you had any opportunity of doing." "O yes," said the other; "*but I knew also your manner of living*. I knew that to maintain such a course of conduct you found it *necessary* to renounce christianity."*

It is well known how very seldom such a thing has occurred as the detection, in any penitentiary crime, of one who had enjoyed the benefit, for a considerable period, of a Sunday school education; although, during the last twenty years, millions, in Great Britain and the United States, have had that privilege. What if all these had been trained, with equal diligence, in schools of infidelity! How differently would the effects of the system have been marked upon the records of crime, and upon the peace, purity, and order of society!

The precise difference between the fruits of christianity and of infidelity, as exhibited in the general assembly of their respective professors, consists in this: There are those who profess to be Christians, and yet are wicked men; but they are wicked in direct opposition to the influence of christianity, as well as to the characters and influence of those with whom they are connected. There are, also, those who profess to be infidels, and yet are men of sobriety, and amiableness, and moral deportment; but they are such, in direct opposition to

* Gospel its own Witness.

the influence of infidelity, as well as to the characters and influence of those with whom, as infidels, they are associated. The former and the latter are alike exceptions to the general rule.

But let us turn from infidels in general, to their teachers and leaders. A stream is seldom purer than its fountain. A river rises no higher than its source. We may consider the chief priests and scribes, the elders, and rulers, and champions of infidelity, who have constructed its various creeds and composed its books of scripture—its Humes, and Tindals, and Bolingbrokes, and Paines, and Voltaires, and Rousseaus—as affording, in the average of their character, a fair standard for the measurement of the moral stature of infidels in general. What, then, was the moral worth of those renowned leaders in the war against christianity? Let us look at their principles.

Herbert maintained that the indulgence of lust and anger is no more to be blamed than the thirst of a fever, or the drowsiness of a lethargy. Thus, *every vicious propensity* was licensed. Hobbes, that every man has a right to all things, and may lawfully get them if he can. Thus, all *theft* was licensed. Again, that a subject may lawfully deny Christ before a magistrate, although he believes Christ in his heart. Thus, all *hypocrisy* was licensed. Again, that a ruler is not bound by any obligation of truth or justice, and can do no wrong to his subjects. Thus, all *tyrannical oppression and cruelty* were licensed. Again, that the civil law is the sole foundation of good and evil; of right and wrong. Thus, moral principle is as various as climate and country, and vice in one, may be exalted virtue in another. Hume maintained that self-denial, self-mortification, and humility, are not virtuous, but useless and mischievous; that pride and self-valuation, ingenuity, eloquence, strength of body, &c., are virtues; that suicide is lawful and commendable; that adultery must be practised, if we would obtain all the advantages of life; that female infidelity, when known, is a small thing; when unknown, nothing. Bolingbroke, that ambition, the lust of power, avarice, and sensuality, may be lawfully gratified, if they can be safely gratified; that modesty is inspired by mere prejudice, and has its sole foundation in vanity; that man's chief end is to gratify the appetites and inclinations of the flesh; that "adultery is no violation of the law, or religion of nature; that there is no wrong in lewdness, except in the highest incest."*

These principles will suffice as specimens of infidel writers in regard to moral obligation. It is fair to judge men by their professions. Few rise above their opinions, in practice; none, in heart. When one contends that he may innocently indulge his vicious propensities, we need not doubt that he does indulge them. These writers either believed what they professed, or they did not. If the latter, they were gross hypocrites, endeavouring to spread what they knew was deadly poison. If the former, then tell me what kind of practice, what veracity, what honesty, what chastity, or any other virtue, can be supposed to have dwelt in men who in grave, philosophical discussions could publish such sentiments to the world? Had we no other evidence of the lives they led, we might conclude with certainty, from these professed opinions, that, while one, here and there, may not have carried them out to their full extent, none could have been, in any sense, good men; while the generality must have been without any regard to truth; guilty of gross hypocrisy and dissimulation; willing to offer any sacrifice at the shrine of ambition and human praise; unbridled in temper and passion; seducers, adulterers, and corrupters of their fellow-creatures. Such is the description which, so far as any accounts of their private characters have been received, is fully sustained by facts.

Hume pretended to a great diligence in search of truth and spent all his powers against the gospel, and yet, says Dr. Johnson, "confessed that he had *never read the New Testa-*

* See Dwight on Infidel Philosophy.

ment with attention." His friend in scepticism, Adam Smith, considered him "as approaching as nearly to the idea of a perfectly wise and virtuous man as perhaps the nature of human frailty will permit." But since, in his estimation, female infidelity, when unknown, was nothing; one needs pretty positive evidence to believe that he was specially pure.*

Gibbon's moral character is seen in his History of the Roman empire; a work full of hypocrisy, perversion, and impurity; the production of a mind as unchaste, as it was insidious. When he could not *find* an occasion to insult christianity, he *made* it, by false glosses or dishonest colourings. "A rage for indecency pervades the whole work; but especially the last volumes. If the history were anonymous, I should guess that these disgraceful obscenities were written by some debauchee, who having from age, or accident, or excess, survived the practice of lust, still indulged himself in its speculations; and exposed the impotent imbecility, after he had lost the vigour, of the passions."† This was no "arrow shot at a venture."

---

* That Hume was virtuous, *without chastity*, is evident from his essays. They contain passages, by way of wit or illustration, not only gratuitously introduced, but forced in by a mere *amateur* taste of the writer, which a chaste mind would not have thought of, and a man of chaste habits and principles would have rejected, as both polluting to his pages and disgraceful to his character. I cannot believe that one who could venture on such sentences before the public eye, and show such pleasure and evident facility in grovelling indecencies of writing, was free from unclean practice where no public eye was to be encountered. And still, in Adam Smith's opinion, he may have been "as perfectly virtuous *as the nature of human frailty would permit.*" What exceptions are included under this last clause, who can say? In an infidel's creed, virtue has no more quarrel with unchasteness, than in the creed of the Spartans, it had with theft. Among the latter, nothing was required to make stealing virtuous but *concealment.* Among the virtuosi of infidelity, what more is required to establish the innocence of impurity?

The person who put out an edition of Hume's Essays in this country, dedicating it to the president of the United States, and lauding Hume and his principles to the skies, showed very plainly how he had profited by his favourite volume, at least by the Essay in defence of Suicide.—He killed himself by drunkenness!

† Porson.

What gross hypocrisy and lying pervade the writings of Herbert, Hobbes, Shaftesbury, Woolston, Tindal, Collins, Blount, Chubb, and Bolingbroke! One while they are praising christianity, exalting Jesus, professing to have the sincerest desire that the gospel may be promoted. At another time, they are scoffing at its essential doctrines; charging its Founder with imposture; and diligently labouring to destroy it. Hobbes affirms that the scriptures are the voice of God, and the foundation of all obligation; and yet that all religion is ridiculous. Shaftesbury says that it is censurable to represent the gospel as a fraud; that he hopes its enemies will be reconciled to it, and its friends, prize it more highly; and yet he represents salvation as ridiculous; insinuates that the designs of Christ were those of deep ambition, and his zeal and spirit savage and persecuting; that the scriptures were an artful invention for mercenary purposes. Collins protests that none are further from being engaged in the cause of infidelity; that he writes for the honour of Jesus, and the defence of christianity; to advance the Messiahship and truth of the holy Jesus, "*to whom*," he says, "*be glory for ever and ever, amen*;" and yet he casts the most scurrilous reflections on this holy One, compares the gospels to Gulliverian tales, says they are full of absurdities, and must be rejected, and the authority of Jesus along with them.*

Such are a few examples of the *honesty* of such men. What if Christians should thus flatter infidelity, and next revile it? When would their opponents cease exposing their hypocrisy? The best of infidel writers cannot be trusted on the score of veracity, when christianity is in question. The corruption of the texts of books, the misrepresentation of facts, the grossest unfairness in citations, are accounted lawful by their Humes and Gibbons in this controversy One of their own fraternity may here be allowed to testify. "If," says Rousseau, "our philosophers were able to discover truth, which of them would interest himself about it?

* Dwight on Infidel Philosophy.

There is not one among them who would not prefer his own error to the truth discovered by another. Where is the philosopher, who, for his own glory, would not willingly deceive the whole human race?" I need not spend time, after all that has been exhibited, in showing that such leaders in infidelity have evinced no spirit of benevolence, no disposition to labour for the benefit of their fellow-creatures; but on the contrary, have lived unto themselves, and almost without exception, cultivated the coldest selfishness.

But to speak more directly of the morals of leading infidels. Bolingbroke was a libertine of intemperate habits and unrestrained lust. Temple was a corrupter of all that came near him, given up to ease and pleasure. Emerson, an eminent mathematician, was "rude, vulgar, and frequently immoral." "Intoxication and profane language were familiar to him. Towards the close of life, being afflicted with the stone, he would crawl about the floor on his hands and knees, *sometimes praying, sometimes swearing.*" The morals of the Earl of Rochester are well known. Godwin was a lewd man by his own confession, as well as the unblushing advocate of lewdness. Shaftesbury and Collins, while endeavouring to destroy the gospel, partook of the Lord's Supper, thus professing christian faith for admission to office! "Woolston was a gross blasphemer. Blount solicited his sister in-law to marry him; and being refused, shot himself. Tindal was originally a protestant, then turned papist, then protestant again, merely to suit the times; and was at the same time infamous for vice in general, and the total want of principle. He is said to have died with this prayer in his mouth: 'If there is a God, I desire that he may have mercy on me.' Hobbes wrote his Leviathan to serve the cause of Charles I.; but finding him fail of success, he turned it to the defence of Cromwell, and made a merit of this fact to the usurper: as Hobbes himself unblushingly declared to Lord Clarendon."* Need I describe Voltaire?—

* Dwight on Infidel Philosophy.

prince of scoffers, as Hume was prince of sceptics; in childhood, initiated into infidelity; in boyhood, famous for daring blasphemy; in manhood, distinguished for a malignant, violent temper, for cold-blooded disruptions of all the ties and decencies of the family circle, for the ridicule of whatever was affecting, and the violation of whatever was confidential! Ever increasing in duplicity and hypocritical management, with age and practice; those whom his wit attracted and his buffoonery amused, were either disgusted or polluted by his loathsome vices. Lies and oaths, in their support, were nothing to his maw. Those whom he openly called his friends, he took pains secretly to calumniate; flattering them to their faces, ridiculing and reviling them behind their backs. Years only added stiffness to the disgusting features of his impiety, coldness to his dark malignity, and fury to his impetuous temper. Throughout life, he was given up "to work all uncleanness with greediness." Such was the witty Voltaire, who, in the midst of his levity, had feeling and seriousness enough *to wish he had never been born.*

What shall we say of J. J. Rousseau?—a thief, and liar, and debauched profligate, by his own "Confession." Educated a protestant, he turned papist for "subsistence;" and afterwards professed protestantism again at Geneva, that he might enjoy the rights of citizenship, while all the while he was a foul-mouthed infidel. He began life as an apprentice. Having robbed his master and others, he fled and became a footman, in which capacity, having again acted the thief, he tried to swear the crime on a maid-servant, who lost her place by his villany. Stealing he never abandoned, however abandoned himself. Late in life, he said: "I have been a rogue, and am so still, for trifles which I had rather take than ask for." Of his intercourse with vile women; how he took advantage of the hospitality of friends to ruin the characters of those who received him kindly; how he coldly committed, one by one, the offsprings of his base connexions to the charity of the public, that he might be spared their trouble and have room for more; how utterly devoid was this talented infidel of all natural affection, as well as all decency; my lecture is too modest to relate. To use his own language, *guilty without remorse, he soon became so without measure.* Such was the man whom infidels have delighted to honour. The friends of Christ have reason to thank him for saying, "*I cannot believe the gospel.*" "For what communion hath light with darkness? And what concord hath Christ with Belial?"

Nothing but the circulation attempted, of late, to be given to the scurrilous writings of Paine, induces me to descend low enough amidst "the offscouring of all things," to speak of the life of that miserable man. His first wife is said to have died by ill usage. His second was rendered so miserable by neglect and unkindness, that they separated by mutual agreement. His third *companion,* not his wife, was the victim of his seduction, while he lived upon the hospitality of her husband. Holding a place in the excise of England, he was dismissed for irregularity; restored, and dismissed again for fraud, without recovery. Unable to get employment where he was known, he came to this country, commenced politician, and pretended to some faith in christianity. Congress gave him an office, from which, being soon found guilty of a breach of trust, he was expelled with disgrace.* The French revolu-

* The statement in the text, the author is informed, is not precisely accurate. Paine was not expelled from his office; but resigned it, to avoid expulsion. The author is much indebted to the Hon. William Jay, for the following valuable extract from a document found among the papers of his father, the Hon. John Jay. The document was written while Mr. Jay was Minister to Spain, about the year 1780, and was an introduction to an intended history of his Spanish negotiations. The annexed extract would make a valuable page in a history of Paine.

"It is proper to observe that Mr. Deane, in consequence of his recall, returned to America in 1778; and that on his arrival, Congress went into an inquiry into his conduct. Mr. Deane published a paper in the Philadelphia Gazette, containing strictures on the delays of Congress respecting his affairs, and heavy accusations against Mr. Arthur Lee, to whose machinations he attributed the conduct of Congress towards him. This publication caused a ferment

tion allured him to France. Habits of intoxication made him a disagreeable inmate in the house of the American minister, where out of compassion he had been received as a guest. During all this time, his life was a compound of ingratitude and perfidy, of hypocrisy and avarice, of lewdness and

throughout America, and very great heats in Congress. The public papers teemed with publications for and against Mr. Deane and Mr. Lee. Among the writers for the latter was a Thomas Paine, an Englishman, who had been a hackney writer in London, and on his arrival in America, was employed by Aikin in compiling and correcting papers for his magazine. In this capacity his attachment to the American cause became suspected. He struck out several passages in papers composed by Dr. Witherspoon, as being too free. He afterwards became attached to some leading men who were most zealous for American Independence. He published a pamphlet on that subject, called Common Sense, and obtained much credit with the people for it. He was afterward made Secretary to the committee for foreign affairs; and when General Washington was retreating before the enemy in Jersey, and the minds of many were filled with apprehensions, he was again so suspected, as that Congress became uneasy lest the Committee's papers in his custody, should fall into the enemy's hands, and took their measures accordingly. The success at Trenton gave things a new aspect, and new courage to Paine.

"On the present occasion, his zeal for his employers carried him too far. The official papers had brought him acquainted with the state of American affairs at Versailles; and in his paper of the 2d January, he very imprudently inserted the following paragraph: 'If Mr. Deane, or any other gentleman, will procure an order from Congress to inspect an account in my office, or any of Mr. Deane's friends *in* Congress will take the trouble of coming themselves, I will give him or them my attendance, and show them in a hand writing which Mr. Deane is well acquainted with, that the supplies he so pompously plumes himself upon, *were promised and engaged*, and that *as a present*, before he even arrived in France,' &c.

"The Minister of France, Mr. Gerard, being aware of the consequences which would result from these assertions, and feeling very sensibly how much the honour of France was wounded by a supposition of her having given gratuitous aid to America, contrary to her assurances to Britain, did on the 5th January, 1779, present a memorial to Congress referring to this publication, denying the assertions they contained, and representing the propriety of their being disowned by Congress. The day following, the memorial was considered, and various debates, not proper to be specified here, ensued. Paine and the printer were ordered to attend at the bar of the House. The former confessed himself the author, and the latter the publisher, of the paper in question. Many motions were made, debated and rejected, before the house adopted the resolutions which finally took place. The subject was interesting to the public, to the house, and particularly to the friends of the parties in adultery. In June, 1809, the poor creature died in this country. The lady in whose house he lived relates that "he was daily drunk, and, in his few moments of soberness, was always quarreling with her, and disturbing the peace of the family." At that time "he was deliberately and disgustingly filthy." He had an old black woman for his servant, as drunken as her master. He accused her of stealing his rum; she retaliated by accusing him of being an old drunkard. They would lie on the same floor, sprawling, and swearing, and threatening to fight, but too intoxicated to engage in battle. He removed, afterwards, to various families, continuing his habits, and paying for his board, only when compelled. *In his drunken fits, he was accustomed to talk about the immortality of the soul.** Probably much of his book against the inspiration of the scriptures was inspired by his cups. Such was the author of "*the Age of Reason*;" such the apostle of mob-infidelity. Unhappy man! Neither he, nor Rousseau, nor Voltaire, is dead, except in the flesh. Their immortal souls are thinking as actively, at least, as ever. We and they will stand, on the same great day, before the bar of God. How awful, in reference to such despisers and scoffers, is that description: "Behold he cometh with clouds; and every eye shall see him, and *they also which pierced him.*"

III. We proceed to speak, in the last place, of the fruits of christianity, *as displayed in the deaths of its genuine disciples, in contrast with those connected with infidelity.*

There is no question to which the testimony of the death-bed is so legitimately applicable, as that between infidelity and christianity; not only because the hour of death is specially to be relied on, as an hour of dispassionate and con-

---

difference, as well as Mr. Paine's patrons; and, as is always the case on such occasions, more warmth than prudence took place. The majority, however, were of opinion that Paine had prostituted his office to party purposes, and therefore ought to be discharged. This did not long remain a secret to him, and to avoid that disgrace he resigned."

P. S. Mr. Jay was a member of Congress at the time of the above occurences.

* Cheetham's Life of Paine

scientious judgment; but, particularly, because it is one of the precious promises of the gospel, that true believers shal. find the sting of death taken away, and experience rich consolation and support, when heart and flesh are failing. Infidelity, also, has published her promises in relation to the trial of death; and her disciples are not a little diposed to boast how confidently and fearlessly they could meet the king of terrors. Let us consult experience on this head. Have Christians experienced the fulfilment of the promises on which they trusted? Have infidels made good their boasts? With regard to christians, it is a most impressive fact that *such a thing has never been known as any one being sorry, in the hour of death, that he had embraced the gospel of Christ.* We have often seen and heard of persons, who had spent their days in the careless neglect of religion, most bitterly lamenting, when they found themselves near to eternity, that they had not been devoted Christians. It is invariably the case that genuine Christians, when they look back on their lives, from the verge of the grave, are sorry that all their days had not been spent in a much more zealous consecration to the service of Christ. Professors of religion are not unfrequently unhappy when they come to die; not because they are, or have been Christians, but only because they see reason to fear that they have not been real Christians. This unhappiness arises from the consciousness of being too much like those who reject the gospel; too little under the influence of its spirit; too much under the influence of a practical unbelief. And they seek consolation, not by endeavouring to banish the gospel from their minds, but by pressing to the feet of Jesus, and seeking to have their hearts filled by his spirit. But among all that ever named the name of Jesus, from the death of the martyred Stephen, to the present hour; the millions upon millions of Christians, who have died under all manner of tortures, and in all manner of circumstances, calculated to try the strength of their faith; not a philosopher or peasant: not a noble or a beggar;

not a man, woman, or child; was ever known to repent that his preparation to die was that of the faith of Christ.

On the contrary, it has been the invariable effect of the religion of Christ that those who, in the days of health, were evidently devoted to its spirit and duties, when death approached, have been enabled to await the event with an humble, submissive, and cheerful mind, keeping a confident eye "unto Jesus," as the Finisher, as well as Author of their faith. They have felt it to be their most precious, their unspeakable consolation that they had been persuaded to be Christians. Nothing did they look back to with such thankfulness, as that, instead of having lived in indifference or infidelity, they had lived a life of faith upon the Son of God. They have felt that however solemn and, to the flesh, painful, was death, to them it was not gloomy nor appalling, nor any thing to be lamented; but only a short valley in the way to their everlasting and blissful rest with God on high. The most timid by nature, have stepped down without fear or doubt, believing in Jesus, and walking by faith. The affectionate parent has found such an accession of strength, in the act of separation from a beloved and helpless family, as to be enabled cheerfully to take the last look, and leave his fatherless children with God. The young man, in the prime and promise of his years, with every thing that earth could give to make life desirable, has had the prospect of a better inheritance presented to his mind with such assurance, that he had a strong desire "to depart, and be with Christ." The nearer Christians have come to eternity, and the sharper the trial of their faith, the nearer have they drawn to Christ; the more closely have they embraced his cross; the more necessary has seemed his death for their sins; the more precious and full of glory the whole plan of redemption. Such is the *medium* statement of the testimony furnished by the death-beds of the disciples of Christ, when disease or the suddenness of departure has not prevented them from all testimony whatever.

But, in innumerable instances, the facts are much more positive. It is frequently the case that dying Christians, as they draw near to eternity, seem to catch the song and share the bliss of heaven. Their faith not only delivers them from gloom and fear, but fills them with joy and triumph. They are not only supported, but exalted; unspeakably happier in the agonies of death, than ever they were in the vigour of health. As the body sinks, the spirit rises in strength of faith and confidence of approaching glory. A smile of joy plays upon the death struck countenance. The tenderest affection, and the most benevolent interest for all around them; earnest prayer that sinners may come to Jesus, and that his gospel may be embraced in all the world, occupy their latest moments. They die, *thanking God, who giveth them the victory through Jesus Christ.*

This is no picture of imagination. It is drawn from facts which the lecturer has frequently had the privilege of witnessing; facts such as have been often repeated in the observation of all whose duty has led them often to visit and converse with the dying, on the subject of religion; facts of which the domestic history of the gospel, in all ages, is full, and of which no effrontery can attempt a denial. Paul, in the near view of a painful death, exclaimed: "I am now ready to be offered, and the time of my departure is at hand. I have fought a good fight; I have finished my course; I have kept the faith; henceforth, there is laid up for me a crown of righteousness, which the Lord, the righteous Judge, shall give me at that day, and not to me only, but unto all them also that love his appearing."* Polycarp, when they would have nailed him to the stake, said: "Let me remain as I am; for he who giveth me strength to sustain the fire, will enable me also, without your securing me with nails, to remain unmoved in the fire." Then, being bound for a burnt offering, he exclaimed: "O Father, I bless thee that thou hast counted me worthy of this day and this hour to receive my portion

* 2 Tim. iv. 6, 7, 8.

in the cup of Christ." Bilney, putting his finger into the flame of a candle, on the night before he was burned, repeated that promise: "When thou walkest through the fire, it shall not burn thee;" and said: "I constantly believe that, howsoever the stubble of this body shall be wasted by it, yet my soul shall be purged thereby; a pain for the time, whereon, notwithstanding, followeth joy unspeakable." Hooper, going to the stake, being addressed by a papist in the language of condolence, answered: "Be sorry for thyself, and lament thine own wickedness; for I am well, I thank God, and death, to me, for Christ's sake, is welcome." Bishop Bedell, apprehending a speedy dissolution, assembled his family, and, with many other words, declared: "Knowing that I must shortly put off this my tabernacle, I know also that I have a building of God, a house not made with hands, eternal in the heavens. Therefore to me, to live is Christ, and to die is gain, which increases my desire, even now, to depart and be with Christ, which is far better. I ascend to my Father and your Father, to my God and your God, through the all-sufficient merits of Jesus Christ, my Redeemer, who ever lives to make intercession for me." Fletcher's continual exclamation, while dying, was, "*God is love! God is love!*" He panted for words to express what he felt in the utterance of that precious truth. Finley, in the act of departing, used such language as this: "A Christian's death is the best part of his existence." "Blessed be God, eternal rest is at hand." "The Lord hath given me the victory. I exult; I triumph. Now I know that it is *impossible* that faith should not triumph over earth and hell." "Lord Jesus, into thy hands I commit my spirit; I do it with *confidence;* I do it with *full assurance.* I *know* that thou wilt keep that which I have committed to thee."* Said the dying Payson: "While my body is thus tortured, the soul is perfectly, perfectly happy and peaceful, more than I can

* See "Deaths of Hume and Finley Compared," by Dr. Mason; in the Tract, No. 190, of the American Tract Society.

possibly express to you. I lie here and feel these convulsions extending higher and higher, without the least uneasiness; but my soul is filled with joy unspeakable. I seem to swim in a flood of glory, which God pours down upon me. And I know, I *know* that my happiness is but begun. I cannot doubt that it will last for ever." And what shall I say more? For the time would fail to tell of Latimer, and Ridley, and Hooker; of Romaine, and Newton, and Scott; of Swartz, and Buchanan, and Martyn; of Oberlin and Richmond; of Evarts and Cornelius; leaders in the faith, "of whom the world was not worthy." But should we go into the more retired walks of Christian life, and consult the annals of every village church, and gather out the examples of holy patience in suffering, and sublime faith, and deep humility, and joy unspeakable in dying, which the eye of God has seen among the poor of this world, in every age, since the death of Christ! what a cloud of witnesses would compass us about, uniting their joyful testimony to Jesus as "the resurrection and the life;" to the gospel as in all its promises, faithful and "worthy of all acceptation!"*

---

* A beautiful exhibition of the effects of the gospel is found in the Narrative of the Loss of the Kent East Indiaman, in 1825. The account is given by Major M'Gregor, who was not rendered the less capable of calmly observing the events he has recorded, or of firmly bearing his part in the dangers of that awful crisis, in consequence of having his soul kept in peace by the precious hopes of a disciple of Christ.

While the ship was burning below, and the magazine was every moment expected to blow up, and not a soul, out of more than six hundred, had a thought but of perishing either by fire or the tempest; while some were standing in silent resignation, or stupid insensibility, and others were given up to the most frantic despair; while "some on their knees were earnestly imploring with significant gesticulations, and in noisy supplications, the mercy of Him whose arm, they exclaimed, was at length outstretched to smite them;" and others had sullenly seated themselves directly over the magazine, that by means of the expected explosion a speedier termination might be put to their sufferings; "Several of the soldiers' wives and children, who had fled for temporary shelter into the after cabins, on the upper decks, were engaged in prayer, and in reading the scriptures with the ladies, some of whom were enabled, with wonderful self-possession, to offer to others those spiritual consola-

Now, let us turn to infidelity. What confirmation has resulted, from the death-beds of infidels, to the truth of their faith, and its ability to support and comfort the souls of its dying disciples? Ah! the change is like being translated from the beauty, and fragrance, and joyful promise of spring, into the coldness, and barrenness, and gloominess, of winter.

Has infidelity ever exhibited a solitary example of that high and delightful consolation; that triumphant, unspeakable joy on the brink of the grave, of which christianity can cite innumerable instances? It seems almost ridiculous to be at pains enough to answer such a question. Infidelity has no doctrine, no promise, out of which such a delightful frame of mind could grow. Infidels feel themselves so infinitely removed from it, that it seems to them, in the distance, as something incomprehensible, or visionary, or fanatical. But are there not examples of such persons dying without fear? Unquestionably there are; but how few of them have any application to the present argument! The great majority of them have been cases in which the lethargy or delirium occasioned by disease prevented the patient from being sensible of his condition; or his death succeeded so immediately after the symptoms of his danger, as to allow no time for the consideration of his eternal interests; or his friends took care that he should be kept in ignorance of the fatal character of his disorder, until it was too late for any thing but insensibility and dissolution; or else the unhappy infidel,

---

tions, which a firm and intelligent trust in the Redeemer of the world appeared at this awful hour to impart to their own breasts. The dignified deportment of two young ladies in particular formed a specimen of natural strength of mind, finely modified by christian feeling, that failed not to attract the notice and admiration of every one who had an opportunity of witnessing it. One young gentleman, having calmly asked my opinion of the state of the ship, I told him that I thought we should be prepared to sleep that night in eternity; and I shall never forget the peculiar fervour with which he replied, as he pressed my hand in his, '*My heart is filled with the peace of God.*'" Comment would only mar such a beautiful testimony to the blessedness of a gospel faith. "Thou wilt keep him in perfect peace whose mind is stayed on thee: because he trusteth in thee." Is. xxvi. 3.

suspicious of his steadfastness when the trial should arrive, surrounded himself with such companions as would guard his bedside from the approach of any minister of better consolations, and keep his mind amused with trifles, and his pride stimulated with the ambition of holding out to the last. Undoubtedly there have been cases to which none of these specifications are applicable; cases of infidels, who, in quietness, with their intellects in sound and wakeful exercise, and with a knowledge of their nearness to eternity, have died without the manifestation of alarm. But this has nothing to do with our point. We could speak of multitudes who believed christianity, and had no idea that they were prepared to meet their God; but, nevertheless, died without alarm. The question is, does infidelity sustain and comfort its disciples in the hour of death? It can hardly be necessary to assert, that whatever calmness any of them may have manifested had no manner of connexion with their infidel principles. They might have had the same, as well without infidelity, as with it. They did not pretend to draw strength and peace from its barren breasts. What was called, in their case, *resignation*, was not the offspring of their principles, as infidels, but of their doom, as mortals. *They had to die, and there was no use in complaining*; this is about the amount of all their consolation. Most gladly would they have entreated to live, could they have supposed that entreaty would have succeeded. Death has never been regarded by such men, except as a necessary evil in every respect, only to be submitted to, because irrevocably appointed. Such is the very best account we can give of the testimony of the death-beds of infidels. It is dreary, desolate, cold. It whispers something that should go to the heart of a sceptic. Its dismal negativeness is positive condemnation. Where, in all this region of emptiness, is the sweet serenity, the cheerful resignation, the positive pleasure and happiness in prospect of death, which so generally attend the dying Christian? Where is your parallel, in a single infidel, to the joyful wel-corre which death has received, in a million cases, at the lips of the followers of Christ, when they have felt themselves almost home, and, in view of heaven, have longed to depart and be with Christ?

No case of a dying unbeliever has been made so much of, by way of a set-off to the testimony of Christians, as that of David Hume. The evident object of Adam Smith, the narrator, is to put up his friend for a comparison with believers. Gibbon says: "He died the death of a philosopher." No thing can be more affected, more evidently contrived for stage effect; or, even on infidel principles, more disgraceful to such a mind as Hume's, than the manner of his death, according to the account given by his friend. He knew his end was near. Whether he was to be annihilated, or to be for ever happy, or for ever miserable, was a question involved on his own principles, in impenetrable darkness. It was the tremendous question to be then decided. Reason and decency demanded that it should be seriously contemplated. How does he await the approach of eternity? Said Chesterfield (an infidel also): "When one does see death near, let the best or the worst people say what they please, it is a serious consideration." Does Hume treat it as a serious consideration? He is *diverting himself!* With what? With preparing his Essay in defence of *Suicide* for a new edition; reading books of amusement; and sometimes with a game at cards! He is *diverting himself* again! With what next? With talking silly stuff about Charon and his boat, and the river Styx! Such are a philosopher's diversions, where common sense teaches other people to be, at least, grave and thoughtful. But why *divert* himself? Why turn off his mind from death? Why the need of his writings, and his cards, and his books of amusements, and his trifling conversations? Was he afraid to let his mind settle down quietly and alone to the contemplation of all that was at stake in the crisis before him? Whatever the explanation of his levity, it was ill-timed, out of taste badly got up; an affected piece of over-acting, intended for posthumous fame, to say the best of it. He died "as a fool dieth." Take his own views, as thus expressed, at the end of his Natural History of Religion: "The comfortable views exhibited by the belief of futurity are ravishing and delightful. But how quickly vanish on the appearance of its terrors, which keep a more firm and durable possession of the human mind? The whole is a riddle, an enigma, an inexplicable mystery. Doubt, uncertainty, suspense of judgment, appear the only result of our most accurate scrutiny concerning this subject." In his own estimation, then, *futurity has its terrors.* Doubt, inexplicable mystery, hung over his future destiny! Whether he was not to be a child of hell for ever, his most accurate scrutiny could only suspend his judgment! In this tremendous suspense, he plays cards, as it were, on his coffin lid! jests about ridiculous fables, as he steps down to the momentous uncertainties, but eternal realities, of the future! If a finger had been about to receive its sentence, whether to be amputated or not, he would at the least have been more grave. How far such a death-bed scene is honourable to philosophy or infidelity, or fit to be compared with that of millions of Christians, I need not say. But this is the fairest aspect of the matter on the side of infidelity.*

* There is reason to believe that, however unconcerned Hume may have seemed in the presence of his infidel friends, there were times when, being diverted neither by companions, nor cards, nor his works, nor books of amusement, but left to himself and the contemplation of eternity, he was any thing but composed and satisfied.

The following account was published many years ago in Edinburgh, where he died. It is not known to have been ever contradicted. "About the end of 1776, a few months after the historian's death, a respectable looking woman, dressed in black, came into the Haddington stage coach, while passing through Edinburgh. The conversation among the passengers, which had been interrupted for a few minutes, was speedily resumed, which the lady soon found to be regarding the state of mind persons were in at the prospect of death. An appeal was made, in defence of infidelity, to the death of Hume, as not only happy and tranquil, but mingled even with gayety and humour. To this the lady said: 'Sir, this is all you know about it; I could tell you another tale.' 'Madam,' replied the gentleman, 'I presume I have as good information as

We said, the case could not be mentioned of any one having regretted, on his death-bed, that he had lived a

---

you can have on this subject, and I believe that what I have asserted regarding Mr. Hume has never been called in question.' The lady continued: 'Sir, I was Mr. Hume's housekeeper for many years, and was with him in his last moments; and the mourning I now wear was a present from his relatives for my attention to him on his death-bed; and happy would I have been if I could have borne my testimony to the mistaken opinion that has gone abroad of his peaceful and composed end. I have, sir, never, till this hour, opened my mouth on this subject; but I think it a pity the world snould be kept in the dark on so interesting a topic. It is true, sir, that when Mr. Hume's friends were with him he was cheerful, and seemed quite unconcerned about his approaching fate; nay, frequently spoke of it to them in a jocular and playful way; but when he was alone, the scene was very different; he was any thing but composed; his mental agitation was so great at times as to occasion his whole bed to shake. He would not allow the candles to be put out during the night, nor would he be left alone for a minute. I had always to ring the bell for one of the servants to be in the room, before he would allow me to leave it. He struggled hard to appear composed, even before me. But to one who attended his bedside for so many days and nights, and witnessed his disturbed sleeps and still more disturbed wakings; who frequently heard his involuntary breathings of remorse and frightful startings; it was no difficult matter to determine that all was not right within. This continued and increased until he became insensible. I hope in God I shall never witness a similar scene.'"—*Christian Observer*, vol. xxxi. p. 665.

There is internal evidence of truth attached to the above. Hume had no opinions with regard to God, or the future, except that all was doubtful. Whether there was a God, a future state, a hell, or annihilation, he did not profess to know. The future had its terrors, he acknowledged. To him they were terrors of darkness and uncertainty. He spoke of "the calm, though *obscure* regions of philosophy." He called the whole question as to man's future destiny, "*a riddle, an enigma, an inexplicable mystery.*" All he could arrive at was, "*doubt, uncertainty, suspense of judgment.*" In this state of mind, nothing could have been more forced or unnatural than the levity described by Smith. That was his stage-dress. If a man lay a hundred pounds upon a game, he is *anxious* till the uncertainty as to its fate be removed. But Hume knew that his ALL, FOR EVER, was at stake; and that he was unconcerned, unanxious, *when not diverted*, is incredible. On the other hand, the account presented above is exactly what nature and reason would expect from the state of mind in which the philosopher described himself, as to all that awaited him. Not to be penetrated with anxiety of the most painful kind, when a few hours were to decide whether he was to be annihilated, or to be carried to the judgment seat of God, and find all that he had ridiculed in the gospel true, and be condemned to eternal misery- a destiny which, on his

Christian. We now say, that cases innumerable have occurred of persons bitterly lamenting, when dying, that they had lived in infidelity. Every where, such instances have occurred. They are too notorious to need citation. The boldest unbelievers have furnished the most numerous examples. They have felt every foundation removed, when heart and flesh began to fail. What they had boasted in life, they found a miserable comforter in death. The earl of Rochester, a scholar and a blasphemer, as deep in vice as in infidelity, when he approached the end of life, became a thorough penitent; and, to one of his former companions, said from his death-bed: "O, remember that you contemn God no longer! He is an avenging God, and will visit you for your sins; and will, I hope, in mercy, touch your conscience, sooner or later, as he has done mine. You and I have been friends and sinners together, a great while. We have been all mistaken in our conceits and opinions; our persuasions have been false and groundless; therefore I pray God grant you repentance." To those who had been drawn into sin, by his example and encouragement, he said: "I warn them no more to make a mock of sin, or contemn the pure and excellent religion of my ever blessed Redeemer, through whose merits alone, I, one of the greatest of sinners, do yet hope for mercy and forgiveness."

Hobbes could never bear to talk of death. His mind was haunted with tormenting reflections. If his candle went out in the night, while he was in bed, he was in misery. As he descended to the grave, he said "he was about to take a leap in the dark."

Struensee, prime minister of Denmark, and Brandt, the companion of his disgrace and imprisonment, had both been poisoned by the writings and society of Voltaire; and both, in prospect of death, renounced infidelity with detestation, and embraced the gospel as all their hope.

---

own principles, was as likely as any thing else—could only be accounted for on the supposition that disease or *friends* diverted his attention from the decision approaching.

Shall I lead you to the horrible spectacle of Voltaire, in the arms of death, and expecting in a few moments to stand at the bar of God. He has just returned from a feast of applause in the theatre, to be laid on a bed of death, in the agonies of an upbraiding conscience. The physician enters. "Doctor," said the apostle of infidelity, with the utmost consternation, "I am abandoned by God and man. I will give you half of what I am worth, if you will give me six months' life." The physician told him he could not live six weeks. "Then," said he, "I shall go to hell." His companions in guilt, D'Alembert, Diderot, and Marmontel, hasten to keep up his courage, but meet nothing but reproach and horror. In spite of the guard of infidels about him, he sends for the Abbe Gautier to come as soon as possible. In his presence, and that of other witnesses, he signs a recantation of infidelity, and professes to die in the church. It is sent to the rector of St. Sulpice and the archbishop of Paris for approval. The Abbe Gautier returns with it, but cannot enter. Every avenue to the dying infidel is defended by those who had shared in his conspiracy against christianity. They want to hide his terrors and their own shame. Now it is, that D'Alembert, Diderot, and about twenty others, of like character, who beset his apartment, never approach him but to hear their condemnation. "Retire!" he often exclaims, with execrations, "it is you that have brought me to my present state! Begone! I could have done without you all; but you could not exist without me! And what a wretched glory have you produced me?" Then his conspiracy comes before him, and, alternately supplicating and blaspheming, he complains that he is abandoned by God and man, and often cries out: "Oh Christ! Oh Jesus Christ!" *He is looking on Him whom he pierced!* He is drinking the cup of trembling! the foretaste of the second death! The Mareschal de Richelieu flies from the scene, declaring it "too terrible to be sustained." The physicians, thunderstruck, retire; declaring "the death of the impious man to be terrible indeed." One of them pronounces that "*the furies of Orestes could give but a faint idea of those of Voltaire.*"*

We shall close these awful scenes, with a few glances at the dying Paine. Once it was his boast that, during a dangerous illness, he thought with new satisfaction of having written the Age of Reason, and found, by experiment, that his principles were sufficient to sustain him in expectation of death. It was an empty boast! Let us see him when really dying. He would not be left alone night or day. If he could not see that some one was with him, he would scream till a person appeared. A female attendant more than once found him in the attitude of prayer. Having asked her what she thought of his Age of Reason, and being answered that, from a conviction of its evil tendency, she had burnt it; he wished all its readers had been as wise, and added: "If ever the devil had an agent on earth, I have been one." An infidel visiter said to him: "You have lived like a man; I hope you will die like one." He turned to others in the room, and said: "You see what miserable comforters I have." The woman whom he had enticed from her husband lamented to a neighbour her sad condition. "For this man," she said, "I have given up my family and friends, my property and my religion; judge then of my distress, when he tells me that the principles he has taught me will not bear me out." Well might she be distressed, when she heard his exclamations. "He would call out, during his paroxysms of distress, without intermission, 'O Lord help me, God help me, Jesus Christ help me, O Lord

* "The nurse who attended him, being many years afterwards requested to wait on a sick protestant gentleman, refused, till she was assured he was not a philosopher; declaring, if he were, she would on no account incur the danger of witnessing such a scene as she had been compelled to do at the death of M. Voltaire. I received this account (adds the Right Rev. Daniel Wilson) from the son of the gentleman, to whose dying bed the woman was invited, by a letter now in my possession."

The above account is abridged from the "History of Jacobinism," by the Abbe Baruel, and has been denied by no one of the many witnesses to the death of Voltaire.

help me,' &c., repeating the same expressions without any, the least, variation, in a tone of voice that would alarm the house."*

And now what need be said in conclusion? You have seen the fruit of the trees. One produces corruption; the other holiness of life. One roots up; the other nourishes and cherishes whatever is good around it. The spread of infidelity is that of vice, and disorder, and all confusion. The spread of christianity is that of purity, peace, and all the virtues of the social state. The more thoroughly an individual embraces infidelity, the more entirely does he become the slave of sin. The more perfectly he embraces the gospel, the more perfectly, does he become the example of whatever is lovely and of good report. No infidel ever rose higher than the chill composure of a Stoic's firmness, in the trial of death. Multitudes and the chief of infidels have, in that honest hour, abandoned their sentiments with horror. On the other hand, no Christian ever regretted, when dying, that he had believed the gospel; all have only wished they had followed it more diligently; and, in cases innumerable, disciples of Christ have risen to the most triumphant emotions of joy and praise, and the most exulting assurance of eternal life and glory, in the very act of departing for eternity.

Is a tree known by its fruits? Then which of these is the tree of life? Which looks like truth? Which is to be cut down, and cast into the everlasting burning?

The whole argument, of this and the preceding lecture, may be well concluded with an applicable and *true* saying of Hume. Being asked by a friend, to whom he used to refer his essays, previously to publication, whether he thought that, if his opinions were universally to take place, mankind would not be rendered more unhappy than they were; and whether he did not suppose that the curb of religion was necessary to human nature; "The objections," answered he, "are not without weight, but ERROR NEVER CAN PRODUCE

* Cheetham's Life of Paine.

GOOD." Such is precisely the text of this and the preceding lecture. "Do men gather grapes of thorns, or figs of thistles?" "The tree is known by its fruits," said the Saviour. "Error never can produce good," said the man who denied him. By this, let the comparative merits of christianity and infidelity stand or fall.

How imperative, then, is the exhortation to all professors of the religion of Jesus: "Let your light shine before men!" "Be careful to maintain good works!" "Let your conversation be as it becometh the gospel of Christ!" To you, is committed the honour; on you, depends the character of christianity among the unbelieving and disobedient. Its most legible and universally imposing evidences are found in the living epistles of those who, under the influence of its saving truth, are seen devotedly "following after righteousness, godliness, faith, love, patience, meekness;" "using the world, as not abusing it;" looking for death, as not fearing it; cheerful in all duty, while they remain on earth; happy when the time comes for them to depart out of it unto the Father? Ah! if all that are numbered among Christians were thus radiant in the beauty of holiness, how soon would the whole earth be filled with the praise of the Lord! Then, indeed, would the church put on strength. Then would the gentiles come to her light, and kings to the brightness of her rising; all they that despise her should bow themselves down at the soles of her feet; and they should call her, "The city of the Lord; the Zion of the Holy One of Israel."*

* Isaiah, lx.

LECTURE XII.

SUMMARY OF THE ARGUMENT, AND APPLICATION TO OBJECTIONS.

In the course of the preceding lectures, I have been enabled, by a kind Providence, blessing me with a more adequate measure of health than I anticipated, to spread before you a comprehensive view of the external evidences of christianity. Although one whole division of our forces, and one of no secondary consequence, has not been brought into the field; and of that which has been employed, several important subdivisions have been held in the back ground for want of room to display them; enough, I trust, has been done to give you an impressive idea of what the strength of the cause must be, when all the immense variety of auxiliaries composing its host are arranged together under command of a mind capable of using them to the best advantage. It would stand like the massive squares of British infantry at Waterloo, to which the boasting enemy rode up again and again, in the full confidence of sweeping them before the impetuosity of their charge. But "their onset and reception was that of a furious ocean pouring itself against a chain of insulated rocks."*

Before relinquishing our course, it is important to take a brief retrospect of the ground we have been over; that we may gather into united and co-operating force the several lines of argument which as yet have been employed only in their separate efficiency.

After having divided the whole field of evidence into the two general departments of *external* and *internal*, and separated the former, as that to which our course would be con-

* Scott's Napoleon.

fined, we proceeded to lay the foundation of all our subsequent reasonings by making good the AUTHENTICITY OF THE BOOKS OF THE NEW TESTAMENT, and the CREDIBILITY OF THE HISTORY contained therein. In reference to the question of authenticity, we instituted an inquiry whether there is sufficient evidence that the several scriptures composing the New Testament were written by the men whose names they bear, the original apostles and disciples of Christ? For an answer to this, we pursued precisely the same method as in determining the authenticity of any other writings. The evidence required in such investigations was shown to be so unaffected by time, that whether a book be ascribed to the christian era or to five centuries earlier or later, a similar description of proof would possess a similar conclusiveness. That for the authenticity of the books of the New Testament was presented under the following heads: They are quoted or alluded to by a series of writers extending, in unbroken succession, from the present to the apostolic age. In the earliest writers of this series, as well as the later, they are treated with peculiar respect, as possessing an authority belonging to no other books, and as conclusive in all questions of religion; they were collected at a very early period into a distinct volume; were publicly read and expounded in the assemblies of the primitive Christians; commentaries were written upon them; harmonies were formed out of them; different copies were carefully compared, and versions were made into different languages, in the first centuries of christianity. Hence it appeared that the agreement of the ancient church, as to what were the authentic books of the New Testament, was complete, and was no more imperfect among the various sects of heretics, than among the orthodox fathers. None of these several heads of evidence attach to any of those spurious writings commonly called *Apocryphal Scriptures;* while the marks of the spuriousness of these can be asserted with regard to none of those which are esteemed as authentic. In confirmation of the mass of testimony, adduced in support of these propositions, we exhibited a most important collection of proofs from the writings of the early adversaries of christianity. The style and language of the New Testament were spoken of, as in perfect agreement with the local and other circumstances of its reputed writers; as in perfect harmony with their known character, and with the age and country in which they lived; and such as could not have been produced in any age subsequent to theirs. In conclusion of the whole argument, we endeavoured to show that such was the necessity of detection, in case of a forgery, during the primitive centuries, that had the books in question been deficeient in the evidence of apostolic origin, nothing less than a miracle in their aid could account for their early and universal currency. The whole train of evidence concluded with this result: that to suppose the New Testament unauthentic or even questionable in this particular, is to resign the authenticity of every other book of the least antiquity; yea, and the sufficiency of human testimony, in its most conclusive form, to establish the authenticity of any such work. Having come to this, it seemed no presumption to proceed in our subsequent lectures, as if the question of authenticity were answered in the affirmative with entire satisfaction.

But in connexion with the apostolic origin, it was important to look into the integrity of the New Testament scriptures; for the purpose of ascertaining to what extent they have been preserved without mutilation or corruption. That they have undergone no material alteration since they were first published, was inferred from the perfect impossibility of such a change; from obvious agreement among the existing manuscripts of the New Testament; and from the harmony of our present text with the numerous quotations in the works of early christian writers, as well as with those ancient translations which are still extant.

But in laying the foundation of our subsequent argument, another question remained: Is the history, contained in these authentic writings, *credible?* In answer to this, we assumed that the credibility of the gospel history is to be ascertained precisely like that of any other history. It appeared that, in questions of this kind, the two great points to be proved are, *a competency of knowledge, and trustworthy honesty*, on the part of the historian; did he know enough to write a true account, and was he too honest to write any other account than such as he believed to be true? These points established, the credibility of the history is settled. The first was easily determined by the consideration that the amount of knowledge required for the writing of the gospel history was by no means great; that the narrative is extremely simple and unambitious; and that those who penned it were personal companions of Christ, and eye-witnesses of almost all they related. In reference to the second point to be made out, we took the position that *there is abundant evidence that the writers of the gospel history were too honest to relate any thing but what they believed to be truth.* Taking the history as written by St. John for a specimen, we discovered a strong internal evidence of the honesty of the writer in the fact that it is in a high degree *circumstantial;* and another, in the incidental characteristic of the writer, that he takes no pains to convince us of his honesty, and makes no parade about it, as if it were possible to be suspected; and another, in the circumstance, that while he could not have been ignorant that he was relating many extraordinary and wonderful events, he betrays no appearance of wonder in himself, nor any expectation of wonder from his readers, thus evincing that he was conscious of narrating events of universal notoriety. In addition to these striking imprints of honesty; we perceived another, in the minute accuracy which distinguishes all the allusions of this narrative to the manners, customs, opinions, political events, and circumstances of the times.

Having thus exhibited satisfactory evidence of the honesty of one of the writers of the gospel narrative; we produced seven other writers, each entirely independent of the rest, and possessing all the internal marks of honesty discovered in St. John; all concurring in their statements so entirely that no contradiction can be detected; and yet with so much incidental variety, that the suspicion of a concerted scheme for mutual support is as unreasonable as if they had lived in different centuries. The fact that they were heartily interested in the gospel; that they so firmly believed what they wrote, as to have lived in zealous devotion to Christ, even to the sacrifice of life, was shown to be the strongest confirmation, instead of the least abridgement, of their united testimony. In their co-operating evidence, we have a proof of the honesty of each writer, and of the credibility of the whole body of facts contained in their pages, such as no history of any individual of the world can equal. *Four histories, written by persons contemporaneous with the subject*, are only found in the case before us. When it is considered that the authors were not only contemporaries but companions of the personage whose history is given; their mutual support and internal evidences of honesty afford a body of proof which, were their narratives untrue, would be morally impossible.

Here, we might have left the question of *credibility*. But we proceeded to show, that to suppose these writers to have published what they did not believe, is to suppose that they acted not only without any conceivable motive, but in direct opposition to all the motives by which the minds of men are ever influenced. And finally, it was made to appear that the gospel history has in its support, not only all the testimony that could fairly have been expected from its enemies all of them yielding at least the evidence of *silence*, when, had they been able, they would assuredly have published a denial; but much stronger testimony than could fairly have been expected from enemies, since several of their most hostile writers positively acknowledge all the facts that are necessary to establish the divine authority of Jesus. But this was not our highest reach of testimony. We found a great cloud of witnesses to the truth of this history in the multitudes converted to the gospel under the preaching of the apostles: witnesses who have this peculiar excellence, that, from having once been enemies, they became devoted friends, by the mere force of their conviction of the facts in question. The whole argument for credibility was finished by showing, from the very nature and circumstances of the history, that had it not been true, its currency for a single year would have been quite as miraculous, and more unaccountable, than any thing related therein.

Having thus cleared our way to the New Testament, by ascertaining the authenticity of its books, and the credibility of its history; we were prepared to open the volume, and investigate its contents. It professes to contain a revelation from God, communicated to mankind by the Lord Jesus and his apostles, as invested with a divine commission for this very purpose. We asked for their credentials. They referred us to their miraculous works. The appeal was confessedly fair. Miracles perfectly proved, are perfect evidence of divine attestation. But, before proceeding to a direct investigation of the testimony in favour of the miracles of the gospel, we found it necessary, on account of the desperate efforts which enemies of christianity have made to escape this argument, to illustrate the following preliminary truths: that there is nothing unreasonable or improbable in the idea of a miracle in proof of divine revelation; that the miracles wrought for this purpose, in the first century, can be rendered credible to us of the nineteenth, by no other evidence than that of testimony; that such evidence is perfectly sufficient to prove a miracle; that the testimony to the gospel miracles has suffered no diminution of force by increase of age; and that we, who are restricted to such means of conviction, are situated in regard to our state of probation and moral discipline, more consistently than if we had been present when the miracles were wrought, and could have proved their reality by the test of our senses.

From these important propositions, we proceeded to the

testimony in regard to THE MIRACLES OF THE GOSPEL. Here we might have stood upon the equitable assumption that, in having established the truth of the narratives, we had proved also the reality of the miracles, of the New Testament; inasmuch as miraculous events are so essentially interwoven with many of them, that to question the latter, is necessarily an impeachment of the former. But as our object was not merely proof, but variety and fulness of proof, we proceeded to the fact that, the religion of the Bible having been established by direct appeal to miracle, in evidence of the divine authority of its teachers, stands alone in this respect among the various religions of mankind; after which, we laid out the materials of our argument under the following propositions. Supposing the wonderful works ascribed to our Lord to have really occurred, they cannot be ascribed to second causes, but must have been genuine miracles. They were of such a nature as admitted of their being brought at once to the test of the senses. They were performed, for the most part, in the most public manner. They were exceedingly numerous, and of great variety. The success, in every case, was instantaneous and complete. There is no evidence of such a thing, as an attempt on the part of Christ or his apostles to perform a miracle in which they were accused of a failure. For seventy years, the miraculous gifts in question continued to be exercised, and to be submitted to the inspection of mankind. During all this time, it is a matter of certainty that they underwent the most rigid examination from those who had every opportunity and every disposition to detect imposition. Every advantage was afforded the adversary by their being published and appealed to immediately after, and in the very places where, they occurred. The persons who performed them were of all others the least qualified, and the least likely either to attempt a series of counterfeit miracles, or to succeed in passing them upon the Jewish and heathen world. Notwithstanding all that was done to break the constancy and extort the confessions of those early Christians who were eye-witnesses of the deeds of Jesus and his apostles; none were ever known to acknowledge they had been deceived, or had found any thing but truth in the miracles by which they were led to embrace the gospel. The benevolent character and holy effects of the miracles; the humble, self-denying, unambitious spirit of those who performed them, are irreconcilable with the supposition of any thing selfish or deceitful. That they were genuine, and to the people of that century undeniable, we have the plainest and strongest confession from the primitive adversaries of Christ and his cause. But confessions stronger, unspeakably, are found in the history of great multitudes in Judea, and every country of heathenism, who beheld in the miracles such incontrovertible certainty as induced them to lay aside the bitterest enmity to the gospel, and make the most painful sacrifices of which human nature is capable, for the sake of embracing the service of Jesus. If with all this evidence, there is not reason to rely implicitly upon the reality of the gospel miracles, we are driven to believe in the most unaccountable violations of the laws of nature, of truth, and of common sense, as necessary to account for the singular events connected with their performance, and for their universal acknowledgment in the era of their first publication. Hence it was concluded that the credentials of Jesus and his apostles were given from heaven; and, consequently, that the New Testament, as an authentic record of what they delivered, is *the book of the revelation of God.*

Here, with perfect safety, might the cause have been considered as determined. But, unwilling to content ourselves with once establishing the divine authority of the gospel, the argument was commenced anew, substituting PROPHECY for MIRACLE, as the source of evidence. Considerations were stated which render the argument from prophecy specially valuable: such as the continual increase of its strength, and the important characteristic of many predictions, that their fulfilment, being a matter of present existence, is evidence before our eyes—addressed to our senses. Before proceeding to the proof of fulfilment, the fact that all other religions have shrunk from attempting such dangerous ground as the publication of prophecy, and yet that, however certain of exposure in case of imposition, it is every where appealed to and rested upon, in the Bible, was treated as a strong presumptive argument that in the Bible is found what no false religion can possess—something to warrant it in venturing where divine omniscience alone is able to tread—*inspiration of God.* We then glanced at the immense extent, and vast embrace, and wonderful minuteness, which characterize the scheme of scripture prophecy; the many ages included; the variety of agents employed; the numerous particulars predicted; and the harmony of all the details. The undeniable fact was asserted, that between the least prediction of the Bible, and any event of history, there is not the smallest evidence of contradiction. We then demanded whether it were credible that imposture would ever have dared to commit its cause to a venture which could terminate successfully only by such a hopeless series of miraculous coincidences.

With all this presumptive evidence on our side, we took up a brief selection of important prophecies, and showed their minute and wonderful fulfilment, from sources of testimony to which there could be no exception. Your attention was specially directed to a great variety of predictions, by different writers, and in all ages of bible history, all centering in Jesus, and determining the time and circumstances of his advent; the character of his life; the particulars of his sufferings and death; foretelling his resurrection, and the increase of his kingdom. After having thus showed the fulfilment of prophecies, of which Jesus was the subject; we proceeded to others, of which Jesus was the author.

In the destruction of Jerusalem, and its subsequent history. we had, prepared to our hands by the writings of unbelievers, a most impressive accomplishment of a series of predictions on the part of our Lord, in which the utmost plainness of meaning is united with singular minuteness of detail. The agreement between the predictions and the events admitted of no denial. The supposition of chance was the only explanation to which unbelief could flee. But it was stated, on the authority of strict arithmetical calculation, that, according to the principles employed in the computation of what are called chances, the probability against the occurrence, at the predicted time, of all the particulars embraced in the prophecies of which we had spoken, exceeded the power of numbers to express; even without the consideration of the providence of One who hateth iniquity, and especially when it is practised under pretence of his authority. The conclusion was inevitable: that the Bible, in thus containing so many genuine prophecies, scattered through its several books, contains revelation from God, and exhibits satisfactory evidences of divine authority; and that Jesus Christ, being in his character and office, as the Saviour of sinners, the great theme of this system of prophecy, and being himself endued with the spirit of prophecy, was, and is to come, no other than what he claimed to be considered, the Son of God, the redeemer of men, King of kings, and Lord of lords.

Here again, we might have rested our cause. But unwilling to withhold the interesting evidence remaining; we commenced the main question anew, and set out to prove the divine original, from the history of THE PROPAGATION OF CHRISTIANITY. The difficulties in the way of its extensive progress were manifest from considering that the enterprise of propagating a new religion, to the exclusion of every other, was perfectly novel, and universally offensive; that the whole character of the gospel, as a system of doctrine and a rule of life, erected a barrier against its progress which, to human force, would have proved insurmountable; that it necessarily arrayed against itself all the influence of every priesthood; all the powers of every government; all the prejudices, habits, and passions of every people; and all the pride, wit, and influence of every school of philosophy in the world. Add to this, that the character of the age was peculiarly adapted to increase the difficulties above mentioned, and to put the truth of such a religion as that of the gospel to the very closest and strongest trial. The agents intrusted with the propagation of christianity were of all others most unfitted for their work, on the supposition that it was one of imposture. They set up their banner when every thing visible on their side only tended to inspire them with despair, and every thing on the side of their enemies was considered as triumphant. The mode they adopted was directly calculated, on human principles, to increase and multiply all their difficulties. They were encountered every where by the fiercest persecution that the malignant ingenuity of enemies could invent, and the principalities and powers of the earth could execute. In spite of all these enormous combinations of resistance, such was the rapid and mighty progress of the gospel, that, in thirty years, the Roman empire was every where pervaded with its influence, and even haughty Rome could yield a great multitude, as her first fruits, for the fires of persecution. The conversions, which ensued in such numbers, were not changes merely of opinion, but of heart and life; they involved individuals of all classes of mind, of learning, of rank, and of opulence. Nothing in any degree corresponding to this work had ever been known before, or has ever been witnessed since; even though efforts have frequently been made, in circumstances and with means, on the supposition that the apostles were not specially favoured of God, much more advantageous than theirs. All these particulars combined, demonstrate that in the labours of the apostles, none but "*God gave the increase,*" because none but God could give such increase. They present a miracle as unquestionable, as if, at the bidding of man, a rock should become a fountain of water.

Thus, a third time, did we finish our proof. Here, again,

might the argument have been safely terminated. But the FRUITS OF CHRISTIANITY presented a source of additional evidence, too important to be omitted. We began, in this department, with THE EFFECTS OF CHRISTIANITY ON SOCIETY IN GENERAL. We surveyed the moral condition of mankind when the gospel era commenced. The most polished, literary, and admired nations of the ancient world were selected as, at least, favourable specimens of all others. Their personal, domestic, and social virtues were placed in comparison with those of civilized nations of the present age, and especially with those which christian influence has most thoroughly pervaded. The contrast was exceedingly impressive. The moral improvements effected in society have been immense and inestimable. We found nothing in the philosophy, or the religion, or the fluctuations, or any other ingredient of the heathen or infidel world, to effect such a change. No heathen nation, left to itself, has ever reformed. The history of the world demonstrates that the whole work must be charged to christianity. The history of christian effort, among heathen nations of the present age, demonstrates that she was capable, and ever will be capable, of accomplishing such blessed results.

From the fruits of christianity on society in general, we turn to those exhibited in *the character and happiness of her genuine disciples*. Undeniable and innumerable transformations, in moral character and habits, were pointed out, which are utterly incapable of explanation, but on the supposition of a divine power accompanying the gospel. A comparison was drawn between the lives of genuine disciples of Christ, and those for which unbelievers are notorious. Another was instituted between the death-bed scenes and testimonies of real Christians, and such as have been witnessed in connexion with infidelity. It appeared that, with a few exceptions, individuals are the slaves of sin, in proportion as they become devoted to infidelity; while it was equally evident that, without any exception, they become servants of righteousness, in proportion as their hearts are surrendered to the influence of the gospel. It appeared that while, on the one hand, no unbeliever ever advanced beyond the negative and comfortless composure of a Stoic, under the trial of death, and multitudes, and the very chief of their profession, have, in that hour, abandoned their sentiments with horror; it was never heard, on the other hand, that a Christian regretted, in his death, having believed and obeyed the gospel; while innumerable disciples of that blessed faith, in the very act of dissolution, have risen to the most triumphant assurance of eternal life and glory. Such are the legitimate fruits of the gospel of Christ.

On the wise principle, therefore, that "a corrupt tree cannot bring forth good fruit," we must pronounce christianity good; and since no religion can be good without being true, or as Hume expressed it: "*error never can produce good*," we must conclude that her assertion of divine authority is worthy of all acceptation. Thus terminated the argument of the last lecture.

And now, while the retrospect, we have been taking, is fresh in your memories, consider:

1st. The *plainness and simplicity* which characterize the evidences of christianity. To understand the meaning, and appreciate the force, of any or all of them, so far as is necessary to a clear, intelligent, and impressive conviction of the divine inspiration of the scriptures, and the divine nature and mission of the Lord Jesus Christ, is a work to which the mind of any thoughtful individual of ordinary information is competent. Willingness to read, readiness to learn, humility to submit to conviction, and an ordinary knowledge of the meaning of words, are the only requisites for a satisfactory investigation of the whole argument. How different, in this respect, is the system of Christ, from all the speculating and metaphysical systems of infidel philosophy! What would plain common sense people do, did their understanding of the grounds of faith and duty depend upon such dark questions, as the sufficiency of the light of nature, the origin of evil, the metaphysical relations of cause and effect, the foundation of virtue, the elements of accountability, the freedom of the will, &c.; questions which must be settled in our own minds, and by our own reason, before we can consistently embrace any other religion than that of revelation; but about which all the philosophy on earth, if it reject the scriptures, may speculate to the end of time, without arriving at sufficient certainty to satisfy a single conscience. The gospel requires no abstract theories to explain its way of salvation, its principles of obligation, or its rule of duty. It simply presents the evidence that Jesus Christ, the Son and the Sent of God, came into the world to teach and to save sinners; and then, to every sinner, publishes this plain direction: *What Jesus in his word has taught, believe; what he has there commanded, follow; and, through his righteousness, thou shalt be saved.*

2d. Consider the *great variety* and *accumulation* of the evidences of christianity. In the lectures to which you have listened, were presented no less than four independent and complete methods of proof, each of which is amply sufficient to bear the whole weight of the gospel. The argument from miracles is conclusive without the argument from prophecy. The latter is in no wise dependent upon the former, or any that succeeded it. The argument from the propagation is complete in itself, as well as that from the fruits of christianity. But under each of these general heads, what a boundless variety of auxiliary evidences might have been adduced! Every single miracle; every fulfilled prophecy; a thousand separate facts in the spread of the gospel, and innumerable examples of its holy fruits in the hearts and lives of believers, would have furnished us with so many effulgent centres, from all of which rays of brilliant evidence are continually meeting and harmonizing in a shining testimony to Jesus, as the resurrection and the life.

But remember that one whole division, out of the two which embrace the field of evidence, has been left untouched. We have found an astonishing variety and accumulation of proof; and yet the whole department of INTERNAL EVIDENCE, that which arises from the search of the New Testament itself—its spirit, manner, dress, and beauty—the simplicity of its character; the benevolence of its temper; its power over the conscience; the suitableness of its contents to the wants of man; the excellence of its doctrines; the purity and elevation of its morals; the character and conduct of Jesus, and the happy tendency of all his instructions: —this immense field of diversified evidence, secondary to none in its influence upon the mind, and superior to all in its direct appeal to the heart, we have not so much as entered. Could we but see all the separate streams united in one; could we measure at once the force of that majestic tide which collects its innumerable tributaries from all ages, and all nations, and all hearts; could we appreciate its strength by an accurate estimate of all the obstructions with which earth and hell, "the prince of the power of the air," and "the rulers of the darkness of this world," have endeavoured to resist its course—the mountains of difficulty which, in every century, it has rent asunder, or rolled away to clear its course; we should wonder, indeed, at what Divine Goodness has done to make us believers, and at what human obduracy has been able to withstand for the purpose of continuing in unbelief.

But this astonishing flood of evidence is perpetually increasing. Every additional benefit which christianity bestows upon any portion of mankind; every additional conversion of a sinner to God; every holy life that is added to the shining ranks of the followers of Christ; every new triumph of christian faith over the trials of life and the terrors of death; every increase in the fulfilment of prophecy; every advance in the conquest of the gospel over the darkness of paganism; every new year of victory over all the resistance of pretended friends and unfaithful professors, of internal divisions, and infidel enmity, is a new stream to swell the many waters, which one day, like the deluge of old, will drown unbelief in its last refuge, and make all nations and kindreds know how precious, as an ark of safety, is He who "came into the world to save sinners."

But who can ask for additional evidence? Did not the question affect the darling idols of the heart; were it one of property, or of science, or of human life; were it some new medicine, to heal the maladies of the body, that laid before us this immense mass of credentials from all generations; or were it a scheme for the acquisition of earthly gain that came to us accompanied with such voluminous evidence of its unfailing truth and wisdom; no man of common sense could hesitate a moment to give it his unqualified belief. All men are continually committing their dearest interests to evidence unspeakably inferior. We intrust our lives to the care of physicians, of whose skill, and wisdom, and carefulness, and honesty, we have no assurance comparable to our proof of Jesus, as the only Physician to save our souls, and as that all-sufficient One, in whose hands none can perish. We believe, without a question, in all the great events of history; and yet their evidence is so inconsiderable in comparison with the proof of the gospel, that if you take away, as unestablished, the great pillars of the argument of christianity, you pronounce the whole foundation of historical knowledge, unestablished; yea, you rob mankind of the whole fruit of human testimony, and write *terra incognita* over almost the whole map of the generations and things of the universe.

III. *How impressive to the mind of every human being, should the evidence of christianity appear.* If he take up any system of faith which men have ever attempted to substitute for the gospel, and compare its evidences, how immediately is it confounded by the contrast. If he attempt to set aside any one of the great proofs on which the noble fabric of christianity is supported, how immediately are his efforts defeated, and his weapons broken? He may invent difficulties, but the arguments of the gospel he cannot answer.

What, then, is the condition of the inquirer? The religion of Christ, thus solemnly and impressively attested, declares him a sinner before a just and holy God; condemned, under sentence of the divine law, to eternal retribution and wo. It tells him, that except he repent, he must perish; except he believe in and follow Jesus, as his Master and only Hope, he cannot be delivered from condemnation. It declares, on the other hand, that if he repent and believe on the Lord Jesus Christ, he shall be saved; the sting of death will be taken away; an inheritance will be given him "that is incorruptible, and undefiled, and that fadeth not away." All this comes to him under the sanction of evidences innumerable; for none of which is he provided with an answer. History informs him that the best and wisest men of all ages have considered those evidences incontrovertible. Immense multitudes assure him, that in embracing the gospel they have experienced the truth of its promises, and realized the holy and happy influence of its doctrines. The probability, to say the very least, must seem immense, even to a sceptic, that should he reject christianity, he would reject the truth of God, and incur eternal ruin. While, on the other hand, the certainty is evident, that should he embrace it, not only would he suffer no loss in case it should prove untrue, but he would gain many precious consolations in this life, of which infidelity is entirely barren. In these circumstances, how serious is the crisis, when he is making the choice whether to be an infidel or a christian! Does he decide for infidelity? He can gain nothing; he certainly loses much; and if the gospel be true, he loses all for ever. Does he decide for christianity? He can lose nothing; he certainly gains a great deal; and if infidelity prove to be true, he has nothing to regret but that truth and happiness should be so directly at war.

Then what a step does he take, who, notwithstanding all the evidences of the religion of Jesus, determines upon its denial? What solemnity and carefulness of investigation;

what candour and impartiality of judgment; what jealousy over one's own inclinations and prejudices; what long and patient consideration; what earnest prayer for divine guidance and help, should precede such a decision! One would suppose that at least the maturest knowledge, and the coolest temperament, and the most sober hours, would be waited for, before coming to a point on which such tremendous consequences are suspended. What, then, is our amazement to see the stupid ignorance, or the senseless levity, or the lazy thoughtlessness, or the intemperate enmity, with which this momentous decision is almost always made! How many become infidels, not only without candid investigation, but without any serious thinking; without so much as an inquiry; without even a decent sobriety of mind! To such persons, I know not a more alarming occupation than that of reading a well ordered exhibition of the evidences of christianity.

Have the evidences of the christian religion been ever answered? Infidels have attacked christianity. But any thing may be attacked. They have slandered her doctrines; ridiculed her word; reviled her precepts; hated her holiness, and influenced many to go and do likewise: but neither hatred, nor reviling, nor ridicule, nor slander, is the test of truth. Have infidels ever resorted to the one only fair and honest mode of meeting, face to face, the whole array of testimony which christianity advances, and endeavouring cooly to prove, as a matter of historical evidence, that the authenticity of the New Testament, and the credibility of its history, are not sustained; that the miracles of Jesus have not been supported with adequate testimony; that the prophecies of the scriptures have met their attestation in no accurate histories; that christianity was propagated by human force alone, and its fruits are those of a corrupt and deceitful tree? I answer, no. There is no such effort in the books of infidelity. I read of speculations, opposed to our facts, insinuations, in answer to our testimonies; sneers, in reply to our solemn reasonings; assertions, where we demanded arguments; levity and presumption, where an advocate of truth would have been serious and humble. But I know of no such thing, as a book of infidelity in any sense corresponding in the nature, or grounds, or spirit of its reasoning, with such arguments for christianity as those of Paley, or Lardner, or Gregory, or Wilson, and a thousand others, to which no man ever dared to attempt an answer. Infidelity, like an insect on the pillar of some stupendous temple, that can see no further than the microscopic irregularities of the polished marble beneath its feet, may busy itself in hunting for little specks in the surface of the noble fabric of christianity; but has no such eye, and takes no such elevated stand, as would enable it to survey the whole plan, and judge of its pretensions by the mutual adaptation of its parts, the harmony and grandeur of its proportions.

IV. But there is a most important feature in all the evidence we have been considering, to which I now direct your special attention. It is strictly PHILOSOPHICAL. By this I mean that the process by which we have arrived at the truth of christianity is precisely similar to that by which the astronomer arrives at the most certain truths of the celestial bodies; or the chymist determines the most fundamental doctrines of his important science. The grand characteristic of the philosophy that Bacon illustrated, and Newton so nobly applied, and to which all science is so deeply indebted, is that it discards speculation; places no dependence upon theory; demands fact for every thing, and in every thing submits implicitly to the decision of fact, no matter how incomprehensible, or how opposed by all the speculations of the world. This is called *inductive* philosophy in distinction from that of theory and conjecture. It collects its facts either by personal experiments and observation; or by the testimony of those whose experiments and observations, and whose fidelity in recording them, are worthy of reliance From these it makes its careful inductions, and determines the laws of science, with a degree of plain, unpresuming authority, to which every enlightened mind feels it ought to bow. The great principle of all Newton's Principia, and that on which he set the ladder that raised him to the stars, was this simple axiom: "Whatever is collected from this induction ought to be received, notwithstanding any conjectural hypothesis to the contrary, till such time as it shall be contradicted or limited by further observations." But why is not this self-evident truth as fundamental in religion, as in astronomy? If Reid and Stewart have been permitted, with universal consent and approbation, to apply the simple principles of induction to the philosophy of the mind; on what possible ground can they be excluded from the philosophy of the soul—the religion of the heart? We beg as a favour, what is also demanded by right, that christianity may be tried by the strictest application of these principles. You are called upon for no greater effort of credulity; no more implicit reliance on testimony, in order to receive the whole system of christianity, as a divine revelation, than you are obliged daily to exercise in believing those innumerable facts in natural science, which you have not the opportunity of testing by your own experiments. In regard to these, you simply ask, what is the statement? Is it accurate? Is it honest? However it may contradict your previous ideas, or seem at variance with previous phenomena, or even with well established laws, you only investigate the testimony with the more carefulness. This confirmed, you receive the facts; and, instead of squaring them by any of your old theories or speculations, you proceed to measure the latter by their line, with as much submission as if every mystery involved in them, were perfectly explained. Only behave thus reasonably in the investigation of the great question we have been considering. Apply to it the measuring rod of sound philosophy. Let every speculation as to its truth be blotted out. Let all conjectural hypotheses, for and against it, be set aside. Let the infidel and the

Christian sit together in the chairs of Bacon and of Newton; and with that stern rejection of mere theory, and lowly deference to fact, which so eminently distinguished those venerable patriarchs of modern science, let the New Testament be brought to the bar. It professes to be the authentic and credible record of the life and doctrine of Christ. In it, Christ professes to have been sent of God. Let the question be put. Not, however, is this religion consistent with our notions of what man wanted, and God might have been expected to reveal? Not, does it contain any thing strange, or mysterious, or apparently contradictory to what we have been accustomed to believe? But, let it be a plain question of inductive philosophy. Is it supported by a competent number of well certified facts? Is there so much credible testimony that we are warranted in determining that the New Testament is authentic; that its history is true; that Jesus did work miracles; that his prophecies have been fulfilled? that no human power, unaided by that of God, can account for the propagation of his gospel; that no corrupt imposture could ever produce the fruit with which its influence has blessed mankind? If there be, then all true philosophy says: "*Christianity ought to be believed, notwithstanding any conjectural hypothesis to the contrary.*" Only confine yourselves to this mode of investigation, and submit yourselves to this simple law of evidence, and, like Newton, you may mount a ladder set on a rock, and reaching to the right hand of the throne of God. Proceed on any other principle, and, like the heavenly vortexes and the immense currents of ethereal matter in the philosophy of Des Cartes, it can only lead you into inextricable confusion. But, if you adopt the true principles; what becomes of the writings of infidels? Buried amidst the rubbish of vain speculations, and ingenious absurdities, and scholastic trifling of the dark ages, when to get wealth by the hypothesis of a philosopher's stone, instead of the homely, experimental realities of diligence and common sense, was the great effort of scientific ambition! Infidelity is all speculation. Reduce it to a residuum of inductive reasoning, and you bring it to nothingness. Strip it of its several envelopes of ingenious hypothesis, and bold assertion, and scoffing declamation, and you find nothing left but a man of straw—an ugly shape to keep the hungry from the bread of life, which you need only approach to discover that it is made of rags, and stuffed with rottenness.

The argument for the divine authority of the gospel is all composed of statements of undeniable facts, and of direct inferences legitimately drawn from them. I defy the ingenuity of the keenest critic to take up the course of reasoning to which you have listened, and point out a single theory, or speculation—any thing, depended on for proof, but plain statements of facts, established as perfectly, and bearing as directly upon the point in question, as any of the observations of Newton's telescope, or of Davy's crucible. Not a word have we said as to what might be supposed or conjectured; what is likely or unlikely; what might have been expected or the contrary; but have simply inquired, *what is historically true.* Let our opponents do likewise. Whether any thing in christianity appears to them probable or improbable; consistent or inconsistent; agreeable to what they should have expected, or the contrary; wise and good, or ridiculous and useless; is perfectly irrelevant. We can by no means consent to make their judgments the standard in such matters. Infidels are thought to entertain very absurd and inconsistent ideas of absurdity and inconsistency, and of what should be esteemed as both good and wise. We ask them to descend from their flights of fancy and speculation, and condescend, in matters of religion, to do what, in those of science, public opinion would force them to, or laugh them out of countenance; to sit down to the plain investigation, on principles of common evidence, of the *facts* which support christianity, determined to believe what may be collected therefrom, notwithstanding any of their conjectural hypotheses to the contrary. Such was once the honest demand of astronomy and chemistry upon all the tribes of theorists and conjecturalists, in those departments of science. It is but a short time since our present fundamental doctrines,on those subjects,were opposed by philosophers whose speculations they rooted up, precisely as the great doctrines of the gospel are still opposed by infidels whose lives they condemn. By and by, it became irresistibly evident that there is no way to science but by the slow and humble path of experiment, obtained either by personal observation, or by the credible testimony of others. As soon as men of scientific minds shall learn to be consistent with their own principles, and to reason philosophically, as well when a law of religion, as a law of nature is concerned, then the contradiction will no longer appear,of a philosopher loving to investigate the works of God, but rejecting His word.*

In truth, the evidence of christianity rests upon a basis which cannot be condemned, without the downfall of many of the most important works of science. The main facts and reasonings of chemistry are considered undeniable, because experimental. But who feels it necessary to make all the experiments, or to see them made, before he will believe? Many of the most important, he receives, and must receive, upon the testimony of others. Thus it is also in astronomical calculations, Seldom are the facts obtained from our own observations. Many of them, we believe, because they are reported by credible witnesses. We come to a certain result, by means of a number taken from a table of calculations made to our hands, with as much assurance, and base our reasonings upon it as confidently, as if we had obtained all the elements by our own labour; and yet the very corner stone of our computation is a mere matter of testimony. On such reliance are eclipses predicted, and nautical observations founded; and yet a man of science who should evince any scepticism with regard to events thus ascertained, would

* On the application of the inductive philosophy to the evidences of christianity, see chapters viii. and ix. of Chalmer's Evidences.

render himself no less an object of ridicule than if he should cavil about the sun's rising to-morrow. What is a page of logarithms, but a page of assertions, the whole value of which is the faith of testimony; and yet upon such data the most momentous calculations in the exact sciences are based without a question.

Pure mathematics are considered as involving complete demonstrations. Mathematical reasoning is regarded as the very perfection of certainty. And yet, in many of its most important operations, elements, on which the whole chain depends, are assumed on a basis not a particle more sure, to say the least, than that on which our belief of the christian miracles is founded. "Who would scruple, in a geometrical investigation, to adopt as a link in the chain a theorem of Apollonius or of Archimedes, although he might not have leisure at the moment to satisfy himself, by an actual examination of their demonstrations, that they had been guilty of no paralogism, either of accident or design, in the course of their reasonings?"* And yet a result, however important, arising from such an investigation, none would suspect. A philosopher would rest his life upon its certainty. But have we assurance of the accuracy and honesty of such men, to whose testimony we thus implicitly yield, whether they be mathematicians, or chymists, or astronomers, comparable in any degree to our assurance of the competent knowledge and immoveable honesty of those original witnesses of the works of Jesus who have borne such devoted testimony to his miracles? Did Apollonius, or Archimedes, or any philosophers of later times, seal their honesty with their blood? Did they suffer the loss of all things in maintenance of their doctrines? Were they willing to be accounted as fools for the sake of their testimony? Did Galileo brave the torture of the inquisition sooner than deny his astronomical discoveries? We do not require such extreme evidence of integrity even in the greatest questions of scientific testimony. It were folly to expect it. We are

* Stewart's Philosophy, ii. 178.

satisfied with a far inferior degree of assurance. And yet such, in ten thousands of instances, is the evidence by which we know the honesty of those from whom comes our testimony to the great facts of the gospel history. They did suffer the loss of all things; they did endure to be treated as the offscouring of all things; they did give themselves to the rack, and flame, and wild beasts, for the testimony of Jesus.

I mentioned, in the announcement of this lecture, that besides a summary of the whole previous course, it would contain an application of the argument to the principal objections brought forward by infidels. This, in substance, has been exhibited. We know of no objection of any importance which is not put to silence and buried, by an appeal from what men *think* to what men have *done;* from *speculation* to *testimony;* from the *ideas of objectors* to the *facts of witnesses.* The simple application of the great principle of inductive philosophy, that *whatever is collected by observation ought to be received, any hypothesis to the contrary notwithstanding,* is the smooth white stone in the sling of David, which no champion of the Philistines, however gigantic in intellect, or learning, or in the boast of either, can stand. I am now speaking of the chief objections. I have nothing to do with the ignorant ribaldry of such an antagonist as Paine. To this man, the purity of the gospel was its chief deformity; and its stern contradiction of his disgusting vices, its most irreconcilable inconsistency. He studied the Bible to defame it, and scraped the common sewers of infidelity for its very lowest and filthiest objections; and then, without honesty even to advert to the thousand answers each had received in its day, served them up with his own dressing of strong assertion and acrid ridicule, and advertised them to the world as his own, and as unanswerable. Such matters we must leave to the writings of those who have had stomach to handle them. In the answer of Bishop Watson, you may see how entirely boasting is their strength. They need but the light, to make all their show of argument fade away. Their best answer is found in the profligate life and despairing death of the poor, miserable man himself.

The *mysteriousness* of certain things in christianity is urged as a strong reason for the rejection of its divine authority. Many will not believe the doctrine of the Trinity; the divinity of Christ; his incarnation; his atoning sacrifice; his resurrection from the dead; his intercession in heaven; the influences of the Holy Spirit upon the hearts of men, and our new creation unto holiness by his converting power, not to speak of many other of the deep things of God, because they are *mysteries.* Mysteries they are unquestionably, and were intended to be so regarded. So far as we have need to understand them, they are as intelligible as the plain truth that man is the union of body and spirit. So far as we are not concerned to understand them, they are as mysterious, but not more so, than the *nature* of the union between body and spirit in man. Religion must have mysteries. "Religion without its mysteries is a temple without its God."

Whither shall we flee to get beyond the region of things incomprehensible? They beset us behind and before. If from revealed religion, we go to natural, they are there! The most essential doctrine of all religion, the existence of God, is mystery to the uttermost. What explanation can be given of his self-existence? His presence in all parts of the universe at once? How he inhabits eternity, having no relation to time—and immensity, having no relation to space? If from natural religion, we go to atheism, they are there also! He who denies the existence of God, plunges at once into the most confounding of all mysteries. What in scripture is more incomprehensible than that this world had no Maker? that all its examples of wise and deep design had no Designer? Will you go from thence, to the experimental certainties of natural philosophy? Mysteries are there also! Explain the attraction of gravitation, the nature of electricity, the elastic power of steam, the secrets of evaporation. What is vegetable, or animal, or spiritual life? In mechanics, we arrive at the utmost certainty respecting the *relations* of force, matter, time, motion, space; while, with the things themselves, we have not the least acquaintance. They are mysteries, as unsearchable to us, as the deepest things of revealed religion. How force is communicated from one body to another, is no more intelligible than how the influences of the Holy Spirit are communicated to man. Matter, in its changes, is as incomprehensible as grace in its operations. "There are questions, doubts, perplexities, disputes, diversities of opinions, about the one as well as about the other. Ought we not, therefore, by a parity of reasoning, to conclude that there may be several true and highly useful propositions about the latter as well as about the former? Nay, I will venture to go farther, and affirm (says a devoted teacher of science) that the preponderance of the argument is in favour of the propositions of the theologian. For while force, time, motion, &c., are avowedly constituent parts of a demonstrable science, and ought, therefore, to be presented in a full blaze of light, the obscure parts proposed in the scriptures for our assent are *avowedly* mysterious. They are not exhibited to be perfectly understood, but to be believed. They *cannot* be understood without ceasing to be what they are. Obscurities, however, are felt as incumbrances to any system of philosophy; while mysteries are ornaments of the christian system, and tests of the humility and faith of its votaries. So that if the rejectors of incomprehensibilities acted consistently with their own principles, they would rather throw aside all philosophical theories in which obscurities are found and exist as *defects*, than the system of revealed religion, in which they enter as essential parts of that '*mystery* of godliness' in which the apostles gloried."*

If from natural philosophy, we ascend to the higher branches of *pure mathematics*, the regions of unmixed light and certainty, where naught is tolerated but strict demonstra-

* Gregory's Letters.

tion, *even there will mystery find us, and its right hand will hold us.*

Explain the *demonstrated* fact that "there are curves which approach continually to some fixed right line, with out the possibility of ever meeting it;" that "a space *infinite* in one sense, may, by its rotation, generate a solid of *finite* capacity;" that "a variable space shall be continually augmenting, and yet never become equal to a certain finite quantity."

These are depths which the mathematician can solve no better than Christians can explain the great mysteries of redemption. But they do not hinder him. He can use, as the elements of his calculation, doctrines thus incomprehensible, without feeling any diminution in the certainty of the result. Why may not a Christian, with equal reason, include among the articles of his belief doctrines no more incomprehensible, without embarrassing his assurance of the duties and consolations which result from them?

If mysteries be valid objections to that which speaks of God and his relations to man, why are they not at least as formidable in all those branches of human knowledge in which created and finite subjects alone are involved? But they are not treated as objections by the mathematician or the philosopher. The former asks no question, but simply, *what is demonstrated?* The latter, *what is proved, either by experiment or by testimony?* If phenomena be well attested, he does not wait to understand their cause, or mode, or effects; he does not suspend belief till he has harmonized their peculiarities with a favourite hypothesis, or with previous observations. He sets them down among the truths of science, and believes; taking for granted, that though *he* may not understand them, there is One that does; and though *he* should never discover the theory by which such events are shown to be in agreement with all others, there is still a harmony which pervades "all things in heaven and earth, and under the earth."

Such is the application of inductive philosophy to the mysteries of nature. Let the mysteries of revelation be treated with equal justice; and instead of employing them as objections to its truth, you will acknowledge them as essential to its nature, and portions of its glory.*

But there are many who object to christianity, not only because they cannot understand the *nature*, but because they cannot see the *reason*, of certain things contained in, or connected with it. For example: It is well known that God is gracious and merciful, and desireth not the death of a sinner, and that He has all power to save whom He will; and yet it is revealed that without the sacrifice of Christ, and without conversion and faith, the sinner cannot be saved. Why, it is asked, this circuitous method, this expense of suffering, when a word from the Almighty would save the world? An intelligent Christian could give many answers to this question; but what if he had none? Would the way of salvation, as revealed in the gospel, be in any degree less credible? Shall we refuse to believe the ways of God, till he has laid all his reasons before us? Why not as well deny His works on the same indefensible ground? Why believe that a sick man cannot recover without a tedious course of medicine? God can raise him with a word! Why cultivate the ground, and seek the mediatorial office of the sun for the raising and ripening of your grain? God can load your fields with harvests without such a circuitous process! Why His power is not exerted immediately for these purposes, you can no more explain than why a sinner cannot be saved but by faith in the sacrifice of Christ. Your belief in the importance of intermediate steps depends as little upon the reasons of the divine appointments, in one case as in the other.

Again: you read that the gospel is of inestimable importance to the happiness of man; a wonderful exhibition of

* See an admirable article on Mysteries in Religion, in Gregory's Letters, vol. i.

divine grace to sinners; and yet there are hundreds of millions who have never heard of it, and it is asked, why, since God is infinitely good and merciful, as well as mighty, such an immeasurable blessing has not been communicated to all mankind? This question is often put as a strong objection to the divine origin of the gospel. Were it taught in the scriptures that those who had never had the gospel will be judged by its law, the objection would have force. But there is no such doctrine. The objection is reasonable only so far as there is reason in a creature's requiring the Creator to explain His ways, and admit him to His councils, before he will believe them. Does a philosopher stand on such grounds? Does he doubt the immense difference between the gifts and blessings, the privileges and improvements, of a native of England, and those of a savage of Kamtchatka, because he knows not for what reason it was so ordained? Does he deny that the former are inestimable, because not universal? Will one refuse to believe that he has a mine of gold in his field, or that the gold is worth his seeking, because all men are not equally favoured? Shall a husbandman despise the genial rain upon his grass, because his neighbour's fleece is dry? If God has not seen fit to reveal the reasons for which He has distributed the gifts of nature, of providence, or of grace with an unequal hand, I find nothing to complain of. I can still believe that those gifts are from above, and are excellent, and distributed under the guidance of infinite wisdom.

That there are no difficulties connected with the scriptures, and with the doctrines of revealed religion, it would be saying too much for the intelligence, education, and study of the general reader, to assert. Until all shall be candid, studious, patient, and humble, some will find many difficulties in christianity. If a child, instead of beginning arithmetic in the elements, should dive at once into the midst of a calculation of algebraic roots and powers, he would scarcely escape being stifled with difficulties. Thus, however, do most objectors to christianity endeavour to appreciate its doctrines. Instead of learning first the first principles, they plunge without ceremony amidst the deepest mysteries of the gospel. Is it wonderful that they come out, exclaiming: "Who is sufficient for these things?" It is well said: "Objections against a thing fairly proved are of no weight. The proof rests upon our knowledge, and the ojections upon our ignorance. It is true that moral demonstrations and religious doctrines may be attacked in a very ingenious and plausible manner, because they involve questions on which our ignorance is greater than our knowledge; but still our knowledge is knowledge; or in other words, certainty is certainty. In mathematical reasoning, our knowledge is greater than our ignorance. When you have proved that the three angles of every triangle are equal to two right angles, there is an end of doubt; because there are no materials for ignorance to work up into phantasms, but your knowledge is really no more certain than your knowledge on any other subject."

If it be a valid objection to religion that, to some minds, it presents difficulties which cannot be solved, then there is no department of human knowledge that may not be legitimately condemned. What is more certain than the existence of a material universe? or of the necessary connexion of cause and effect? But even in these, wise heads have succeeded in discovering difficulties which it would puzzle much more sensible people to remove by a process of reasoning. That matter is infinitely divisible, is assumed in science as fundamentally certain. That the doctrine, however, involves very great difficulties, is palpable to all common sense, inasmuch as, to suppose a foot measure divided into an infinite number of parts, requiring an infinite number of portions of time to pass over them, and yet to be passed over in a moment, is to make a moment infinite, in other words, eternal; for although it should be said that the portions of time would be infinitely small, still they would be portions of time, and an infinite number of any portions of time must make an infinite duration. Who will pretend that in this, there is no room for perplexity and doubt? In the mean time, the operations of science, in which the infinite divisibility of matter is assumed, proceed with as much confidence as if there were no difficulty connected with it.*

Much is said of the certainty of mathematical demonstra tions; but if difficulties that cannot be solved are sufficient objections, even here also must sentence of condemnation be pronounced. It might be shown how trifling are even the definitions of geometry, the most exact of all the mathematical sciences. Its definitions might be alleged, upon no inconsiderable grounds, to be nonsensical and ridiculous; its demands or postulates, plainly impracticable; its axioms or self-evident propositions, controvertible, and controverted indeed even by themselves. But why are not these things objected to the truth of mathematics? What is there in the religion of Jesus more encumbered with difficulties?

Were the dispositions of the human heart and the idols of a sinner's devotion as much opposed by the demonstrations of mathematics, as by the doctrines of christianity, it would be just as difficult to convince men of the truth of the former, as of the latter. The folly of speaking of a something that has length without breadth; of a point that has no parts; of lines for ever approaching and never meeting, &c.; the futility of basing a certain demonstration upon elements so unintelligible and impossible, would be trumpeted to the ends of the world. The wicked would no more believe a proposition of geometry, than they will now, a doctrine of redemption. The scoffer would find as much to ridicule in Newton's Principia as in Paul's Epistles.†

---

* "The divisibility, *in infinitum*, of any finite extension, involves us, whether we grant or deny it, in consequences, impossible to be explicated, or made in our apprehensions consistent; consequences that carry greater difficulty, and more apparent absurdity, than any thing that can follow from the notion of an immaterial substance."—*Locke on Human Understanding.*

† See an interesting piece of reasoning, *apropos* to the above, in one of the tracts of the American Tract Society, entitled "Conversation with a Young Traveller," No. 203.

But we do injustice to the good cause in which we are engaged by standing exclusively on the defensive. Infidelity has too long been indulged with the privilege of attack. It is the stratagem of weakness, to put on a bold front and make a desperate assault. Any arm can strike, but not every breast can repel a blow. It is high time infidelity were accused and brought to the bar. What proof of a single feature of doctrine or of moral principle can it produce, after having rejected such evidence as that of christianity? What satisfactory argument for the obligation of any thing connected with natural religion; what reason for believing in a future state; what proof even of the existence of God, can be offered as worthy of reliance, without a shameful inconsistency, by men who, in the immense power of evidence sustaining the divine authority of the gospel, can find nothing to convince them?

We have shown that the argument for christianity is strictly philosophical, because entirely experimental. It might easily be shown that every system of infidelity, so far as it pretends to any religious doctrine or precept, is wholly destitute of all claim to such a character. What a catalogue of theoretical assertions, and unsustained conjectures, and positive contradictions, and gross absurdities, and inexplicable difficulties, might be drawn up against the most rational of the infidel systems! The Deist professes to believe that the light of nature is sufficient for human guidance in all matters of moral obligation; and yet he believes that notwithstanding such all-sufficiency, some among those who have attempted to follow it have contended for the immortality of the soul, and others have denied it; some have maintained that God created all things, others that matter is as much from eternity as Himself; some, that He governs and will judge the world, others that He does not concern himself about it; some, that God should be worshipped, others that all worship is weak superstition; some, that virtue is virtuous, and vice vicious, others, that there is no distinction in principle between them;

that sin is but a matter of custom and opinion, and that the indulgence of the lowest passions is no more to be blamed than the thirst of a fever or the drowsiness of a lethargy.

Some infidels deny that Jesus ever lived, and yet they believe that the whole nation of the Jews, bitter enemies of christianity as they have always been, acknowledge that they put him to death on the cross. Some confess that there was such a person, but accuse him of a most barefaced system of fraud and imposture; and yet they cannot but concede that his character was eminently pure and excellent. Others, to escape such a contradiction, maintain that he was a pure, but weak and visionary enthusiast; and yet they acknowledged that he composed and inculcated a system of morals very far superior to that of the wisest of the ancient philosophers. Infidels profess to believe that the apostles of Christ were instigated by mercenary considerations, and yet that they willingly suffered the loss of all things; by ambitious considerations, and yet they submitted cheerfully to all ignominy and shame! According to infidels, they were devoted to a selfish scheme of personal benefit, and yet were always going about doing good, without the least regard to their own convenience or pleasure. They were gross deceivers, it is said, and yet they endured all sufferings, and sacrificed their lives, in confirmation of their sincerity. They were weak fanatics, and yet the strongest and most learned minds could not resist the power and wisdom with which they spake. Infidels deny that Jesus ever wrought miracles, but cannot deny that his bitterest enemies, who had infinitely better opportunities of judging than they can boast, confessed the contrary. Infidels pretend that the prophecies of the Bible were nothing more than guesses, and that all correspondence between them and subsequent history was a mere matter of chance; and yet they cannot find, among all the guesses in the Bible, a single failure; while they cannot deny that many of its guesses have succeeded, in the minutest particulars, in spite of a proportion of chances against them too great for numbers to express. Infidels contend that the gospel is against all reason and common sense, as well as truth; they laugh at the efforts of modern apostles to convert the nations of heathenism to the faith of Christ, as visionary and fruitless. Nothing seems to them more impossible than that such an enterprize should succeed. And yet, according to their wisdom, when only twelve missionaries, with none of the education, or experience, or human support and countenance; with none of the facilities for multiplying books, and disseminating knowledge, which modern labourers possess; when twelve despised, persecuted Jews, undertook a similar work, not among ignorant barbarians, but polished Greeks; and when, in less than forty years, their cause was coextensive with the known world; then what is so impossible now *was nothing wonderful or unaccountable;* it was a mere matter of human contrivance and enthusiastic perseverance; the work of men alone, and of weak, superstitious, credulous, simple, and deceitful men, though the only work of the kind since the creation of the world!

It were easy to proceed much further with this array of the contradiction and difficulties into which men are necessarily brought by rejecting the evidences of christianity. But we have said enough to show, that if infidels were put upon the defensive a little more frequently, they would have much less time to be creeping, with poisoned arrows, around the outworks of christianity. Let them point out, in the belief of the gospel, any thing like the contradictions and absurdities involved in a profession of infidelity, and it shall be renounced as unworthy the countenance of a rational being.

LECTURE XIII.

INSPIRATION OF THE SCRIPTURES, AND CONCLUDING OBSERVATIONS.

The external evidences of christianity, as a system of faith, divinely revealed, we consider to have been closed with the lecture next preceding the last. On that subject, we shall offer no additional argument. But there remains one very important matter of inquiry.

Christianity and the scriptures are essentially associated. Without the latter, we should not have received the former. But however inseparable in the use of their benefits, they are quite distinct in the proof of their infallible origin. It is one thing to show that the *doctrines* taught in the scriptures are divine; and another, that the *books* containing those doctrines are divine. The former, we think, has been fully established. The latter has not yet been attempted. We have proved that the books of scripture are authentic and credible; the works of the authors whose names they bear; and correct narratives of such matters of fact as they profess to relate. But were we to stop here, we should leave the Bible on a level, in point of authority, with many other books of the christian religion which contain the truth, and, so far as we can judge, contain nothing else; and yet have no pretension to any other than a human origin. In this case, we should have no ultimate and sure appeal for either doctrine or duty; a door would be open for all manner of interference, on the part of "man's wisdom," for the perversion and corruption of the truth; the most essential features of the gospel, on the easy plea that the apostles, being men, may sometimes have misunderstood their Master, would be accessible to the most ruinous suspicions of overstatement or misconception.

We have need, not only of a divine system of religion, but of a divine teacher of that system. The latter was possessed by the apostles in the person of Christ, while he continued with them; and subsequently in the special presence and guidance of the Holy Ghost, whom the Saviour promised as a Comforter, to lead them into all truth. In place of the privileges thus possessed, what remains to which may confidently be referred every question of religious doctrine and duty, and by which our minds may be safely led to the whole truth as it is in Jesus? Are the scriptures *infallible?* In other words, are they *divine?* Have they been "*given by inspiration of God?*" This brings us at once to the main point of the present lecture—THE INSPIRATION OF THE SCRIPTURES—a subject which, however eminently important, has had so much done, preparatory to its consideration, in our previous lectures, that it need not occupy at present a large portion of your time.

The distinct proposition to which your attention is called, I would express partly in the language of St. Peter: *The scriptures came not by the will of man: but holy men of God wrote as they were moved by the Holy Ghost;* or in the words of St. Paul: "*All scripture is given by inspiration of God.*"

By *inspiration* is understood: "Such a communication by the Holy Spirit to the minds of the sacred writers, of those things which could not have been otherwise known, and such an effectual superintendency, as to those particulars, concerning which they might otherwise obtain information, as sufficed absolutely to preserve them from every degree of error in all things which could in the least affect any of the doctrines or precepts contained in their writings, or mislead any person who considered them as a divine and infallible standard of truth and duty."

This definition is perfectly consistent with what a critic would regard as a fault of style in a book of scripture; or a philosopher, as scientifically inaccurate; or a rhetorician, as a departure from the rules of rhetorical writing. It is entirely compatible with the evident fact of the several authors having written in such various idioms and styles as their respective talents, habits, associations, or circumstances rendered most easy and natural: while, at the same time, it places all the sacred writers, however various their modes and minds, on the same footing of divine authority; and gives to all portions of the Bible an equal claim to be received as the oracles of God. Thus, over the just interpretation of each single verse, is written, *infallibility.*

In examining into the degree of authority to be attached to the scriptures, we are favoured with a very direct appeal. We may go to the scriptures themselves. Having already established their credibility; we have a full warrant to depend on them for a true statement of the words of the Saviour and his apostles. Having established also the fundamental doctrine that the Saviour and his apostles were divinely sent and attested, we have a right to rely implicitly on their words, as truth divinely sealed and certified. Our way, therefore, is plain. We must search the scriptures for any words of the Lord Jesus and of his apostles concerning the subject before us. We have but one question to answer: *Does the New Testament bear witness that the several books composing the Bible were treated or represented by the Saviour or his apostles as divinely inspired?* This determined in the affirmative, the inspiration of the scriptures is decided, until the whole argument of the preceding lectures shall be proved inconclusive.

I. Let us divide the question, and begin our inquiry with the Old Testament scriptures.

1st. It is undeniable that the Saviour and his apostles regarded the Old Testament with at least as much reverence, as did the Jews in their day. They reproved the latter for many errors of doctrine and of practice; for mutilating the scriptures by false interpretations; and for making them of none effect through their traditions; but nowhere do we read the least insinuation of their having censured the Jews for paying too much respect to the scriptures, or for allowing them too much authority. On the contrary, they evidently joined in, most earnestly, with the Jewish mind on this subject; and, instead of attempting to unsettle, aimed directly at increasing its habit of implicit submission to the Old Testament writings. But had the Jews been erroneous in that high degree of reverence with which they regarded those sacred books; such countenance and example on the part of our Lord and his ambassadors could not have been showed, consistently with the perfect truth and openness which marked all their dealings.

Now, be it observed, that the Jews, in the time of Christ, considered the writings of the Old Testament as *divinely inspired;* not merely in respect to their doctrines, but their whole matter and substance. Josephus says, that in his time they were universally believed to have been written by men "*as they learned them of God himself by inspiration,*" and were justly believed to be "DIVINE." He draws a wide distinction between the histories of the Jewish people which were written since the time of Artaxerxes, and those contained in the Bible, and gives, as a reason why the former had not been received as having so much authority as the latter, that since Artaxerxes there had not been a succession of *inspired men.* "How firmly we have given credit," he says, "to these books of our own nation, is evident from what we do; for during so many ages as have already passed, no one hath been so bold as either to add any thing to them, to take any thing from them, or to make any change in them; but it is become natural to all Jews, immediately and from their very birth, to esteem those books to contain divine doctrines, and to persist in them, and if occasion be, willingly to die for them."* Hence we see that Jesus and his apostles, in coinciding with, and in employing and promoting the current sentiment of the Jewish people in their days, must be considered as having, really and in the

* Cont. Apion, b. i. §§ 7, 8.

broadest sense, espoused and confirmed the doctrine of *the divine inspiration* of the Old Testament scriptures.

2d. But, unanswerable as is the above attestation, we have a direct assertion on the part of St. Paul of still greater importance. Having reminded Timothy, that from a child he had known "the *holy scriptures*," which were able to make him wise unto salvation through faith in Christ Jesus, he makes this positive and conclusive declaration: "*All scripture is given by inspiration of God*, and is profitable for doctrine, for reproof, for correction, for instruction in righteousness: that the man of God may be perfect, thoroughly furnished unto all good works."*

Here, then, is the plain testimony of one, whose knowledge and veracity we have ascertained, that whatever in his time was included under the name of "scripture," or "holy scriptures," was of divine inspiration. We have only to ask, therefore, to what books Paul applied that name. It was a name of common use in his day. Josephus and Philo frequently speak of "the divine scriptures," and "the holy scriptures." It is manifest, therefore, that Paul meant to be understood as asserting the divine inspiration of that collection of sacred books to which the Jews notoriously applied such names; in other words, the books of the Old Testament. He regarded them all as scripture. He declared them all inspired.

Now, that under the same title we have the same collection of writings is certain; not only from the important fact that on this head there is a perfect agreement between our bibles and those of the whole Jewish nation at the present day; but also from the testimony of Josephus, who, although he has not mentioned the names of the several books considered as scripture in his time, has given us their number, and so described them that their identity with ours cannot be mistaken. He takes care to speak of them "as of divine authority."† In addition to this, we have the testimony of

* 2 Tim. iii. 15, 16, 17. † Cont. Apion, b. i. § 8.

the New Testament as to the canon of the Old. For besides the books of Moses, which the former expressly mentions as of divine authority, it also specifies almost all the other books of our Old Testament as belonging, in the time of Christ, to the sacred canon of the Jews. Some are omitted, only because the mentioning of any is incidental. Nothing but a formal enumeration can be expected to be complete. That none are excepted against, is proof that all were received by the Lord and his apostles.

Hence, we are fully warranted to believe that "*all scripture,*" in the mouth of St. Paul, meant all the books of the Old Testament which Jews and Christians at present unite in receiving as divine oracles; consequently, we have apostolic authority in proof that they were all "given by inspiration of God."

Much additional evidence to the same point might be added; but with any who acknowledge the argument of the previous lectures, and thence believe that whatever St. Paul asserted, as a doctrine of christianity, is true, the above simple reasoning will be amply sufficient for the divine inspiration of the Old Testament.

II. Let us proceed to the second division of our subject, and carry our inquiry to the books of the New Testament.

1st. *The inspiration of the New Testament may be naturally and reasonably inferred from that of the Old.* In this, we argue by analogy. No reason can be given why those holy men of old, who composed the books of the other Testament, should have written, not "by the will of man," but "as they were moved by the Holy Ghost," that does not apply with much greater force to the writers of the later volume. The economy of the Old Testament was to cease at the advent of Christ; that of the New will endure to the end of the world. The former was intended only for a single nation, and adapted but to a country of narrow boundaries. The latter was framed to include all nations, and is intended of God to be coextensive with the globe. The law had only "a shadow of good things to come;" the gospel has "the very image of the things;" the first was a system of types, "which stood only in meats, and drinks, and divers washings, and carnal ordinances imposed, until the time of reformation;" the second (the time of reformation being come) is a system of direct revelation; the veil has been rent in twain, so that it may be said, in comparison with the previous dispensation, that we "no longer see through a glass, darkly, but face to face." One grand distinction of the economy of the gospel is, that it is the dispensation *of the Spirit*. That peculiar feature in which its covenant is "a better covenant, established upon better promises"—"a new covenant"—is found in this, that it is a *spiritual covenant;* its promises, its privileges, its duties, its parties, are all spiritual. Its character, in this respect, is seen in that stipulation of its Divine Author: "I will put my laws into their *mind*, and write them in their *hearts*." So much, therefore, does this "ministration of righteousness exceed in glory" all that preceded it, that although there had never risen, under the Old Testament system, a greater than John the Baptist; yet "he that is least in the kingdom of God (i. e. under the New Testament system,) is greater than he."

Now, is it supposable that, under a dispensation so limited in extent and duration as that of the law; so carnal in its ordinances; so obscure in its revelations; serving only "unto the example and shadow of heavenly things;" the sacred books should have been given by inspiration of God; and yet, that under the far better covenant of the gospel, designed for all mankind, and to stand while the world endures; a dispensation so eminently distinguished for the outpouring of the Spirit; for the spiritual gifts of its earliest ministers, and the spiritual duties and blessings of all its members: we should be left to a standard of truth and duty, dictated only by the wisdom, composed only under the superintending care, of fallible men? Surely the inspiration of the New Testament is naturally and reasonably inferred from that of the Old.

2d. The same conclusion necessarily arises *from the evident inspiration of the apostles in their preaching and other official actions.*

It was expressly promised by the Lord, that when they should stand before enemies, in defence of the gospel, they should speak by *inspiration of God.* In such circumstances, their direction was: "Take no thought how or what ye shall speak. For it is not ye that speak, but the Spirit of your Father which speaketh in you." "The Holy Ghost shall teach you in that same hour, what ye ought to say." "I will give you a mouth and wisdom, which all your adversaries shall not be able to gainsay, nor resist."* We have no reason to suppose that these promises of inspiration were confined to the special circumstances referred to in the passages above quoted. The apostles were to be placed in many others for which they would be quite as needful. Certain circumstances were particularly spoken of by the Lord; because in them the faith of his apostles would be particularly tried.

But inspiration was promised by the Saviour, in terms of the most comprehensive kind. A little before his crucifixion, when the hearts of his disciples (Judas having left them) were greatly troubled at the assurance that he was soon to be taken from them; he promised to send them a Comforter —the Holy Spirit—who should abide with them for ever. This blessed Person, he called repeatedly "the Spirit of truth." He was distinctly promised to the apostles, as a substitute, in all respects, for the presence, the guidance, the instructions of their Lord himself. The great consolation of such a substitute consisted in his being to the apostles, *invisibly*, just what Jesus had been to them, *visibly*; so that they might consider themselves to be divinely directed and instructed under his influence, in a manner quite as direct and infallible, as if they had still the Master's voice to hear, and his footsteps to follow. They were assured that "the

* Mat. x. 19, 20. Luke xii. 12; and xxi. 15.

Spirit of truth" would teach them whatever knowledge their duties might require. "*He shall teach you all things.*" "*He will lead you into all truth.*" Had they forgotten any portion of their Lord's instructions? "*The Spirit of truth,*" said he, "*shall bring all things to your remembrance whatsoever I have said unto you.*" "*He shall take of mine, and shall show it unto you.*" Even the knowledge of the future was promised to the apostles, by the inspiration of the Holy Ghost. "*He will show you things to come.*" They were directed to tarry in Jerusalem after his death, until they should receive "*power from on high.*" Now all these promises are positive proofs that the apostles were inspired in their ministry, as soon as their fulfilment took place. Thus, when the day of Pentecost was fully come, and the Spirit descended upon them, "they were all filled with the Holy Ghost," and "began to speak as the Spirit gave them utterance." By this inspiration, they were enabled to preach, in all languages, the wonderful works of God. The sermon of Peter, on that day, was spoken under this influence. By the same help, he discerned the spirit of Ananias and Sapphira. Their lie was unto the Holy Ghost, in as much as, it was unto one whom the Holy Ghost inspired. Directed by the same Spirit, Peter journeyed from Joppa to the house of Cornelius, and first opened the door of faith to the Gentiles. Paul, by inspiration, went forth on his mission from Antioch to the lesser Asia; being "full of the Holy Ghost," he searched the conscience of Elymas, the sorcerer, and punished his wickedness with blindness. When the apostles, and elders, and brethren were assembled in council about the question sent up from Antioch for their decision; they consulted and determined as they were guided by inspiration of God. "*It seemeth good to the Holy Ghost,*" was the solemn sanction annexed to their sentence. They claimed to be always received, as inspired. Their speech and their preaching, they asserted, were "in demonstration of the Spirit;" "not in the words which man's wisdom teacheth, but which the Holy Ghost teacheth." It is expressly declared by St. Peter, that his brethren and himself "preached the gospel with the Holy Ghost sent down from heaven." All these statements, and many others which might be adduced, abundantly confirm the position, that the apostles, in their preaching and other official actions, were in the highest sense *inspired.*

Hence it would seem to be very naturally and reasonably inferred, that when they *wrote* for the permanent guidance of the churches, they were inspired also. Can it be supposed that St. Paul, in preaching to the Ephesians or Corinthians, spake as he was moved by the Holy Ghost; and yet was entirely bereft of that divine aid, when he sat down to the much more important work of composing epistles to those churches? When it is considered how entirely all the oral communications of the apostles ceased to be remembered, in a short time after they were uttered, except as they were recorded in the scriptures; and how their written communications to the churches have remained unmutilated, these eighteen hundred years; and are now circulated in upwards of one hundred and seventy languages; and will continue to be the guide and treasure of the church to the end of the world; can it be believed that in these the apostles were left to their own fallible wisdom, though guided in the others by the inspiration of God? Such an opinion would be absurd in the extreme.

It seems to be a necessary conclusion, from the above premises, that the authors of the New Testament were divinely inspired, as well when writing for all people and all ages, as when speaking to the congregation of a single synagogue.

3d. If the apostles did not intend to impress the church with a belief that they wrote by divine inspiration, they adopted the very means that were most likely to lead its members into a most important heresy. St. Paul, in an epistle to Timothy, which he knew would be universally circulated, published the broad assertion: "*All scripture is given by inspiration of God.*" Now it is worthy of note, that the epistle, containing this declaration, is generally supposed to have been written after all the other works of St. Paul, and but a short time before his martyrdom at Rome. At any rate, it was one of his latest works. The Gospel of St. Matthew had been written and circulated at least twenty years. Those by St. Mark and St. Luke were already in the possession of the churches. The same is true of the Acts of the Apostles. We know of no part of the whole New Testament that was written subsequently to the uttering of the above declaration, except the gospel, epistles, and Revelation by St. John.

In connexion with this, be it observed, that when the primitive christians received an epistle or gospel from one of the apostles or evangelists, they regarded it as a portion of *holy scripture.* By this familiar name, it was universally known, and with this high honour, it was always treated. Precisely as the writers of the New Testament speak of the books of the Old Testament, calling them *the scriptures,* do the christian writers, who were contemporaneous with the apostles, continually quote their books. This cannot be questioned. Then, consider the circumstances of the churches. They have in possession, and in daily use, a number of writings which have been sent them by the apostles and evangelists, the greater part of them by St. Paul himself. It is well known to the latter, that those writings are universally revered and read as *holy scriptures.* In these circumstances, he declares that "*all scripture* is given by inspiration of God." How are they to understand him? Shall they say: He speaks in that passage only of the Jewish scriptures? His primary reference was unquestionably to them. But in what sense can his assertion be true of *all* scripture, if so large a part as that comprising the New Testament, and which was universally denominated *scripture,* came only "by the will of man?" But this is not all that the apostles did to promote the belief of the inspiration of their writings.

The christian churches were accustomed to appeal to the Old Testament as an inspired volume. A large number of their members had been educated in the Jewish faith, and by habit, as well as reflection, always associated the idea of divine inspiration with that of a book of scripture. Consequently, when the writings of the New Testament were received; when they came to occupy, in regard to the christian church, a corresponding place to that of the Old Testament books in regard to the Jewish church; when they were honoured by universal consent, with the same title of "holy scriptures" as was applied to the sacred books of the former dispensation; it was extremely natural that the churches should treat them precisely as they treated the older books, and believe them also to have been written by inspiration of God. That they did thus regard them is indisputable. Clement, bishop of Rome, a contemporary of the apostles, says: "Look into the holy scriptures, which are the true words of the holy Ghost. Take the epistle of the blessed Paul, the apostle, into your hands; verily he did by *the Spirit* admonish you." The primitive christians rejected from the canon of scripture certain books, because, though true and edifying, they were not inspired by the Holy Ghost. They habitually spoke of the New Testament as "The Word of God," "The Voice of God," "The Oracles of the Holy Ghost."

Now, in such circumstances, how would the apostles, as men of common honesty and candour, have acted in case they did not consider their writings to be inspired? Knowing the natural tendency and the actual state of public opinion among the churches, could they have been even silent on this subject? Must they not have warned their disciples against a disposition so dangerous, and a heresy so conspicuous? Would not the most ordinary measure of humility and faithfulness have impelled them to draw the line of distinction, too plainly to be mistaken, between what they had written by their own wisdom, and what holy men of old had written "as they were moved by the Holy Ghost?" What course do they pursue? Not only do they allow the natural disposition of those accustomed to attach inspiration to the scripture to have its way; not only do they say nothing having the least tendency to correct the universal impression of the churches on so vital a point; but they adopt the very course which was calculated directly to confirm all their prepossessions. They introduce their writings in a manner of authority precisely similar to that of the inspired men of older times. Witness the beginning of the Epistle to the Galatians: "Paul an apostle (not of men, neither by man, but by Jesus Christ and God the Father who raised him from the dead) unto the churches of Galatia," &c. Peter, speaking of the epistles of Paul, as familiarly known among christians, expressly numbers them among "*the scriptures*," and puts them upon a level with "*the other scriptures*,"* which Jews and Christians alike considered to have been written by inspiration. Paul speaks of the writings of the "*apostles and prophets*" as constituting together that good foundation on which christians were built, "Jesus Christ himself being the chief corner stone."† And after Peter has particularly included the epistles of St. Paul among *the scriptures*, the latter publishes his declaration that "*all scripture* is given by inspiration of God."

If those holy men did not intend to promote the belief of the inspiration of their writings; if they were desirous of teaching the churches to make a wide distinction between their works, as merely human and fallible, and those of Moses and the prophets, as divine and infallible; how singularly did they mistake the way! how exactly did they inculcate what they wished to contradict, and build up what they were bound to destroy!

In what manner the primitive churches understood their

* 2 Peter, iii. 16. † Ephesians, ii. 20.

instructions, is manifest; and on the supposition that the apostles taught that their writings were *not inspired*, it forms a singular proof of the great obscurity with which they must have expressed themselves. Justin Martyr, a contemporary with St. John, says that "the gospels were written by men full of the Holy Ghost." Irenæus, a few years later, declares that "the scriptures were dictated by the Spirit of God, and that, therefore, it is wickedness to contradict them, and sacrilege to alter them." "The gospel," he says, "was first preached, and afterwards, by the will of God, committed to writing, that it might be, for time to come, the foundation and pillar of our faith."

Enough, it is believed, has now been exhibited to satisfy any reasonable mind that it was the intention of the writers of the New Testament, and of their blessed Master, that the church should regard their works as having been dictated and rendered infallible by divine inspiration. To those who acknowledge that Christ and his apostles were commissioned and taught of God, this is perfect evidence of the great doctrine at which we have been arriving. For those who, after all that has been said in our preceding lectures, shall still refuse to acknowledge the Lord Jesus and his apostles as divinely commissioned and endowed, we have no more argument. Much additional reasoning might be offered; but such is the conclusiveness of what has been adduced, that it may be said without presumption, if they believe not upon such evidence, "neither would they believe though one rose from the dead."*

We may now conclude a course of lectures, which has already extended far beyond the anticipations of the author. Having arrived at the divine authority of christianity, and the divine inspiration of the scriptures, we have not only *a religion revealed from God*, but *an infallible expression of*

* For a much more extended and able view of the inspiration of the New Testament, see *Dick on the Inspiration of the Scriptures*, and *Lectures* on the same *by Leonard Woods, D. D., Andover.*

its doctrines and duties. We have the guide, as well as the way, to everlasting life—both equally certain, equally divine.

Let us be thankful for such unspeakable gifts. Next to the mercy of a Saviour—able and ready "to save to the uttermost all that come unto God by Him"—is the book of the inspiration of God, which, as a lamp to our feet, and a light to our path, conducts to such a Friend, and teaches us, without mistake, all that we must do to be saved.

Let us consider our obligation to study this blessed book, with most serious attention and care. What can be more ungrateful, more disobedient, more sinful, in the sight of God, than the total neglect, or the careless reading of a volume which His own Spirit indited for our express guidance and consolation? "Search the scriptures!" is the injunction, as well of our reason, as of the Lord Jesus. "Let the word of Christ dwell in you richly in all wisdom," is a command as delightful in its obedience, as it is authoritative in its declaration.

Let us yield implicit submission to the decisions of the scriptures. In them we read the oracles of God—the mind of the Spirit—infallible wisdom. As inspired pages, their authority is absolute. It is plain duty, therefore, to bring every question of truth or practice to their judgment; and to bow, without a question, or a murmur, or the least reserve of mind or heart, to whatever they require. To proceed on any other principle; to bring any thoughts of ours into the least competition with the decision of the scriptures; to submit to one portion of the Bible, more than to another; to withhold assent to any of its doctrines, till we can fully perceive their necessity, or reasonableness, or their consistency with certain notions of human wisdom, is a practical denial of the divine authority of the whole volume, and deserves no other name than that of unbelief.

Let us search the scriptures *daily;* for they were made to be daily "profitable for doctrine, reproof, correction and instruction in righteousness." It is only when taken as an intimate companion and friend, that the Bible throws off its reserve, and appears in all its excellence. Then it speaks to the heart, and begins to develope treasures of consolation as numerous as the wants of sinners, as endless as the grace of their Saviour. We can well perceive the hand of God in the general construction of christianity, while standing without, and looking only upon its walls and bulwarks; but, like the temple of Jerusalem, we must enter within the holy place to "behold the fair beauty of the sanctuary;" the fine gold of its workmanship; and the glory of Him "who dwelleth between the cherubim." "The secret of the Lord is with them that fear him; and he will show them his covenant."

Let us search the scriptures with *prayer;* "praying always with all prayer and supplication in the Spirit," that we may be "filled with the knowledge of His will in all wisdom and spiritual understanding." The key of the ark, in which are laid up the tables of testimony, is prayer. By this alone can we get into "the secret place of the Most High," and be taught of God. He who, without prayer, should seek to enter within the veil, and obtain a view of the divine glory as it shines within the scriptures, would act no less presumptuously, than Aaron, the high priest, had he attempted, without his brazen censer and his incense, to pass the veil of the holy of holies, and stand before the mercy-seat. "My son," saith the scripture, "if thou criest after knowledge, and liftest up thy voice for understanding; if thou seekest her as silver, and searchest for her as hid treasures; then shalt thou understand the fear of the Lord, and find the knowledge of God."

We began these lectures with prayer to God for his Holy Spirit to guide our way and help our infirmities, that all of us might see and embrace the *truth.* We recommended prayer as one of the chief means to be used by all who would study the evidences of Christianity in a right spirit. We are now just at the last words of a course, which, we trust, God has not permitted to be heard by you without precious benefit, as well in increasing your impression of the solemn claims of the gospel upon your hearts and lives, as in strengthening your conviction of its truth as a revelation from God for the salvation of men. Take, we beseech you, the Holy Scriptures, wherein God speaks, by his Spirit, to every generation, as your unfailing guide, your most dear treasure, the appointed means by which, as the inspired vehicle of God's truth, it is His revealed purpose to carry on, through the inworking of the Holy Ghost, the sanctification of them that believe in the name of His only Son, our Saviour, Jesus Christ!

"BLESSED LORD, who hast caused all holy scriptures to be written for our learning, grant that we may, in such wise, hear them, read, mark, learn, and inwardly digest them, that by patience, and comfort of thy Holy Word, we may embrace and ever hold fast the blessed hope of everlasting life, which thou hast given us in our Saviour, Jesus Christ." *Amen*

THE END.

www.ingramcontent.com/pod-product-compliance
Lightning Source LLC
LaVergne TN
LVHW020100110826
845151LV00001B/37

* 9 7 8 1 4 2 5 5 4 4 7 5 1 *